Christmas 1964
from Mum –

D0295156

SELECTED PAPERS

Baron Cooper of Culross of Dunnet in the County of Caithness,
Lord Justice-General of Scotland and Lord President of
the Court of Session, 1947-1954

SELECTED PAPERS

1922-1954

The Right Honourable

LORD COOPER OF CULROSS

Lord Justice-General and Lord President
of The Court of Session, 1947-54

OLIVER AND BOYD

EDINBURGH: TWEEDDALE COURT

LONDON: 39A WELBECK STREET, W. I

First collected Edition 1957

Printed in Great Britain by
Oliver and Boyd Ltd., Edinburgh

Acknowledgments

M<small>Y GRATEFUL THANKS</small> are due to Dr H. W. Meikle, the Historiographer-Royal for Scotland, Professors W. Croft Dickinson and A. H. Campbell of Edinburgh, Professor T. B. Smith of Aberdeen, and Baron Keith of Avonholm for their invaluable advice upon the selection and arrangement of the Papers and Opinions appearing in this volume. Acknowledgment must also be made to Thomas Nelson & Sons Ltd. for granting me permission to re-print the four Addresses which have already appeared in *Supra Crepidam* published by them in 1951. I have also to thank the editors, publishers, institutions and societies mentioned in the Bibliography for permission to re-print contributions to their publications. Acknowledgments are also due to Messrs Drummond Young Ltd., Edinburgh, Messrs Elliot & Fry, London, and the Planet News Ltd., London, for agreeing to reproduction of the photographs.

J. M. C.

Contents

★

Photographs

Biography

On 8th June 1891 John Aitken Cooper, c.e., of Culross, Fife, married Margaret Mackay, of Dunnet, Caithness. Sixty-four years later, their elder son, Thomas Mackay Cooper, took his seat in the House of Lords with the title of Baron Cooper of Culross of Dunnet in the County of Caithness.

John Aitken Cooper was educated at Dollar Academy and, after a long technical training, followed by practical experience in Dollar, Edinburgh and Glasgow, was appointed Burgh Engineer of Edinburgh in 1881. During his tenure of office he was responsible for many important developments. The power stations at Dewar Place and Macdonald Road were built under his supervision—both remarkable for their time, as his son was to recall more than forty years later when, as Lord Advocate, he opened the final extension to the much larger and more modern power-house at Portobello.

When, in 1900, John Aitken Cooper was invited to become President of the British Association of Municipal and County Engineers and Surveyors, reference was made in the *Scottish Local Government Gazette* of 18th August 1900, to " his fairness, and unflinching integrity, his unerring precision derived from his long and unique experience, and his extraordinary capacity for hard work "—qualities which his son inherited in the fullest measure.

Margaret Mackay had come to Edinburgh in 1880 with her parents, her sister and her youngest brother. Her oldest brother John, who died at an early age, was already in the office of Messrs John C. Brodie & Sons, w.s., whilst her second brother Tom, who was to become the senior partner of Messrs Macpherson & Mackay, w.s., was with Messrs Tods, Murray & Jamieson, w.s. There was thus a strong legal connection on that side of the family.

Mr and Mrs John Cooper's eldest son, Thomas Mackay Cooper, was born at 15 Cumin Place, Edinburgh, on 24th September 1892, and their second son, James Murray Cooper, who was also to become senior partner of Messrs Macpherson & Mackay, w.s., was born on 2nd April 1895.

Tom was deeply attached to his father whom he would constantly question on this, that, and everything. Family friends often recalled watching with delight as father and son walked across Bruntsfield Links on a Sunday morning to " sit under " their favourite Dr Hood Wilson of the Barclay Church, both of them deep in argument and totally oblivious of their surroundings. Even Dr Hood Wilson experienced some anxious moments seeking for suitable replies to some of Tom's probing questions on the scriptural quotations which happened to be troubling him at the time.

Two outstanding events in Tom's early life in the closing years of last century were to be recalled by himself at a function half a century later. One was when he was taken to Princes Street to watch the first motor bus making its journey from the Waverley Steps to Haymarket and back ; the other when he travelled on the first cable car to make the journey up Lothian Road, and was then deeply troubled in his conscience because it was a Sunday morning when the test was being made.

But to his abiding sorrow Tom was to lose his father all too soon : for, after a protracted illness, John Aitken Cooper died from pernicious anæmia on 9th July 1901, at the early age of forty-nine. On his death bed he committed to Tom, then only eight years old, the care of his mother and brother. How faithfully and amply Tom fulfilled that trust the years that followed were to show.

After her husband's death, Mrs Cooper and her two sons removed to 42 St Alban's Road, and in 1902 Tom Cooper entered the Junior School of George Watson's Boys' College, his brother simultaneously entering the Elementary School. For the next eight years they walked daily to and from school —a quarter-of-an-hour's walk each way, whatever the weather, without any help from the various forms of transport provided for the present day school child. Money was scarce, for John Aitken Cooper had not died a rich man, and, whilst his widow had relatives only too willing to help, she was an intensely proud and independent woman. Thus, when he entered Watson's Tom realised that he must play his part in easing the family budget by striving his best to win bursaries and foundations, and he succeeded in doing so every year until he left school. Throughout his whole life he never forgot those early years and the care and devotion of his mother. As he strove to help her then, so, later, she was always first in his thoughts.

Tom's last year at Watson's and his entrance to Edinburgh University the same year were indicative of his future. Apart from medals and other special prizes, ten in number, he was, as *The Watsonian* recorded at the time, the first pupil of the School, so far as the records showed, to become Dux of the School in his first year in the " Sixth." Simultaneously he won the leading Watson's Bursary of £100 to Edinburgh University, and a month or two later, in the University competitions he headed both the Open Bursary List and the John Welsh Classical List. During his University career this early promise was maintained. Medallist in all his classes, he took a brilliant First-Class Honours in Classics at the age of nineteen, LL.B. " with distinction " at twenty-one, a Vans Dunlop Scholarship and the Lord Rector's Prize.

The question of Tom Cooper's future career in life arose when he was completing his M.A. degree. There can be little doubt that, had his father lived, Tom might well have become a scientist or engineer : for, as later events were to show, he had a keen bent for mechanical and electrical engineering, and indeed for any form of scientific work. But his uncle, the late Mr T. M. Mackay, a well-known figure in Parliament House and then the senior partner of Messrs Macpherson & Mackay, W.S., was anxious that Tom should read for the Bar, knowing how much vital help he could give his nephew at the very beginning of his career.

Accordingly, at the conclusion of his University career, Tom Cooper spent a year in his uncle's office which enjoyed

an extensive Court practice. Thereafter, along with his intimate friend, the late Lord Macgregor Mitchell, he began to
" devil " to the late Mr C. E. Lippe, K.C., then the leading
Junior Counsel at the Scottish Bar. He was called to the Bar
in 1915. Rejected for military service on medical grounds, he
temporarily gave up his practice, closed his house in Edinburgh,
and went with his mother to London where he worked in the
Blockade Department of the Ministry of Trade, receiving the
O.B.E. at the end of the war. During the war, his life was not
easy. His working hours were long, his salary small, life in a
London hotel was expensive and food was scarce. It was a
" treat " for him and his mother when his brother, on
occasional leave from the Army, brought meat coupons
which enabled them to supplement their monotonous civilian
diet.

Returning to the Bar in 1919, Tom Cooper rapidly acquired
a large practice. His first official appointment came in 1922
when he was made Junior Legal Assessor to the City of Edinburgh and in due course Standing Counsel to many other
Local Authorities. With expanding practice, he took Silk
in 1927 and became no less popular as a leader. His unusual
knowledge of technical subjects (for he had not neglected his
early interest in science and engineering) gave him great
advantages in cross-examining expert witnesses ; and his
amazing capacity for mastering any subject often confounded
the experts in their own fields.

Apart from an odd debate in the University Union, Tom
Cooper, who had always been a staunch Unionist, had had no
time to take a really active part in politics but, with the
reputation he had by now acquired in London as well as north
of the Border, he was approached in 1930 to state if he would
be prepared to stand for Parliament and, after consenting,
he was adopted later that year as prospective Unionist Candidate for Banffshire, then a Liberal seat. As was to be expected,
he threw himself strenuously into this new field of operations.
He was a fluent and untroubled speaker at all times, possessed
of a pawky humour and a sureness of touch which enabled
him immediately and effortlessly to select the jest or argument

PLATE II

Mr T. M. Cooper, Advocate, 1919

most apt to his audience, and at his adoption meeting he
delighted a somewhat hostile audience by some of his remarks.
In the *Banffshire Journal* of 9th December 1930 he is reported
as saying, *inter alia* :—

One thing that appeals to me in Applied Unionism is that it has the
common honesty and the common sense to accept and act upon the wisdom
of the old Scottish saying about " Keeping our ain sea guts for our ain
sea maws." . . . If a man has farmed land and raised stock in Banffshire
all his life and his father and grandfather before him, I do not believe
he has anything to learn from all the Government clerks in Whitehall,
and, if you do not believe me, do as I did last night and go to the Fat
Stock Show in Edinburgh.

Asked by a heckler if we would not be much better with a
Parliament in Scotland and Home Rule of our own, he replied :
" If you guarantee to make me Prime Minister of Scotland, I
will be very pleased to support your views." But all his careful
nursing of the constituency was to go for nothing, for, at the
subsequent General Election, in accordance with the Baldwin
pact with the Liberals in October 1931, he withdrew in favour
of the Liberal candidate.

Resuming his legal activities, Tom Cooper began to appear
regularly at the Parliamentary Bar in London and, as the
result of his handling of the promotion of a number of Provisional Orders, he received many English retainers and was
pressed to practise exclusively there. One of his proudest
moments occurred when, during the promotion of one Order,
he quoted with effect the evidence given by his father in an
Order promoted some forty years previously. But his heart
was in Scotland and he decided to return to Parliament House
where his services were to prove in still greater demand. It is
impossible to mention here all the important cases in which
he appeared. One reference must suffice. The late Lord
Alness in an Appreciation published in *The Scotsman* of 17th
July 1955, recalling the famous " Silks " trial conducted before
him by the late Lord Aitchison (then Lord Advocate) wrote :
" Lord Cooper's client was named first in the indictment and
therefore he had the right to cross-examine first. There were
eight or nine other Counsel in the case. Yet, when Cooper

b

sat down, there was not one of them left with a question to ask, they all adopted simply his cross-examination."

The time had now come when Tom Cooper was to re-enter politics. At a by-election in 1935, he was adopted as National Government candidate for West Edinburgh, and, after a vigorous campaign, was duly elected by a large majority. On taking his seat he immediately became a Front Bencher as Solicitor-General for Scotland. At the General Election which followed only a few months later, he increased his majority and became Lord Advocate for Scotland and a Privy Councillor.

Throughout these two political campaigns which followed so closely on one another, Mrs Cooper, his mother, faithfully accompanied him wherever he went, and, at the conclusion of every meeting, the pair of them made a point of leaving the platform in order to have a chat with their principal Socialist hecklers who pursued them nightly from hall to hall, with resultant expressions of esteem and friendship on both sides, politics temporarily forgotten. Therein lay one of Tom Cooper's principal assets. At all times modest, friendly and approachable, he became equally " Tommy " to the Socialists as to the Tories, and his mother was just as warmly received. He often recalled with pleasure one occasion when, having arranged to meet his mother at the House of Commons, he sought her for some time in vain and eventually found her happily presiding over a tea-table on the Terrace where her Labour hosts were Jimmy Maxton, David Kirkwood, Willie Gallacher and George Buchanan. One of his proud possessions was a copy of Mr Gallacher's *Revolt on the Clyde*, inscribed " With the warm regards of the author to T. M. Cooper, an honest and generous political opponent."

Tom Cooper's life was now a full one. In addition to his duties in his constituency, at the Crown Office, and as Lord Advocate in the House, he found himself taking a prominent part in several important United Kingdom Bills in which he was associated with and warmly thanked by Sir Samuel Hoare and Mr Hore Belisha. About this time he was consulted by the Cabinet and attended the Privy Council

PLATE III

The Rt. Hon. T. M. Cooper, K.C., M.P.,
Lord Advocate, 1935

meeting when the question of the Abdication of King Edward VIII arose.

On the eve of the outbreak of the Second World War, Tom Cooper, then in Edinburgh, received his " Absolute Government Priority " telegram. Having, as on all occasions, mastered in advance his extensive instructions, he was able immediately to hold the necessary consultations with Scottish Command, to set in train the last minute preparations and, some twelve hours before the country was actually at war, to telephone to London from the Headquarters of the Regional Commissioner, " Preparations completed."

The coming of war made life more strenuous still. For a time Joint Regional Commissioner for Scotland, in addition to his work at the Crown Office and in his constituency, he had now to handle a mass of Emergency War Legislation in the House, and to travel continually between Edinburgh and London. Family illness added to his anxieties, both his mother and his brother being in nursing homes. At the same time he was removing to his final residence in Hermitage Drive, Edinburgh. He would leave London on a Thursday night, superintend the removal, visit the two invalids, attend to his duties at the Crown Office, go twice to Church on the Sunday, and catch the Sunday night train back to his work in London. During the bombing of London, his room at the House of Commons was destroyed, as was also his room at the Scottish Office in Dover House. His walk from Dover House to his club was often far from pleasant. Nor were his night train journeys always restful. He used to recall one night when he lay awake in his sleeper, the train having halted on the bridge over the Tyne at Newcastle while enemy aircraft tried to bomb the bridge.

The long strain of his heavy responsibilities, frequent sleepless nights, and constant travelling were bound to tell upon a man who had never possessed a robust constitution ; and it must have been a relief to him when, on the death of Lord Aitchison in 1941, he was offered and accepted the office of Lord Justice-Clerk, taking his seat with the forensic title of Lord Cooper.

With the end of his Parliamentary career, the Press of the day referred to his time in the House of Commons in the following terms :—

He was only six years or so in the Commons and it is seldom that a new member has made his mark so quickly or in so short a time left so high a reputation.   There were two things which helped Lord Cooper to do this.   One was his capacity and indeed enthusiasm for hard work, the other was his friendly and generous nature.   Law Officers are frequently called on to give assistance or advice to Back Benchers seeking solutions to some of their constituents' difficulties.   They found the Lord Advocate, as he then was, both ready and willing to do all he could for them, and his courtesy and helpfulness were extended equally to the political journalists whom he met in the Parliamentary lobbies.

When he left the Commons to become a Judge, a leading Civil Servant in England remarked—" There goes the finest brain at the disposal of the Government."   The comment confirmed what was an open secret at the time, that he was frequently consulted by the Cabinet on problems which had no relation to Scotland and that his opinion was highly valued.

Lord Cooper held office as Lord Justice-Clerk for five years. During that period, besides presiding in the Second Division, he took many criminal trials of public interest, including the notorious Aberdeen " Coffins " case, when his seat on the Bench was hemmed in by coffin lids, shrouds and other funeral appurtenances.

It was his opinion that " Scots Criminal Law can challenge that of any other country."   Called upon more than once to pronounce the death sentence, Lord Cooper, in giving evidence before the Royal Commission in 1950, deponed :—

I attach the utmost importance to the maintenance of capital punish-ment. . . . Sane people in Scotland do not commit murder as readily as sane people in England. . . . Psychiatrists are getting too many charges of murder reduced by making exaggerated and unproved claims.

In 1946, on the promotion of Lord Normand to be a Lord of Appeal, Lord Cooper was appointed Lord Justice-General of Scotland and Lord President of the Court of Session. During his tenure of office, as Lord Justice-Clerk and as Lord President, Lord Cooper was regularly in Parliament House about nine in the morning in session and even in recess, following the lesson taught him by the late Lord Scott Dickson to whom he had so often acted as Junior.

Although a busy man all his life, Lord Cooper was not a man without recreations or hobbies. Thanks to the enthusiasm of his uncle, he started to play golf, when only eight, with a discarded iron and any ball he could lay his hands on. For many years thereafter, the family summer holidays were always spent at golfing resorts and Lord Cooper's golf steadily improved until he had worked down to a reliable handicap of nine. He gave up the game on medical advice about 1935. But, as he told the Merchant Company Golf Club at a dinner a year or two before his death, whenever he felt depressed he visited the clubhouse of the Royal Burgess Golfing Society and gazed with pride at a handsome Cup bearing his name.

At an almost equally early age he became interested in astronomy. When he was ten, his mother's birthday present to him was Sir John Ball's *Story of the Heavens*. Having thoroughly assimilated the contents, he then saved up every penny until he was able to purchase a second-hand telescope which he put into action every starry night. From then onwards he slowly collected a small library of astronomical works and the knowledge he thus acquired was to be skilfully applied to his later research work. When he became a Fellow of the Royal Astronomical Society, he often visited the Observatories at Calton Hill and Blackford. Only a few years ago, through the generosity of the Society, he was lent a large and powerful telescope which was duly erected in his garden. He spent many happy hours with it and often dragged out his long-suffering mother or his brother on a cold night to have a peep at some stellar phenomenon which had thrilled him.

Another of Lord Cooper's recreations was angling. Sponsored by his great friend the late Lord Macgregor Mitchell, he purchased all the necessary equipment in 1926 and went off with this experienced angler for a fishing holiday. He continued to fish for a number of years but, becoming impatient with a sport which seldom yielded the quick results which his nature always demanded, he gradually gave it up.

When the better wireless sets started to come on the market, Lord Cooper purchased one and, being dissatisfied with its performance, promptly stripped it. Having closely examined it, he considered that the circuit could be improved upon, and, after drawing many diagrams, produced a final drawing which he sent to the manufacturers. To his amazement he received an enthusiastic invitation to meet them as they considered his improvement could be followed out to their mutual benefit. He replied that he was not further interested, but that they were welcome to make any use they liked of his idea and in due course he received an intimation that they were embodying it in the new sets they were constructing.

Lord Cooper was keenly interested in hydro-electricity and shortly after he became Lord Justice-Clerk he was appointed to preside over the Government Committee to enquire into the possibility of hydro-electric development in Scotland. The " Cooper Committee " Report which followed upon the Committee's extensive enquiries, and which is a model of clarity, provided the basis for the subsequent legislation which brought the North of Scotland Hydro-Electric Board into being. In later years, when touring in Scotland, he never missed a chance of visiting the various power stations constructed or in course of construction, and of drawing the resident engineers into talk.

An enthusiastic traveller when time permitted, Lord Cooper made several journeys abroad. After a tour through France with Mr J. S. C. Reid, now Baron Reid of Drem, and a visit to the United States and Canada with the late Lord Birnam, he later made several trips through the Mediterranean and toured various areas in North and West Africa. On board ship his technique never varied. He made a practice of asking for a seat at the Chief Engineer's table. In due course an invitation to the engine room would follow where his intimate knowledge of ships' engines never failed to impress. Generally, there followed an invitation to the bridge from the Captain, and here again he was far from being out of his depth, having in his time digested many books on Navigation and, during his practice, conducted numerous " collision at sea " litigations.

Notwithstanding the wide scope of his activities, Lord Cooper was an omnivorous reader of poetry and prose alike. He was a well-known figure in all the bookshops in Edinburgh and his friends were constantly surprised by the extent of his reading and his critical literary judgment. Most of his reading was done on Saturdays and in bed nightly, but he was a quick reader with the happy faculty of being able to remember what he had read.

Lord Cooper found another outlet in music. Without any formal lessons he taught himself at an early age how to play the piano, and he continued to play right up to his last illness. Whilst he enjoyed all good music, his favourite was " The Messiah," and if he could not attend the concert where it was being rendered, he would listen raptly to a broadcast, with the score open in front of him. He also owned a two-manual American organ, and, as a half-hour's relaxation from his work, he went almost nightly to his organ or his piano. Nothing pleased him more than to be given a chance to play on a church organ provided the church was empty.

From his school days, Lord Cooper liked to sketch. Ships and engines were for long his favourite subjects and many such drawings were found on odd scraps of paper after he had left his seat at the Bar or on the Bench. Later in life he took his sketch book and paint box with him on holiday and he made some hundred water colours of scenes that took his fancy — paintings for which he certainly never claimed any special merit but which gave him soothing pleasure in their execution. Lord Cooper also took up colour photography, purchasing a projector and screen, and, as another half-hour's light relief, he would sometimes entertain the family by running through his collection. Keenly interested in his garden, he was out every morning before he left for Court consulting and planning with his gardener, and in the evening when opportunity offered he himself worked there.

He was a life-long cat lover. If he met a cat in the street or in a house, he never failed to speak to it and the cats seemed to sense that they had found a friend. He regularly attended cat shows, but his own two cats were strays found starving in the Hermitage of Braid. His last stray " Tinker," who is still alive, was very dear to him and for some time after Lord Cooper's death " Tinker " was inconsolable.

Countless stories have been told about Lord Cooper's great love of children and of their love for him. Never talking down to them, he had an amazing knack of winning their confidence and of sharing their thoughts and hopes. When he went for his Sunday afternoon walk, he came home a very disappointed man if he had not encountered some children quite unknown to him with whom he had succeeded in spending a happy half hour. If he met strange children playing in a house or a hotel, he would sit down near them, fetch out a piece of paper and start drawing a ship, an engine, or an animal. Sooner or later the children would drift across to him and, the ice once broken, demands for drawings and stories would pour in. It was a regular occurrence, when his car was out of action, to see him walking along Hermitage Drive with a small school-bound child in either hand. However busy, he always found time to answer immediately the letters he received from his small friends, and he devoted much thought to the selection of their Christmas presents.

One incident in particular which caused Lord Cooper much amusement and delight is worth recording. A dog engaged with a bone had had it snatched from him by a child and, although of hitherto irreproachable character, the dog had promptly bitten the child. A lower court had ordered the dog to be destroyed, but its owner took an appeal by way of Stated Case to the High Court of Justiciary. In a short opinion, which received much Press publicity at the time, Lord Cooper, supported by his colleagues, championed the dog's cause, indicating that no self-respecting dog could be expected to stand by without protest whilst his dinner was appropriated. The following evening a small girl, a complete stranger, called at Lord Cooper's house and asked to see him. Ushered in to him, she explained that the report of how he had spared this dog's life had been read to her, that she possessed a doggie of her own, and that she had felt that she must call and thank him for being so merciful. Only a small child could have had the courage to call upon the Lord Justice-General in order to discuss one of his opinions with him.

All his life a devout Churchman, Lord Cooper was an elder in St George's West during the ministry of the late Dr James Black and was always warmly welcomed during his regular visits to the members in his district. When he came to Hermitage Drive, Lord Cooper joined North Morningside Church and worshipped there twice every Sunday until three weeks before his death.

In the course of his academic career, Lord Cooper received many distinctions. An LL.D. of Edinburgh (1951), Glasgow (1951), and St Andrews (1953), Universities, he was the first Scottish Judge since the sixteenth century to be honoured with the Doctorate (honoris causa) of the University of Paris (1951). An Honorary Bencher of the Middle Temple, he was at various times Vice-President of the Royal Society of Edinburgh and Vice-President of the British Association. He was also a Trustee of the National Library of Scotland, and of the National Galleries of Scotland, Chairman of the Executive Committee of the Scottish Committee on the History of Parliament, Chairman of the Ancient Monuments Board of Scotland, 1946-49, and President of the Scottish History Society, 1946-50. He was also an Honorary Member of the Society of Public Teachers of Law, of the Merchant Company of Edinburgh and of the Institute of Municipal Engineers.

His ability to grasp the essential points in any problem, his wisdom in suggesting how difficulties might be overcome and his ease and clarity of exposition led to a demand for his services in many ways, notably as Chairman of the Hydro-Electric Committee already referred to, of the Committee on grants to the Scottish Universities, and of the Clyde Estuary Committee. In 1949 the Secretary of State appointed him to report on the difficult problem of St Andrews University and University College, Dundee. Although unwilling, he gave of his best and whilst his report and recommendations were not accepted, they paved the way for the later Royal Commission presided over by Lord Tedder.

As far back as 1934, Lord Cooper contributed an article to the *Scots Law Times* on the proposed foundation of a Stair Society to encourage the study and to advance the knowledge of the history of Scots Law—a project in the subsequent development of which he was to take so prominent a part, especially by his various contributions to its publications and as Chairman of its Council. Naturally, perhaps, his classical and legal scholarship led to a further hobby in the study of early Scots Law and the history of its development. He was always happy in reading and analysing the early legal cases reported in the ecclesiastical cartularies and his *Select Scottish Cases of the Thirteenth Century* was a by-product of this reading. His four addresses to the Scottish History Society (reprinted as *Supra Crepidam* and hereinafter) were models of their kind as well as gentle reproaches to the historians : for in them he showed how other disciplines—*e.g.* astronomy, cartography, and the Latin cursus—could be used as an aid to historical research. These and other publications are listed in the appended Bibliography, and a selection of his many contributions to legal and historical subjects are reprinted in this volume. His reputation extended far beyond Scotland, and not a few of his papers have been translated and reproduced in foreign countries at the request of eminent jurists. His judicial decisions are, of course, fully reported in *Session Cases* from 1941 to 1954. Perhaps the best known, the " E. II. R." opinion, is reprinted in this volume, along with one or two other opinions in criminal cases.

In addition to his work on the Bench and in the many other spheres to which reference has been made, Lord Cooper was constantly in demand to give lectures, unveil memorials, make presentations and deliver public speeches all over Scotland and in England as well.

Not many men, even if endowed with a like intellect and industry, could have got through so much work. Lord Cooper was peculiarly favoured in three respects. In the first place, he possessed an amazing quickness of apprehension. A member

PLATE IV

Lord Cooper, at the Sorbonne, Paris, 1951, being congratulated by M. Vincent Auriol, President of the French Republic.

of the Bar once remarked, " Before you have spoken a dozen words the Lord President has grasped the point you are going to make." His critics, especially if they had lost an argument before him, complained that he was too quick for a judge. In the second place, once he had grasped the points involved in a judicial or administrative problem, he could swiftly and unhesitatingly discard the irrelevant and marshal the relevant in clear, logical order. And finally, when the moment came to speak or write, he could clothe his thoughts immediately in fitting words. His extempore judgments needed no subsequent " touching up " to improve their grammar or style. So too, when he took up his pen or, in later years, sat down before his typewriter—characteristically taken to pieces, re-assembled and always serviced entirely by himself—in order to compose a judgment, a report, or a scholarly article, there was no fumbling for words, no erasing and no re-writing. The composition came straight out in its final form, orderly, lucid, precise and elegant. He himself attributed this to his classical reading, especially in Latin. He said that when he had anything important to write, having arranged his thoughts, he would attune himself to composition by reading a few pages of Latin prose, after which well-balanced English sentences seemed to form themselves in his mind without conscious effort. Incidentally, he would express the opinion that the universal use of Latin as a learned language would not only facilitate communication between scholars of different nations but would in many subjects make for greater precision of thought.

On more than one occasion he might have been promoted to the House of Lords as one of the Lords of Appeal, but he was reluctant to transfer himself to London and thought his services should be to Scotland, being a " Nationalist " in the true sense of the word. Life in his native city, where he was in contact with so many administrative and public activities, offered more satisfaction to his energetic and versatile nature.

Yet he once said, " I am a shy man. Professionally I am not shy, but socially I am." It was not apparent to those who saw him conversing easily on a social occasion. Nevertheless it is true that he derived little pleasure from the trivialities of social intercourse, and, after dining out, he would sometimes humorously complain of having wasted an evening which might have been spent on work or on his hobbies. It was otherwise if, during the evening, he had met someone with whom he could exchange ideas or from whom he could learn something to add to his store of technical information. When able to get away from Parliament House at midday he would lunch at his club, where he had his circle of friends, yet even there it was often necessary to " have a word with " some fellow-member of a Board or Committee on a matter of pending business, or there was a problem of historical scholarship to discuss with the professional historians or a point of legal theory on which he wanted to hear the opinion of an academic lawyer.

Eventually the years of unremitting labour began to take their toll. A heart affection which had troubled him slightly for some years now grew more serious. Only his great courage kept him on the Bench on the occasions of these attacks and he often came home in the evenings a very exhausted man. The sudden death of his mother in October 1951 came as a terrible shock to him. Loyal to the promise he had given to his father, his main aim in life had been ever to be with her and to give her the best in life, just as she had devoted her whole life to her sons.

After his mother's death Lord Cooper threw himself back into his work on the Bench and into all his other activities and the climax to his career came when, in the June 1954 Birthday Honours List, he was raised to the Peerage. It was a great regret to him that his mother had passed away before this honour was conferred, for he knew how intensely proud she would have been, but he little thought that his own life was nearing its close. After his Peerage was announced, he had a short holiday and returned to Edinburgh at the end of August 1954. On 2nd September he had a meeting with Lord Carmont and later with Lord Normand in the morning, worked in his garden in the afternoon, and attended a B.B.C. function in the evening, during the course of which he was suddenly struck down by a cerebral thrombosis. Unconscious for several days, his life was despaired of and the doctors held out no hope. The first time he became conscious was when his brother tried to tell him about a telegram from Sir Winston Churchill, who had previously telephoned enquiring as to his condition. His brother read out the telegram two or three times and finally Lord Cooper opened his eyes, stretched out his hand for the telegram and lay looking at it, although quite unable to read. Ultimately he smiled and then went off to sleep and thereafter his condition improved slowly but steadily. By November he was well enough to travel to Harrogate for a change and on his return he faced his doctors demanding their decision as to his prospects. Their intimation that his strength would never again be adequate for the responsibilities of his high office was a crushing blow to one who still had so many plans and ambitions for the future ; but unhesitatingly he immediately intimated his resignation.

From that time onwards it became increasingly obvious that he was a very sick man. Though he never complained, it was painfully clear that he felt the contrast between his old life of perpetual activity and the life now forced upon him by ill-health. His one remaining ambition was to take his seat in the House of Lords whilst Sir Winston Churchill, who in 1946 had sent him his own Medal as a member of " The Great Coalition," was still Prime Minister. Accordingly in March 1955, with his old friends Baron Reid of Drem and Lord Keith of Avonholm as his Sponsors, he was able, notwithstanding his great weakness, to go through the long ceremony without faltering, and, amidst many old friends on both sides of the House to whom he still was " Tommy," he took his seat as Baron Cooper of Culross of Dunnet in the County of Caithness.

Whilst on holiday at Kinlochrannoch two months later, however, he had a severe relapse and had to be conveyed by ambulance to an Edinburgh Nursing Home. Once again he rallied and seemed to be getting better but on the morning of 15th July 1955 he had a sudden coronary thrombosis, became unconscious and passed away within half an hour.

Typically, Lord Cooper had left instructions that he did not wish a public funeral and, accordingly, after a short service in his house conducted by his old College friend the Very Rev. Dr Charles L. Warr, he was laid to rest on 18th July 1955, beside his mother in Grange Cemetery. In addition to his brother with whom he had lived all his life, his pall bearers, by his own request, were Lord Normand, his predecessor, Lord Clyde, his successor, Lord Thomson, the Lord Justice-Clerk, Lord Russell, Lord Hill Watson, Lord Wheatley, and the Rt. Hon. W. R. Milligan, Q.C., the Lord Advocate. A large and representative assembly of mourners gathered to pay their last tribute to a great Scotsman, a great lawyer and a great Judge who had passed away all too soon to his final rest.

J.

The Contribution of Lord Cooper of Culross to Scottish Law [1]

by

T. B. SMITH, Q.C., D.C.L., M.A. (OXON)

Professor of Scots Law in the University of Aberdeen

I SHOULD not do justice to the memory of the man who was probably the outstanding Scottish judge of our time if I were to speak tonight in the language of eulogy. The temptation to do so—which is strong when there is the sense of recent loss—must be resisted. Lord Cooper's personal qualities have been brilliantly and sympathetically recorded in obituary notices by men who had been intimate friends of a lifetime ; and for such as myself—a junior disciple—to dwell upon these qualities would be almost an impertinence. My aim is to assess the contribution made by Lord Cooper of Culross to the Law of Scotland—not only in discharge of the highest judicial offices of the country as Lord Justice-General of Scotland, as Lord Justice-Clerk and as Lord President of the Court of Session—but also in the field of Scottish legal scholarship. Whether my evaluation is justified depends not only on the past but on the future. On the morrow of Corunna how would a soldier have assessed the achievement of John Moore ? A Napier or a Hardinge would not have judged it merely by the gains and losses of a Peninsular campaign— but according as to whether Moore's enlightened and humanely efficient training of the Light Division at Shorncliffe would establish a viable tradition. Posterity will judge the achievement of Lord Cooper, not only by his work for the law of

---

[1] This public Memorial lecture was delivered in the University of Aberdeen at the opening of the Winter Session, 1955. (Published in the *Juridical Review*, vol. lxvii, 1955, pp, 249-270).

Scotland, but by the flowering or withering of that law to which he devoted his life. We, and especially those of us who are lawyers, cannot take too much for granted in this respect; and the future is largely in our own hands.

Thomas Mackay Cooper was born in 1892. Outstanding both at school and at University, he very quickly made his mark on admission to the Faculty of Advocates, and took Silk in 1927. His sure mastery of law and of a lucid and logical forensic style ensured rapid and deserved success at the Bar. In 1935 he became successively Solicitor-General for Scotland and Lord Advocate, proving in these offices his great talent for administration. In the same year he was sworn of the Privy Council. On the death of Lord Justice-Clerk Aitchison in 1941, Lord Cooper was appointed to succeed him and presided in the Second Division until 1946, when he followed Lord Normand as Lord Justice-General of Scotland and Lord President of the Court of Session on the latter's appointment as Lord of Appeal in Ordinary. In June 1954 Lord Cooper was created Baron Cooper of Culross of Dunnet in the County of Caithness, but, unlike Lord Dunedin earlier in the century, he was not to enjoy the opportunity of sitting judicially from time to time in the House of Lords while retaining supreme judicial office in Scotland. Before the sittings of the court resumed last year, he was suddenly struck down by a serious illness, from which he never recovered. In December he resigned his judicial offices, and on 15th July 1955 he died.

I need not greatly elaborate this brief factual statement except to note that Lord Cooper's talents were employed extensively outside the normal judicial field. His capacity for hard work was prodigious. To him fell, for example, the preparatory work for the hydro-electric development of the North of Scotland; he sat on the Committee of Inquiry which sought to resolve the St Andrews University dispute; he was most actively concerned with the administration of the National Library and of the National Galleries of Scotland. Between 1946 and 1949 he was President of the Scottish History Society; as Chairman of Council of the Stair Society he was tireless and undaunted in his efforts on behalf of Scottish legal history.

Baldly stated, these facts might imply no more than the *cursus honorum* of a very able Scottish lawyer. My submission, however, claims much more. I believe that the state of Scottish law and of Scottish affairs generally when Lord Cooper assumed judicial office was such that he alone had the necessary combination of qualities to check certain trends and to reorientate the course of development. He was only granted some thirteen years on the Bench, and though he worked with almost superhuman energy and application we cannot say for certain that this time was sufficient for the task he attempted. Lord Cooper believed that the law of Scotland—especially private law and criminal law—was a " typical product of the Scottish ethos." He considered that this law (though needing reform in certain respects) was an important part of our national heritage, a safeguard of our liberties, and in itself a guarantee of our nationhood. He also believed—and with good reason—that on its merits Scottish law should be preferred on impartial comparative evaluation to the law of England, which was increasingly encroaching on the Scottish system. Therefore he was concerned above all to preserve the Scottish legal tradition. Few men can have had a deeper understanding of that tradition, and the published results of his researches into medieval Scottish law—especially that of the thirteenth century—are so far our surest guide in that field. By contrast with the medievalist—or, should I more truly say in supplement of the medievalist—we find in Lord Cooper the mind of the reformer, or, as he himself put it, of the iconoclast. He was not addicted to ancestor worship for its own sake, nor to favouring a legal doctrine merely because at some phase in Scotland's legal development it had gained recognition. There was much of the spirit of Bentham in the late Lord President. He had the intellectual honesty for example, to admire what is good in Stair, the greatest of our institutional writers, but to deny him that semisuperstitious reverence which— associated with incantations to institutional writers generally and to Roman law—one finds most frequently among those

Scottish lawyers who know least about Roman law or of the contents of the folio treasuries of our common law. Roman law Cooper regarded as having been a valuable formative influence in Scottish law. In modern times, as he observed,[1] " borrowing still goes on, but under the impact of the new interest in comparative jurisprudence the lawyer in search of new ideas has now the civilised world at his disposal and is not confined to Justinian and Gregory IX." Strongly opposed to uncritical Anglicisation of Scottish law, Lord Cooper fully recognised the contributions made in recent years by Anglo-American legal scholarship in refining legal principles.[2] In appropriate cases he gladly accepted the lead of English writers and judges, but he was sensitive [3]—possibly, though understandably, hypersensitive—to the danger of indiscriminate borrowing. If I may peril myself on a medical analogy, if there is transfusion from an unsuitable blood group or with infected blood, one may kill the patient. Thorough testing by experts is a necessary preliminary. From preference, however, Lord Cooper was concerned to encourage the traditional intellectual contacts of Scottish lawyers with the legal thought of the Continent. It is significant that Lord Cooper was the first Scottish judge since the sixteenth century to receive a Doctorate from the University of Paris. In his relations with English lawyers, though he valued his election as Honorary Bencher of the Middle Temple, he was probably more at home with those from the Law Schools of Oxford, Cambridge and London than with the Chancery or Common Law practitioner in whom he sometimes suspected a conservative complacency.[4]

Concerned not only intellectually but emotionally to preserve the Scottish legal tradition against encroachment,

[1] (1950) 63 Harv.L.R. 469.

[2] e.g., B.M.T. v. Gray, 1951 S.C. 586 ; 1951 S.L.T. 247 (restraint of trade) ; Watt v. Jamieson, 1954 S.C. 56 ; 1954 S.L.T. 56 (nuisance).

[3] e.g., Macdonald v. North of Scotland Bank, 1942 S.C. 369 ; 1942 S.L.T. 196 (prescription of bank account) ; McLaughlan v. Craig, 1948 S.C. 599 ; 1948 S.L.T. 483 (Rylands v. Fletcher liability) ; Winks Exors. v. Tallent, 1947 S.C. 470 ; 1947 S.L.T. 316, also Salvesen's Trs. v. Wye, 1954 S.C. 440 ; 1954 S.L.T. 299 (charitable trusts) ; Famer v. Mill, 1948 J.C. 4 ; 1948 S.L.T. 133 (interpretation of Vagrancy Act).

[4] " Scottish Legal Tradition " (1949) at p. 30.

yet zealous for the reform—using modern comparative methods —of all that was out of keeping with current social developments, Lord Cooper was called to high judicial office at a critical time. The field of human activity controlled by the principles of Scottish law had greatly diminished since the nineteenth century when Inglis, for example, had undertaken a task comparable to Cooper's. Further, the defences were in the mid-twentieth century in an indifferent state of repair. United Kingdom statute law, including much emergency legislation, had in many branches of the law replaced well-established principles. The English doctrine of absolute sovereignty of the King in Parliament had not been seriously challenged in a Scottish court. Administrative law and tribunals had in many instances ousted the jurisdiction of the Supreme Courts ; nationalisation and voluntary amalgamation of industrial and mercantile enterprises had led to increasing exclusion of Scottish law from application even in Scottish affairs—through arbitration clauses in contracts and so forth. The Scotsman under arms—volunteer or conscript— was by a statutory provision of general reference subjected not just to a British military code but generally to an alien system of criminal law. In the administration of the principles of Scottish common law by some judges in the Scottish courts and the House of Lords, there had long been a tendency to assimilate Scottish to English law through citation of English precedents and by the facile assumption—made frequently without argument by qualified experts on the point, and sometimes without full comprehension—that the principles of Scottish and English law on the matter *sub judice* were identical.[1] Now, of course, these various factors had operated long before the mid-twentieth century and had exercised the attention of Scottish lawyers since the Union, but they had become increasingly prominent during the twentieth century.

The defences against such encroachment were not well manned. In particular the Law Schools of the Universities

---

[1] Thus it was assumed without argument in *Donoghue* v. *Stevenson*, 1932 S.C. (H.L.) 31 ; 1932 S.L.T. 317, that the Scottish principle of *culpa* and the English tort of negligence were identical—which is demonstrably inaccurate.

—which in other countries may be relied on for the maintenance of a critical censorship of the law commanding the
respect of the profession ; for the production of treatises and
articles of authority ; and for the enthusing of new generations
of lawyers—in Scotland did not without exception rise to the
occasion. Legal scholarship relied in Scotland on the work
of a very few enthusiastic or disillusioned men. More and
more the tendency increased to live exclusively on the capital
of the past—which may lead to parochialism—or to borrow
from the nearest neighbour without calculating the consequences. These consequences are bankruptcy and absorption.

Such then is the background of Lord Cooper's contribution to Scottish law—the background to his preservation
of a valued heritage and to his reform and advocacy of further
reforms where he found the system defective. To these tasks
he brought a sense of mission ; a clearness of thought and
lucidity of style—which make his printed judgments a joy to
read [1]—and intense application to work. It is common
knowledge that he preferred to preside in the courts of Scotland
rather than—like a number of his predecessors as Lord Advocate
or Lord President—to accept appointment to the House of
Lords as one of the Lords of Appeal in Ordinary. This preference distinguishes him from such Scottish judges as Lord
Robertson, and suggests the comparison of Lord Cooper's
contribution with that of Lord President Inglis. Like Inglis
in the Bute Guardianship case,[2] it fell to him to defend the
jurisdiction of the Court of Session against the House of Lords
and to emphasise the Scottish view that the Treaty of Union
is still a valid constitutional document. (In passing, one may
question whether Scotland can afford to spare two of her
ablest judges for permanent duty in the House of Lords—which

[1] Particular reference may be made to his opinions in complex cases of property
trust and succession, *e.g.*, *Cochrane's Ex.* v. *Cochrane*, 1947 S.C. 134 ; 1947 S.L.T.
69 ; *Tennent's J. F.* v. *Tennent*, 1954 S.C. 215 ; 1954 S.L.T. 161 ; *Petries Trs.* v.
Mander's Tr., 1954 S.C. 430 ; 1954 S.L.T. (Notes), 72 ; *Sturgis's Tr.* v. *Sturgis*,
1951 S.C. 637 ; 1952 S.L.T. 37 ; *Ballantyne's Trs.* v. *Ballantyne*, 1952 S.C. 458 ;
1952 S.L.T. 425 ; *Magistrates of Banff* v. *Ruthin Castle*, 1944 S.C. 36 ; 1944 S.L.T.
373 ; *Elliot's Ex.* v. *Elliot*, 1953 S.C. 43 ; 1953 S.L.T. 91.

[2] (1861) 4 Macq. at pp. 76-77 ; see also *Orr Ewing* v. *Orr Ewing's Trs.* (1884)
11 R. 600.

hears annually only a trifling number of Scottish civil appeals, and, of course, no Scottish appeals in criminal matters.) Again like Inglis, Cooper presided first in the Second Division before his promotion to the Lord President's Chair, and thus knew intimately the judicial psychology of his colleagues in both Divisions.

The technique of a great judge cannot be taken to pieces like a machine ; yet, so to speak, checks and balances also play their part in the judicial process.   Though it may be clear that justice and modern conditions would suggest one solution, even a court which is not enslaved to precedent may be compelled with reluctance to decide according to the unambiguous terms of a statute or according to some established rule of professional practice.[1] If the decision must be shared by a bench of judges, then the interpretation of the law by each must lead to adjustments in the decision of all. Thus it is that an analysis of Lord Cooper's decisions produces, on the one hand, instances of judicial reorientation of law, and, on the other, instances of reluctant acquiescence in obsolete or obsolescent doctrines.   Moreover, the ablest of judges is not infallible, and Lord Cooper was no exception.[2] Being a bachelor, for example, he possibly set the standards of married life rather higher than the average man who has actual experience of it would consider reasonable.[3]   In exercising criminal jurisdiction his greatest difficulties probably arose after a verdict of " guilty " had been recorded in certain types of case and in *McCudden* [4] it may be thought that he overstrained the law regarding corroboration by evidence of similar acts.

I propose then to deal with Lord Cooper's influence on various aspects of the law—developing, preserving, defending,

---

[1] *e.g., Borland* v. *Borland,* 1947 S.C. 432 ; 1947 S.L.T. 242.

[2] See, *Ross's J. F.* v. *Martin,* 1954 S.C. 18 ; 1954 S.L.T. 49 ; 1955 S.L.T. 117 (an understandable but fallacious endeavour to give effect to the supposed meaning of the testatrix rather than to the wording of the will).

[3] *Jamieson* v. *Jamieson,* 1951 S.C. 286 ; 1951 S.L.T. 174 ; rev. 1952 S.C. (H.L.) 44 ; 1952 S.L.T. 257 ; *Wallace* v. *Wallace,* 1952 S.C. 197 ; 1952 S.L.T. 165. On the other hand in *Riddell* v. *Riddell,* 1952 S.C. 475 ; 1953 S.L.T. 9, the late Lord President gave a masterly exposition of the law regarding collusion and lenocinium.

[4] 1952 J.C. 86 ; 1952 S.L.T. 357.

and indeed counter-attacking, as he considered the case required. His judicial opinions are only one of the sources on which I have drawn.

Criminal Law

It is obvious that Lord Cooper maintained a very close interest in Scottish criminal law even after he had demitted office as Lord Justice-Clerk and assumed that of Lord Justice-General. This chapter of Scottish law has been greatly developed during the last thirty years by decisions of individual judges and by appellate sessions of the High Court of Justiciary. No appeal lies in criminal matters to the House of Lords, and so the Scottish judges are masters in their own house—unless Parliament should intervene. That, I think, was the main reason why his Lordship opposed codification of Scottish criminal law while favouring in theory codification of Scottish private law—if carried out in Scotland by a competent Scottish body. Criminal law, he feared, might be codified on a United Kingdom basis to the serious prejudice of the more enlightened principles of Scottish law. In his evidence before the Royal Commission on Capital Punishment [1]—a masterly clarification of our law—the late Lord Justice-General stressed a number of these principles. The Scottish law of murder is in effect confined to cases of intentional killing ; " constructive malice " is unknown ; the anachronistic McNaughton rules regarding insanity do not bind a Scottish court ; insanity is practically never in Scotland a contested issue because of the plea of diminished responsibility ; the illogical verdict of " Guilty but insane " has no place north of the Tweed ; the scope of the death penalty is restricted within very narrow limits ; pre-trial and re-trial publicity are avoided. It is ironical that the conflicting views of English law, which are themselves condemned by enlightened lawyers in the South, should have been perpetrated so far as soldiers and airmen are concerned, including Scottish soldiers and airmen, by the Army Act

[1] Minute of Evidence 18—1950.

and Air Force Act of this year[1] which had to be defended on these points in Parliament by the present Lord Advocate. His task was an unenviable one. Lord Cooper's apprehensions regarding the effect on Scotsmen of codification of criminal law in Britain were, it would appear, amply justified.

From the many leading contributions made by the late Lord Justice-General to Scottish criminal law, I can select only a few. Best known, I expect, in Aberdeen was the case of *Dewar*.[2] It was urged for the defence in that case that the indictment for theft of numerous coffins and coffin lids, appropriated by the manager of the Aberdeen Crematorium after bodies had been committed for cremation, could be met by the defence that the accused believed that he was justified in so acting. He thought, it was said, that he could treat these coffins and lids (for which of course, the executors had paid) as " scrap." The jury was left in no doubt by the judge's charge that—while error or mistake might in law be a good defence—such a defence as was advanced by Dewar could only avail if the belief could be proved to be reasonable—as to which the onus was virtually impossible to discharge in the circumstances.

In *Crawford*,[3] the law regarding provocation and self-defence—which had been somewhat confused in the earlier case of *Hillan*,[4] due to the fact that the background to such pleas is often similar—was clarified by a court presided over by Lord Cooper. Provocation, it was stressed, cannot exculpate but can only palliate crime—justifying, that is to say, a lesser punishment. Self-defence must exculpate completely or fail completely.

Giving the leading opinions in *Fox* v. *Patterson*,[5] and *Brannan*,[6] Lord Cooper made clear the scope of the doctrine of " recent possession " which, when it applies, may throw on an accused found in suspicious circumstances "in possession" of recently stolen goods the onus of giving an explanation compatible with his innocence. This doctrine is of very

---

[1] *i.e.*, Army Act, 1955, 3 and 4 Eliz. 2, c. 18, esp. s. 70 ; Air Force Act, 1955, 3 and 4 Eliz. 2, c. 19.　　[2] 1945 J.C. 5 ; 1945 S.L.T. 114.
[3] 1950 J.C. 67 ; 1950 S.L.T. 279.　　[4] 1937 J.C. 53 ; 1937 S.L.T. 396.
[5] 1948 J.C. 104 ; 1948 S.L.T. 547.　　[6] 1954 J.C. 87 ; 1954 S.L.T. 255.

considerable practical importance in the suppression of crime
—and the solution reached by the court reconciles common
sense with adequate safeguards for a person unjustifiably
suspected. It is not necessary that the stolen goods should
have been actually found by the police upon the person or
under the immediate control of the suspect—provided, for
example, it can be proved that he had parted with possession.

In *Galletly* v. *Laird*,[1] his Lordship had to consider the vexed
contemporary problem of obscene literature, and his views
were later adopted by Lord Goddard in England. His concern was not primarily with the nature of the work attacked,
but rather with the question whether it was being circulated
among those likely to be corrupted. Works which were
condemned by " the morose Puritan " might in law be un-
objectionable so far as the educated reading public were
concerned.

Two of Lord Cooper's charges to juries in murder cases
may be mentioned as models of clarity. Reading them, one
is struck by his facility in presenting complex legal issues in
exact and easily comprehended language. In *Braithwate*,[2]
he was concerned with the defence of " diminished responsibility "—that is to say a defence falling short of a plea of
insanity, which will justify a court in treating as a mitigating
factor some lesser impairment of the mind or mental aberra-
tion. After his charge, stating the limits of the defence, the
jury convicted of murder. *Rutherford*,[3] was indeed a unique
case. The defence was that the deceased woman had
" pestered " the panel (or accused) to strangle her ; and that he
had (according to his own story) to frighten her put a tie
round her neck, pulled it, and had inadvertently throttled
the deceased. Lord Justice-Clerk Cooper (as he then was)
gave very clear directions on the limits of murder, culpable
homicide, casual homicide and assault—ruling out assault
and casual homicide from the jury's consideration. He further
clarified the distinction made in criminal law between motive
and intention. The jury convicted of culpable homicide.

[1] 1953 J.C. 16 ; 1953 S.L.T. 67.   [2] 1945 J.C. 55 ; 1945 S.L.T. 209.
[3] 1947 J.C. 1 ; 1947 S.L.T. 3.

Some of the most controversial criminal decisions of Lord Cooper—controversial because of major importance as the liberty of the citizen is involved—concern the admissibility of evidence elicited by police interrogation or during examination of police surgeons, or as a result of unauthorised search of premises. His Lordship had to reconcile two often conflicting interests ; one, that the citizen should be protected from illegal or irregular invasion of his liberties by the authorities ; and the other, that the interest of the State to secure evidence bearing upon the commission of crime should not be withheld merely on technical grounds. In seeking a just solution a number of interesting distinctions have been made by the High Court of Justiciary in recent years. So far as material evidence is concerned (*e.g.* possession of salmon in the close season), even if the evidence has been obtained in circumstances of which the law disapproves, the court *may* in its discretion admit the evidence.[1] This discretion to admit is subject to the qualification that material evidence discovered as a result of improper interrogation and linked with it is not admissible ; and also to the qualification that, while the police refrain from arresting an individual (and the decision to arrest limits police powers of questioning) material evidence obtained from the accused person prior to arrest will not usually be admitted.[2] As the Lord Justice-General observed of such cases, " Unless the principles under which police investigations are carried out are adhered to with reasonable strictness, the anchor of the entire system for the protection of the public will very soon begin to drag." May I underline the increased sensitivity to protect a suspect when his actual person is immediately concerned. This is again apparent in the strict rules laid down by a court presided over by Lord Cooper regarding procedure as to medical examination and evidence elicited during medical examination of persons suspected of driving while under the influence of drink and drugs.[3] In his last year of judicial office the late Lord Justice-General

[1] Compare *Lawrie* v. *Muir*, 1950 J.C. 19 ; 1950 S.L.T. 37 ; and *Fairley* v. *Fishmongers of London*, 1951 J.C. 14 ; 1951 S.L.T. 54.

[2] *McGovern*, 1950 J.C. 33 ; 1950 S.L.T. 133.

[3] *Reid* v. *Nixon*, 1948 J.C. 68 ; 1948 S.L.T. 295.

convened a Full Bench to consider the admissibility of evidence elicited by police interrogation prior to arrest of a boy who was suspected as the likely perpetrator of a murder.[1] It was held—admittedly hampering the police in their investigation— that at the stage when suspicion has definitely focused on a particular individual, only a voluntary statement made without pressure or inducement is admissible—while after arrest the accused must not be questioned at all. Prior to arrest it would also seem that a citizen may decline either to answer questions or to accompany the police to the station " to assist them in their inquiries." It seems to me that Lord Cooper was not happy—as his earlier views in *Rigg* [2] (another case of murder) seem to confirm—about the spontaneity of admissions made by persons in the hands of the police. Professor Dewar Gibb has with some justification criticised his attitude of " undue tenderness " [3] to accused persons as unreasonably hindering the investigation of crime. Lord Cooper's solution would probably have been to revive the older Scottish practice of preliminary judicial examination of suspects before an impartial judge—the sheriff—and this solution has much to commend it. Another good example of his concern for fairness to the suspect is apparent in his condemnation of pre-trial press comment on matters which might embarrass the defence by influencing the minds of those who were to serve on the jury. In *Macalister* v. *Associated Newspapers*,[4] which preceded the so-called Scottish Nationalist " Conspiracy Trial," he intervened to curb the pre-trial comment of a paper which had followed un-Scottish standards in such matters by publishing a series of articles calculated to create alarm and antagonism regarding the so-called S.R.A.

Civil Law

Scottish criminal law was, compared with civil law, late in maturing, and has not been so restricted by precedent as have many chapters of civil law. Let us observe how Lord Cooper dealt with a number of problems in the civil law where application of the established legal rule would not do justice in a

---

[1] *Chalmers*, 1954 J.C. 66 ; 1954 S.L.T. 177.
[2] 1946 J.C. 1 ; 1946 S.L.T. 49.   [3] 66 J.R. 199.   [4] 1954 S.L.T. 14.

particular case. Where the rule was clear and unambiguous and was relied on in professional practice, he felt unable to override law with equity even in " hard cases." Conveyancing is a formal and conservative branch of the law in any country—possibly particularly so in Scotland. Thus Lord Cooper insisted on exact fulfilment of the strict formalities of notarial execution of deeds—though he admitted that the result of insisting upon the strict letter of the law might be to frustrate what was the genuine expression of a testator's last wishes.[1]

On the other hand, where probative writing was required to complete a contract for the sale of a house and it was sought to take advantage of a technicality, his Lordship denounced the rule regarding the requirement of probative writing of both parties as " a fossil relic of feudalism, explicable, if confined within the field of strict conveyancing, but completely out of touch with realities when it intrudes into the field of mutual contract." The circumstances of the case made it possible on a rather strained construction for him to hold that the technical rule had in fact been satisfied.[2]

The same attitude of respect for settled law and intolerance of anachronism can be found in the late Lord President's attitude to questions regarding the property of married women.[3] Formerly the law had tended to treat married women rather like wayward children where property was concerned—and elaborate trusts were contrived to put a woman's capital beyond her reach, restricting her to a liferent even if there were no children of the marriage and she was left a widow. With the ever-decreasing value of money, many childless ladies of middle age (and, I must add, their husbands) had occasion to deplore the caution of the bride's father in tying up her property on marriage some thirty years earlier. In *Beith's Trs.* v. *Beith*,[4] the First Division, led by Lord Cooper, considering the changes in the position of married women

---

[1] *Hynd's Tr.* v. *Hynd's Trs.*, 1954 S.C. 112 ; 1954 S.L.T. 113 ; *Finlay's Trs.* v. *Finlay*, 1948 S.C. 16 ; 1948 S.L.T. 182.

[2] *McGinn* v. *Shearer*, 1947 S.C. 335 ; 1947 S.L.T. 255.

[3] *Dempster's Trs.* v. *Dempster*, 1949 S.C. 92 ; 1949 S.L.T. 110.

[4] 1950 S.C. 66 ; 1950 S.L.T. 70.

generally during the past seventy-five years, declined to follow a precedent laid down by seven judges in 1875. Applying in effect the maxim *cessante ratione legis cessat lex ipsa*, the First Division refashioned the law, and held that in a marriage where there could no longer be children the wife could call on the trustees of the marriage contract to pay over her capital. The conditions governing the liberation of the wife's capital from the fetters of a trust have been worked out in subsequent cases—in which the need to reorientate the law and also to respect such established doctrines as " alimentary " protection have been taken into account.[1] In *Preston* v. *Preston*,[2] Lord Cooper clearly regarded as unsatisfactory the existing law restricting the wife's participation in the revenue of the household. Though acquiescing in this law in the case before him, he looked forward to the day when legislation or judicial decision in a more authoritative court would introduce a limited form of *communio bonorum*.

The one case in contract which I have time to mention,[3] I again select, not for what the court actually decided, but for Lord Cooper's suggested challenge to the tyranny of " contracts of adhesion." By this I mean that in many trans- actions to-day, notably contracts of carriage, the operator, by printed conditions which are never the subject of negotia- tion, purports to exclude his liability in contract or delict for any mishap to the person paying for the service. In *McKay* v. *Scottish Airways*,[4] Lord Cooper reserved his opinion

---

[1] *Kennedy* v. *Kennedy's Trs.*, 1953 S.C. 60 ; 1953 S.L.T. 131 ; *Sturgis's Tr.* v. *Sturgis*, 1951 S.C. 637 ; 1951 S.L.T. 37.

[2] 1950 S.C. 253 ; 1950 S.L.T. 196.

[3] Among many other important decisions of Lord Cooper in the field of con- tract, the following may be particularly noted :—*Martin* v. *Scottish Transport and General Workers Union*, 1951 S.C. 129 ; 1951 S.L.T. 132 (*ultra vires*) ; *Winestone* v. *Wolifson*, 1954 S.C. 77 ; 1954 S.L.T. 153 (interest on I.O.U.) ; *Langford* v. *Dutch*, 1952 S.C. 15 ; 1952 S.L.T. 72 (repudiation of contract) ; *Sinclair* v. *Juner*, 1952 S.C. 35 ; 1952 S.L.T. 181 (edictal liability, *locatio custodiæ, locatio operis faciendi*) ; *Anderson* v. *Lambie*, 1953 S.C. 94 ; 1953 S.L.T. 82 ; rev. 1954 S.C.(H.L.) 43 ; 1954 S.L.T. 73 (error in expression) ; *James B. Fraser* v. *Denny Mott & Dickson*, 1943 S.C. 293 ; 1944 S.L.T. 139 ; aff. 1944 S.C.(H.L.) 35 ; 1945 S.L.T. 2 (frustration of contract—on which also see Lord Cooper's article (1946) 28 Journal Comp. Leg. 1).

[4] 1948 S.C. 254 ; 1948 S.L.T. 402.

on the point (which had not been argued) whether public policy might not be pleaded to restrict the sweeping exemptions from liability which are encountered in many leonine bargains through the operation of " ticket conditions."

Delict or reparation is another chapter of the law to which Lord Cooper has made an important contribution in somewhat difficult circumstances. The basic principle of the Scottish law of reparation is that liability depends upon fault or breach of duty by the defender. Liability for *culpa* or negligence may arise in very different circumstances, but this does not alter the basic principle.[1] Through decisions of the House of Lords, however, extraneous categories which really reflect the incomplete development of the English law of torts have been superimposed on the Scottish system in certain respects—such as the liability of occupiers or lessors of premises for injury caused to persons entering on the premises ; or in cases of liability for the escape of dangerous agencies from land. It is a paradox that the English Law Reform Committee [2] is now (without considering the former Scottish law) recommending a solution to problems of occupier's liability very similar to that adopted by the Scottish courts before the intervention of the House of Lords. Lord Cooper felt strongly that the intrusion of English precedents into the Scottish law of reparation had led to an unsatisfactory state of our law. " Either oil or water," he said [3] " is preferable to the unsatisfactory emulsion which results from attempts to mix the two." Wherever he was free to do so, he sought to re-establish the general principle of *culpa* or fault as the measure of liability in the Scottish law of reparation.[4] In this connection he was clearly troubled by the doctrine of *respondeat superior*—that is

---

[1] *Lockhart* v. *Barr*, 1941 S.C. 578 ; 1941 S.L.T. 414. Whether breach of statutory duty is appropriately designated " negligence " is arguable—but see Lord Cooper's *dicta* in *Hamilton* v. *Anderson*, 1953 S.C. 129 ; 1953 S.L.T. 77.

[2] Cmd. 9305, 1954.

[3] " The Scottish Legal Tradition " at p. 23.

[4] *McLaughlan* v. *Craig*, 1948 S.C. 599 ; 1948 S.L.T. 483 ; *cf. McPhail* v. *Lanarkshire C.C.*, 1951 S.C. 301 ; 1951 S.L.T. 32. The law of nuisance was latterly regarded by Lord Cooper as an aspect of the law of neighbourhood independent of the principle of *culpa*—see *Watt* v. *Jamieson*, 1954 S.C. 56 ; 1954 S.L.T. 56 ; *cf. Davie* v. *Magistrates of Edinburgh*, 1951 S.C. 720 ; 1952 S.L.T. 74.

that an employer will be held vicariously responsible in certain circumstances to third parties injured by the wrongdoing of a servant or an agent—even though the employer was not personally at fault.[1] This doctrine can only be explained on grounds of expediency these days—when in some cases an employer may be precluded from selecting, from dismissing or even from controlling the actual work of the employee for whose wrongdoing he is held vicariously responsible. I cannot analyse Lord Cooper's many important judgments on such questions—but may mention specifically the question of "hospital liability." As is generally known, until a decision of the First Division presided over by Lord Cooper last year, it was supposed that a hospital authority was not responsible in Scotland for the negligence of professional staff while acting in a professional capacity. The difficulty often was to determine where the frontier ran between professional and administrative functions. The decisions in *Macdonald* v. *Glasgow Western Hospitals Board* and of *Hayward* v. *Edinburgh Royal Infirmary Board of Management* [2] have rejected these distinctions and lay down, rightly I submit, that where duties are imposed by statute through the Secretary of State on Hospital Boards, they are responsible for the proper discharge of these duties, and cannot elide responsibility by pleading the professional status of persons whom they employ to carry out the actual treatment or nursing. If I may say so, though the result of Lord Cooper's interpretation of the law may not please all the medical profession, his careful and conscientious examination of the rules and principles involved is to my mind convincing. The National Health Service (Scotland) Act, 1947, applies in circumstances very different from those in which the voluntary hospitals operated.

In the law of reparation I may be permitted to mention

[1] See, *e.g.*, *Short* v. *Henderson*, 1945 S.C. 155 ; 1946 S.L.T. 71 ; *Kilboy* v. *S.E. Fire Area Joint Committee*, 1952 S.C. 280 ; 1952 S.L.T. 332 ; *Malley* v. *L.M.S. Ry.*, 1944 S.C. 129 ; 1945 S.L.T. 313 ; *Matusczyk* v. *Nat. Coal Board*, 1953 S.C. 8 ; 1953 S.L.T. 39 ; *Mair* v. *Wood*, 1948 S.C. 83 ; 1948 S.L.T. 326 (which is a valuable authority on the nature and liability of partnerships) ; *Power* v. *Central S.M.T.*, 1949 S.C. 376 ; 1949 S.L.T. 302 (where, however, the defender's contract with the pursuer does not seem to have been considered).

[2] 1954 S.C. 453 ; 1954 S.L.T. 226.

just one further instance of Lord Cooper's moulding of the
law in accordance with the needs of contemporary society—
Steel v. *Glasgow Iron and Steel Co.*[1] Here Lord Cooper gave the
leading judgment recognising that a man, who lost his life
in the effort to save from destruction property imperilled by
another's negligence, did not by his conduct bar a claim for
damages on the plea *volenti non fit injuria*.   After a masterly
analysis of the law of England and America he continued,
" The question being therefore for us an open one, it must be
answered by the application of our native principles of the law
of reparation ; and by following these principles to their
logical conclusion I consider that the solution can be found." [2]

Within the limits of one lecture one could not range over
many of the leading judgments of Lord Cooper—but, on the
other hand, one cannot omit reference to his judicial pronouncements on the constitutional position of Scotland and of
Scottish law within the framework of the United Kingdom.

In many of Lord Cooper's judgments there will be found
passages repudiating sharply the suggestion that Scottish law
should follow English precedents and revolve as a satellite
of the Anglo-American Common Law.   It may even be that
on occasion he reacted without full justification.   This sensitivity is more readily understandable after perusing contemporary opinions of the House of Lords, where the opposite
tendency is exaggerated—that of using in Scottish appeals
English technical terms " for convenience," or often of assuming—unless the contrary is expressly argued and established—
that the principles of Scottish and English law coincide.   A
recent example which irked the late Lord President was the
House of Lords decision reversing the Court of Session in
I.R.C. v. *Glasgow Police Athletic Association.*[3]   This case decided
that though the word " charity " is used in English law in a
highly technical sense—distinct from the popular sense in
which the term is used in Scotland—the highly technical
English meaning is that to be read into United Kingdom
taxation statutes.   Probably not since the Treason Act of

---

[1] 1944 S.C. 237 ; 1945 S.L.T. 70.   [2] *Ibid.* at p. 247.
[3] 1952 S.C. 102 ; 1952 S.L.T. 136 ; 1953 S.C.(H.L.) 13 ; 1953 S.L.T. 105.

Queen Anne's reign [1] have Scottish courts and practitioners been faced with so perplexing a situation. The Scottish courts are bound to apply as British law a technical English doctrine as to the definition of which there is considerable uncertainty in England—but are precluded from hearing evidence as to the meaning of the vital technical terms in English law [2] or from referring the question to the English Courts. Situations such as this were calculated to gall Lord Cooper—as likewise did the English practice of declaring to be wards in Chancery, irrespective of domicile, pupils and minors who had ventured within the jurisdiction of the English courts. [3]

From a constitutional standpoint, however, Lord Cooper will probably be remembered by posterity for the views which he expressed *obiter* in the so-called E. II. R. case— *MacCormick* v. *Lord Advocate*. [4] The First Division led by Lord Cooper heard in that case an appeal from the Lord Ordinary on the question whether Her Majesty was lawfully designated Elizabeth II in Scotland. It was held that in fact this designation—whether or not historically accurate or politically desirable—did not depend on statutory provision at all ; and therefore the court was not called on to decide whether a particular statute contravened the Act and Treaty of Union. Lord Cooper, however, dealt with the general question as to whether Parliament could lawfully override the entrenched provisions of the Union. He rejected the doctrine of unlimited Parliamentary sovereignty as inconsistent both with pre-Union Scottish theory and with the Treaty which had called into being the new Parliament of the United Kingdom. He pointed out with justice that what happened in 1707 was not just the admission of Scottish representatives to the Parliament of England, and rejected the theory that Parliament could lawfully legislate in defiance of the fundamental and essential

---

[1] 7 Anne, c. 21.

[2] Normally English law must be proved, *McElroy* v. *McAllister*, 1949 S.C. 110 ; 1949 S.L.T. 139.

[3] But in *McLean* v. *McLean*, 1947 S.C. 79 ; 1947 S.L.T. 36, Lord Cooper expressed himself with considerable restraint on this point.

[4] 1953 S.C. 396 ; 1953 S.L.T. 255.

conditions of the Union.[1] These views, if upheld in the future, will modify profoundly the doctrine on which most of us lawyers have been nurtured in our student days. They are the first articulate statement in two and a half centuries of the fundamental law of the British Constitution.

So much for the judicial contribution of Lord Cooper—and how inadequate a survey it is ! My outline of his influence would be incomplete, however, if I did not at least mention his constant activity against what he regarded as anachronistic,[2] inefficient and dilatory in our legal procedure. The civil jury he disapproved of in particular,[3] and rightly observed that it was imposed on Scotland in the interests of the House of Lords a century and a half ago when that House was familiar only with the English system where the jury was regarded as the palladium of the constitution. It is another paradox of English influence on Scottish law that to-day many if not most of the cases which in Scotland are tried by civil jury would be tried in England by a judge. In the interests of the litigant—whose concern with litigation is too often overlooked by lawyers—Lord Cooper advocated that simple issues involving moderate sums should be determined by a procedure less elaborate and less expensive than is appropriate for complex matters involving great sums.[4] His attitude to strict judicial precedent—another legacy of the House of Lords—was also somewhat uninhibited by modern standards ; and, as I have illustrated, he would not readily acquiesce in the application of a Scottish precedent which he regarded as out of date and unsatisfactory. He might distinguish, reject the *ratio* as obscure, or apply the maxim *cessante ratione legis cessat lex ipsa*.[5] He was not violently opposed to administrative courts for the speedy determination of appropriate issues provided that the Supreme Courts were empowered to check

---

[1] Though the courts could not always restrain the illegality.

[2] *e.g.*, *Armstrong* v. *Lithgows Ltd.*, 1954 S.C. 233 ; 1954 S.L.T. 37.

[3] " Scottish Legal Tradition " at p. 25.

[4] See his address to the Society of Public Teachers of Law " Defects in the British Judicial Machine " (1953) 2 Journal S.P.T.L. (N.S.) 91.

[5] *Beith's Trs.*, *supra*, n. 34 ; *McGinley* v. *Pacitti*, 1950 S.C. 364 ; 1950 S.L.T. 276 (assessment of damages) ; *Hopkinson* v. *Napier*, 1953 S.C. 139 ; 1953 S.L.T. 99 (reputed ownership and hire-purchase).

manifest injustices and to interpret questions of pure law. He disliked undue concentration of power in any one of the three organs of government.[1]

In such leisure as he allowed himself from modern law, Lord Cooper researched deeply into the history of Scottish law—especially that of medieval times—and into questions of mutual interest to historians and lawyers. He did not accept the existence of rigid frontiers in the empire of the mind and cheerfully disregarded the maxim *ne supra crepidam sutor judicaret*. Those brief and lucid passages in his judgments by which he was wont to put the modern law in its historical perspective were the by-product of his research.[2] Probably of greater value even than the published fruits of his own scholarship—such as the Stair Society volumes and his contributions to *The Juridical Review* and *Scottish Historical Review*—is the inspiration which he has given to others to continue where he left off. He has put questions to the historians and to the lawyers which will, I earnestly hope, provoke answers of importance to both. He felt deeply the reflection that Scottish law had never produced its Pollock, Maitland or Holdsworth. Had he been granted a longer life, he might well have laid down judicial office to devote himself to the writing of a comprehensive work on Scottish legal history.

In conclusion, I may observe, Lord Cooper took an enthusiastic interest in Scottish legal education, and deplored that our law schools had not been equipped or organised to take the lead in legal development in the manner of the Universities of Paris, Harvard, Rome and Oxford. If an appeal lies from the House of Lords, surely it is to the Master of University College, Oxford, as Editor of *The Law Quarterly Review*. His Lordship was keenly interested in the institution of a comprehensive academic first law degree which would rank with, and indeed above, all others in the Universities of

---

[1] 1954 S.L.T. (News) 189.

[2] See *Campbell's Trs.* v. *Campbell's Trs.*, 1950 S.C. 48 ; 1950 S.L.T. 82 (*valentia agere*) ; *Graham* v. *Cuthbert*, 1951 J.C. 25 ; 1951 S.L.T. 58 (legal aid in criminal causes) ; *Price* v. *Watson*, 1951 S.C. 359 ; 1951 S.L.T. 266 (possessory remedies) ; *Miller* v. *MacRobbie*, 1949 S.C. 1 ; 1949 S.L.T. 2 (leasehold) ; *cf.* " Supra Crepidam," p. 4 ; *Riddell* v. *Riddell*, *supra*, n. 12 (oath of calumny).

Scotland. He encouraged every progressive step—and urged those concerned with legal scholarship to further personal efforts. The Society of Public Teachers of Law, recognising his contribution to legal education, conferred on him the rare tribute of Honorary Membership.[1] His criticism was always constructive ; his help and advice were most generously given. When, for example, a lectureship in Comparative Law was instituted here, I recall that his Lordship gave the inaugural lecture in a subject which had for him great academic and practical importance. He was, incidentally, returning as Lord President to lecture in a faculty where he had been examiner in the days of Professor Mackenzie Stuart. In his lecture Lord Cooper regretted that Scottish legal scholarship in the twentieth century had neglected comparative legal studies. Though, he said, no man can be completely master of more than one system of law, an understanding of the principles of other legal systems is essential to the development of modern Scottish law—and, indeed, without the stimulus of comparative law the Scottish system would surely die.[2]

On the Bench and as a scholar Lord Cooper of Culross gave himself unsparingly for the law of Scotland—which was, as has been said, the great love of his life. His judgments and his many published works of legal scholarship remain as his memorial. Above all, however, there is the inspiration of what he conceived the destiny of our Scottish law to be. The value of that contribution will in the future be assessed largely by reference to the response of the present generation of Scottish lawyers—especially law students in Scottish universities—and of their successors to the lead of a man who was indeed one of the choice and master spirits of this age.

[1] Lord Cooper died during the Society's Edinburgh meeting—at which it had been hoped his Lordship would take a leading part. An eloquent tribute was paid to his memory by the President.

[2] I am grateful to Dr J. Fackenheim for notes of Lord Cooper's lecture.

SELECTED PAPERS

Legal Education in Scotland : A Criticism

IN his recent inaugural address to the Juridical Society of Edinburgh the Lord Justice-General epitomised the ideal to which the legal profession should strive to attain in the phrase, " the favourable conjunction of trained intellect and courageous character." No man, of course, by taking thought, can suddenly acquire for himself, or directly impart to others, the qualities which go to the formation of " courageous character." These are the fine fruits of too subtle influences to be capable of forced cultivation. The " training of intellect," however, stands on a different footing ; for in this field there will always be ample scope and pressing need for well-directed educational activity on the part of our legal associations. But the duty which they owe, both to themselves and to society at large, to contribute of their best towards progressively perfecting legal education, and so adapting the machinery of the law adequately to perform its ever-widening functions, is one which for long has been virtually ignored.

At any time this attitude of detachment and indifference would be reprehensible ; but at the present moment it is doubly so. The last fifty or sixty years have witnessed the inauguration of a period of transition in our jurisprudence. Under the increasing pressure of modern legislation, feudal law, in the widest sense of that term, including all those doctrines and topics which form the foundation of our institutional works, is slowly but surely receding into the limbo of legal antiquities ; but, though the " old order changeth, giving place to the new," it has still vitality enough to make insistent demands upon student and practitioner alike. Simultaneously with the decline of the older law, there has been in progress the rapid and infinitely multifarious development of mercantile law ; and the present-day student is accordingly compelled not only to cover all—or nearly all—the old ground, but also to

3

explore in detail whole continents of which Stair and Erskine never dreamt, or were vouchsafed only the most fleeting of " Pisgah glimpses." But, notwithstanding the patent need for a complete review of educational methods to meet altered conditions, and notwithstanding the advance which has been made in recent years in the study of the science of teaching, it is a truly remarkable and lamentable fact that the requirements of our legal associations from their intrants, and the legal curricula of our Universities, are substantially the same to-day as they were a generation and more ago.

No legal body in Scotland provides organised instruction in law. All except one—the Signet Society—accept substitutes for their entrance examinations. Consequently the direction of legal education in Scotland falls upon the Law Faculties of Edinburgh, Glasgow, and Aberdeen Universities, although the character of the training which these institutions afford is deeply influenced by the regulations for admission to the legal societies, as well as by the direct control exercised by representatives of these societies on the governing bodies of the Universities. Accordingly, in what follows, reference is made almost exclusively to the law curriculum of the Universities, and particularly of the University of Edinburgh.

The education of the law student naturally falls into three parts, viz., (1) general education ; (2) theoretical instruction ; and (3) practical training. The line of demarcation is not a hard-and-fast one, and all three members of the triad are closely interrelated. But any educational scheme which fails to make adequate provision for each branch is radically defective.

1. *General Education*

In these days of high pressure and utilitarian sentiment, the temptation to premature specialisation in professional studies is a strong one, and it is not surprising that the Universities have partially succumbed to it. The student who contemplates graduation in both arts and law is now free to offer two legal subjects as part of the five required for graduation in arts, thus reducing his arts curriculum proper to three distinct subjects. This concession is, of course, designed to shorten the time required for the double degree ; but is it justifiable in principle ? If there is one quality more than another which makes for success in the practice of the law it is mental adaptability. The catholic outlook which is derived from a liberal education combining breadth with a modicum of depth, is a *sine qua non* for any one who may be called upon at short notice to assimilate rapidly and to expound intelligently subjects so diverse as electrical engineering and physiology, or advanced accountancy and navigation. A competent knowledge of these and numberless other subjects is, needless to say, unattainable ; but there is nothing unduly ambitious in the attempt to acquire the disciplined habit of mind and the intellectual breadth which enables a man confidently to attack any problem, however unfamiliar and however technical. These qualities, and, above all, the proper development of the analytical faculty, which is the practising lawyer's indispensable auxiliary, cannot be attained under any narrow and restricted educational scheme. For these reasons, it is suggested that, so far from countenancing overlapping between the arts and law curriculum, or sanctioning specialisation by law students in single groups of subjects, the academic authorities would promote the best interests of the average student by insisting upon the postponement of legal study until the arts curriculum had been completed, and by requiring aspirants to the double degree to select their curriculum upon the most comprehensive basis consistent with the student's aptitude.

2. *Theoretical Instruction*

Theoretical instruction and practical training in law are mutually complementary. The futility of a merely doctrinaire knowledge of legal principles is too obvious to require exposure. Much less obvious, but no less real, is the futility and inadequacy of a curriculum which presents law mainly from the practical standpoint of an applied science. Just as a sound knowledge of anatomy is the almost invariable pre-requisite of training in surgery and clinical medicine, so it is essential that the law student in his early days should view the juris-prudence of Scotland as an organic whole, that he should see its various branches logically analysed, and their correlation scientifically expounded, and there should be inculcated into him at an early stage a sound appreciation of the ratio of legal principles in their origin and subsequent development. This is a need which the Scottish Universities do not adequately supply. In their present curriculum and lecture system an unfortunate attempt has been made to give theoretical instruc-tion not as an end in itself, but as a means of imparting practical training, and the result presents the excellencies of neither branch and the defects of both. The student is denied the opportunity of studying Scots law as a system of jurisprudence and is invited instead to learn his business by means of a protracted series of oral " correspondence courses," with the additional drawback of having to take down each " course " to the dictation of his lecturer. To-day, as in Lord Shaw's student days, " law is taught as a trade and learned as a trade." Now, as then, the image of Scottish jurisprudence, " serene, splendid, and august, is never beheld, even in a vision."

This unsatisfactory state of affairs is due in part to the almost fantastic confusion in the arrangement of courses. Taking Edinburgh University as an example, there is sub-stantial overlapping between the subjects dealt with in Scots law on the one hand, and (1) mercantile law, (2) industrial law, (3) accounting and business method, (4) landlord and tenant, and (5) banking, on the other hand. The first, third and fifth of the latter group of subjects also mutually overlap. Such topics as sequestration, liquidation, and negotiable instruments are expounded by at least three different lecturers in three different classes. In place of a well-thought-out and logical scheme of study, the curriculum is forced to conform to the haphazard arrangement in which the chairs were founded—several of them in the eighteenth century. Further, the requirements of the academic authorities as to attendance at classes is equally incapable of justification. To Scots law, which is by far the most important and comprehensive class, only eighty lectures are assigned ; and precisely the same amount of time has to be devoted both to civil law (two-thirds of which is truly Roman antiquities), and also to constitutional law and history (which is simply British history *minus* foreign policy). If the whole realm of Scots law is deemed capable of being surveyed in eighty lectures, the allowance of forty lectures for such relatively restricted subjects as administrative law and forensic medicine seems somewhat excessive. Finally, there is apparently nothing in the regulations to prevent a student taking the courses in any order he likes.

The plain truth of the matter is that the present scheme is palpably illogical, and wholly out of touch with modern conditions and requirements. What is required is not merely reform, but complete reconstruction. The present curriculum is founded upon the principle of unequal emphasis, and is maintained in existence by sheer force of inertia. Difficulties there may well be in altering foundations and allocating endowments ; but there are such things as provisional orders and private Acts of Parliament.

3. *Practical Training*

It has been stated that the compromise adopted in the Scottish Universities is to attempt to provide practical training by means of theoretical instruction. While the method of approaching the study of law from the standpoint of an applied science largely detracts, as we have seen, from the real value of the theoretical instruction, the practical training equally fails to meet the necessities of the case. An acid test of the character of the training is to be found in the degree examination questions. A perusal of the questions set over a period of years discloses a marked tendency to a stereotyped and periodically recurring form of inquiry calculated to elicit as an answer a short extract from the lectures on the subject in question. The more faithful the reproduction, the higher are the marks awarded. The student who attains complete success under this method will have a rude awakening when he realises on entering upon the practice of his profession that actual problems do not present themselves in stereotyped form, but that by far the most difficult question which the lawyer has to meet is to ascertain what the real problem is by isolating the true issue from a confused mass of partly relevant material.   Another defect of the present system is that it is a direct encouragement to the student to apply himself to the study of the lectures alone.   It is possible—*experto crede*—to graduate with distinction in law without having acquired even a nodding acquaintance with the law reports and the standard works which the student will have to handle familiarly for the rest of his life, without having seen a closed record, and without having heard of, much less understood, the term " relevancy."

Apart from the school of experience in a lawyer's office or the Parliament House, these deficiencies might be supplemented in various ways.   The substitution of the concrete problem for the stereotyped inquiry, insistence upon the study of current law reports, attendance in law Courts, organised debating societies, and work in " legal dispensaries "—all these would help to clothe with flesh the skeleton training with which the student has at present to rest content.

The above reflections are offered not in any spirit of captious criticism, but in the hope of provoking discussion and arousing among the members of our legal societies a sense of the duty which they undoubtedly owe to their profession to ensure that those who come after them will be adequately equipped for the practice of the law.   The study of law is, of course, a task for which a lifetime is far too short.   But it is a matter of the supremest importance for the future of the profession that the foundations of such a lifework should be well and truly laid in a sound professional training.   In the present position of matters a student may graduate as a Bachelor of Laws of a Scottish University without being competent to handle intelligently the simplest piece of professional work, and without even knowing where to procure the information how to do it.   Is the perpetuation of this system creditable, or even tolerable ?

1922

Accountancy Evidence from an Advocate's Point of View

THERE ARE MANY POINTS at which, in the exercise of our respective professions, the accountant and the advocate are brought into business contact. As auditor, liquidator, trustee in bankruptcy, or judicial factor, you operate in a region in which legal difficulties, more or less complex, are constantly encountered ; and examination of your syllabus shows that your Society's deliberations possess a definitely legal flavour ; and however assiduously you may have attended the Law classes, a member of *your* profession may occasionally find it expedient to seek the advice of a member of *mine*. But the presentation of expert accountancy evidence, upon which I have been asked to address you to-night, is not a task which arises in the normal exercise of your professional duties ; and in its performance we do not meet in the customary relationship of counsel and client. It is a special operation of peculiar delicacy and difficulty, in the execution of which, if we would work to any purpose, we must meet not merely as allies in a common cause but as partners in a joint adventure ; and in which the measure of our joint success will largely depend upon the completeness and intimacy of the mutual understanding which can be established between us. I therefore welcome this opportunity of briefly reviewing the subject from the standpoint of the Bar, and of telling you *what we want, what we do not want, and why.*

At the outset may I make two introductory observations.

1. The presentation of accountancy evidence is a branch of your work which few of you can afford to neglect and none to despise. There *was* a time when it was the fashion to deride expert testimony of all kinds ; and you are all familiar with the three categories into which liars have traditionally been divided. Even in the latest edition of the leading English

authority on evidence, there has been left standing a passage which I wish to quote as an instance of the repute in which the expert witness was until lately regarded in high quarters : " The testimony which least deserves credit," says the learned author, " is that of skilled witnesses. If is often quite surprising with what facility and to what an extent their views can be made to correspond with the wishes or interests of the parties who call them. Their judgments become so warped by regarding the subject from one point of view that, *even* when conscientiously disposed, they are incapable of forming an independent opinion. Being zealous partisans, their Belief becomes synonymous with Faith as defined by the Apostle—the substance of things hoped for, the evidence of things not seen." Whatever justification may have existed for these strictures in the bad old days, I doubt whether the charge could ever fairly be levelled at accountancy witnesses, whose training and habit of thought tend to produce a cold impartiality, and who have never been addicted to the practice of riding the hobby-horses of pet theories. In any event, the reproach has long since been redeemed. It is generally accepted to-day that scientific knowledge and special skill, conscientiously applied under the government of high principle, is an invaluable auxiliary to the ends of justice. And among those who are habitually retained as accountancy experts at Westminster, in the Strand, and in the Parliament House are to be found the keenest wits and the strictest code of honour in the profession. The field is one which offers unlimited scope, not only for technical dexterity but for the widest and most liberal exercise of your special knowledge as men of figures ; and there must be few to whom the peculiar interest and infinite variety of the work does not offer a strong attraction. Finally—if I may be permitted to allude to mercenary motives—the rewards are by no means to be despised.

2. My second observation is a corollary from the first. The Scottish School of Accountants has produced in the past, and can offer to-day, many expert witnesses of outstanding ability who have justly earned the confidence and admiration of the courts, and your Societies number among their present

and past Presidents and Honorary Presidents several gentle-men whose eminence and skill as expert witnesses may be equalled but will never be surpassed.

In this matter the younger generation, to which many of my listeners belong, have a high tradition to uphold. With the multiplicity of interests and the wide variety of pursuits which your profession now offers, many of you may be tempted to discard forensic work in favour of other duties to which your inclinations or special aptitudes may attract you ; and this temptation may be all the stronger when you recall that work in the Law Courts demands skill, experience, and ability of a special order, which can only be acquired " not without dust and heat." But to those of you who stand at the threshold of the profession I would say not only that it is your duty to respond to the stimulus of the example of your prede-cessors by emulating their success in this field of work, but that you will find it a peculiar privilege to breathe the tonic air of public controversy, and to submit your technical knowledge as frequently as possible to the salutary, though sometimes humiliating, process of relentless criticism. Nothing, I am confident, is better fitted to correct your perspectives, to clarify your ideas, to broaden your outlook, and to sharpen your wits than work of this kind.

Now let me suppose that you have been requested to act as an expert accountancy witness in a substantial cause—it may be in an ordinary litigation or arbitration, or in a criminal prosecution for embezzlement, or in an inquiry into a Parlia-mentary Bill or Provisional Order. I wish to trace the progress of your work through its three main stages of (1) the prepara-tion of your precognition ; (2) your examination-in-chief ; and (3) your cross-examination, and to suggest such practical hints and warnings as my experience has shown to be of value and importance. And if as I proceed my tone impresses you as offensively didactic, may I take the liberty of reminding you that it is the prerogative of counsel in charge of a case to dictate both strategy and tactics—even to his expert witnesses —and the sooner you get used to it the better !

The Preparation of the Precognition

It is no exaggeration to say that this, the initial step in the process, is frequently by far the most valuable to your associates in a litigation. When an accountancy expert is called in he may safely assume one or other of two things : either the lawyers in charge of the case have found themselves unable without skilled assistance to discover from books or accounts the facts upon which their claims and contentions are to be based, and look to their expert to disentangle and extract these basic facts ; or else a series of facts and figures, the results of which are sufficiently ascertained, require to be sifted, marshalled, rearranged, and presented to the tribunal in artistic and orderly form, and in such a way as will most effectively support the conclusions which it is sought to establish. In either event, it is at this stage that the accountant has the fullest scope for his ingenuity and initiative, and can contribute most notably to the success of the cause which he has espoused.

My first point may seem an obvious one, but it is none the less vital. The accountant is entitled and bound, before commencing his task, clearly to envisage in all its aspects the issue upon which parties have joined. In a case of any degree of intricacy a bare instruction to ascertain and prove certain specific facts cannot ordinarily be carried out to the best purpose. The accountant should procure and study the printed pleadings, and the Memorandum on the Line of Evidence, if any, which has been prepared by counsel. If necessary he should seek an interview with the agents, or even a consultation with counsel, as to any elaborate lines of investigation upon which it may seem feasible to embark, or which have suggested themselves to him as a result of a preliminary examination of the case. For I have known of a fruitful line of inquiry or a new ground of action or of defence being discovered for the first time by the accountant who was called in to deal with a different matter altogether, but who accidentally unearthed other facts the significance of which he fortunately recognised. In many cases it may be expedient to submit for criticism and discussion a skeleton interim report, briefly embodying the result of the expert's investigations, and offering alternative methods of vouching the conclusions or of establishing ancillary points. Above all—and this is a warning which has constantly to be repeated—let these things be done in sufficient time to permit of the completion of the work and the execution of any additional investigations before it is too late to make adequate use of them.

In approaching his task the accountancy expert should keep prominently in view that his evidence may consist in part of evidence of fact and in part of evidence of opinion. The pure fact to which the expert will normally have to speak will usually consist of summarised conclusions from the records contained in books and accounts. The whole responsibility for the accuracy of such data and the soundness of the conclusions drawn from them will rest with the expert alone, and he must see to it that his results will stand the fire of the hottest criticism which his ingenuity can suggest. In many cases, however, the expert witness's conclusions do not wholly depend upon facts which he has himself deponed to and vouched, but upon facts derived from other witnesses or from some independent source. You are fully entitled to utilise such facts, and to say so in evidence ; but it is of paramount importance that you should make it abundantly plain in your precognition what these independent facts or assumptions are.

As regards the *form* in which the evidence is to be presented or the information conveyed to the client's legal advisers, it is hardly necessary to observe that circumstances vary infinitely. But with the possible exception of an arbitration before another accountant, the golden rule is to remember the limitations of judges, juries, arbiters, Parliamentary Committees, and even of advocates in the handling of figures in the mass, and constantly to aim at the most limpid lucidity and simplicity. For securing this end no method is better adapted than the preparation of a series of tables, diagrams, or graphs, copies of which can be reproduced in sufficient numbers and handed in as part of the witness's evidence, and which can be explained item by item with a clarity to which oral evidence on figures cannot possibly attain. The preparation of such tables affords an opportunity for unlimited ingenuity and skill not only in accountancy but also in the science of statistics ; and the witness should not hesitate to avail himself of the whole resources of typography and of the graphical method of presentation in the endeavour to set forth in vivid and emphatic shape the facts and conclusions which he wishes to drive home. In applying the tabular method, never attempt to include in one table or graph more information than can easily and conveniently be handled and assimilated, for to do so is to reintroduce the confusion of thought which the table is designed to dispel. In skilful hands it is possible—I have seen it again and again—to epitomise the real essentials of the most intricate case on half a dozen sheets of paper, and so to confine the issues in a nutshell, and, what is more, to keep them there.

It may be of interest to you to learn how this operation is performed on the heroic scale. The most elaborate judicial investigation within living memory was the inquiry by a Select Committee of the House of Commons into the Glasgow Boundaries Bill of 1925. This Homeric contest commenced on the 12th of May, and ended on the 22nd of July of that year. The leading accountancy witness for the promoters was Mr Arthur Collins of Westminster, whose eminence as an expert witness has long been universally acknowledged, and who, I trust, will forgive me for using his work as an object lesson in the preparation of accountancy evidence. His object was to justify on financial grounds the annexation by Glasgow of large areas of Lanarkshire, Renfrewshire, and Dunbartonshire, and his evidence was presented to the Committee in forty-one printed tables and graphs neatly bound and indexed. Let me tell you what these tables contained. Eight tables were devoted to showing in parallel columns the area, population, and valuation of the city and of the adjoining administrative areas as they were, and as they would be if the annexation were sanctioned by Parliament, with the valuation figures reduced for purposes of comparison to common denominators of valuation per acre and valuation per head of population. Four tables contained analyses on comparable bases of the remunerative and unremunerative loan debts of the four authorities minutely classified under parallel headings and compared on the basis of debt per head of population. Four tables displayed in parallel columns an analysis for thirteen consecutive years of the rating accounts of the four authorities, showing the aggregate expenditure and the equivalent rate per pound under each several head of assessment. Twelve tables were devoted to an analysis over the same period of the accounts of the common good and of each of the trading departments conducted by the authorities, and a similar set of tables was provided with reference to the Education Authorities and Parish Councils. So far, you will observe, the witness was engaged in marshalling voluminous and intractable statistics, and presenting them in the form which best facilitated comparison and contrast between the present position and past records of the competing parties in relation to all the public services, and readily permitted of an easy and accurate forecast of the financial consequences which would result to the city and the counties from the annexation of the " added areas." But Mr Collins did not stop there. To reinforce and illustrate his evidence, and the claims which through his lips were being urged upon the Committee, he furnished a statement of comparative data relating to nine other selected cities ; a table classifying the various types of heritage to be found in the four areas ; a stupendous compilation showing the comparative poundage rates levied in each of the eighty-six different rating areas during the preceding thirteen years ; a table comparing the statistics of the county areas after amalgamation with the parallel statistics of the ninety-nine other counties and county districts in Scotland ; and finally a *pro forma* set of municipal accounts prepared on the basis of the estimated additional expenditure and added yield of assessments to be anticipated if and when the city's boundaries were extended in accordance with the promoters' scheme. In the result Mr Collins' tables became the financial Bible of the inquiry ; for within their limits it was easy to discover in what respects and to what extent the inhabitants of any given district would benefit or suffer from the proposed change, and what the future held in store for each district under the old or new régime.

There you have an example of the best Parliamentary practice. Will you allow me to give you another example of a different type of case ?   Eighteen months ago there took place an arbitration under the Lands Clauses Act before a sole arbiter for the purpose of valuing a waterfall which had been compulsorily acquired as a source of hydro-electric power, the claimant being the owner of one bank of the river and one-half of the falls.   I have no concern to discuss to-night the exceedingly interesting question as to how such a subject as the potential energy of falling water should be translated into cash value ; but as an example of expert accountancy practice let me tell you how the claimant's witness—a celebrated London accountant—went about his task.   He produced in tabular form estimates prepared in collaboration with the engineers, of (1) the cost of constructing the works on the right bank of the river ; (2) the cost of constructing similar works on the left. There you will observe the witness was necessarily dependent not upon his own knowledge or investigations, but upon the estimates supplied to him by others.   These figures he ulti-mately used as the basis of allocating the estimated value of the falls between the two riparian proprietors.   He then pro-duced detailed estimates of the *operating costs* on each side of the river ; and with these four tables as a basis and on the assumption of a known output and various hypothetical selling prices for the current, he constructed a fifth table bringing out the estimated maintainable revenue of the hypothetical undertaking.   To justify the multiplier of seventeen and a half years which he then proposed to apply to this maintainable revenue, he finally produced a table showing the market price and yield per cent. of some twenty comparable securities. Assuming the basis of this calculation to be sound in law, nothing could be clearer than its presentation in evidence. But even the most expert accountant is not infallible, and you may be interested to hear how this artistic and polished thesis was attacked and how the respondents turned it to their own use.   In the table of operating costs, the witness properly included an item for local rates. When questioned in cross-examination as to this figure, he produced a seventh table showing a *pro forma* valuation of the undertaking for rating purposes. Unfortunately for him, his valuation had been calculated according to the English and not the Scottish method ; and within a few minutes it became plain that the valuation and consequently the figure for rates were well below the mark, with the result that the maintainable revenue was shown to be overstated by a substantial sum. The moral is obvious. In the first place, and you will all, I expect, agree with me in this sentiment, so perish all who employ English accountants to do Scottish work ! But that is hardly fair ; for the blame must rest as much with the counsel who elicited the evidence as with the witness who deponed to it. In the second place, please observe how great is the risk that elaborately constructed arguments of the kind which accountants are frequently required to devise, may not only fail in their object, but, if vitiated by a single vital flaw, may, if that flaw is detected, recoil with quite irresistible force against those who present them.

I have now given you an example of Parliamentary work and of a typical civil claim. My last instance relates to quasi-criminal proceedings, for criminal prosecutions, properly so called, lie outside the range of my professional experience. The case I have in mind was decided last spring, and related to the managing director of a company who died a few years ago, leaving a large fortune. The investigations of the Inland Revenue authorities into the company's books disclosed the most remarkable irregularities which crystallised in a claim for unpaid excess profits duty of upwards of £25,000, the profits which should have borne that duty having been misappropriated during the war years by the deceased managing director. I pause to observe that a leakage of some £33,000 in the course of three years had been passed by the auditor without comment. The action came into court in the form of a claim by the company against the representatives of the deceased managing director for repayment of the £30,000, and a well-known Glasgow accountant was called in to prove

B

the defalcations. In this case, differing from those with which I have already dealt, there were no facts or statistics to marshal. All we could do was to introduce our accountant to the officials from the Investigation Department of the Inland Revenue, to present him with the books of the company, the accounts of certain of its customers, and the bank and investment accounts of the deceased, and to ask him to find the missing £30,000 ; and not merely to find it, but to prove by legal evidence that every halfpenny of that sum passed from the company's coffers into the pockets of the managing director without the authority of the company or its board. The accountant disappeared for a month or two, and then turned up with a handful of tables, on the strength of which decree was ultimately obtained for the whole sum claimed with the exception of certain items, which were abandoned on purely legal grounds. These tables provided an absorbing study in detective methods, no doubt familiar to you in your work as auditors. The plan of action was to adopt that disconcerting line of inquiry which the Inland Revenue are now applying with such embarrassing results to taxpayers— viz. to start with the deceased's estate at the date of death, and to trace it backwards, separating capital from revenue and disentangling reinvestments from new investments. This furnished material for the first set of tables, which disclosed a large and unaccountable capital accretion during the critical years. The second group of tables was devoted to the deceased's deposit and current accounts, from which and from numerous transactions in treasury bills and other short-dated securities it was possible to fix the dates and amounts of the capital accretions. Another table disclosed a series of improperly vouched withdrawals from the company's funds which tallied in amount and date with many of the items in the deceased's books ; while a fourth contained an analysis of the accounts of customers of the company who had paid sums to the com- pany which reappeared not in the company's accounts but in the pocket of the managing director. The investigation was of unusual difficulty ; for the deceased had carefully covered his tracks by means of defective vouchers, by booking letters which were never despatched, and by accumulating the proceeds of several peculations before depositing or investing the misappropriated sums. But the testimony of the expert's final table was so precise and irrefragable that evasion of the claim proved quite impossible, and the money is, I believe, in course of being paid.

These three examples, drawn from three different types of judicial process, will serve to illustrate the methods which forensic experience has proved to be best calculated to produce the desired result. I shall now pass to one or two final recommendations as to the preparation of the precognition.

In preparing your precognition never forget that you have *two* objects and *not one* in view. Your first object is to provide your counsel with the framework upon which he can lead your evidence if and when you enter the witness-box, which you may never do. Your second object—and it is every whit as important as the first—is to provide your counsel so far as in you lies with the information upon which to construct his own arguments and to cross-examine the opposing expert. Forgive me for emphasising this point so strongly ; but there is no more common source of justifiable annoyance to counsel, and no more fruitful cause of lost litigations, than the expert witness who carefully conceals from his own instructors some hidden pitfall or difficulty, and who, when urgently appealed to for information while his opposite number is in the box, can only reply : " Leave it to me, and I shall deal with it in evidence." What is so often forgotten, and with such damaging results, is that the rules of pleading require that a defender's case must be fairly put to the pursuer's witnesses in cross-examination ; that the first aim of an advocate, particularly when acting on the defensive, is to prove as much as he can out of the mouths of his opponent's witnesses ; and that a separable issue not so put may not be allowed to be proved at all when the defender's evidence comes to be led. Make it your business accordingly when preparing your evidence not merely to concentrate upon the testimony which *you* expect to give, but to forecast and to meet by anticipation the evidence which may be given on the other side. If there are difficulties, pointedly draw attention to them whether you know the answer or not. If you cannot make up your mind how to deal with them, your advisers may be able to suggest the answer. If there is no answer to any special point, it is essential that your counsel should be warned in advance in order that he may mature his plans for meeting the difficulty.

Further, do not be afraid to incorporate the favourable and the adverse, the positive testimony and the suggested criticisms, the anticipated difficulties and your proposed solutions, in your formal precognition or report. You will not be taken over it all when your turn is reached ; and you will have abundant opportunity of discussing with counsel in consultation how much of your proposed evidence may profitably be led, and how much should be kept in reserve or totally discarded. The main thing is to supply your associates in the fight in reason with *all* the ammunition and defensive armour which your investigations have disclosed or your ingenuity can suggest, and to do so in sufficient time to permit of the whole of it being mobilised before the case begins. If you do not, you may have the mortification of seeing the case closed without some essential item of evidence which was in your possession all the time. Unforseen difficulties must be dealt with when they arise to the best of an advocate's ability ; and in an intricate accountancy case that may not amount to much. But to leave your counsel unwarned of the existence of a concealed trap from which you know the way of escape is to commit the unpardonable sin, and, I fear, to seal your fate as an expert witness. In most cases of any size or difficulty, the consultation before the proof will give you the chance of indicating the points of danger which you have discovered, and of considering how these dangers may best be averted or overcome. As an opinion witness, you are, of course, entitled, as I have already said, to offer your evidence on the basis of stated assumptions which you may infer for yourself or which may be supplied to you. It is of great importance that such assumptions should be very carefully scrutinised and considered, for they are the necessary foundation of the evidence which you give. And if there are conceivable alternative assumptions which are capable of being advanced, it is always advisable to re-think the argument and recalculate the figures on the different bases so as to be prepared for cross-examination. In the Greenock Extension Bill last summer a section of accountancy evidence evaporated into thin air when it was discovered that a certain local authority could borrow on a $4\frac{3}{4}$ per cent. basis instead of the $5\frac{1}{4}$ per cent. which had been assumed without proper verification. It may not be your province to establish the assumptions on which your evidence is based. It rarely is ; but it is your province to make it abundantly clear to those in charge of the case what your underlying assumptions are, in order that they may provide for their proof in the proper way.

Examination in Chief

So much for the preparation of evidence. I now turn to your duties in court, and, in particular, to your examination in chief. If you are the first accountant expert to be examined, and if you have observed the suggestions which I have ventured to lay before you as to the preparation of your evidence, the examination in chief should present no difficulty and calls for little comment. But as you are usually discoursing to a lay tribunal, uninstructed in the subject-matter of dispute, upon a topic which is traditionally mysterious and bewildering, it is well to make due allowance for the deficiencies of your audience, and to expound the position and to vouch your conclusions step by step with all the lucidity at your command, carefully following the lead of the questions put to you, but ready to answer freely and fully in the direction which the examining counsel is indicating. Marshal your evidence along broad and distinct lines, plainly leading to the conclusion which you are seeking to justify. Do not, in the first instance at least, obscure the main issue by seeking to substantiate in undue detail every step in the argument. It is usually preferable and always sufficient to depone merely that you are prepared, if so desired, to explain the detailed calculations ; and unless these calculations are vital to the argument, hold them in reserve. The effect of the evidence may be seriously impaired by an air of manifest hesitancy, lack of confidence, or indecision ; but the danger above all others to be guarded against is the slightest trace of bias, undue zeal, or over-statement. To be detected in exaggeration even on matters of immaterial detail is to incur the risk of being totally dis-credited so far as vital matters of opinion are concerned ; for many tribunals are excessively sensitive to the suggestion that they may have been deliberately misled. Indeed, it is tactically unsound, as well as morally reprehensible, to conceal any relevant factor in the problem which may possibly tell against your client, even if that factor is likely to elude the detection of your opponents. It is *not* your business deliberately to go out of your way to damage the case which you have been retained to assist ; but it *is* your business to present the facts as fairly as it is possible to do so and as favourably as you can for the interests which you support, and to invite the tribunal to draw no conclusions which are not in your opinion properly deducible from these facts. You will never be asked to do more ; and the general effect of your evidence will be greatly enhanced if it is plain that you are striving to be scrupulously just in the presentation of your evidence.

The question is sometimes asked whether it is legitimate for an expert witness or counsel to support a case which he *knows* to be bad. Of course it is not, and it is never done. If in the opinion of his advisers a client's case is bad *in law*, he is so informed, but he need not take that advice, and the advice may well be wrong. He is entitled to the judgment of the court, and it is the duty of his counsel to present the case in argument in the most favourable possible light, leaving it to the court to decide. I do not know whether it is a reflection on the Bench or on the Bar, but many a case is won or lost against the confident beliefs of every counsel engaged in it. If, on the other hand, the case is bad *in fact* and is *known* to be so, the case does not proceed, for no counsel or agent would incur the risk of the professional consequences of wilfully misleading the court. In civil causes such a situation hardly ever arises in practice ; but if it does, the expert accountancy witness may rest assured that he will never be requested to stretch his conscience, much less to commit perjury, for the benefit of his client.

One final suggestion which I would place before you is part of the artistry of expert testimony. One or more steps in your argument may be open to a challenge to which you know the answer. In some instances it may be judicious to face the music in chief by deliberately suggesting the difficulty and furnishing the answer yourself. This is generally the safest way of taking the edge off a criticism when the best answer you can offer is not too convincing or conclusive. But if your explanation is decisive and complete, the preferable course is to pass the matter over in silence, and to reserve the crushing retort for your opponent when he falls into the trap and tables the challenge in cross-examination. One or two experiences of that kind are exceedingly disconcerting to a cross-examiner, and the results are often strikingly effective.

So far I have been assuming that the imaginary accountancy expert whom I am advising has been the first to enter the witness box ; and that is obviously the easiest case. Let us now turn to the converse situation of the witness for the defence, whose task is fundamentally more difficult. In such a position it will be the duty of the accountant to attend during the examination of the opposing experts, and to devote his attention to doing two things at once as quickly as is humanly possible. In the first place, he must endeavour to convey to his counsel instantaneously and in tabloid form any additional points which may emerge for cross-examination purposes, making tactful allowance for the fact that the harassed advocate is probably writing, thinking, and speaking at one and the same moment. If the senior is on his feet, the junior is the person into whom the condensed information should be pumped at high pressure. In the second place, the accountant must all the time be mentally adjusting his evidence and ideas to meet the new contentions and arguments, if any, which his opponent is expounding, with a view to making such alterations or additions to his evidence as may be required in the interval before his own turn is reached. There is no royal road to success in such a task, and no rules for the guidance of the uninitiated. It calls for the quick thinking and decisive action which experience alone will mature ; and there is no stage in a case in which complete mastery of the issues at stake and of the whole facts on which they depend is more indispensable if the witness is to afford his side the fullest value of his services.

Cross-Examination

Cross-examination is an ordeal which most witnesses enjoy as fully as a visit to the dentist ; but there is no reason why it should hold any terrors for the accountancy expert who has really familiarised himself with the facts and figures of the case. It is very unlikely that the witness will be asked in cross any questions on the mathematical or actuarial side of his evidence. Counsel have too much sense and too little time to choose such unfavourable ground for a battle of wits except in such rare cases as a Parliamentary inquiry last spring, when I watched an accountant—a municipal, not a chartered accountant—writhing beneath the mortifying experience of having to admit a serious error in the addition of the final column of his principal table. I do not know why the opposing accountant thought of checking the totals, but the effect of his discovery was distinctly disconcerting. The attack to which you are much more likely to be subjected is an investigation of the theory and assumptions which underlie your evidence on the figures, and a demand for your justification of the basis on which at each step you have proceeded. If you survive this test, you will probably be invited to accept a fresh set of assumptions, and to indicate how these would affect your conclusions. In the ordinary case it is a profound mistake to refuse to follow the cross-examiner obediently down his own avenues of inquiry. If you consider that these avenues are for any reason illegitimate, do not fail to say so, and you will be given a chance by the court or in re-examination of indicating why. But your evidence will best serve the interests of your client if you promptly and courteously submit your theories to every test which your opponent advances, and resolutely refuse to be ruffled by any provocation to which he may mischievously subject you. Never underrate your opponent. He is probably not so foolish as you think ; and, even if he is, above all conceal your opinion. If you are faced with an undoubted flaw in your case, readily admit it ; for the rest of your evidence will unquestionably suffer if you attempt even temporarily to defend the indefensible. Finally, and as you value the good opinion of the average judge or arbiter, enunciate slowly and distinctly, cultivate a relevant mind, and exactly answer the questions which are put to you before embarking on qualifications or explanations.

My time and my ideas are alike exhausted. My random suggestions have ranged from the obvious and inevitable to the counsel of perfection ; but I shall consider myself fortunate indeed if this informal address has provided some of you with a few hints towards perfecting yourselves in the execution of this delicate and, in many cases, unfamiliar branch of your professional duties.

1928

The Limitations of the Judicial Functions of Public Authorities

ISPARITY between theory and practice has always
been an arresting and distinctive feature of the British
Constitution. It has never been safe to study the
fundamental elements of the subject except from the three
different points of view of the formal, the conventional, and the
actual. At the present day certain of the gaps which separate
these three aspects of the problem have expanded to an extent
which has already evoked more than one spirited protest
from the official judicature, and which is now beginning to
challenge general public attention. To the student of orthodox
political science and history the idea that the Executive should
wield extensive and largely uncontrolled judicial powers is
utterly foreign to the spirit of the British Constitution. To the
late Professor Dicey, who placed in his thesis of " the Rule of
Law " an implicit confidence which, even when he wrote,
was not wholly warranted by the facts, the title of this paper
would have seemed an affront. But the present generation
has lived to witness the feverish development in multifarious
directions of the administrative activities of central and local
authorities, and, following upon that development, and as a
necessary consequence of it, a remarkable and increasing
tendency by the Executive to encroach farther and farther upon
the legislative and judicial functions of government.

Let us recognise at once that some such process was in a
sense an inevitable one. Under the pressure of modern
economic and political theory, the wisdom or unwisdom of
which it would be irrelevant to discuss, the sphere of the
State's activity is constantly being widened to keep pace with
the growing complexity of the social structure. Juridical
relationships which affect only two or more individual citizens
are slowly being superseded in numbers and importance by

juridical relationships in which the State, in the person of a Central or Local Authority, asserts, and must be conceded, an active title and interest. It may be that we are witnessing the first stages in a revolutionary change in the basic concepts of jurisprudence. This new and important phase in our corporate life received a great impetus during the War, and is now an established factor in the problem of government ; and it is not a factor which is peculiar to Great Britain, but one which has recently forced itself upon the attention of the public in many leading countries of the world. To meet this changed situation it would seem futile to fall back upon any doctrinaire theory of the " separation of powers," still less upon vague ideas of the spirit of an unwritten constitution evolved under different circumstances and in contemplation of different problems. The practical question for us, and for every modern State, in the altered conditions of post-war life, is by what expedients the conflicting principles of *imperium* and *libertas* can best be reconciled, conformably with the genius of national and constitutional traditions.

The problem in its different phases has been a frequently recurring one in British History ; and the first stage in its active solution has usually been one in which all governmental agencies tacitly conspire to shut their eyes to its existence. That is the stage through which we in Great Britain are passing at the present time. In America the difficulty was quickly appreciated and deliberately met by carefully devised modifications in the constitution, designed on the one hand to secure that expedition, economy and technical expertness which are the *raison d'être* of a system of administrative law, and on the other hand to preserve to the subject free access to the ordinary courts, by means of appeals on questions of law, and ample security from injustice or irregularity in proceedings conducted before the tribunal of first instance, by means of the " due process " clause and the jealous supervision of the official judicature. In France the authorities found a ready-made solution of proved efficiency in a highly developed system of administrative law and in a hierarchy of special tribunals by means of which their citizens have confidently enjoyed for two generations a measure of security and privilege which has too often been misrepresented and unfairly decried. But we in this country have adopted the characteristic and perilous policy of doing one thing and saying another ; of creating half unconsciously and step by step an intricate but wholly unsympathetic structure of administrative law while hotly asserting that we are doing nothing of the kind ; and of clinging with pathetic loyalty to the outworn shibboleth of " equality before the law " at a time when in a hundred different respects the Executive has become a law unto itself and a judge in its own cause. Having no ready-made system, we have sedulously refrained from attempting to manufacture one, but have sought to habituate the patient public by twenty years of hurried and slovenly legislation to the belief that the unexplained, and occasionally inexplicable, *fiat* of a Government Department or of a local authority must be the authentic voice of the public interest. In the main—and thanks to the discipline imposed by the emergencies of the War—these ideas have so far been accepted with dumb submission ; but it would be dangerous to assume that the shadow of DORA has permanently darkened the counsels of the present generation, or that further advances in the direction of an administrative despotism, however benevolent, will be tolerated without an insistent demand for the drastic revision of our system of public law.

To come a little closer to the question, a general review of the judicial and *quasi*-judicial functions now confided to public authorities reveals, as one would expect, a perplexing variety and lack of system in the methods adopted by the Legislature in conferring these new powers and duties. The *ad hoc* statutory tribunals—*e.g.* the Railway Rates Tribunal or the Industrial Court—set up for the purpose of determining special types of dispute, may be ignored as falling outside the immediate scope of the present inquiry. But the Statute Book, and particularly the collection of private and local Acts, already presents a most impressive array of instances in which the personal and proprietary rights of individual citizens are exposed to the risk of being deeply affected by the exercise by a Central or Local Authority of their statutory powers, and in which the determination of the resulting dispute is confided either to that authority, with or without a right of appeal from a local or subordinate authority to a central department, or to a central department direct. In most instances resort to the ordinary courts of the land is expressly excluded ; sometimes a limited right of appeal is permitted on questions of law ; occasionally provision is made for raising before the Courts the question whether an administrative discretion has been " reasonably exercised " ; still more rarely an appeal is available upon the whole merits of the controversy.

Fortunately, the common law—in Scotland at least—still affords the citizen a certain measure of paper protection against arbitrary, capricious, or illegal treatment. The paramount appellate jurisdiction of the Supreme Courts can only be excluded by the clearest and most specific enactment ; and even where that jurisdiction is undeniably inoperative, the Courts can be invoked and will interfere, whenever the statutory authority has acted *ultra vires*, or in those obscure and imperfectly defined types of cases where the proceedings can be shown to have been vitiated by " oppression " or " corruption," or by actings which are deemed to be " contrary to the principles of natural justice." Further, the Supreme Court will in suitable circumstances interpose to compel the inferior tribunal to discharge its statutory duty by hearing and determining a case " according to law."

But experience soon demonstrated how limited and narrow are the scope and value of these theoretical safeguards. So long as the administrative tribunal professedly acts as the parties' judge and not as their oracle ; so long as the public authority can be said to have " preserved a judicial temper and performed its duties conscientiously and with a proper feeling of responsibility " ; so long, in short, as there is no overt and flagrant defiance of the more elementary standards of equity and fairness, the judicial hands are tied. But the matter does not end there. Not only are the limits of the Court's effective interference closely restricted, but it is possible to detect a growing and quite intelligible reluctance on the part of the Court to interfere at all. Finding themselves again and again expressly debarred from trespassing in a region of some technicality and complexity, the Courts have begun to recognise that under the conditions imposed by recent legislation they are often " ill equipped " (as one eminent judge has put it) to weigh the merits of certain types of practical administrative issues, and powerless to champion the interests of the subject who claims protection from alleged oppression at the hands of a public authority. Two comparatively recent decisions in the House of Lords have thrown into startling relief the weakness of the supervision which the courts are already content to exercise over administrative jurisdiction ; for it is now established that the public authority is under no duty to conform to the rules of evidence and procedure which tradition and long experience have recognised as best adapted to the administration of justice and the ascertainment of truth, and that the administrative tribunal is in general under no obligation to disclose either the basis or the reason for its decision.

The policy of the executive departments in invading the judicial sphere has thus been (1) to disclaim judicial methods of procedure and to substitute nothing in their place but an unlimited and indefinable discretion ; (2) to assert the right to finality in judgment and so to deprive themselves voluntarily of the invaluable discipline and stimulus of having to furnish decisions which will bear the scrutiny of a court of review ; and (3) to replace open publicity and reasoned judgments by the methods of obscurantism.

Having thus been empowered if not encouraged, to work in the dark according to devices of its own invention, and having the assurance that its determinations are normally incapable of being brought under review and can only in the rarest circumstances be effectively challenged, the public authority vested with judicial powers indeed enjoys the powers of a giant. Does it use them like a giant ? Speaking in the recollection of several memorable years spent in a Whitehall department, and in the light of subsequent forensic experience gained partly on the side of the appellant citizen but mainly on the side of local authorities, I have no hesitation in replying to this question with a general negative. In the great majority of cases I am convinced that administrative tribunals—whether local authorities acting as judges of first instance or central departments exercising an appellate or confirmatory jurisdiction—have conscientiously striven to hold the balance fairly between the public and the private interest, and that these efforts have attained substantial success.

But this statement is by no means universally true : and, even if it was, the question under consideration would still require to be carefully examined. Isolated instances of startling injustice and grave irregularity have come before the Courts in sufficient numbers to raise the liveliest apprehensions as to the working of the system as a whole ; while for every citizen who is wealthy enough and courageous enough to challenge a public authority in open battle, there must be many who suffer in silence rather than engage in so costly and unequal a contest. So long ago as 1923 the *Quarterly Review* published an outspoken attack from the layman's point of view upon the system described in the title of the article as " Bureaucracy Triumphant." Two years later so eminent and responsible an authority as Professor J. H. Morgan, writing in his introduction to a notable work upon *Public Authorities and Legal Liability*, complained in pointed terms of the " growing arbitrariness of temper . . . which is in flagrant contradiction with the most elementary principles of justice," and compiled a depressing collection of recent judicial *dicta* on the subject, suitable (as he cynically phrased it) for inclusion under a rubric headed " The Distempers of the Bureaucracy." Within the last few months there has been published by Dr Port a comprehensive work on *Administrative Law*, in which he recognises the pressing need for positive safeguards, and strongly advocates their early adoption. It was only the other day that the *Times* devoted a leading article to the " very formidable problem " which has been created by " the cryptic introduction of an uncodified and arbitrary departmental *droit administratif.*"

Finally and most important of all, it is already, I fear, undeniable that the present system no longer enjoys public confidence ; and without that fundamental support no system can long survive. Nothing has contributed more to this result than the impenetrable obscurity in which the operation of administrative jurisdiction is almost always involved and the complete absence of reasoned decisions. The impression is gaining ground that, before an administrative tribunal, the private citizen does not get a square deal ; that the local authorities are too often committed in advance to the prosecution of schemes and lines of policy to which, in their view, private interests must in general subserve ; and that the central departments are in league with the local authorities and in honour bound to support them through thick and thin. However unfounded this impression—and it is not entirely without foundation—the mere fact that it exists is a sufficient justification for a peremptory demand for reform. The appellant who questions whether it is even worth his while presenting his case to a particular type of administrative tribunal, and the appellant who comes away from such a tribunal feeling that he has not only lost his case but that he never had a chance of winning it, are critics whom no argument will ever convince ; and of these I have met not a few. I am well aware that these statements will elicit dissent, but if proof is required of their validity it will be found in the first public utterance of the newly appointed Lord Chancellor, who announced his intention at the judges' banquet three weeks ago of initiating an investigation into the matter in order " to allay the anxiety which no doubt prevailed in the public mind."

So far I have been examining the position from the outside. It is interesting to observe that dissatisfaction with the present system is not confined to the litigant before the administrative tribunal. Writing in the *Journal of Public Administration* of October 1924, the Town Clerk of Birmingham, after pointing out the evil effects which would follow further attempts at over-centralisation, advocated the complete emancipation of local authorities from central control exercised by means of the appellate jurisdiction, and suggested the substitution of local appellate tribunals. To the same number Mr I. G. Gibbon contributed a paper in which an able but guarded defence of the present system was coupled with the admission that the process had gone quite far enough. Thus the representative of the local authority exhorted the executive official to confine his attention to his proper business of administration, while the representative of the central department expressed the fervent wish that he might be permitted to do so !

Turning from the critical to the constructive aspect of the problem, and before attempting to formulate any conclusions or suggestions, it is advisable to glance briefly for guidance at those forms of the administrative tribunal which have met in practice with a measure of success.

In Scotland a solution for many of the difficulties has been found in a large number of cases by confiding administrative jurisdiction to " the Sheriff of the county." For the benefit of those unfamiliar with the Scottish judicial system, it is sufficient to say that the " Sheriff-Substitutes," of whom there are nearly fifty, each exercising an extensive civil and criminal jurisdiction within defined areas, correspond approximately to the English County Court judges but enjoy considerably wider powers. Recruited almost exclusively from the ranks of the Bar, the Sheriff-Substitutes are whole-time judges, holding office in practice for life, and residing within the area of their jurisdiction. For each county or group of counties there is in addition a part-time official of higher dignity and authority in the person of " the Sheriff " or " Sheriff-Principal," who is almost invariably a King's Counsel of standing, free to practice his profession and to reside where he pleases. In addition to acting as a judge of appeal from his Sheriff-Substitutes and to exercising an original jurisdiction in various circumstances, the Sheriff is the local representative of the Crown, and discharges either personally or, less commonly, through his Substitutes a great variety of customary and statutory duties of an administrative character. The practice of constituting the " Sheriff " as the appellate or confirmatory judicial authority in administrative questions is one of long standing in Scotland, though serious inroads have latterly

C

been made by the central departments. This change is deeply to be deplored. The Sheriff undoubtedly enjoys the confidence of the public, for his independence is beyond dispute and there is no room for the suspicion of bias in favour of the constituted authorities as against the public. Being widely experienced in the performance of ordinary judicial work, the Sheriff can be trusted not only to conduct the enquiry judicially and with cold impartiality, but also—and this is not less important —to create the impression that he is doing so. In addition he is in sufficiently intimate touch with local circumstances and requirements to be able to apply to the case a severely practical and intelligent scrutiny. The proceedings are conducted formally but expeditiously and in the wholesome light of complete publicity, while the decision is customarily embodied in a reasoned judgment. On the other side of the account it may be urged that the utilisation of the Sheriffs as administrative judges cannot make for harmony and uniformity in the trend of decisions, and that the Sheriff cannot bring to his task the specialised skill of the administrative expert. I am not satisfied that these criticisms are well founded, or that, if they are, the objections are crucial. I have yet to see an administrative issue more complex and technical than those which are daily arising in the Courts of law and are being satisfactorily determined. Equally it is by no means clear that uniformity in a series of decisions relating to different circumstances and different local conditions may not be too dearly purchased.

Another Scottish experiment in the utilisation of the official judicature for the determination of *quasi*-administrative disputes is to be found in the Lands Valuation Appeal Court—a tribunal consisting of three judges of the Supreme Court who sit once or twice a year to hear appeals by Stated Case against the valuation for rating purposes placed by local Valuation Committees on heritable property. The personnel of the Court is usually preserved unaltered for a considerable number of years at a time, with the result that the members possess to a conspicuous degree a highly specialised knowledge and experience which enable them to dispose of the cases inexpensively, summarily, and according to uniform principles, and in doing so to build up by means of their reported decisions a very valuable and elaborate system of valuation law for the guidance of the assessors and local committees. This is neither more nor less than the *droit administratif* on a small scale ; and its practical success is beyond question.

In stressing these examples in which the " legal mind " has demonstrated its complete capacity for the adequate performance of administrative work, I do not wish to suggest that the " official mind " is necessarily or usually unfitted for the successful discharge of judicial duties. If proof were needed to controvert such a suggestion, it would be found in the general public confidence which has been won under unpropitious auspices by the Special Commissioners of Income Tax, whose appellate tribunals provide a supreme model of fairness and efficiency. Further, there are fields of enquiry so highly technical that it is hardly practicable to entrust them to any but those whose lives have been devoted to their study. A dispute between the Central Electricity Board and the owners of a " selected station " as to the load factor at which the generating plant should be operated is a matter which is properly left to the Electricity Commissioners ; and no one will envy them the task. But when one exchanges the rarified atmosphere of kilowatts and transformers for such mundane topics as advertisement stances, traffic bye-laws, compulsory acquisition of land, pilotage dues, or omnibus licences, it is difficult to see why any executive official should be supposed to possess peculiar aptitude for acting in a judicial capacity in the determination of the familiar disputes which arise in connection with such matters. One cannot but feel that the withdrawal of responsible civil servants from their special duties in order that they may occasionally experiment as amateurs in the performance of delicate functions which no professional judge ever finds easy is always a waste of valuable time and talent, and too often a conspicuous example of putting a round peg in a square hole. If notable counter-balancing advantages were secured by the exercise of judicial functions by executive authorities the position might be different ; but are there any such advantages ? As contrasted with, say, proceedings before the Sheriff, there is no saving in expense (for the parties are in general obliged to pay the expenses of the enquiry, as well as their own costs) and certainly no saving in time ; while on the score of efficiency the probabilities are all in favour of the experienced professional judge and against the casual amateur. I am aware in making this statement that the official conducting the enquiry usually reports to his superior, and that the ultimate decision is alleged to enshrine the collective wisdom of an entire Government Department. But the man in the street is constitutionally incapable of the sublime act of faith involved in the acceptance of this theory ; while, speaking as an advocate, I am in a position to say that there is no more fruitless and disheartening task than arguing before an official sent down to conduct a local enquiry in the full knowledge that the decision does not rest with him at all. It is impossible to convince or impress at second or third hand ; it is equally impossible to dispense justice under such conditions. Direct contact must be established either orally or in writing between the litigant or his advisers and the judge. Too often the local enquiry serves no purpose except the oblique and indirect one of enabling the parties to ventilate grievances from which there is no means of escape.

My conclusions may be summarised as follows :—

(1) The time has come for abandoning the policy of drift, and for deliberately determining upon a settled and systematic line of action for the treatment of the very large and growing volume of administrative disputes. In the words of Lord Sankey, " some new method *must* be devised either by adapting old law to modern situations or creating a new code to deal with them."

(2) The practice of confiding uncontrolled or partially controlled judicial powers to administrative officials or bodies, under conditions which enable them to proceed according to their own devices and to base their decisions upon grounds which they do not disclose is fundamentally unsound and

indefensible, and has already incurred the risk of the final condemnation of public opinion.

(3) Apart from special circumstances—*e.g.* where the subject matter is of high technicality or where the dispute involves only two or more subordinate authorities without affecting any private interest—judicial powers, whether original, appellate, or confirmatory, should never be entrusted to administrative authorities.

(4) The administrative judge in the normal case should be an official of the type of the Scottish Sheriff, *i.e.* an independent and permanent trained judge of lower rank, authorised to conduct the proceedings in a summary and informal fashion where that is appropriate, but bound to adhere to the fundamentals of judicial procedure and to issue a reasoned judgment on fact and on law.

(5) Where necessary, the administrative judge should be provided by the appropriate Department with a skilled assessor to advise him on technical questions or matters of policy and practice. Such a step would probably be unnecessary except in special cases and on the request of the judge or of the parties.

(6) Appeal should *always* be available by Stated Case on any question of law emerging during the proceedings or involved in the judgment. The appeal could be in England to the ordinary Divisional Court, or in Scotland, to the Inner House of the Court of Session ; or, if the work expands to a sufficient extent, a specially constituted tribunal could be formed on the lines of the Lands Valuation Appeal Court.

These proposals are in no sense revolutionary. Singly or in partial combination they have been in successful operation in Scotland under certain statutes for many years. Their general adoption would remove many of the objections to which the present system is exposed. The citizen will be confirmed in his enjoyment of *libertas*, while the public authorities need have no apprehensions that their *imperium* will be improperly curtailed, unless their position to-day is to be the extreme and indefensible one that they cannot and will not submit their conduct and methods to the scrutiny of an independent tribunal.

In advancing these few suggestions I have made no attempt to divest myself of professional predilections, but have purposely stated the case as it appears to me from the Scottish legal and unofficial standpoint. I think that I may claim that the views which I have ventured to express are widely held. An eminent judge recently complained that " the liberties of the subject are determined in the ' third floor back of a Government Department.' " Let me borrow a title for this paper from Mr Jerome K. Jerome. It is a plea for " The Passing of the Third Floor Back."

1929

Some Classics of Scottish Legal Literature

MY SUBJECT was suggested to me by your secretary, and I have readily adopted it in the desire to deepen your interest in one fascinating and important chapter of Scotland's distinctive contribution to the life and thought of the modern world. For there never was a time when there was greater need to stimulate and to foster all that is best in Scottish ideals, Scottish sentiment, and Scottish traditions, if the spirit of Scotland is to survive and to rise superior to the material influences which are at present combining to stifle our independent national life. In matters commercial, industrial, financial and political, we are rapidly succumbing to a process which can only end, if unchecked, in degrading Scotland to the level of a minor and decaying English province. We have lost our railways. We have lost many of our shipping interests. We are even losing our banks and our insurance offices. The *Daily Mail* is sold in our streets. The voice of the cockney is heard in the land. Heirs though we are of a great national culture, of a romantic historical tradition, and of our own distinctive art, literature, and jurisprudence, we shall soon be associated in the mind of the supercilious southerner with nothing more inspiring than the grouse, the haggis, and that perennial fount of post-prandial merriment, Aberdonian thrift.

Now this is not the election address of a Nationalist candidate. It may well be that the prevailing drift to the omnivorous Metropolis is merely a symptom of that tendency to centralisation which is so prominent a characteristic of the post-war world. It may well be that in certain matters we are too small, too weak, and too impoverished to stand alone. But speaking as a Scotsman to Scotsmen on a peculiarly Scottish topic, I venture to remind you at the outset that the Scottish race has always spiritually thrived in an atmosphere of almost aggressive individualism ; that it is only in that native air, and not in obsequious subservience to imported ideas, that further independent development and achievement may be looked for ; in short, that our national emblem is a thistle and not a " third single " to Euston.

It is accordingly at once our privilege and our duty to turn—as I now invite you to do—with renewed earnestness and enthusiasm to the study of our past, not in any spirit of mere antiquarianism, but in order that, as we expand our horizon and widen our experience, we may find in the record of these distinctive achievements a basis and an inspiration for further advances under the beneficent influence of a vision which will be sought in vain in the dead levels of a false internationalism.

But first, a word of explanation and defence. To you, whose business contact with the legal profession is habitually made at points which disclose only the dingier and less inspiring vistas of Scots Law, it may seem a misuse of language to apply the terms " literature " and " classics " to the repellent tomes that oppress the shelves of a lawyer's study ; and up to a point you would be right. It has been judicially admitted with ironical caution that " Shelley has given greater prominence to the element of music than has Stair." It cannot be denied that in the graver crises of human life few " turn for fortitude or consolation to the numbered lyrical effusions " of George Joseph Bell. Although no chapter of human enquiry is richer than jurisprudence in the raw material of tragedy, comedy, history, and philosophy, it is the fact—for all Lord Kames' protests—that law does tend too often to be studied and expounded as " a dry, intricate and crabbed science." As a thinker, the lawyer is apt to rely unduly upon the exercise of the analytical faculty ; and in the relentless pursuit of logical accuracy, his ideal insensibly becomes the avoidance of error rather than the apprehension of the deeper truths. As a writer, compelled to handle familiarly an uncouth and cacophonous medley of English, Scotch, Law Latin, and Law French, it is surely pardonable in him that he should choose a vehicle of expression more remarkable for its severity and technicality than for grace of diction or stateliness of composition. Stair himself confessed that " a quaint and gliding style, much less the flourishes of eloquence . . . could not justly be expected in a treatise of law, which of all subjects doth require the most plain and accurate expression."

There is thus a measure of truth in the popular conception of law and legal works immortalised in *Aylmer's Field* and depicted in mordant caricature in *Bleak House* ; and it is not surprising that it was only in 1922 that there appeared for the first time in the person of the present Lord Moncrieff an exponent of " The Poetry of Law." But while the nature of the subject and the inevitable methods of approach combine to impose upon legal writers conditions under which the production of " literature " on the higher planes is a virtual impossibility, it is nevertheless true that Scotland has produced several great jurists whose works are not only justly pre-eminent as authoritative expositions of the subjects with which they deal, but are also well worthy to be ranked high as models of philosophic prose, characterised in a notable degree by the rare qualities of transparent clarity and unerring precision. It is to certain of these works and their distinguished authors that I wish to direct your attention briefly this evening ; and I have been led by considerations of time and space to confine my selection almost exclusively to three outstanding masterpieces—the *Institutions* of Stair, the *Institutes* of Erskine, and the *Commentaries* of George Joseph Bell.

The names of these three men dominate the three main divisions of Scottish legal history ; for with Stair, we associate the sudden rise of Scots Law as a separate and coherent system of jurisprudence ; with Erskine, the final development of the old Feudal and Roman Law ; and with Bell, the creation of our modern system of Mercantile Law. Stair belongs to the seventeenth century, Erskine to the eighteenth, and Bell to the nineteenth ; and all three are characteristic products of the successive eras in which they lived and worked. No legal system owes more to its literature than Scots Law does to its institutional writers. And it is not only upon Scots Law that these writers and their works have left their mark ;

for their labours in formulating, in moulding, and in developing—one might almost say in constructing—our independent national system of jurisprudence have contributed in no small measure to the fashioning of the economic and social history of the country.

First, then, let us take the earliest and greatest member of our trinity—Sir James Dalrymple, First Viscount Stair, and President of the Court of Session during the " golden age " of Scots Law. He was born in 1619, and died in 1695, his career thus coinciding with what was probably the most eventful period in the political and religious history of Scotland. At an early age he entered the Army, but soon abandoned military pursuits for the more congenial atmosphere of a Scottish University ; and for six years he occupied the Chair of Philosophy in the University of Glasgow. Called to the Bar at the age of twenty-nine, he had the good fortune soon after to be appointed Secretary of the Commission which was sent to Holland to treat with Charles II as to his return to the throne, and thus early entered the arena of public life, in which he was destined to play a very considerable part. Having thereafter attained eminence as an advocate, he was recommended to Cromwell by General Monk in 1657, for appointment as a judge of the Court of Session at the modest salary of £300 per annum. Re-appointed after the Restoration, Stair felt himself compelled by conscientious scruples in regard to the oaths of office to tender his resignation, which was accepted ; but he was shortly afterwards restored to his position and created a Baronet of Nova Scotia. In 1671, Stair succeeded Sir John Gilmour as President of the Court, and at the same time received the questionable honour of being appointed a member of the notorious Privy Council. His services in the former capacity were recognised five years later by the Town Council of Edinburgh, who resolved to mark their approval of " the manie signall good offices don . . . to the commonweil of this citie in its just concern," by paying the rent of his house (situated in Potterrow), and by giving him a free sitting in Tolbooth Church. Unfortunately the political horizon darkened during the troublous years which ensued, and in

1681 Stair was obliged to retire to his country seat, and shortly afterwards he fled to Holland, being subsequently outlawed for treason. These were the days when an aspirant for political honours not only incurred the risk of forfeiting his deposit, but imperilled his fortune, his liberty, and even his life. Returning with William of Orange, Stair was restored to office and created a Viscount ; but his later years were clouded by the implication of his son, and indirectly of himself, in the Massacre of Glencoe, and by a campaign of pamphleteer persecution after the manner of the day, in which his association with Monk, with Lauderdale, and with the new dynasty successively was made the ground for publicly vilifying him as a changeling and a time-server. Truly, as Lord Shaw observed in a recent judgment, " no one knew better than Stair what troublous times were " ; and his domestic life was almost as troublous as his public career, for his wife was popularly, but most unjustly, reputed to be a witch, and it was the painful and tragic history of his daughter Janet that furnished Sir Walter Scott with the plot of the *Bride of Lammermoor*.

So much for the man. I turn to his work. Stair's *magnum opus*, his *Institutions of the Law of Scotland, deduced from its originals and collated with the Civil, Canon and Feudal Laws and with the Customs of Neighbouring Nations*, was published in 1681. It has long been accepted as the fountain-head of Scots Law. Its outstanding feature is the emphasis consistently laid upon first principles, and the systematic development of these principles in harmony with the most enlarged and comprehensive views of comparative jurisprudence. The *Institutions* are no mere compendium of Scots Law ; for Stair made the whole science of jurisprudence his province. " No man," as he himself shrewdly remarked, " can be a knowing lawyer in any nation who hath not well pondered, and digested in his mind, the common law of the world." He ranged in a spirit of philosophic eclecticism over an immense field of enquiry, extending from the basic axioms of religion and ethics to the intricacies of early Scottish forms of process, and reduced the whole to an orderly and scientific system which has furnished the model and basis for all subsequent treatises of its kind.

In conception and execution, the work was far in advance of its time. As Lord Dunedin has more than once observed, the key to the proper understanding of legal systems founded upon the Common Law of England is the fact that the right depends on the existence of the remedy, and not the system on the existence of the right ; and such systems have slowly evolved under a process which placed adjective law and procedure in the forefront, and the doctrines of substantive law a long way behind. The fortunate circumstance that we in Scotland have developed a code of law on the philosophic basis of beginning with the right and ending with its vindication is attributable in very great measure to the synthetic genius of Stair, who in the very infancy of Scots Law provided Scotland with a ready-made legal system.

The magnitude of Stair's achievement becomes all the more evident if we consider the material upon which he had to work. Fortunately for him, and for the system of which he is virtually the founder, he had ready to his hand two sources of sterling value. In the *Corpus Juris* and in the commentaries of the famous Continental school of jurists, he had the most elaborate and profound body of law that the world has ever seen ; and the debt which he owed to this source is evident on every page of his work. Again, as he himself readily acknowledged, " our learned countryman, Craig of Rickertoun, hath largely and learnedly handled the feudal rights and customs of this and other nations in his book *De Feudis* " ; and on this work—the *Jus Feudale*, as it is commonly known— Stair placed much reliance in dealing with land rights. But so far as the Common Law of Scotland was concerned, Stair was virtually a pioneer. Sir James Balfour of Pittendreigh, it is true, had given his name to a collection of *Practicks*, prepared in the sixteenth century ; and Sir Thomas Hope of Craighall, an early contemporary of Stair, had produced a similar compilation. But valuable as these early manuals are as sources of historical information and antiquarian lore, they can have afforded little, if any, aid in the preparation of a comprehensive and systematic treatise ; and Stair was obliged to fall back upon his native genius, his philosophical training, and his long and rich experience as an advocate, a legislator, and a judge. " It is but little short of forty years," observed the learned author, " since I have followed the study and practice of law constantly and diligently, so that those who will not deny me reason and capacity can hardly deny my knowledge and experience of the subject I write of." As one of his biographers has justly remarked, " his opportunities had been unrivalled, and he used them all ; . . . it is in the highest degree improbable that to equal talent there will ever again be granted equal experience."

Though Stair's *Institutions* could hardly be described as a work " which holdeth children from play and old men from the chimney corner," it nevertheless possesses a deep and abiding interest for a far wider circle than the legal profession. " My design," said Stair, " is to give a description of the law and customs of Scotland, such as might not only be profitable for lawyers and judges, but might be pleasant and useful to all persons of honour and discretion." His scheme was novel but strictly scientific. The first broad division is concerned with the constitution of rights ; the second, with their transmission amongst the living and from the dead ; and the third, with their enforcement ; and though the emphasis in the treatment of particular subjects is laid rather differently from the manner in which it would be laid to-day, the consummate skill in the arrangement of topics, and the wisdom and transparent lucidity of the exposition, have compelled the unanimous and enthusiastic admiration of generations of readers. Though he himself participated in enacting numerous salutary and important statutes, Stair believed in the cautious method of " trial and error," and entertained a marked preference for " judge-made " law, " wrung out," as he phrased it, " from debates upon particular cases, until it comes to the consistence of a fixed and known custom." Those of us who have faced the task of perusing say, the Local Government Act of 1929, will wistfully echo Stair's prophetic protest against the creation of " a labyrinth of many and large statutes, whereof the posterior do ordinarily so abrogate and derogate from the prior that it requires a great part of a life to be prompt in these windings, without which no man with sincerity or confidence can consult or plead, much less can the subjects, by their own industry, know where to rest, but must give more implicit faith to their judges and lawyers than they need or ought to give to their divines."

Stair's style has a characteristic rugged vigour which aims at force and clarity rather than smoothness. His diction is pithy and picturesque, but deeply coloured by the law Latin of the Civilians, and it only faintly reflects the purity and splendour of Elizabethan English, and the dignity of the Authorised Version. His illustrations are drawn copiously from the Bible. When he seeks to justify the rules of heritable succession, he recalls the Pauline peroration, " If children, then heirs." Jacob's espousal to Leah affords an illustration of essential error rendered unavailing by reason of supervening consent. The doctrine of general mandate is explained by reference to Abraham's commission to Eleazar ; and the limitations of proof by oath by the story of Achan and the Babylonish garment. The fundamental rule of parole evidence is traced to its source in the injuction that " in the mouths of two or three witnesses " must every word be established. Even the *jus mariti* is explained by the Divine announcement to Eve in the Garden of Eden ; while considerable time and trouble are devoted to reconciling the legal effect of desertion upon the marriage tie with the New Testament doctrine of divorce. And it was not only to the Bible that Stair habitually turned for precept and example ; for the classical writers, both of Greece and of Rome, are extensively drawn upon—Solon, Plato, and Aristotle being his favourite authorities in the literature of Greece, and Caesar, Seneca, and Cicero in that of Rome.

Time forbids me to pursue the examination of Stair's work ; and I pass to the second chapter of the Trilogy, in order that by comparing and contrasting the two works we may gain further light on both.

John Erskine of Carnock, the second of the Institutional
writers whom I have selected for consideration, was born in
the year in which Stair died.   His works furnish his sole
claim to immortality, for his career was the sheltered and
uneventful one of the Professor of Scots Law in the University
of Edinburgh, a position which he filled for twenty-six years,
from 1737 to 1763.   He died in 1768, having devoted the
later years of his life to the composition of his *Institute of the
Law of Scotland*, which first appeared in 1773, five years after
his death.

In passing from Stair to Erskine, we leave the seventeenth
century, with its tension and its vivid colouring, for an age
which was only relieved from the humdrum by the two
Jacobite Rebellions ; and we exchange the practical sagacity
and keen insight of the philosopher, who was also an active
man of affairs, for the cold exactitude and unwearying industry
of a University professor, whose erudition was rescued—
but triumphantly rescued—from pedantry by an inexhaustible
fund of good sense.   Long before Erskine wrote, the commercial ardour of the later seventeenth century had been
damped, if not extinguished, by the failure of the ambitious
schemes which preceded the Union of 1707 ; and the energies
of the legal profession had been diverted from the Law
Merchant to the Law of Heritable Rights by the wholesale
forfeiture of estates which followed upon " the '15 " and " the
'45."   To meet this changed situation, the old Common Law
of Scotland in both its divisions—" the one resting on the
Roman Law, and the other adapted from Feudal Customs "—
reached its highest development ; and it is as the final and
authoritative exponent of the older law that Erskine still stands
supreme.

Two comprehensive treatises on Scots Law bridge the gap
between Stair and Erskine.   In 1684 the redoubtable Sir
George Mackenzie of Rosehaugh, founder of the Advocates'
Library, and familiarly known for other reasons as " the bluidy
Mackenzie," published his *Institutions of the Law of Scotland* ;
but this work, which was confined " within the compass of a
small duodecimo," could not bear comparison with Stair's

Institutions, and has long since disappeared into virtual obscurity. Curiously enough, Erskine appears to have held Mackenzie's *Institutions* in the highest repute ; for he frequently cites it, and refers to it as having been "justly received with universal approbation." Further, in 1751, there appeared a much more notable treatise, the *Institute* of Lord Bankton, which attained considerable celebrity, and survives to this day as an important authority, though " overshadowed " by Stair and Erskine.

These works, a number of specialised treatises which had from time to time made their appearance, and above all the gradual accumulation of a great mass of precedents, at once facilitated and rendered much more complex the task to which Erskine set his hand. His method of treatment was, as one would expect, predominantly academic ; and the present generation of law students is the first since Erskine's day who have not learned the rudiments of law from his pages. In Erskine's hands, the scheme of arrangement acquires the conventional lines which have ever since been followed—the law of Persons, the law of Heritable Rights, the law of Moveable Rights and Obligations, and the law of Actions—a simple workmanlike classification which readily lends itself to the exhaustive analysis in detail of the innumerable sub-heads. Conformably with this scheme, and resolving to identify himself fully with the existing conditions around him rather than to take his stand in the van of progress and constructive legal speculation, Erskine set himself to record plainly, accurately, and completely the law of Scotland as he found it ; and in this limited but very onerous task his success was complete. He does not, and probably could not, display the philosophic breadth of Stair or the bold insight of Bell. His attitude is cautious rather than subtle, exact rather than profound. His style—be it said in all humility—sets the standard of the undistinguished pedestrian prose only too familiar to the reader of the modern legal text-book. But the name of Erskine is still one for reverence. Than Erskine's *Institute* no other volume in Scottish legal literature has been accorded a respect more nearly approaching that due to verbal inspiration. Within his limits he is unshaken and unassailable.

But limits he had ; for Erskine failed to realise that, even as he was writing, the centre of interest in legal study was rapidly shifting from the Law of Property to Commercial Law, which in his work received scant consideration and very imperfect treatment. The task of supplying this deficiency fell to the third of the great Scottish lawyers, George Joseph Bell, to whom I now turn.

Bell was born in 1770 and died in 1843. Though acknowledged as one of the greatest masters of commercial jurisprudence of all time, he never attained either worldly prosperity or any of the prizes of the profession of which he was so distinguished an ornament. Called to the Bar in 1791, we first hear of him in 1800 when he published his *Treatise on the Law of Bankruptcy in Scotland*, which was subsequently expanded into his famous *Commentaries* ; and from this time he achieved eminence not only as a pleader and consultant, but as an accepted authority on Mercantile Law. Twenty-two years later—perhaps with a pang of disappointment—he accepted, on the nomination of his colleagues at the Bar, the position of Professor of Scots Law in the University of Edinburgh ; and in 1831, having seen at least nine of his juniors promoted to the Bench, and being at last reconciled to that strange destiny which denies the race to the swift and the battle to the strong, he was constrained, apparently by reduced family circumstances, to accept the relatively inferior post of a Principal Clerk of Session, which he occupied until his death twelve years later. One can only wonder whether his contemporaries at the Bar and on the Bench during these years appreciated the grim humour of the fate which relegated Bell at the summit of his powers to the position of a spectator in the Inner House, and whether they realised the tragedy of wasted talent which was daily being enacted before their eyes.

The main project to which Bell devoted a lifetime of research was one which offered full scope for even his profound learning and conspicuous ability. During the latter half of

D

the eighteenth century Scottish commercial enterprise had been steadily growing with increasing vigour. It was this period, as you know, that witnessed the rise to importance of the older Scottish banks. But Scotland was still virtually devoid of any system of Mercantile Law worthy of the name. For some strange reason—perhaps only because of their traditional conservatism—the legal profession was not only oblivious to the need for reform, but actively hostile to any innovation. It was not until 1772, and then only in the face of determined opposition, that a tentative and imperfect Act was passed introducing the process of sequestration of a bankrupt estate. By the time Bell first turned his attention to the question, the need for the development and elaboration of Commercial Law was clamant ; and he determined to collect and to systematise the universal Law Merchant, to extract its principles and practice from English and Foreign sources, and to reconcile these principles with the fundamental doctrines of Scots Law. This ambitious and exceptionally difficult project required that the learned author should not merely set out the law as it had been declared to be, but the law as it probably was, and as it ought to be ; for he had practically no detailed and technical authoritative precedent upon which to rely. It is truly remarkable to observe how the work expanded and developed in his hands. Beginning as a treatise on Bankruptcy it grew through five different editions during the author's lifetime into a Commentary on the whole law of Scotland. " I have been able," said Bell, " on the one hand, to dismiss much reasoning that, by the authoritative recognition of the principle, had become unnecessary ; and, on the other, gradually to extend my Commentaries to other questions as they rose into importance or as room was left for their discussion by the abridgment of what had become familiar and established." The truth is that for thirty years Bell enjoyed the position, while still living and writing, of being recognised as an authority almost as commanding as a supreme court ; and he had the unique experience of watching his reasoning and conclusions being absorbed year after year into the common law of the land.

The scheme of his *Commentaries*, as presented in the final edition which he prepared, has no parallel, so far as I am aware, in any comprehensive treatise before or since. He begins with a general review of what he calls the law of debtor and creditor, describing the methods of compelling the payment of debt and executing diligence when prosecuted by an individual creditor. The second book is devoted to the various kinds of property of which creditors may avail themselves for payment of their debts. Bell then turns to the rights of personal creditors, and so passes to a general exposition from this unusual angle of the law of contract in all its aspects, ending with a detailed examination of the principles and practice of Bankruptcy Law. Though Bell in this manner surveys practically the whole field of Scots Law, the dark spectre of insolvency broods over every chapter, and constantly reminds the reader of the initial and abiding object with which the author wrote.

The work displays throughout a mastery of the vast and previously unknown stores of legal lore contained in the case law of England, and particularly the decisions of the new school of commercial lawyers of whom Lord Mansfield was the founder. Bell thus paved the way for that process of *rapprochment* between the two systems which has since enured so greatly to the advantage of both. He has been called " the lawyer of precedent " ; but the description is unjust if it suggests that undue and invertebrate dependence upon the leading strings of authority which is too often seen to-day ; for no one ever used precedents as they ought to be used with more sagacity and discrimination than Bell. His style, though possessing no outstanding literary professions, has the crisp precision of a mathematical treatise, and many of his polished maxims and definitions have passed into the current coin of legal speech. A century of multifarious progress has familiarised us with ideas and doctrines undreamt of in Bell's philosophy ; but his work stands to this day as a unique and permanently valuable contribution not merely to the exposition, but to the creation of the latest and most important chapter of our law. It is not too much to say that the work of Bell was an essential link in the chain of causation which rendered possible the great expansion of Scottish industry, commerce, and banking which took place during the latter half of the nineteenth century.

Looking back over the ground we have briefly surveyed, one cannot avoid the humbling reflection that "there were giants in these days." It was of Blackstone's *Commentaries* that it was said that in their presence all successive professors of law felt very small. I do not know with what feelings the lineal successors of Erskine and Bell contemplate the achievements of their predecessors ; but I am sure that no intelligent reader can rise from the perusal of the Scottish institutional works without realising the relative insignificance of our vaunted twentieth century progress when viewed in comparison with these great monuments of the solid learning of the past.

May I end on the note on which I began ? I fear that, in my endeavour to infect you with enthusiasm in the study of a topic which is predominantly of purely professional interest, I have forgotten that I am not addressing an audience of lawyers. But if you are not all lawyers, you are nearly all Scotsmen—if not by domicile of origin at least by domicile of choice ; and you are all, without exception, the "persons of honour and discretion" for whom Stair wrote. In recommending to your further study the subject on the fringe of which I have touched to-night, I would close with the exhortation addressed to a similar audience many years ago by Lord President Inglis, the greatest Scottish judge of the nineteenth century—"No man can be well read in the history of his own country who has not acquired some knowledge at least of the history of its jurisprudence."

1929

The Length of the Chancellor's Foot

" One Chancellor has a long foot, another a short foot, a third an indifferent foot."—SELDEN : *Table Talk*

THE law of Scotland and England and of the countries which have derived their law from England has been developed primarily as a system of case law, founded upon respect for the common law and for the judicial precedents which constitute its most important source. It may be, as a Paris professor has recently asserted, that British respect for the common law has degenerated into a blind and superstitious veneration. It may be that the orthodox judicial attitude towards statute law tends to be one of thinly veiled hostility. But the fact remains that judicial precedent is the heart and core of our jurisprudence, and that, if we ceased to be case lawyers, we should cease to be lawyers at all.

This was not always so. It is sometimes forgotten that so recently as Erskine's day the binding force of precedent was repudiated, and it was only grudgingly that value was conceded to a " uniform tract of decisions " as evidence of custom (Inst. I. 1. 47 ; Prin. I. 1. 17). Thrice over in the middle of last century Lord St Leonards, with the tepid support of Lord Brougham and Lord Loughborough, declared that, though the House of Lords might not be able to reverse its own decisions, it was not bound to persevere in a demonstrable error (*Bright* v. *Hutton*, (1852) 3 H.L.C. 341 ; *Wilson* v. *Wilson*, (1854) 5 H.L.C. 57 ; *Scott* v. *Maxwell*, (1854) 1 Macq. 791). It was not until 1898 that the House decided in terms that its erroneous decisions could only be set right by an Act of Parliament (*London Street Tramways* v. *L.C.C.*, [1898] A.C. 375). Even after that it was still possible for Lord Halsbury to assert, in a desperate attempt to evade the implications of a previous decision, that a case is only authority for what it actually decides. " I entirely deny," he said, " that it can be quoted

for a proposition that seems to follow logically from it.　Such a
mode of reasoning assumes that the law is necessarily a logical
code " (*Quinn* v. *Leathem*, [1901] A.C. 495, 506).

But interesting as it is to glance backwards over the road
we have traversed, and at the sporadic and ineffectual attempts
which have from time to time been made to arrest or reverse
the march of progress, there can be no question as to the
position which we have now reached.　The legal philosophers
may find it difficult to rationalise, or to confine within the
limits of a formula, the relation of the judge to the common
law, and the process by which a decision, professedly declaratory
of the existing law, may nevertheless involve a perceptible
modification and development of previous conceptions.　But
these metaphysical subtleties present no practical difficulty
to the rank and file of the profession.　By long tradition we have
become habituated to that method of approach which depends
on the tacit assumption that somewhere in the mass of decisions
there lies hidden a rule of known law, which, if we can only
find it, will precisely fit the facts of the case in hand.　The
search, be it observed, is a search for a principle and not
necessarily for a direct authority.　The principle, once it has
been discovered and applied, may by that very process be
expanded or contracted in its significance and value.　The
system as a whole will in process of time evolve and develop
in many new and unexpected directions.　But, *plus çac hange,
plus c'est la même chose.*　For better or for worse, the genius of our
law demands that, as each fresh case presents itself, the enquiry
should be, What *is* the law ?　and not, What ought the law to
be ?

In the light of these reflections it is instructive to examine
the process by which in the recent case of the " snail in the
bottle " (*Donoghue* v. *Stevenson*, 1932 S.C.(H.L.) 31) the House of
Lords opened a new chapter in the law of reparation in relation
to a topic which necessitated the review of a mass of previous
decisions.

Lord Buckmaster, who delivered the leading dissenting
judgment, defined his attitude to the problem with conspicuous
clarity.　" The law applicable is the common law," he observed,

" and though its principles are capable of application to meet new conditions not contemplated when the law was laid down, *these principles cannot be changed, nor can additions be made to them*, because any particularly meritorious case seems outside their ambit." Lord Tomlin, who concurred in this view, added : " The reported cases—some directly, others impliedly —negative the existence as part of the common law of England of any principle affording support to the appellant's claim, and *therefore* there is, in my opinion, no material from which it is legitimate for your Lordships' House to deduce such a principle." Lord Thankerton, though differing in the result, only did so because he found the existence of the alleged legal duty to be in conformity with the principles derivable from the decided cases.

In contrast with these views it is possible to detect in the opinions of Lord Atkin and Lord Macmillan evidence of a new and different conception. Lord Atkin prefaces his examination of the authorities by a note of caution which recalls Lord Halsbury's blunt declaration in *Quinn* v. *Leathem*. " It is very necessary," he says, " in considering reported cases in the law of torts that the actual decision alone should carry authority . . . lest the inherent adaptability of English law be unduly restricted." Having thus unshackled the fetters of precedent, his Lordship proceeds : " I do not think so ill of our jurisprudence as to suppose that its principles are so remote from the ordinary needs of civilised society and the ordinary claims it makes upon its members as to deny a legal remedy where there is so obviously a social wrong." It is not surprising that an investigation of the cases conducted under these auspices produced sufficient material to support—or at least insufficient material to invalidate—the *a priori* conclusion which his Lordship admittedly set out to justify.

Lord Macmillan, who concurred with Lord Atkin and Lord Thankerton in the majority judgment, pursued a middle course in his definition of the problem. In his Lordship's view, the current of decision was not unbroken and consistent, but had set at different times in different directions. In this inconclusive state of the authorities, the question, viewed as a new question, fell to be determined " from the point of view of the principles applicable to this branch of law," and in accordance with the doctrine enunciated by Lord Esher in *Emmens* v. *Pottle* (1885), 16 Q.B.D. 354, that " any proposition the result of which would be to show that the common law of England is wholly unreasonable and unjust cannot be part of the common law of England." Starting accordingly with a clean slate, Lord Macmillan asserted, rather than deduced, the existence of the alleged legal duty, mainly upon the ground that to refuse recognition to it would be in his opinion consonant neither with justice nor with common sense.

The writer has no quarrel with the conclusions of the majority, still less with the dialectic brilliance of the opinions which have made so notable an addition to the law of reparation and of torts. The interest of the case rather resides in the method adopted in reaching the conclusion, and in particular in the readiness displayed by Lord Atkin (and in a lesser degree by Lord Macmillan), to formulate a proposition in law for which no positive British precedent could be adduced, which ran counter to the *ratio decidendi* of several of the authorities cited, and which was ultimately referred by Lord Atkin to the standard of " the sound common sense " of anyone " who was not a lawyer," and by Lord Macmillan to the opinion of " any twelve reasonable men."

It is doubtless essential that " the inherent adaptability of English law " should be vindicated, and that full recognition should be accorded to the fact that " the categories of negligence are never closed " ; but the question which suggests itself is whether the pursuit of flexibility along the lines so courageously followed in this case is not attended by an element of risk. It is a little difficult to believe that the problem presented by this case was of so novel a character that no weight should have been given to the fact that the existence of the alleged duty had never before been affirmed in terms. The " sealed container " and its counterparts have been familiar articles of commerce for half a century, and there would therefore seem to be justification for the question which the dissenting judges raised when they asked themselves why, if the principle contended for by the appellant was part of the common law, it had not been successfully asserted on many previous occasions. The only sources to which the man in the street and his legal adviser can refer for information as to the principles of the common law are the reported decisions and the text-books of authority ; and if, amid the wealth of precedents in the law of reparation which these now afford, no answer is given to the question whether a given right or remedy exists, it would seem a reasonable assumption that the common law does not recognise the right nor afford the desired remedy, and that it is to the Legislature that the aggrieved party must look. But if, under such circumstances, it is necessary to reckon with the further possibility that the courts may be disposed to supply the deficiencies of the common law by emulating the function of the Prætor dispensing edicts, a new and disturbing factor is at once introduced. It is impossible to forecast with any degree of confidence whether any given new principle will be regarded by the Court as " consonant with justice." In the case under consideration, five of the nine judges who heard the argument took one view, and four the other. And if the relevancy of a pursuer's averments falls to be tested by a conjectural enquiry as to the probable view which would be taken on this question of law by " anyone who was *not* a lawyer," or even by " any twelve reasonable men," the anchor of the entire system begins to drag.

Fortunately or unfortunately, it is unlikely that many opportunities will present themselves for the exercise of the judicial function as thus more liberally interpreted. But it may be permissible to voice a feeling of regret that so widely different a conception must have prevailed when the House of Lords decided *Cameron* v. *Young*, 1908 S.C.(H.L.) 7—a decision which could not survive any of the tests proposed by Lord Atkin and Lord Macmillan, and which the latter dismissed with the remark (which was true in more senses than one) that it belonged to " a different chapter of law."

1933

Trial by Jury in Scotland : Is there a Case for Reform ?

THE SUBJECT of my address to-night was selected not by me but by your Syllabus Committee ; and I welcome its choice as evidence of the active interest which is being shown to-day by so many sections of the non-legal community in every aspect of the principles and institutions which form the fabric of the system under which we live and work. As a profession, there is nothing we lawyers need more than an occasional tonic blast of lay criticism. From the days of the Twelve Tables until now every legal system has displayed an ineradicable tendency towards petrifaction, which has required to be fought both from within and from without. So long as life advanced at a leisurely pace, it proved possible for lawyers, if periodically stimulated by a jog on the elbow from the impatient public, to improve and adapt their technique, their mechanism, and even their principles in such fashion as to meet the changing conditions of the times and the fresh demands of a growing society. But we of the present age have witnessed, and are witnessing, social, economic, political, and administrative developments so swift, so fundamental, and so incalculable that the task of equipping our legal system to satisfy the requirements of the new standards and new ideals of a new, but imperfectly defined, social philosophy presents unprecedented difficulties. " We are now," said Lord Haldane a few years ago, " on the threshold of an epoch of profound legal transformation." If that transformation is to be successfully achieved, there must be brought to the task not only the wisdom and experience of the professional expert with his innate respect for stability and tradition, but also the constructive criticism of the lay citizen, in whose efficient service every legal system must find its sole justification. This is the spirit in which I would invite you this evening to devote a short time to a consideration of a small, but important, element in our judicial mechanism—Trial by Jury.

Our first effort must be to acquire a proper perspective of our subject both in time and in space. Within the limits of this address I cannot attempt to survey, however rapidly, the immense field of legal history and comparative jurisprudence. Suffice it to say that, from an early date in the development of organised civil communities, recognition and effect have been accorded by many different systems to the idea that the private citizen ought to participate actively in the administration of justice. Historically this idea takes precedence over the democratic principle that the individual citizen should take part, directly or indirectly, in the enactment of statute law. Its germ is found in the primitive community, and it underlies such widely diverse institutions as the Athenian *dikastae*, the Roman *judices*, and the English jury. Its justification from the political and social standpoint is claimed to be that it is good for the juryman and good for the law. It is good for the juryman to cultivate the judicial habit of mind ; to realise vividly the active duties which he owes to society ; and to acquire in the school of experience a wholesome respect for law and order. On the other hand, it is good for the law that it should never again become an esoteric cult monopolised by a professional oligarchy ; that it should be saved from over-refinement by being constantly brought into contact with every-day common sense ; and that its simplicity and intelligibility should be guaranteed by the working partnership between the expert and the untrained layman. It is by arguments such as these that the political theorist would explain and justify the introduction and retention of the principle that the judicial function should be discharged to some extent by the amateur ; and the validity of the arguments is beyond question, though it is very doubtful how far they were consciously present to the minds of those who introduced and developed the mechanism for giving effect to the abstract principle.

Before pursuing my analysis further, it is desirable to discriminate between the Civil and the Criminal Courts.

In the case of major crimes involving an offence against society and imperilling the life or liberty of the accused, there is a manifest appropriateness in the idea that the outraged community should itself take the responsibility of pronouncing a verdict of absolvitor or condemnation. The issues, however complex, are normally within the range of the practical experience of every citizen. Questions of prejudice and intimidation apart, the accused can rarely have just cause for complaint if a representative selection of his fellow citizens, duly instructed as to the few simple rules of law which usually fall to be observed, are satisfied that he has broken the law and deserves to suffer an appropriate penalty. In cases of this kind—and it must never be forgotten that they represent a very small fraction of the total volume of litigation—the Jury System has obtained wide popularity, and, in this country at least, is unlikely to be modified except in detail. It is true that a Criminal Jury presents most of the defects of the Civil Jury, to some of which I shall subsequently revert ; but these defects count for little by contrast with the wider expediencies which render it both impracticable and undesirable to suggest any material alteration of our traditional system of administering the criminal law in cases of major offences. In criminal procedure, further, our law provides the most ample guarantees against the risk of a miscarriage of justice. The deeply rooted traditions of the Crown Office, the presumption of innocence, the stringent onus of proof, and the ubiquitous shadow of the Court of Criminal Appeal ensure that the proceedings will be conducted with the most scrupulous avoidance of everything which might impair or prejudice in the slightest degree the right of the accused to a fair trial. It follows that a verdict of guilty, which is either not appealed or appealed unsuccessfully, is as likely to be a just verdict as human foresight and care can secure. It must be very rarely indeed, under modern conditions, that the innocent man is convicted ; and if the guilty occasionally escape, no irreparable harm is done. So far as the Criminal Jury is concerned, therefore, I would leave well alone. What I have still to say is directed to the system of trial by jury in civil cases.

The Civil Jury as the means of determining disputed issues of fact is a distinctive characteristic of English common law. As is the case with so many popularly cherished institutions, its gradual evolution was the result of a haphazard and accidental process of which the finished product bears so little resemblance to its early forms that the origin and development of trial by jury is still a favourite topic of controversy with the historians. Though its use seems to be less frequent than in the past, it survives to-day as a central feature of English Law and of the systems which have been framed on the English model. In France and Germany, on the other hand, the institution never took root, and has long since been discarded. To the French lawyer trial by jury is an ancient institution, the retention of which by those who are habituated to its use may be excused by the respect due to antiquity, but by nothing else.

In Scotland, the civil jury, borrowed from England, can be faintly discerned through the mists which obscure our early legal history ; but it had fallen into disuse by the seventeenth century, owing, no doubt, to the influence of the Continental ideas which were then widely prevalent in this country. In 1815, however, the civil jury was reintroduced as a temporary experiment under a new tribunal, the Jury Court, which was separate and distinct from the Court of Session. This separate court, which consisted at first of three, and latterly of five, judges, with a separate establishment of officers, was abolished in 1830, since when the Scottish civil jury has exhibited most of the features which it preserves to this day.

I pause to emphasise two facts which are apt to be overlooked. *First*, the civil jury, so far from being in general use in modern states, is the offspring of English common law, and is employed only in those systems which are modelled on, or have borrowed from, English law. *Second*, the civil jury is not indigenous to Scotland, but is an alien importation, introduced within comparatively recent times as an experiment, and subjected to more or less continuous experimental modifications ever since.

The list of causes appropriated for trial by jury in Scotland was first enumerated by section 28 of the Judicature Act of 1825, which is still law, though profoundly modified by subsequent statutory provision and by practice. It is a remarkable list ; for it includes, in addition to those actions of damages which we naturally associate with trial by jury to-day, all actions on account of injury to moveables or land ; actions affecting the responsibility of carriers, inkeepers, or stablers ; actions brought for nuisance ; actions on policies of insurance ; actions on charter-parties and bills of lading ; actions for freight ; actions on contract of carriage ; and actions for the wages of masters and mariners of ships and vessels. For a time this very miscellaneous assortment of suits was faithfully remitted for trial by jury ; but in 1850 the need for substantially narrowing the scope of the new method of procedure received recognition in the Court of Session Act of that year, which rendered it competent to substitute proof on commission for jury trial in all cases except actions for libel and nuisance or such as are properly and in substance actions of damages. The drift away from the jury proceeded a step further in the Evidence Act of 1866, in which it was provided that it should be competent in any case, with consent of parties or on special cause shown, to dispense with a jury. The discretion thus conferred on the Court has been exercised with various degrees of freedom at different times. Until the war the tendency was in the direction of withdrawing cases from a jury on comparatively slight pretext. This tendency was reversed by the views expressed in the House of Lords in a case decided in 1916, and until quite recently the current set in the opposite direction. Latterly the deficiencies of trial by jury in cases of complexity have been illustrated so conspicuously in one or two notable instances that the pre-war view is beginning to revive.

As a result of these progressive developments in practice, the actual position to-day may be summarised as follows : With the exception of an occasional action for reduction of a will, and the comparatively rare action of damages for slander or breach of promise, the great bulk of the jury trials conducted in the Court of Session are now concerned with the action of damages for personal injury or for " solatium " to relatives in the case of accidental death. Of these cases, a very large proportion arise out of traffic accidents ; a fair number out of alleged defects in private property or places of public resort ; and the balance out of alleged deficiencies in plant, materials, or systems of working, as a result of which workmen sustain injuries in factories, coal mines, and the like. I think that statistics would bear me out in the estimate that nine out of every ten juries have to determine whether a motorist committed a mistake. Whether we like it or not, the jury in Scotland has come to be in the main an accessory of the internal combustion engine, and a desperately expensive accessory at that.

Will you consider next how the civil jury normally works ? In order to decide a question which, as I have already explained, very frequently takes the form of an enquiry whether John Smith blew his horn or applied his brakes in time, thirty-six citizens of the counties of Midlothian, Haddington, and Linlithgow are compelled under divers pains and penalties to leave their homes and avocations—perhaps at a very early hour and at the expense of untold personal inconvenience— and to repair to the Parliament House at 10 a.m., twenty-four of them will be released about 11 a.m., having suffered nothing worse than a wasted forenoon ; while the balance will be empanelled for a period varying from one to three days, or even longer, during which they are virtually immobilised as useful members of the community, receiving in exchange free meals and drinks and 10s. per day provided by the unsuccessful litigant. Out of regard for the inexperience of the jurors, the proceedings are tediously protracted, and cumbered with tiresome ceremonial, with two speeches a side, laborious setting of the stage in evidence, and a charge from the presiding judge, followed by an interval of silence frequently lasting for hours, during which the jury deliberates upon its verdict. If the case presents the opportunity for doing so, one side or the other will ask directions from the judge and, if need be, " except " to the directions which he gives, a proceeding which is frequently followed by a costly and often protracted attempt to upset the verdict in the Inner House and occasionally in the House of Lords. A similar right of review is not infrequently resorted to by the unsuccessful litigant in cases where he thinks that he can demonstrate to the Inner House that the verdict is " contrary to the evidence," or that the damages are " excessive " ; and in all such cases a verbatim report of the evidence has to be reproduced. Even when matters take end with the jury's verdict, the procedure normally costs about £400 for a one-day trial, exclusive of the consequential loss arising from the withdrawal of the jurors from their usual work. And a large part of this utterly disproportionate expense ultimately falls upon the community at large ; for it is met in many cases by insurance companies, who pass it on to the public in the form of insurance premiums. To complete the picture, it is only necessary to add that the sum awarded usually falls short of the cost of the proceedings, and rarely exceeds £1000.

Let us now endeavour to divest ourselves of all prepossessions, born of long familiarity with the usage of generations, in order to assess dispassionately the merits and demerits of this system of procedure.

It is said that the jury is an institution so popular and so deeply rooted in British sentiment that no far-reaching departure from tradition would be tolerated by the public. As regards the criminal jury, as I have already admitted, this is no doubt true. In the case of the civil jury, however, I do not believe that any sentimental attachment which may exist in the public mind would long survive an exposure of the actual facts with regard to the working of that overrated and misunderstood device. There would always be some, of course, who would make vague and unintelligent references to Magna Carta and to the Treaty of Union, but such historic irrelevances and our instinctive respect for tradition could not prevail against the insistent demand of the present age for efficiency, expedition, economy, and—may I add—commonsense methods in the discharge of all kinds of public business. And, after all, what principle of public policy can possibly be alleged in support of the continuance of the system within the extremely narrow and artificial limits within which it actually operates ? The theoretic idea of trial by one's peers, or of invoking the judgment of the community, is not realised by a system of procedure which confers the exclusive privilege or burden of jury service upon a limited number of residents in Edinburgh and the surrounding towns and villages, to the total exclusion of the remainder of Scotland from which the bulk of the cases come. In a city state like Athens, or in a country such as England, in which circuit courts are held in all parts of the country for the discharge of civil judicial duties, trial by jury may have at least a semblance of theoretical justification. But the people of Glasgow and Aberdeen and Dundee should awake to the realisation of the fact that what we enjoy in Scotland is not so much trial by jury as trial by Edinburgh citizens. And as for the argument based on the educative value of trial by jury, and the cultivation of a sense of social responsibility, it is probably sufficient to say that these are at best by-products of the jury system, and that, if the lessons which trial by jury can teach require to be learned by the present generation, they can and should be taught in many other ways, at much less cost, and to a much wider and more representative section of the population than the citizens of the capital. Finally, I would ask, how is it possible to reconcile the alleged intrinsic value of the civil jury with the fact that it is rarely employed except in one arbitrarily selected type of case ? What magical potency resides in the verdict of a jury that it should be regarded as appropriate for the determination of issues in fact in cases involving personal injury or death, and in practically no other class of litigation ? In nearly every other type of action involving disputed issues of fact, questions of equal or greater intricacy and subtlety are as a matter of ordinary routine determined by the arbitrament of single judges or sheriffs sitting alone ; and the material and personal issues depending on such judgments are often of infinitely greater importance than those which fall within the province of the average jury. It cannot be suggested that the present practice in the use of juries can be explained or justified by the assumed suitability of the collective wisdom of the jurors as a solvent for the particular class of problem upon

E

which they are asked to pass judgment ; for the problems presented to juries exhibit no features differentiating them from those which arise in proofs, except that they are usually much simpler, much more trivial, and much less far-reaching in their consequences. In matrimonial causes and actions of filiation, which habitually give rise to the most delicate issues of fact and credibility, calling for the broadest and wisest insight into the interplay of human motive, the decision rests not with the jury but with a judge ; and the decision may mean not a few hundred pounds but lifelong happiness or misery, not merely to the actual litigants, but to others whose status or condition in life may be profoundly affected by the decree which is pronounced. In the field of contract and commercial law the financial stakes affected by decisions on pure fact are frequently enormously greater than those which are entrusted to juries ; and yet the responsibility is invariably discharged without a jury's aid. Not only so, but in such cases the remedy which the law affords often takes the form of an award of damages, assessed, as we say, " on a jury basis " but this assessment is made not by a jury but by a judge. In short, it would be impossible to mention any type of controversy within the entire field of human relationships which is not treated according to our present law and practice as within the competence of a judge or sheriff in Scotland. And the determination of the dispute frequently requires that the judge should discharge the characteristically " jury function " of deciding what is " just and reasonable " in a given state of circumstances ; but again it is a judge and not a jury who is entrusted with this arbitral function.

The only possible conclusion is that we have appropriated to trial by jury a group of causes, relatively large in number, but selected on no intelligible principle. In particular, it is incontrovertible that the dividing line between proof and jury trial has been drawn across, and not along, the only conceivable boundary which has ever been suggested as separating the function of the judge and the function of the jury—viz. the line which divides fact from law. If it were true, as some have affirmed, that no man's judgment on a question of fact can reflect the truth as faithfully as the joint conclusion of a casually chosen group of twelve men and women ; if, in other words, twelve heads are invariably better than one, irrespective of the quality or contents of the heads, then *all* issues of fact should be sent to juries, and the alleged intellectual limitations of judges should be publicly recognised.   But no one, I am confident, will be found to advocate such an extension of the use of the jury in this country.

Once again, I would ask, is the average jury peculiarly fitted by special knowledge and experience for the discharge of the duties which we impose upon it ?   Is it nearly as well qualified as the average judge ?   Plainly not.   Many jury trials involve difficult questions of medical fact and opinion, but we are at pains deliberately to exclude medical men from jury service.   Many jury trials give rise to intricate technical issues of an engineering nature ; but that bare fact would be sufficient warrant for either the pursuer's or the defender's counsel objecting to the presence on the jury of any person possessing technical experience or qualifications.   Many jury trials relate to accidents in coal mines ; and in such cases care will be taken by watchful counsel to exclude from the jury even those whose address on the jury list suggests that they may have practical acquaintance with the coal mining industry. In the ubiquitous motor accident trial we have, of course, no method of distinguishing the motorist from the pedestrian ; but we certainly take no steps with a view to securing a jury of Kaye Dons presided over by a Hore-Belisha.   In plain English, our methods are so devised as to secure not that the jury shall be specially qualified to deal with the issue, but rather that it shall possess as few special qualifications as possible, and shall be composed of persons whose only practicable method of deciding the case is by choosing between the conflicting bodies of evidence led for the parties.   They may lack the education and experience necessary to enable them to appreciate a technical issue.   They may have neither the capacity nor the desire to weigh evidence.   They certainly have not enjoyed an infinite part of the experience possessed by the judge in discharging such a duty.   But the theory still prevalent amongst us demands that the highly trained expert should scrupulously refrain from interference with the tyros as they try their hand at an unaccustomed task.

I pass to an argument which is constantly employed in justification of the continued use of the civil jury, and I shall never cease to marvel at the confusion of thought which underlies it. It is claimed that the chief value of a jury's verdict resides in its finality. It seems to me that three obvious fallacies vitiate this contention : (1) In the first place, finality is not an intrinsic quality of any judicial determination, whether by a judge or by a jury. It is a consequence of the rules which regulate the right of review by an appellate tribunal. The verdict of a jury and the decree of a judge can be given just as much, or just as little, finality as we choose. (2) In the second place, though a jury's verdict can only be upset on certain prescribed conditions, it does not in fact possess the finality claimed for it. Scores of cases have occurred in recent years in which new trials have been ordered because of the alleged perversity of juries' verdicts ; and it is by no means unknown for a case to be tried twice before successive juries, and for the verdict to be upset on two separate occasions. In relation even to the award of damages for solatium for the death of a relative, the Court has even gone so far as to lay down a species of tariff, and to declare that a verdict will be upset if the jury gives more than twice as much as the tariff rate (*Elliot* v. *Glasgow Corporation*, 1922 S.C. 146). As a sidelight upon the efficiency of the civil jury as a method of administering justice, this naïve but formal admission of 100 per cent. allowance of error calls for no comment. (3) In the third place, the quality of the jury's verdict which the advocate of the system mistakenly describes as its *finality* is truly its *inscrutability*. This very dubious characteristic has for some obscure reason been developed in Scotland far more extensively than in the true home of juries across the Border. It is the practice in England for the presiding judge to put to the jury a whole series of articulate questions from the answers to which it is frequently possible to infer the process of reasoning which has been applied, and to correct any errors which may have been committed. In Scotland such a process is practically unknown. The general verdict either " for the pursuer " or " for the defender " is the almost invariable rule ; and, as few cases arise in which the ultimate conclusion can be reached otherwise than by a series of distinct stages, it is impossible to discover by which of several possible routes—some valid, and others demonstrably illegitimate— the jury have arrived at their final conclusion. The result is that many a verdict stands for no other or better reason than that the jurors are mercifully excused from the necessity of indicating the grounds on which they have proceeded. I do not think that it is going too far to say that this feature of jury practice is a fatal defect. The administration of justice is a rational process, and should be rationally conducted ; and a method of administering justice which requires to be justified on the ground that it issues in an oracular pronounce- ment which may, or may not, be based on relevant and logical premises, does not differ widely in essence from the spin of a coin or the throw of a dice. Surely we of the present generation have outlived the atmosphere of the Delphic cave, the inspection of the auspices and the trial by ordeal ?

Lastly, we may be told that the judges and counsel, who are most familiar with jury practice, combine in asserting that, on the whole and in the long run, a jury's verdict is more often right than not. It seems to me that this is the sort of faint praise which ought to be the final condemnation of the institution. When deciding (as the jury invariably does in Scotland) on a general issue there are only two possible verdicts, and every jury has therefore an even chance of being in the right. In other words, if the civil jury cannot score at least 50 per cent. of hits, it is positively a public menace, being less reliable than the spinning coin. In addition to the 50 per cent. of cases in which the law of averages requires that the verdict should be right, there is a considerable proportion of cases in which in the course of the trial the evidence turns out in such a way as to admit of virtually only one verdict. Once again, if the jury cannot return the obvious verdict in such cases, they are impeding, and not advancing, the dispensation of justice. As regards the balance of cases in which the issue is an open one, I for one decline to accept the proposition that the jury is right as often as a judge would be, and no one can prove that I am wrong. Where the scales are so evenly balanced that a decision in favour of either side could be justified, it is difficult to see why that decision should not be taken in a straightforward way from the reasoned opinion of a judge rather than from the obscurantist verdict of a jury. Of course, a jury relieves the judge from the responsibility of making a decision, and for this service merits a word of tepid praise and gratitude from the judge. An occasional jury trial introduces a little light relief into the weary existence of the practitioner, and on that account it enjoys a measure of popularity in the Parliament House. And the notorious susceptibilities of juries afford ample scope for a special technique in advocacy which those who possess the necessary gifts are naturally anxious to exploit. Such considerations, however, can be allowed little, if any, weight in an enquiry into the merits of a judicial institution.

The question with which I opened this evening was : Is there a case for reform ? I might have approached that question from the standpoint of an enquiry into the details of jury procedure, the formation of the jury, the appropriate form of the issue, the majority verdict, the review of the verdict, and a hundred other topics which from time to time have arisen for consideration. All these topics I have deliberately discarded in favour of a reasoned argument to support the conclusion, which I have long held and which is confirmed by my daily experience, that the public interest in Scotland would be well served by the total abolition of the civil jury, and by the general recognition of the fact that, even within the narrow limits within which it is still permitted to operate, the experiment of 1815 can no longer satisfy the reasonable demands which are made upon it. I have endeavoured to support my thesis by a sober recital of facts which are readily capable of verification ; and if my argument has carried conviction to your minds, I trust that you will lend the weight of your influence to securing a reform which I have long regarded as overdue.

1934

The Administration of Criminal Justice in Scotland

My LORDS AND GENTLEMEN : I think it was Lord Bacon who said that it is a happy thing in a state when states do often consult with judges and when judges do often consult with the state. And so, as a humble representative of the State, I wish to consult for a little with you, as representative judges, regarding the performance of that essential public function in which we both share a responsibility—the administration of criminal justice in Scotland.

I need not urge you to magnify your office. Out of 126,000 persons brought to trial in Scotland in 1937, no less than 86,000 were dealt with in Police, Justice of the Peace, or Juvenile Courts ; so that you are the arbiters of the fate of 70 per cent. of the offenders against our laws. And though the offences with which you deal are the minor offences, your task is not on that account any the easier, nor your responsibility lighter, in the attempt to dispense even-handed justice in a spirit of wise humanity and impartial discrimination, and with due regard to your paramount obligation to the community which you serve. That is an ideal which demands unremitting efforts on the part of those who seek to attain it : for the best designed machine will sometimes operate harshly, and the best intentioned expedients may gradually fall out of step with the demands of a progressive community and an awakening social conscience.

Let us see whether a rapid survey of the machine of summary criminal justice will reveal any remediable defects.

I begin by noting certain striking facts which emerge from the study of the Criminal Statistics of the last few years. In 1930 the percentage of Probation Orders to cases tried was only 2·6. Notwithstanding the passing of the Act of 1931, which was expected to result in a material increase in the use of

Probation machinery, the Scottish percentage had actually fallen by 1937 to 2·4 per cent.   There are important districts in Scotland where the Probation machinery is virtually in disuse, partly because of the inadequate provision made by the local authorities, and partly because the Courts appear to be still unaware of its proved merit and value.   Over the whole country the Probation Acts are very sparingly used in the case of both juvenile and adult offenders.   Against these facts I put the equally remarkable point that nearly 40 per cent. of the cases before Juvenile Courts ended in a bare admonition, and that some 8000 persons were sent to prison in default of payment of a fine, in whole or in part, the corresponding figure for England and Wales, with eight times the population, being approximately the same.

Without multiplying examples, I should like to suggest to you the question whether the powers which the Courts already possess are being employed, at least in some parts of the country, to a sufficient extent or with the exact discrimination which public opinion to-day expects.   On the one hand it is difficult to believe that some of the offenders who were only admonished should not have received either some more specific proof of the community's disapproval, or the chance of the corrective treatment or supervision which might have ensured their restoration to the ranks of responsible citizenship. On the other hand it seems undeniable that too little has been done to adjust the amount and conditions of payment of fines to the delinquent's capacity to pay.   The broad tendency seems to have been to think in terms of only one or two of the older types of penalty, and in their employment to vacillate between the extremes of undue leniency and undue severity, without a sufficient regard to the numerous intermediate expedients by the fuller use of which it is often possible not only to " make the punishment fit the crime " but to make the punishment fit the individual criminal.

I venture to repeat, Mr Chairman, that enlightened public opinion to-day expects a closer and more exact discrimination in the treatment of the offender.   Without that the judicial function cannot be faithfully discharged : for in its absence some offenders will leave our courts with diminished respect for the law they have violated, while others will be embittered by a just sense of grievance.

As you know, Parliament has just placed in your hands new powers designed to meet the most fatal criticism that can be directed against any judicial system, viz. that there is one law for the rich and another for the poor. Under the Criminal Procedure Act of last year, you are empowered in many cases to dispense with the personal attendance of the accused, and in others to transfer your powers to a more convenient court ; and so to avoid the unmerited loss which might otherwise be inflicted on those who can ill afford the expense of a journey, and whose livelihood might be imperilled by enforced absence from work. Further, that Act has emphasised and extended your powers to allow time for payment, to accept payment by instalments, and, if need be, to review a sentence in the light of fuller information or new facts. Now I know well that there are many cases where imprisonment is properly imposed. But there is no case in which a man can properly be deprived of his liberty *solely* because he is unable to produce a certain amount of ready cash at a given moment. The short term of imprisonment which follows upon failure to pay a fine may not only involve that the punishment falls upon the offender's innocent dependants but it may also entail, directly and indirectly, a deplorable waste of public money in the maintenance of prisons and the payment of relief.

And so I would plead most urgently for a full and free use of these powers. But they are more than powers ; they are duties involving new responsibilities on the Courts. I am well aware that their use will impose upon you—and also upon the Court officials—a good deal of additional trouble and work, and that there is always a temptation to dispose of a case outright in the fashion which will occasion the minimum of difficulty to all concerned. But such considerations, I am confident, will have no weight with you in the discharge of your duties.

One word on a different point. May I commend to your earnest consideration the desirability of extending the practice of holding evening courts? I am certain that an effort to overcome the local difficulties which often exist would be well worth while. A more extended use of the practice would enable a wider range of qualified persons to take part in judicial work. It would greatly facilitate the attendance of witnesses, and it would often obviate hardship to the accused. As a supplement to, rather than a substitute for, the ordinary procedure, I would urge you to explore this question further in your several areas.

Finally, a word on the Criminal Justice Bill. It is very gratifying to note from the leading article in your Bulletin for January that the provisions and scope of that measure have been appreciated by you with an accuracy and an enlightened understanding which stand in marked contrast to the astonishing misconceptions which have gained currency in recent controversy. The statement has been repeatedly made that the object and effect of the Bill is to abolish all punishment for juvenile offenders—with the single exception of the attendance centre—even in the case of serious crime. The truth, as I need hardly tell you, is that under the existing law there are fifteen different methods by which a summary court may deal with a juvenile delinquent, and that, under the new Bill, this number is increased to seventeen or eighteen. So far as serious crime and the higher range of ages are concerned, there is not one word in the Bill to prevent the imposition by the competent courts in suitable cases of the entire range of existing penalties, up to and including the penalty of death. The suggestion that the Bill represents the abandonment by the State of its primary function of vindicating the law and protecting the community is destitute of foundation. There is room for discussion as to the wisdom of abolishing the birching of boys, as to which I shall say a word in a moment. There may be room for discussion (though I doubt it) as to the proposal to raise from fourteen to sixteen the minimum age for sending a juvenile to an ordinary prison, and from sixteen to seventeen the minimum age for the attachment of conditions to the award of such a sentence. There is room for discussion as to the prospects of success which may be expected of the new forms of penalty which it is proposed experimentally to introduce. In these respects the Bill simply carries one stage further the process of reform already embodied in existing legislation regarding children and young persons ; and the deliberations on these important questions will not be assisted by the introduction of false issues. So far from tying your hands in the effort to repress real crime, the Bill amplifies the range of your powers and discretion and widens the opportunity for the exercise of that more exact discrimination for which I am pleading this afternoon.

I know that some of you are interested in the question of birching, and think that on this, as on many other matters, Solomon was right. But it is a significant fact that in England, where boys are endowed with much the same quota of original sin as in Scotland, it has been virtually discarded except in some rural areas, and that it is used in less than 2 per cent. of the cases in which it might be applied. Last year in Scotland, out of 16,500 juveniles brought before a court, only 146 were whipped, and the bulk of those cases came from a small number of courts. Add to that the conclusion of the Cadogan Committee, based on an elaborate expert investigation, that there is no proof that corporal punishment has any deterrent or reformative effect upon the victim ; and you will be obliged to admit that there is at least a formidable case for leaving the rod in the competent hands of the stern parent, and trying out some of the alternative expedients which already exist and which the Bill proposes to supplement.

My time is up. Yours are arduous and exacting duties and I am afraid that we in Parliament are making them more arduous and more exacting every year. But in our several spheres we are all exerting our best endeavours to perfect the machinery for the performance of a vital public service : and it is in grateful recognition of the public spirit and devotion which inspire your labours that I cordially wish you well in the work awaiting you in the year that lies ahead.

1939

The Legal Profession

THERE ARE certain occasions on which originality in the choice or treatment of a theme is impossible ; and this, it seems to me, is one of them. When a senior member of a great and honoured profession is privileged, as I am to-night, to address an audience composed in the main of young men and women who have chosen the pursuit of that profession as their life work, and are engaged in equipping themselves to enter upon its practice, his thoughts inevitably travel back to his own student days, to the mistakes he made, the wrong turnings he took, and the false aims he imperfectly pursued, and to the losses which all these things inflicted not only upon himself but upon the professional ideal which, one and all, we strive to cherish.

And so I make no apology for adopting a serious and didactic tone in my remarks to-night. Each one of us must laboriously construct his own experience and his own pattern of professional life ; but it sometimes happens that those who are a little further along the road and who enjoy the wider prospects which open out when you get a little further up the hill, can drop a hint or suggest an idea which may be helpful to others at the beginning of their professional pilgrimage.

Many years ago, when the Juridical Society was still an active debating society, Lord Clyde delivered to it in my hearing an address of which a copy should be in the hands of every law student. In that address he epitomised the aim of legal training as " the favourable conjunction of trained intellect and courageous character." Now none of us by taking thought can suddenly acquire for himself, still less impart to others, the qualities which go to the formation of courageous character. But trained intellect stands on a different footing ; and in large measure the training of your intellects is in your hands now, to make or to mar.

I say " in your hands " advisedly. For I am not thinking at the moment of organised legal instruction, here or elsewhere, or of the projects for the improvement of the legal curriculum to which much thought is being devoted at the present time. I am thinking rather of that deeper education which never ends so long as life persists, and which every man must provide for himself by deliberately forming and assiduously cultivating the widest cultural background compatible with his tastes and intellectual aptitude. The one thing above all others which Law needs to-day is a broader and richer cultural background in its practitioners ; the catholic outlook, the disciplined habit of mind, the mental flexibility and adaptability, and the breadth of view, which alone will save Law from degenerating from a profession into a trade or a mere mechanic art.

There are several grounds on which that statement could be justified, but I shall mention only two.

In the first place, every honest lawyer will admit that the day-to-day practice of our profession in any of its many branches does threaten to produce in the lawyer that incipient ossification of the brain which is politely referred to in lay circles as " the legal mind." Logic, symmetry, stability, and tradition are our guiding lights. We would rather avoid error than reach the truth. The lawyer's innate caution and respect for precedent—not bad things in themselves—do go some distance towards justifying Dicey's celebrated sneer that statutes reproduce the opinion of yesterday and judge-made law the opinion of the day before. I should never dream of saying such things outside, and I am far from suggesting that these defects are universal or even general. But the blunt truth is that here are your besetting sins. You, who are crossing the threshold of the professional family, are entitled to an early glimpse of the skeleton in the cupboard.

The second point is this, and it applies to you and your generation more forcibly than it did to mine. The tempo of life has recently been immeasurably quickened. In this age of swift and bewildering transition, there is hardly an institution, hardly a belief, hardly a principle—however respectable its antiquity—which is not being openly challenged and required to justify its continued acceptance by demonstrating its fitness to be incorporated into new and imperfectly conceived social philosophies. People will no longer take things for granted as they used to do, or accept without question the rule that what has been done for a long time may rightly continue to be done again and again. This is a new situation ; and it may well be your generation who will have to face it squarely and grapple with the task of moulding and adapting the principles of Scottish jurisprudence until you have fashioned a reconditioned fabric, fitter to sustain the stresses and to meet the needs of the new age on which we seem to be entering.

May I illustrate my point with a personal note ? For the last three and a half years I have been a Law Officer, and I have often had the experience of being asked in conference by some of my lay colleagues, rich in experience of public life, what the Law of Scotland is on a certain point. And on occasions, when I have replied by stating some doctrine which is second nature to us and which we have probably derived from a seventeenth century institutional writer, and treat with all the respect due to Holy Writ, it has happened that my reply has been greeted with a slight lifting of the eyebrows, and the extremely disconcerting question : " Why ? "

The truth is that the time has come when we in Scotland, and the lawyers in every developed country in the world, will have to put to ourselves rather more often than in years gone by that disconcerting and sometimes unanswerable : " Why ? "

And so I come back to my emphasis on the need for the cultural background and the mental adaptability and flexibility which it alone can afford. How can it be acquired ? Let me offer three practical suggestions.

First, may I counsel you against premature specialisation and excessive absorption in the technicalities of your craft ? *Ars longa, vita brevis*, you may say. Personal and financial problems may force your hand. I know the difficulties. Nevertheless I would urge you to lose no opportunity during those early years of dipping as deeply as you can and as widely as you can into subjects which interest you and which have no necessary or obvious connection with the practical pursuit of your chosen profession. I care not whether your interests are scientific, or technical, or literary, or philosophical, or artistic. There is hardly a subject taught within these walls a competent acquaintance with which will not be of real value to you in your professional work and which will not contribute to the development of these finer qualities and habits of mind for which I am pleading. Let your tastes and aptitudes govern your choice. Of course there are some subjects of which it is better to " drink deep or taste not the Pierian spring " ; but there are very few of which it can be said that even a superficial acquaintance is not worth while. The fact is that the competent lawyer must be a Jack of all trades if he is to be a master of one ; for he may be called upon at any time to assimilate rapidly and intelligently, and to employ with confidence, highly technical information upon nearly every topic under the sun.

In the second place, I would urge you, if I require to do so, to make up your minds now to take an interest, and if possible actively to participate, in some form of public life. This does not mean that you should all immediately secure your adoption as candidates for Parliament or for a local council. But it does mean that the mental equipment of a lawyer is inevitably incomplete and one-sided if he is not making constant personal contact with the practical administration of the law which he applies and interprets in the quiet of his study, and if he is not being forced by the sheer pressure of actual experience to suggest and devise improvements in the system which he is striving to master.

Lastly, remember that, for doing any of the things which I have ventured to press upon your attention, there is literally no time like the present. I know that you are all anxious to be done with books and study, to get into an office or on to the floor of the Parliament House, there to apply in actual practice the knowledge you have acquired. It has always been so ; and most of us have discovered too late that the all too meagre seed which was sown here fell amongst thorns which sprang up and all but choked the seed. The student in his University days has chances which will never come again, and it is very rarely indeed that the habits of study and the capacity for its sustained pursuit survive immersion in a reasonably successful professional career. We all need to be reminded, in the words of R. L. S., that perpetual devotion to a man's business is only to be sustained by perpetual neglect of many other things.

No one who has laboured long in the profession of the law can have anything but the keenest enthusiasm for its progressive perfection as an instrument for the service of society. It is in the hope and belief that you too will be fired with the same enthusiasm and will be enabled to transmute that enthusiasm into practical action, that I sincerely wish you well in the careers which lie before you.

1939

Melrose Abbey *versus* The Earl of Dunbar

THERE ARE FEW Scottish litigations which illustrate so many phases of medieval law and practice as the keenly contested dispute which was fought out nearly 750 years ago between the Monks of Melrose and Patrick, Earl of Dunbar. If the impression is still held that in the early thirteenth century the juristic concepts and methods which obtained in Scotland were rudimentary and barbaric, that impression can hardly survive the study of the report which it is possible to reconstruct from the charter records.

First the background must be sketched in. In the north-most area of Roxburghshire enclosed between the Gala, the Tweed and the Leader there lies a stretch of arable land and hill pasture about eight miles square. Until the middle of the twelfth century the chief value of this area lay in the sporting rights. Like Ettrick, Selkirk, and Traquair it was described as a " forest," and it doubtless formed part of the domains of Earl David which became merged in Crown property on his accession to the throne in 1124. By the second half of the twelfth century the characteristics of this area were changing. Agriculture, and especially pastoral farming, was encroaching on the game preserves from every side. The charter references are no longer to the " forest " but to the " pastures " between the Gala and the Leader, and it is with sheep and cattle, pasturage and pannage, timber and peat that they are mainly concerned instead of with the wolf, the boar, the hart, the hind, and the æries of falcons and tercels of which we hear in the earlier records dealing with these Border forests.

The boundaries of this area were for long imperfectly defined, but from an early date we can trace the following neighbouring properties :—

(1) To the north-west lay the territory of Wedale with its centre at Stow, whose church, with its special rights

of sanctuary, first appears as a possession of the Bishops of St Andrews.

(2) To the north-east in the vicinity of Lauder were the lands of the de Morevilles.

(3) To the east, in the vicinity of Earlston, lay the lands of the Earls of Dunbar, who had seemingly succeeded the Lindsays in the ownership of these estates.

(4) To the south lay various lands belonging to the Abbeys of Melrose, Dryburgh, and Kelso.

With the exception of Kelso Abbey, all these proprietors claimed rights of property or of servitude within the forest area. Melrose Abbey, founded by David in 1136, had received as part of its endowment a portion in the south-east, with rights (*aisiamenta*) to pasturage, pannage, and timber-cutting within the forest (*Melrose Charters*, No. 1). Dryburgh Abbey, founded in 1150 by David and Hugo de Moreville, obtained a portion in the east and certain vague rights of pasturage (*Dryburgh Foundation Charter*). Other rights, of which the record has been lost, were also granted, for we know that Alan, son of Walter the Steward, asserted an interest in the pastures, while the de Morevilles and the Dunbars had claims both as agriculturists and as sportsmen. Accordingly, when William the Lion ascended the throne in 1165, there were all the makings of a prodigious multiplepoinding to determine the rights of the rival claimants to this coveted fund *in medio* and to reconcile the conflicting interests of sport and farming. We can trace the stages by which the problem was progressively solved.

The monks first put their own house in order by settling the boundaries as between Melrose and Dryburgh Abbeys by an agreement concluded in 1170 and confirmed by the Bishop of Glasgow, within whose diocese the property lay (*Dryburgh Charters*, No. 113).

The next ten years were occupied with what the monastic chronicle described as the " *magna controversia* " between Melrose and Richard de Moreville, and it was King William (and not an ecclesiastical dignitary) who, on 30th March 1180,

recorded the settlement of this controversy in his presence and
court at Haddington following a perambulation of the marches
conducted by the King in person, the Bishop of Glasgow, and
others.

Four years later came the turn of " the men of Wedale,"
and once again a civil and not a church tribunal was invoked.
A perambulation was made and reported *per juramenta fidelium
hominum*, twelve in number, and their verdict was confirmed
by Royal Charter dated 18th October 1184 (*Melrose Charters*,
No. 112 ; *Melrose Chronicle*, p. 93).

The next to be dealt with was Alan, son of Walter the
Steward, who at some date between 1189 and 1196 abandoned
his pretentions in favour of the Monks of Melrose in the
presence and court of King William at Edinburgh (*A.P.S.* i.
388).

There now remained only the Earl of Dunbar. Patrick,
the fifth Earl, a descendant of Malcolm II. through the Gos-
patricks of Northumbria, the husband of one of King William's
daughters, and the ancestor of a long line of Earls of Dunbar,
Earls of March, and Earls of Moray, was probably the most
powerful magnate in all Lothian, and, as the Monks found to
their cost, he was not an easy man to deal with. It was
perhaps out of respect for so redoubtable an antagonist that
they were so long content to observe an armed neutrality, but
at length they were emboldened to take the offensive, which
they did in the opening years of the thirteenth century (the
exact date being unknown), and this time they adopted new
tactics by appealing not to King William but to the Pope,
alleging that the Earl had violently dispossessed them of their
rights of pasture. In accordance with customary practice
the Pope nominated as judges delegate to determine the dispute
the Bishop and Archdeacon of St Andrews and the Archdeacon
of Lothian.

The Earl received the usual preliminary and peremptory
citations to appear before the tribunal, but he paid no attention and was eventually presumed—with ample justification—
to be *contumax*. The next step would normally have been an
order of *missio in possessionem* in favour of the Monks ; but

the judges delegate, as they tell us, were advised that in this case such an order would lead to bloodshed. They therefore adopted the competent alternative of laying the Earl's lands (*maneria*) under ecclesiastical interdict, thereby penalising all his vassals and dependants. This was too much even for the Earl, who found caution *judicio sisti*, but in so doing expressly reserved his defences. The sentence of interdict was at once recalled and a peremptory diet assigned for the statement of the Earl's dilatory pleas.

At this diet the Earl tendered a plea of " no jurisdiction " on the threefold ground (*a*) that he was a layman ; (*b*) that the subject in dispute was a lay holding ; and (*c*) that " *actor sequi debet forum rei.*" In claiming as he did the benefit of the common law (*juris communis*), the defender was doubtless indignant at the attempt of the Monks to treat him differently from de Moreville and Alan, and even the " men of Wedale," all of whom had been sued in civil courts. But the argument was not a very hopeful one to present in a church court, and the plea was repelled by an interlocutory judgment which proceeded upon the ground that " in those parts " the general custom hitherto observed was for clerics to convene laymen in an ecclesiastical forum, especially with regard to subjects gifted in pure alms.

This is one of the very few echoes which we hear in Scotland of the bitter controversy which had been raging in England and elsewhere between Church and State. The judgment (in which the Pope later indicated his concurrence) bears the impress of political expediency. In so far as it proceeded on the assumption that the subjects were held in pure alms, it involved a *petitio principii*, for the merits had not yet been investigated and the defender's averment was that the subject was a lay holding. In so far as it proceeded upon custom " in those parts," it is true that the principal contested civil disputes of the thirteenth century were in fact litigated in the Court Christian, but it is far from clear that this custom had become established at the date of the judgment. As we have seen all the parallel disputes had been dealt with in civil courts, and even during the later years of the thirteenth century the perambulation of bounds was a type of process usually left to the civil courts. But, right or wrong, the judgment was in favour of the Monks and the Earl fell back on his second line.

His next step—and it was fortunate for him that the plea of " competent and omitted " was not taken against him—was to decline the jurisdiction of the president of the tribunal as suspect on account of certain action alleged to have been taken by him in another dispute relating to the patronage of a church ; and whenever it became apparent (as the Earl must have expected) that this plea also would be repelled, he appealed to the Pope. If the object was to indulge in obstructive tactics, the Earl's advisers knew their business. An accusation of this kind was bound to be taken seriously by the Papal See, and the appeal on this side-issue pursued its way for some distance until it was held up by the failure of the Earl to appear at a diet fixed for proof. After an interval a procurator for the Earl did appear, and seemingly satisfied the Vatican authorities that the declinature was *prima facie* justified, for the next step was the unusual one of the issue of a fresh Papal mandate, this time in favour of the Abbot of Holyrood, the Prior of Inchcolm, and a Rector of Dunkeld, with authority to them to review the whole proceedings with special reference to the objection taken to the Bishop, and to determine the cause, enforcing their decision by ecclesiastical censure.

This second tribunal did their best, but found the task beyond them. After taking evidence and hearing parties they remitted the case back to Rome, fixing Quasimodo Sunday (29th April), 1207, as a diet for the appearance of parties. One of the Cardinals was deputed to hear the case, the process was transmitted, and appearance was duly made for the Monks ; but once again the Earl failed to attend or to send a procurator, " though they waited for a long time."

Matters had now reached a stage at which it was for the Pope at all costs to vindicate his authority. With the express object of avoiding further trouble and expense to the parties, the Pope took the extreme course of granting a third mandate, which is dated 12th September 1207 (*Calendar of Papal Letters*, i. 93), this time in favour of a single nominee—Brice, Bishop of Moray—the choice of a dignitary from this distant diocese being obviously dictated by a desire to exclude any further attempts to attack the impartiality of the court. The same object clearly underlies the instructions to Bishop Brice, for he was enjoined to ignore the earlier proceedings, and to allow the parties fifteen days within which each should nominate as a colleague to act as a judge a " *virum idoneum et honestum,*" under certification that if they, or either of them, failed so to tender a nominee, Bishop Brice should proceed with the case at his own hand—if need be in the absence of either or both of the parties (*Melrose Charters*, No. 101).

At this point there is a regrettable gap in the story. The Bishop's *attestatio* curtly narrates that he allowed the parties the fifteen days in which to present their nominees ; that they did not do so ; that he proceeded with the case ; and that " *tandem lis in hunc modum conquievit.*" Whether the compromise was attributable to Brice's skill as a mediator, or, as is more likely, to the fact that both parties had had enough and felt that honour was satisfied, we do not know. But the elaborate joint minute or *cirographum* was complete by 6th July 1208 (*Melrose Charters*, No. 102), and the remarkable fact is that, although the entire proceedings had been conducted before ecclesiastical tribunals, it was in presence of the King in his full court at Selkirk that the settlement bears to have been concluded. Moreover, the *cirographum* is witnessed by the King and confirmed by a Royal Charter dated 6th November 1208 (*Melrose Charters*, No. 103). And so the Earl got his way in the end, for there can be little doubt that it was by his insistence on the point as part of the compromise that the case took end in a civil court and not before an ecclesiastic.

The terms of settlement disclose a genuine compromise with a full measure of give and take. The Monks received the arable land of Sorulefield, which the Earl conveyed to them by separate charter (*Melrose Charters*, No. 104), and rights of pasture for prescribed numbers of stock in a defined area. No buildings were to be erected on the pasture and none of it was to be cultivated. The Earl's cattle and sheep were to be taken home nightly to Earlston unless prevented by storm or flood, and the Monks were allowed to take a specified quantity of peat annually from a named moss. Nothing was said as to expenses, though the Monks had twice been needlessly dragged to Rome, and the customary oaths to observe the settlement and the voluntary subjection of the parties to ecclesiastical jurisdiction were, as one would expect, omitted. On the whole the honours were with the Earl.

The report of this case, though unusually well documented, is by no means unique. Many others could easily be disinterred from thirteenth century charters, which exhibit to us the operation of a highly developed judicial mechanism and a relatively mature legal system. The mechanism and the system were not Scottish but Canonist, for at this time and for long after the Courts Christian supplied in Scotland the lack of an efficient system of Royal justice and consequently of a native common law ; but the practice of the methods illustrated by this and other cases must have had a profound influence in shaping the native institutions which slowly emerged in the centuries which followed.

1943

The First Law Reform (Miscellaneous Provisions) Act

ON 3rd December 1318 there were enacted at Scone twenty-nine " statutes " which had as their manifest object the carrying into effect of part of the reconstruction plans framed in prospect of the early termination of the Wars of Independence, and which might fittingly be characterised collectively by the title at the head of this article. These measures are well authenticated as to source and date ; for Bernard de Linton, who as Bruce's Chancellor must have participated in their enactment and perhaps in their drafting, was Abbot of Arbroath at the time and caused a record of the statutes to be engrossed in the *Registrum Vetus* of the Abbey.

The cross-bearing afforded by this record is of special value. It is now accepted that the arrangement and chronology adopted for the statutory contents of the first volume of the Folio Acts rest on a very insecure foundation which further research is more likely to undermine than to reinforce. We have therefore little direct and reliable evidence bearing upon the legislation of the thirteenth century, and as this period is one of peculiar significance in the early history of Scots Law, it is worth while trying to cast a reflected light upon it by examining the assumptions on which the amending legislation of the early fourteenth century was based.

The code covers a wide variety of subjects, one or two of which may be selected for closer inspection. Let us begin with Chapter XXIII, which may be freely translated as follows :

Amendment of the law regarding brieves of Mortancestor.—Whereas the brieve of mortancestor has heretofore been available only in claims by a petitioner to succeed to his father, mother, brother, sister, uncle or aunt, it is hereby enacted that for the future the brieve shall also be available to a petitioner claiming to succeed to his grandfather or grandmother : Provided always that this provision shall not be retrospective in effect but shall apply only where the ancestor in question died seised in the lands after the date hereof.

The possessory assise of Mortancestor (which is of course the lineal predecessor of the petition for service of an heir) was borrowed from England, and, as the charter evidence amply demonstrates, was extensively employed in thirteenth century Scotland. Initially it was restricted to claimants within the close degrees of relationship to the deceased ancestor specified in the preamble to this section. The demand for a relaxation of this restriction was met in England during the first half of the thirteenth century by the invention of the writs of aiel, besaiel, and cosinage, by which the remedy was successively extended to claims to succeed to a grandfather, a grandmother, and eventually to collaterals of any degree. All this was the work of the English Justices (notably William of Raleigh), and the reforms were not effected without much forensic controversy, the echoes of which reverberate in the pages of Bracton and in some of the reported cases on which he relied.

What was the position in contemporary Scotland ? The law as laid down in Regiam Majestatem follows the original and unamended practice as expounded by Glanvill towards the close of the twelfth century, and no trace has been noted in any Scottish contemporary record of a reference to the supplementary writs of aiel, besaiel, or cosinage. It seems probable that, as the above section asserts, the limitation to the nearest degree of propinquity prevailed in theory, though extensions of the remedy to more remote relations were winked at in practice. Thus in 1284 we find the procedure applied to a case of grandnieces and grand-uncle (*Reg. de Passelet*, 191). But the points of special interest about the amendment of 1318 are (i) that it accepts the position that down to that date Scotland had not adopted the changes which had been introduced into England some seventy years before ; (ii) that it proceeds to adopt only a part of the English improvements ; and (iii) that it does so by a method of its own without introducing the terms and the forms of process which by this time were familiar in England.

Take next the more elaborate provision dealing with the parallel remedy for wrongous ejection. It reads as follows :—

Amendment of the law regarding brieves of Novel Disseisin.—(i) Whereas under the existing law and practice the brieve of novel disseisin is available only when brought against the person in actual possession of the lands in dispute, whether he be the original intruder or some person deriving right from the original intruder, it is hereby enacted that it shall be competent for the future to call as defenders to a brieve of novel disseisin (*a*) the original intruder, (*b*) the person in actual possession of the lands, and (*c*), if he is still alive, the person from whom the lands were derived by the person in actual possession.

(ii) If several persons have participated in a single act of intrusion and the principal intruder has died before the pursuer recovers possession of the lands, the pursuer shall not on that account lose the right to proceed by brieve of novel disseisin provided that he can find still living either a person in possession of the lands or a person who took part in the original intrusion.

(iii) If while a brieve of novel disseisin is pending a defender infeft under a charter brings a brieve of warrandice against his author, the assise in the brieve of novel disseisin shall not on that account be sisted but shall proceed on the first day as accords.

(iv) Where the pursuer in a brieve of novel disseisin obtains decree against more than one intruder, such intruders shall be liable in damages in proportion to the length of the time during which each was in wrongful possession of the lands.

(v) Every person who after the date hereof is found guilty of intrusion by force of arms shall be liable to imprisonment and to such fine as the King may impose.

(vi) This section shall not be retrospective in effect.

Throughout the thirteenth century Novel Disseisin was the most popular form of action known in England, and the Plea Rolls indicate that there must have been many hundreds of such actions in the Royal Courts every year. But in Scotland, though there are one or two references in the " statutes," there is nothing (so far as has been noted) in the charters of the period or other contemporary records to exhibit this form of action in actual use prior to the time of the English occupation. The present section, however, makes it plain not only that Scotland knew a great deal about the assise, but also that Bruce's advisers were familiar with the identical problems which had arisen in England two generations before and which

English Law had gradually solved, in part by the invention of the writ of entry, in part by the decisions of the Justices, and in part by the Statute of Westminster of 1285—including such questions as the applicability of the remedy against singular successors of the person initially responsible for the ejection, and the odd requirement that the original intruder must be alive when the action is commenced. All this and much more we can read in Bracton ; but once again we find the striking facts (i) that the Scottish amending Act of 1318 accepts the position that the pre-existing Scottish law had not kept abreast of the changes which (as we now know) had long ago been effected in England ; (ii) that some only of the English reforms were accepted ; and (iii) that Scotland devised its own version of the solution and did not slavishly copy the English model.

Lastly, let us glance at the procedural reforms in Chapters XIV to XIX. Each of these aims at the sweeping away of formalities and technical objections and the reduction to the simplest form of the action of damages for breach of contract, the action for delict, and the brieve of right. For example, it is enacted that the pursuer in an action on a contract should no longer be liable to be met by challenges or exceptions provided that he made his case relevant by averring (a) the date and nature of the agreement, (b) the breach, and (c) the damages claimed ; and in an action for payment of a debt the mimimum but sufficient requirements of relevancy were declared to be an averment of (a) the date and amount of the debt, (b) the source from which it arose, (c) the due date of payment, and (d) the damages claimed.

The enquiry might be carried further both into the legislation of 1318 and in other directions, but enough has been said to indicate the nature of the evidence which points to the following tentative conclusions as to the position of Scots Law at or about the time of the Wars of Independence.

(1) The impression commonly held that the juristic ideas and practice which prevailed in the developed parts of thirteenth century Scotland were primitive and elementary has no foundation, for in many branches of civil law matters

had been carried to an advanced stage of refinement and sophistication—in some respects to a higher level than was again attained until the seventeenth century.

(2) Doubtless as the result of defective communications and the absence of law reports or periodicals, there was a time lag, amounting perhaps to two generations, between the emergence in England of new remedies or legal conceptions and their application in Scotland.

(3) While ready to adapt any good idea or successful experiment Scotland from the first cultivated a detached and critical standpoint, rarely appropriating an English remedy as it stood and exhibiting a pronounced distaste for the fictions, formalities, and technicalities beneath which so much English Law was becoming partially smothered even by the time of Edward I. In this latter attitude it is possible to trace the persisting influence of the best period of Canonist practice and of the work of the Papal Judges Delegate who during the first half of the thirteenth century successfully handled a large part of Scottish civil litigation and left marks upon the Scottish legal tradition which have not even yet been effaced.

1944

Curiosities of Medieval Scots Law

As the subject of an address to a non-professional audience law may not seem a very hopeful subject, and medieval law may strike you as positively repulsive. But it is not my purpose this evening to look at early law and legal institutions through a lawyer's spectacles, or a historian's microscope, but to use certain aspects of these topics as the medium for illuminating the customs and habits of thought of our forefathers in Lowland Scotland in the twelfth, thirteenth and fourteenth centuries. That is a period of our history of which we ought to know more, and which, I always feel, would have yielded a rich harvest of fruitful and inspiring ideas had it received the detailed research which has been lavished on such romantic subjects as Mary, Queen of Scots, the Covenanting period, and the Jacobite Rebellions. But the records are pitifully meagre, and those that have survived have never been so exhaustively studied as they deserve. Looming through the mists of the twelfth century we can dimly descry the outline of one majestic figure, King David, whose memory in Scottish history held for centuries the high place which in the story of their race the Israelites of old ascribed to his namesake. William the Lion and the Alexanders are, for most of us, little more than names, though the shabby monument at the foot of the cliff near Burntisland commemorates the tragic death of a Scottish King whose reign was long wistfully recalled as the golden age of Scottish history. The Wars of Independence and the epic of Wallace and Bruce are well enough documented in English sources ; but we look back at these stirring days through a shimmering haze of legend and romance, and know far too little of the ordinary men and women who then peopled this land and who took part in the shaping of the Scottish nation. Of fourteenth century Scotland, with its welter of wars and intestine strife, the average person knows literally nothing.

I, therefore, invite you to join with me for a little this evening in piecing together some selected scraps of authentic legal information which can be traced back to that period, for the purpose of discovering what manner of men these people were, and whether, after all, they were so very different from their more sophisticated, but in some respects less civilised, descendants of the present day. To borrow the thesis of Dr Trevelyan's latest work, let us aim at *social* history, using legal history as the medium of interpretation.

I am glad to be able to assure you at the outset that there were plenty of lawyers in twelfth and thirteenth century Scotland. Unlike his modern counterpart, the medieval Scots lawyer was not a member of a separate, organised, learned profession, but was almost always a Churchman, who studied and practised law as a side line. Still more unlike his modern counterpart he gave his services gratuitously—at least in theory. The earliest practising Scottish solicitor to whom I have traced a reference was (appropriately enough) a Glasgow man, Adam Urri by name ; and if his name suggests an Aberdeenshire origin he was at any rate a cleric attached to the diocese of Glasgow. Of him we read in the old Chronicle of Lanercrost, under the date 1283, when Alexander III was still on the throne, that he was so deeply versed in the law of Rome that he preferred the doctrines of Ulpian to the commandments of God, and—what was thought to be far worse— that he actually accepted fees from his clients. It is thus plain that even at this early date such wares had a market value. The story ends on a happy note, for the chronicler adds that the sinner repented before he died.[1] Thirty years earlier, about the year 1250, we catch another glimpse of the vital subject of lawyer's fees. In a letter written from Oxford University, where he was a student, a nephew of Bishop de Bernham of St Andrews writes to his man of business at Inchture, near Perth, instructing him to raise certain actions for recovery of monies due to him, and authorising him to retain out of the proceeds as remuneration for his services the sum of half a mark, the sterling value of which was the still celebrated

---

[1] *Chron. Lanercrost, Anno* 1283.

sum of " six and eightpence." [1] It thus appears that the basic figure of the modern lawyer's account of expenses is nearly seven hundred years old ; and I trust that the Faculty of Procurators of Glasgow will not allow this glorious septcentenary to pass without some fitting celebration.

But whether they were paid or not, the medieval Scots lawyers richly deserved a fee ; for sufficient traces of their work have survived to enable us to say that, as a class, they were competent and resourceful practitioners. Let us glance at a few of the problems they had to solve and the solutions which they found.

I begin with a very queer case, which is reported again and again in the old records, and which is attributed in some of them to the reign of David I, who died in 1153, though it was still being reported anew in the seventeenth century.[2] I have never been sure whether it was a hypothetical problem in law or the report of an actual occurrence, but you may possibly think that it is much too tall a story to have been invented. A certain man, we are told, was passing along a public road driving in front of him two sheep tethered together by a piece of rope. A horse with " a sair back " had lain down on the roadway, and the sheep proceeded to pass the prostrate horse, the one on the one side and the other on the other. The result was that the rope between the two sheep " kittled " the horse's " sair back." Justly exasperated by this treatment, the horse rose to his feet and bolted, with a sheep dangling at the end of the rope on each side of him, and ran hither and thither through diverse places until he came to a mill which was open and unattended. Into this mill rushed the terrified horse, scattering a fire which was burning within it, and setting fire to the premises, with the result that mill, horse, and sheep were all destroyed. The question for decision was : Who is to bear the loss ?—and the case to-day would give rise to quite a nice problem in remoteness of damage. The answer of the medieval lawyers was short and to the point. The owner of the horse, they said, must pay for the sheep, because he had no right to

---

[1] *Oxford History Soc.* (New Series), vol. V. ii. 472.
[2] Skene's *David II*, c. 26. *Balfour's Practicks*, p. 509.

allow his horse to lie down on the King's highway : and the owner of the mill must pay for the horse and bear his own loss, because he should not have left his mill open and unattended with a fire burning within it.   I do not know whether that judgment would be affirmed to-day, but this at least is plain, that there is a good deal of sound sense behind it ; and the same is true of other examples of what we should now call the law of delict or reparation.   For instance, it was laid down in the thirteenth century [1] that, if a man riding through a town on horseback knocked down and killed a pedestrian in front of him, he must pay to the relatives full damages calculated according to a fixed tariff dependent on the rank and status of the victim.   But if the victim of the accident was behind the horseman and was injured by the hind legs of the horse, only one-fourth part of the value of the horse was due in damages, the principle, as laid down, being that the horseman's duty was to avoid obstacles in front of him and to keep the forelegs of his horse under control, but that the pedestrian who did not keep clear of the hind legs of a horse in front of him had only himself to blame if an accident happened—a clear anticipation of the modern doctrine of contributory negligence.

Occasionally, however, the relevant factors in determining liability are obscured by survivals of archaic rules which recall the Book of Exodus.   For instance, if a *restive* horse bolted with its rider over a crag or into a river and the rider was killed, the horse was forfeited to the King ; but if the horse was a *docile* animal to which the rider had applied his spurs, no forfeiture ensued, because, as we are told, the horse committed no fault, while the rider had received his punishment " in so far as he is perished and deid."   The same strange confusion between reparation and punishment, and between conscious and unconscious guilt, is seen in the express proviso that, if a man falls into a mill dam and is killed or drowned through being carried down to the mill wheel, the mill is not to be forfeited, " seeing it is ane dead thing which may not commit a trespass

---

[1] *Regiam Majestatem*, iv. 30 ; *Balfour's Practicks*, p. 514 ; *Hope's Major Practicks*, ii. 298 ; *Bankton Inst.*, i. 246-7.

to any man." [1] I need hardly add that views of this kind find expression in many other early legal systems of this period.

Few subjects recur more frequently in the early " statutes " of the period than the regulation of fishing ; and the provisions present a curious combination of sound substance with very odd expression. From the time of William the Lion, about the year 1200, the requirement was [2] that there should be a weekly close time from Saturday at evensong until Monday at sunrise, and that at all times the stream of water should allow the passage of fish, and should be kept so free from obstructions that a three-year old pig, well fed, should be able to turn himself round about in the channel without his snout or his tail touching either side. You will find a reference to this very odd rule in Scott's *Antiquary*. I have often tried to picture the spectacle of an official test being carried out with the aid of a pig of the statutory dimensions, and have wondered how the pig was induced to lend his willing co-operation to the authorities. Anglers will be interested to learn that there was not only a weekly close time but an annual close time as well—15th August to 21st November for salmon, and 15th April to 24th June for netting smolts—the penalties for infringement being destruction of nets for a first offence, six months' imprisonment for a second, twelve months' for a third, and so on. [3] Nothing was needlessly wasted in these days, for the old Acts go on to provide that if any man brought to market a rotten salmon, the condemned fish should be given by the bailies to the lepers, and, if there were no lepers (or, presumably, none who felt equal to eating it), the fish was then to be destroyed. [4]

They knew a thing or two in these days about preservation of game. In 1235 there was a litigation before Alexander II at Kirkliston between the Monks of Melrose and the great

---

[1] *Quoniam Attachiamenta*, c. 32. *Balfour's Practicks*, 553. There is actually a recorded decision of the Lords of Session so late as 1481 refusing to forfeit a horse which had thrown its rider into a river, because a Linlithgow jury had found that the rider had applied his spurs to the horse and, therefore, that the horse was not to blame. (*Acts of the Lords of Council in Civil Cases*. p.c.).

[2] *Assise Regis Willelmi*, c. 10. *Balfour's Practicks*, p. 544.

[3] A.P.S., i. p. 752.   [4] Skene's *Robert III*, c. 40.

G

landowner, Roger of Avenel, as to the extent of the former's sporting rights in Eskdale ; and it was then laid down on a construction of the Abbey charters that the monks must not employ in the hunt packs of hounds or nets, nor might they invite guests, nor must they employ snares, except for the purpose of trapping wolves. Even more interesting is the incidental decision that, if a hawk or falcon once nested in a tree, the tree must not be interfered with until sufficiently late in the following spring to make certain that the birds were not coming back to their old nest.[1]

A more practical note is struck by the form in the Bute MS.[2] instructing the sheriffs to hold enquiries as often as might be necessary into the question whether any sheep within the sheriffdom were affected by the disease of sheep-scab ; and, if they found any, to require the destruction of the infected flock, and to impose a " standstill " order against the movement of other stock from their pastures. That is, of course, an almost exact replica of the present procedure under the Contagious Diseases of Animals Acts, for dealing with foot and mouth disease.

Before parting with these sporting and farming topics we may note in passing that there is a great deal in these early records about dogs—not only the sleuth hounds which were used for tracking thieves and robbers,[3] but ordinary dogs as well. Before the middle of the twelfth century it was laid down by David I with poetic justice that any man who wrong- fully killed another man's dog should be compelled for a year and a day to discharge the duties of the deceased dog by keeping watch over its owner's midden, with the further duty of paying for any loss that might be incurred owing to the absence of a real dog.[4]

Twice over within living memory the present generation has been familiarised with emergency legislation passed in times of national stress and danger ; and that is a subject of

---

[1] *Melrose Abbey* v. *Roger of Avenel* (1235). *Sel. Sc. Cases*, p. 44.

[2] Bute MS., No. 74.

[3] *Robert I*, c. 7 ; *Balfour Practicks*, 525 ; *Hope's Major Practicks*, ii. 285 ; *Regiam Majestatem*, iv. 28.

[4] *Assise Regis David*, c. 33.

which, naturally, our ancestors were rich in experience. Air Raid Wardens, Fire Guards, and Special Constables will note with approval and sympathy that, as early as the twelfth century, it was the rule [1] in the four burghs of Berwick, Roxburgh, Edinburgh, and Stirling, and, doubtless, in many others, that every inhabited house should make provision for a watchman of man's age, who should come forth at curfew armed with two weapons, and watch carefully and discreetly until dawn. The penalty for failure was fourpence, and women were only exempted if they were widows—why, I do not know. But it was in the later stages of the War of Independence in the legislation passed at Scone in the summer of 1318 that we find the closest parallels to our modern extremities. Then, as now, it was a case of total war ; but there were neither " Wrens " nor " Ats " ; for Bruce was content to apply compulsion to able-bodied men, by laying down a graduated means test, beginning at the landed proprietors and ending with the man who owned goods to the value of one cow, the latter's obligation being to equip himself at his own cost with a bow and twenty-four arrows, or, alternatively, a spear, and to be ready for action.[2] Export of arms or munitions of any kind to England was very properly prohibited under pain of death.[3] Even Regulation 18B was anticipated in a provision that any person inventing or spreading rumours calculated to cause discord between the King and his people should incontinent be cast into prison and kept there during the King's pleasure.[4] Though inferior to us in the technique of the blitz, our ancestors had ample experience of devastated areas and of planned programmes of reconstruction ; and I take from the fourteenth century a striking example of their methods. The writ, which occurs in the Bute MS.,[5] cannot be identified or dated with exactitude ; but it possibly related to the partial sacking of the town of Dundee by John of Gaunt in 1385. Anxious to re-populate and restore the life of the burgh, what Robert II did was to instruct the sheriffs to announce on market days and court days, whenever they could find a crowd collected,

---

[1] *Leges Quatuor Burgorum*, c. 81.   [2] *Robert I*, c. 27.   [3] *Robert I*, c. 29.
[4] *Robert I*, c. 21.   [5] Bute MS. Styles, No. 48.

that if any man of Scottish origin was willing to settle in Dundee and would go there within the next six weeks, he would at once be provided by the King's officials (that is, the fore-runners of the Department of Health) with a house suitable to his station in life, or, if no such house could be found, with a grant from the King's treasury of 100s. to enable him to build a house ; and that he would also receive the freedom of the city. Observe that there was no attempt at compulsion, and no " directing " of mobile labour to Dundee under threat of summary prosecution. The limit set for the rehousing pro-gramme was not, as now, ten years, but six weeks, and the Treasury subsidy was, according to the standards of the time, a generous one. Finally, there was a means test, for every man was to get a house suitable to his personal rank and status. Needless to say, the freedom of the city, which was thrown in as an added inducement, meant much more in these days than a ceremony in the town hall followed by a civic luncheon.

I now pass to another subject, legal procedure, which is commonly supposed to have remained throughout the Middle Ages involved in archaic formalities and occult superstitions such as trial by battle and the ordeal. It is, of course, true that the legacy of the Dark Ages cast its shadow forwards for centuries, and has not even yet wholly vanished : but by the end of the thirteenth century it is perfectly plain that a great deal of the judicial work was conducted by thoroughly business-like and efficient methods, the investigation of disputed facts being usually performed by sworn inquests or juries, who knew their business and did it well. The examples which might be given are legion, and I content myself by citing from a rather later period the case of a jury which justifiably lost its temper.[1] In 1464 a controversy arose with regard to an almshouse in Angus, and on 4th November a jury of twenty-one was empanelled at Arbroath, to which there were put ten specific and complicated questions with regard to the origin, constitution, and character of this almshouse. To six of these questions the jury returned as their verdict the flat answer : " We do not know." One of the remaining questions was :

---

[1] *Registrum Nigrum de Aberbrothoc*, No. 160.

" Why were the almshouse and its chapel erected outside the monastery ? " to which the exasperated jurors returned as their verdict the answer : " We do not know the reason for building the almshouse and chapel outside the monastery, unless it was that the builders preferred to have it so." That was perilously near to contempt of court, but the verdict was duly recorded in Latin without comment. I shall give one other quaint characteristic of the early procedure. It has always been a feature of certain appeals from a lower court to a higher that the prospective appellant should on the spot intimate to the lower court his desire to subject their judgment to review, and this feature survives to this day before such tribunals as the Income Tax Commissioners and the Valuation Appeal Committees, to whom it is customary and necessary for the dissatisfied litigant through his solicitor or counsel formally to intimate his dissatisfaction as a preliminary to an appeal. In medieval Scotland they did exactly the same thing, but they did it in a more forthright fashion ; for the formula which the disappointed party was required to utter " before turning his toes where his heels had been " was : " This doom is false, stinking and rotten." [1] These are precisely the sentiments entertained by most defeated litigants when they get a judgment against them, and it is in some ways a pity that they are no longer encouraged to give such pithy expression to them ; for as long ago as 1503 [2] a mealy-mouthed Parliament intervened to substitute for the time-honoured formula the bowdlerised version : " I am greatumlie hurt and injured by the said doom, therefore I appeal."

In the sphere of criminal law one finds, as is to be expected, very severe repressive tendencies, especially against the crime of theft, but the basic principles are surprisingly modern in tone, and more than once we glimpse traces of humanitarian tendencies strangely out of harmony with the spirit of the times. For instance, one of the oldest rules was the law of Burthinsak,[3] by which it was provided that the usual penalties for theft

---

[1] *Forme and Manor of Baron Courts*, c. 15.   *James I*, c. 116.
[2] *James IV*, c. 99.
[3] *Regiam Majestatem*, iv. 12 ; *Assise Regis Willelmi*, c. 13.

(and these often included death), should not be exacted from the thief who only took a calf, or a sheep, or as much food as he could carry on his back—the idea apparently being that, while stern justice must be meted out to the bold cattle-riever who operated on the grand scale, the authorities had no particular quarrel with the poor man who only stole to satisfy his hunger. Similarly in the Ayr MS.,[1] which gives us the position about the end of the thirteenth century, we find a form of summons or brieve by which the friends and relations of a man who had fallen into poverty were required to contribute according to their means towards relieving his distress, and even towards defraying a fine which he had incurred for committing homicide. It is a painful commentary upon the impoverishment of old Scotland that we hear so much in the early records about the poor and their relief; and though these measures are imperfect enough when judged by modern standards, they indicate a more sympathetic pre-occupation with the social problem than at this period we should expect to find. It was so long ago as 1424 [2] that James I enacted that "if there be any poor creature for fault of cunning or dispenses that cannot or may not follow his cause, the King, for the love of God, shall ordaine the judge before whom the cause should be determined, to purvey and get a leal and a wise Advocate to follow such poor creature's causes." It is still under the authority of that 500-year-old statute that week by week Lord Normand and I sign scores of orders assigning " poor " cases in the Court of Session to solicitors and members of the Bar who conduct them gratuitously. Then, as now, the problem was to distinguish the deserving case from the lazy, masterful beggar; and the position of the religious houses became so acute that a form is preserved in the Ayr MS. for the appointment by the King of a janitor for monasteries to exclude " gate-crashers," who unjustifiably claimed meals or alms, and to restrict admission to the genuine poor.[3]

    Some of these old forms of process have enjoyed an amazing longevity, which you may regard as a tribute either to the skill

---

[1] Ayr MS., Styles, No. xliii.   [2] 1424, c. 24.
[3] Ayr MS., Styles, No. lxxvii.

of the original draftsman or to the ingrained conservatism of the legal profession. For instance, a widow in Scotland has long been entitled to the liferent of one-third of her deceased husband's lands or other heritable subjects. The form of brieve or summons for enforcing this right against the husband's heir first emerges in the time of Alexander III. It reappears again and again throughout the centuries,[1] always in substantially the same terms. It was actually employed in an action in Aberdeen Sheriff Court which was brought on appeal to the Court of Session in 1891,[2] and this means that the same machinery for achieving the same special object was in use with us for over 600 years. Theoretically some of these old forms might still be used, though there are now few with the requisite nerve to try the experiment. Again, as early as the beginning of the thirteenth century, it was the practice in Scotland under the Canonist procedure for the court to confirm or approve a compromise of a pending action by pronouncing an order "interponing authority" to the terms of settlement.[3] The exact phraseology of that order, in English and not in Latin, is employed in every court in Scotland every day when an action is taken out of court by joint agreement.

The problems of juvenile delinquency which perplex the city fathers and Advisory Councils of the present day were not unknown to their ancestors. In 1312, two years before Bannockburn, a youth was brought before the Regality Court of the Abbey of Arbroath indicted under a charge which is not specified but which involved the penalty of death or loss of a limb. It was pleaded on his behalf as a preliminary defence that he was not amenable to trial on such a charge because he was under age; and this plea was evidently a novel one, for it gave rise to prolonged debate. The decision was that the burden of proving that he had not attained majority was on the accused—no light burden in these days—and that, if he succeeded in discharging that burden, he must either find security that he would answer to the charge when

---

[1] Ayr MS., Styles, xxvii. Bute MS., Styles, 102. *Balfour's Practicks*, 642. *Stair*, IV. iii. 11.

[2] *Craik* v. *Penny*, (1891) 19 R. 339.

[3] *Select Scottish Cases*, Introd., p. xxxvi.

he did attain majority, or else remain in custody. The accused satisfied the court that he was not yet twenty-one years of age, but he was unable to find security for his later appearance, and he was, therefore, ordered to be incarcerated in the Abbey prison to await his twenty-first birthday.[1] What happened then, we do not know.

Let me now give you a specimen of an early building contract. In 1380, the Abbey of Arbroath was destroyed by fire as a result (so the old charters record) of the mischievous activities of the Devil. The monks had to go as evacuees to neighbouring religious houses, drastic economies had to be introduced, and much time was absorbed in collecting the necessary funds for rebuilding. It was not till 1393 that the work could be put in hand, and on 16th February of that year a formal contract was executed in the vernacular between the Abbot and a Border plumber, who had settled in St Andrews, named William of Tweeddale. The job which the plumber was taken bound to perform was to thatch the great choir of the Abbey with lead, to provide gutters, and, after the stone parapet had been formed by the masons, to " dight " it about with lead. The plumber was to provide his own mate, and the Abbey undertook to provide a second labourer, and also all necessary tools and materials. The contract price was 35 marks—about £25—together with a gown with a hood ; and, in addition, the plumber was to get 3d. for each stone of lead, and 1d. for his lunch on each working day.[2] Every time I look at one of these inspiring architectural monuments of the Middle Ages, I recall the labour and the craftsmanship of such forgotten tradesmen as William of Tweeddale, who wrought with their own hands for a few pounds, a cloak with a hood, and a 1d. lunch, and left behind them memorials which are the admiration and the despair of later generations, but who were canny enough to get their bargain embodied in a formal written contract, executed in duplicate, sealed and delivered.

An immense amount of interesting legal information is embedded in the charters or title deeds of the old religious

---

[1] A.P.S., i. 745-6.　　[2] *Registrum Nigrum de Aberbrothoc*, No. 43.

houses, which were printed by the historical clubs over a hundred years ago, but have never been read except by a very few ; and as a sample, selected almost at random, let me give you a conveyance granted in 1299 by the Abbot and Chapter of the Monastery of Arbroath in favour of Richard of Stirling.[1] Arbroath Abbey was very richly endowed, and we learn from this chapter that they owned a piece of land in Stirling, which they had feued, as we should now say, to a man called John of Drylaw. John died, and his son, William, made default in his liabilities to the Abbey and eventually resigned the lands in their hands. The Abbey then looked around for a new vassal, and granted the lands to Richard, the son of Christinus, on the following remarkable terms :—
The feuduty was fixed at 4s. 6d., payable, as now, one-half at Whitsunday and the other at Martinmas, but the principal obligation imposed on the vassal was to provide suitable accommodation for the use of the Abbot and monks or their clerks, bailiffs, or attorneys, when visiting Stirling on the business of the Abbey—including a dining-hall with tables and trestles and other furnishings ; a pantry and cellar ; dormitories ; a kitchen ; and stabling for 30 horses. In addition, fires were to be provided in the dining-room, the dormitory and the kitchen (there was no Fuel Controller in these days) ; and the vassal had also to furnish a supply of white wax candles ; rushes or straw in lieu of carpets and bedding ; and salt for use at table. All this is solemnly set out at length in the conveyance of the lands, though much of it would be more appropriate in a letter to the manageress of a hotel ; and the great caution with which the details of the bargain were adjusted is shown by two conditions which are added—(1) that if anybody stayed for more than three consecutive nights, he could claim no more fires or candles, and (2) that the Abbey's messengers and runners were to be entitled to lodging in the hostel, but were to provide their own board. That single deed affords a more authentic and vivid impression of the domestic manners and customs of thirteenth century Scotland than any historical work of which I am aware. The

[1] *Registrum Vetus de Aberbrothoc*, No. 321.

experiment must have been a success, for the Abbot of Arbroath did not rest content until he had established a chain of similar hotels in Peebles, Inverkeithing, Dundee, Edinburgh and Aberdeen, and the Abbot of Melrose copied his example.

The subject of legal education is much in the air to-day, and I close with a specimen of an examination problem, set at Oxford University about 1250 to students studying law there, some of whom have been identified as Scottish, and two of whom rose in later life to be Bishops in the Scottish Church. I am sorry to have to go to Oxford for this example, but there were no Universities in Scotland in 1250 when the problem was set. As you listen to it, please remember that these students were probably all priests or at least prospective priests, looking forward to getting as soon as possible a lucrative benefice or two ; and it is fairly clear that the teacher's purpose was to teach more than law. The question was this :—

A certain clerk asserted that he had studied civil and canon law for twelve years and more, and that he had read all the law books and decretals. He further stated that he knew how to conduct all kinds of cases. The Bishop of the town in which this clerk lived, relying on these assurances as true, conferred on the clerk the benefice of a larger church in these words : " I, believing that the needs of the church can be met by you and that you are qualified to give all requisite advice and assistance, hereby confer upon you the prebend of our larger church." In course of time the Bishop discovered that the said clerk was incompetent and wished to deprive him of the benefice. Could he do so ? [1]

What the expected answer was I do not know ; but the moral which the question was plainly intended to teach was that all good students should diligently apply themselves to their studies lest a like fate should befall them.

Most of these examples may be taken as belonging to the system of law and practice which had emerged and was in process of being developed in Scotland up to the fatal years when the aggression of Edward I altered the whole course of Scottish history and arrested further legal progress for roughly two hundred years. I have called them " curiosities " ; and they have been chosen primarily for their odd and unfamiliar

[1] *Oxford Formularies* (*Oxford Hist. Soc.*), ii. 472.

qualities.   But please do not imagine that in these quaint oddities you have a representative sample of Scotland's first effort to establish an independent legal system, still less that we can afford to survey that effort with a patronising smile. The most striking " curiosity " of the first phase of Scots Law is to be found in the success with which the lawyers of a small and distant country, not then fused into a homogeneous national or social unit, and completely overshadowed by the example of England which then led the world of law, had already contrived to strike out boldly on lines of their own and to subject to critical modification and adaptation many of the more technical English expedients which were being slavishly copied elsewhere.   If that process of rationalisation had not been rudely cut short by wars and centuries of threatened anarchy, it is, at least, in my view, more than probable that we should not have had to wait for Stair in the closing years of the seventeenth century for Scotland's original contribution to jurisprudence, and that Scots Law, in the full sense of the term, would have been recognised as a distinctive and original system in the course of the fourteenth or fifteenth centuries.   It would probably have been a system much less Roman, much more Canonist, and much more English than that which we eventually adopted : but it would have been distinctively Scottish.   To the unknown lawyers who toiled over the foundations and substructure of that unfinished and forgotten legal edifice we can surely spare a passing tribute of respect and admiration. ·

1945

The Sheep, the Horse, and the Mill

THE RESOLUTE STUDENT who has fought his way through the first 509 pages of Balfour's " Practicks " will there be rewarded by the astonishing spectacle of a smile on the lips of the author. In the title " Anent Burning and Fyre," Balfour (or his anonymous collaborator) first assembles the usual anthology of " Statutes," practicks, and extracts from the Auld Lawes, and then adds a final paragraph with the apologetic sidenote : " A merrie question anent the burning of a miln." As if ashamed of his seeming levity, he hastens to add as his authority for the paragraph references to the Assise of David I and the Statutes of David II. The paragraph reads as follows :—

Gif it happin that ony man be passand in the King's gait or passage drivand befoir him twa sheip festnit and knit togidder, be chance ane horse havand a sair bak is lying in the said gait, and ane of the sheip passis be the ane side of the horse and the uther sheip be the uther side, swa that the band quhairwith thay ar bund tuich or kittle his sair bak, and he, thairby movit, dois arise and carryis the said sheip with him heir and thare untill at last he cumis and enteris in ane miln havand ane fire without ane keipar, and skatteris the fire, quhairby the miln, horse, sheip and all is brunt : *Quæritur* : Quha sall pay the skaith ? *Respondetur* : The awner of the horse sall pay the sheip, because his horse sould not have been lying in the King's hie-streit or commoun passage ; and the millar sall pay for the miln and the horse and for all uther damnage and skaith, because he left ane fire in the miln without ane keipar.

Leaving aside the surprising facts on which the point of law is raised, there is no doubt that the case is of great significance as an early recognition of *culpa* as the basis of delictual liability, and it is small wonder that the compiler of the " Practicks " thought that the case was " reportable." Thirty years later Sir John Skene thought so too for he included a fuller report as ch. 26 of his Statutes of David II, noting that he took it from " ane buke pertaining to Sir David Carnegie of Kynnarde." The decision or opinion was thus incorporated under the most respectable auspices in the early common law of Scotland.

108

Whatever Balfour's MSS. Statutes may have shown, there are no grounds for believing that the case was included in the authentic Assise of David I or in the Statutes of David II. Thomas Thomson searched in vain amongst the MSS. at his disposal, and excluded the story from vol. I of the Acts of Parliament. Where, then, did Sir David Carnegie find it?

The clue is to be found in a note contributed by the late Dr Neilson to that admirable but long-forgotten periodical, *Scots Lore* (Glasgow, 1895, p. 266), where a reference is given to ch. 163 of the *Gesta Romanorum*—that famous collection of moralised folklore and fable, which circulated widely throughout Europe in medieval times, and later furnished the raw material for some of the best work of Chaucer, Gower, Shakespeare, Schiller, and many others. In the " Gesta " the anecdote, embellished with details, and many indications of sympathy with the horse, is imbedded in the tale of Celestinus, the son of Alexander, who, when strolling one day with the philosopher who acted as his tutor, actually witnessed the tragic occurrence and was required by his tutor, under pain of heavy punishment, to record the story in verse and to show who was responsible for the burning of the mill. Finding himself unequal as a versifier and a lawyer to this task, Celestinus adopted Faust's expedient of selling himself to the Devil, the purchase consideration being a set of elegiac couplets. As these represent the only known specimen of a legal rubric composed by the Devil in person, they are worthy of quotation if only for the diabolic cleverness with which the decision and the *ratio decidendi* were compressed within the limits of the closing pentameter. They are as follows :—

Nexus ovem binam per spinam traxit equinam,
  Læsus surgit equus, pendet utrumque pecus.
Ad molendinum pondus portabat equinum
  Dispergendo focum se cremat atque locum.
Custodes aberant : *Singula damna ferant.*[1]

The unknown author of the " Gesta," having another object

[1] A rope tied between two sheep was drawn by them over a horse's back. The horse, feeling it sore, sprang up with a sheep hanging on either side of him, and bore his load into a mill where he scattered the fire and burnt himself and the whole place. The keepers were not there ; let each bear his own loss.

in view, was completely blind to the legal significance of the story, for the only moral which he drew was that " the philosopher is any prelate ; the mangy horse a sinner covered with sins ; the two sheep are two preachers bound by the cord of charity ; the miller's house is the world ; and the fire, detraction." Such allegorical endings are provided for all the tales in the " Gesta," which were used merely as pegs whereon to hang a homily. But just as successive generations of poets found in the " Gesta " a quarry for plots, so some early Scots Lawyer must have detected their possibilities as texts, not for monkish sermons, but for legal expositions. But the queer thing is not merely that this ancient fable was thus appropriated by Sir David Carnegie, and doubtless by the earlier writer from whom he borrowed, as the basis of a legal report, but that the Scot had the courage to dissent from the Devil. Satan thought that the loss lay where it fell—*singula damna ferant*—but the Scot preferred a more subtle solution under which part of the loss fell primarily on the owner of the horse, and the whole loss fell *subsidiarie* on the miller. In face of this regrettable conflict of authority, we can only await the views of seven judges. But it is refreshing to discover from what unconventional sources our early law drew its inspiration.

1945

Cromwell's Judges and their Influence on Scots Law

ONLY THIRTY-FIVE YEARS separate the death of Sir Thomas Hope from the publication of Stair's *Institutions*, and it is certain that this great work must have been in preparation for many years before it appeared. To the student of legal history the main interest of the brief intervening period is that it marks a singularly abrupt transition from the medieval to the modern worlds.

Hope, as Lord Clyde put it, " is the son of Balfour and not at all the father of Stair." It is true that he had absorbed the new learning of the *Jus Feudale* and made full use of the slowly growing volume of " practicks." But Hope's work was broad-based upon the auld lawes, and, as we read it, we breathe the atmosphere of Balfour's *Practicks* and of the old material which Balfour had wrought into the fabric of his treatise and which Skene later republished in his collection of 1609. Stair, on the other hand, hardly spared a glance at his country's early law and practice, but preferred to erect a new legal edifice from the foundations upwards, and in so doing, to create the system which became modern Scots Law. In the third quarter of the seventeenth century Scots Law thus suffered a complete transformation. Up to 1650 its patron saint was David I. After 1681 David was dethroned by Stair.

Making every allowance for the original architectural genius of Stair, we cannot but find it a little disconcerting to encounter in the development of any legal system a change so swift and so sweeping, involving to all appearances a complete break with the past and a fresh start ; and it is natural to inquire whether any causes were at work in the intervening quarter century which might have contributed to giving to legal thought an entirely new set of the current. There is certainly one such cause which at first sight seems capable of having led to a reorientation of legal thinking. For over ten years during the Protectorate the supreme court of Scotland was in abeyance, and for seven of these years its place was taken by Cromwell's " kinless loons." Is it possible to detect in connection with this momentous happening any evidence to connect it casually with the legal revolution which soon afterwards ensued ?

The broad facts are well vouched. The Court of Session sat for the last time in February 1650, and during the next two years the English invasion and its sequels were incompatible with civil judicial administration. In the spring of 1652 the " surcease of justice " came to an end with the appointment of the Commissioners for the Administration of Justice to the people of Scotland. They were seven in number, three Scots and four Englishmen ; and though the personnel changed from time to time as vacancies arose through death or removal from office, the general composition of the tribunal remained unaltered until it ceased to function in 1659, when there was a second " surcease of justice," ending with the resumption of sittings by the Court of Session in the spring of 1661. Amongst the nine Scottish members who successively received commissions between 1652 and 1658, there were seven who had held, or who later held, judicial office in Scotland, the most celebrated being Sir John Hope, who acted for a time as president of the Commissioners, and Stair himself, who was appointed in 1657. The English Commissioners were of no outstanding distinction, but it would be interesting to know more about one of them, Mr Marsh of Gray's Inn, who, on being removed from office in October 1653, promptly joined the Faculty of Advocates !

We shall never know exactly what these Commissioners did until a modern Job has examined the mass of original Acts and Decreets. But a good deal of information can be gleaned from a volume, which was published anonymously and with an apologetic preface in 1762, containing " The Decisions of the English Judges during the Usurpation." This collection contains about 600 reports covering the period 23rd November 1655 to 23rd February 1659, more than half the period of the

Commission's activities, and for this period it must be tolerably complete, for no single court in these days could pronounce much more than 175 final interlocutors per annum. But we have meantime no information regarding the period prior to November 1655 ; and it is doubtless to this period that we must attribute several references in later series of reports to " decisions by the English judges " of which the collection of 1752 seems to include no trace.

But accepting this collection in default of anything better as giving at least a representative cross-section of the work of the Commission, we can draw several clear conclusions. The work was done substantially as it had been done before the Protectorate and as it was later done after the Restoration. The seven Commissioners sat together like the " haill fifteen." The procedure was purely Scottish. The pleaders were advocates. The problems submitted, and the arguments presented to aid their solution, were often aggressively Scottish, and must have severely taxed the capacity of the immigrant judges. The decisions proceeded on familiar lines. From first to last there is nothing to suggest that we are not reading one of our native law reports of the period except the concluding formula : " The Commissioners found . . ." It would seem that the tribunal was controlled by the Scottish members. The Englishmen may have had a majority in number, but they did not have a majority in value. The broad impression con- veyed by the reports is that the Commissioners attempted no innovations, but strove to maintain and apply the traditions and the law and practice of the court which they had super- seded. Indeed there is independent evidence for the view that, from the standpoint of purity and impartiality, they represented a marked improvement on their predecessors, and it is plain beyond doubt that the litigating public of Scotland very freely availed themselves of their services.

Support for all these conclusions is afforded by the action taken after the Restoration, when the reaction of strong political feelings might have been expected to find expression in violent measures. No such action was attempted. On the contrary the first Parliament of Charles II formally ratified

H

the decisions of the Commissioners, subject only to the right of any dissatisfied litigant within one year from the sitting of the Court of Session to have any decision of the Commissioners reviewed. But lest it should be supposed that the Commissioners could do no wrong, this proviso was expressly justified upon the ground that " they did sometimes proceed in an arbitrary way, contrare to Law and Justice, and at other times, many of them being strangers and ignorant of the law, did proceed unwarrantably and unjustly betwixt parties." In the circumstances this can only be described as an extraordinarily faint criticism.

It would be interesting to know how many decisions were thus challenged and with what result ; but once again the answer must await a laborious analysis of the original records. A partial answer can be given from an examination of Sir John Gilmour's *Decisions*, which cover the period from July 1661 to July 1666 ; but it is only a partial answer, for the Lord President only reported cases which he regarded as of permanent interest and value. From these reports we find that the review took the form of a complete re-hearing of the case. Only seven cases in Gilmour's reports were so reviewed, and of these the Commissioners' decision was affirmed in three cases, reversed in three, and varied in one. An eighth case is given by Fountainhall (the *Pitfoddels* case in 2 Brown's Supp. 347), but the intricacies of this case are such that it is hard to tell whether the Commissioners were affirmed or reversed. We can therefore conclude that, so far as cases of legal importance and interest were concerned, the statutory right of review was very sparingly invoked, and that, when it was, the Commissioners showed up none too badly considering the complexity and difficulty of some of the cases they were called upon to decide.

The next point to be noted is that, so far as has been traced, there is not a single reference in our institutional writers to any of the decisions of the Commissioners. In all their citations of cases the years of the Protectorate are a blank. A conspiracy of silence seems to have sealed the lips of later Scots lawyers with regard to what happened to our law during

that period.   The one writer who might have been expected
to have betrayed clear evidence of his association with the
English judges and their system is Stair, and there are a number
of passages in his *Institutions* which disclose an acquaintance
with, and even an appreciation for, points of English doctrine.
But it would be impossible even to suggest that this typically
Scottish treatise owed anything specific to English influence or
transmitted that influence to the law of Scotland.   In the
apologia which Stair published long afterwards to meet the
charges of time-serving which had been brought against him,
he certainly evinces no pride in his labours as one of the
Commissioners.

     To return to our starting-point, the evidence so far available
does not support the suggestion that the change in outlook
which overtook Scots Law in the later seventeenth century
was inspired or affected by the seven years' sojourn in Edinburgh of the English judges or by the work which they did.
To the Scots lawyer of these days and of the succeeding
generation the Protectorate was evidently regarded as nothing
more than a regrettable interlude which interrupted the
normal course of judicial administration, and when the Court
of Session resumed for the Summer Session of 1661 the thread
of the story was picked up at the point at which it had been
abruptly severed eleven years before.   Indirectly, of course,
the experiences of these troublous times must have profoundly
affected the life and thought of the Scottish nation, and the
new contacts and widened horizons doubtless led to the changes
which were to come.   But so far as direct and tangible consequences to the law of Scotland are concerned, the years
between 1650 and 1661 were years which the locusts had eaten.

1946

The King *versus* The Court of Session

O N 30th May 1921 Lord Chancellor Birkenhead appeared in the Throne Gallery at a session of the General Assembly of the Church of Scotland, and was invited by the Moderator to address the members. In the characteristic oration which he then delivered he displayed a mastery of Scottish political and ecclesiastical history which must have amazed his audience. The theme was civil and religious liberty. The text was the decision of the Court of Session in the case of *Bruce* v. *Hamilton* in 1599, when James VI intervened in person in the debate. After quoting from the opinion of the Lord President, Earl Birkenhead concluded : "A nobler and more courageous expression of judicial independence was never made."

Coming from such a source this was indeed a striking tribute. The Lord Chancellor assumed that the story was familiar to most of his listeners. I wonder if it was. To-day it has been so completely forgotten that more than one well-informed critic to whom I have recounted it dismissed the whole episode as apocryphal. But so far from being a romantic legend, the case and its remarkable circumstances can be vouched from original sources, and it is high time that it was given the authentic setting which it rightly deserves.

Narrative accounts in more or less detail will be found in several of the leading standard works—*Tytler*, vol. ix. pp. 289-90 ; *Lang*, vol. ii. p. 438 ; *Calderwood*, vol. v. p. 733 ; *Anderson's Scottish Nation*, vol. i. p. 432, and *R.P.C.*, vol. v. p. lxxxviii, amongst others—but despite its dramatic possibilities the story seems to have escaped the notice of Sir Walter Scott, and probably on that account it has never been incorporated in popular tradition.

The only authority cited by the historians is a contemporary letter from George Nicolson to Sir R. Cecil, which is a rather unconventional source for a law report. But the letter plainly records the immediate impressions of an eye-witness, and it has the ring of undoubted authenticity. This letter is calendared by *Thorpe* (vol. ii. p. 767), and the original (like so much else that ought to be in Princes Street) is still in Chancery Lane (*Public Records, Scotland : Elizabeth*, vol. 64, nos. 38 and 43).[1]

Let Nicolson tell his story in his own words. Writing on 9th March 1598-99, he says :—

> Yesterday Mr Robert Bruce suiting for his stipend got it (*illegible*) with him before the Lords of the Session. The King being there in his contrary was angry and raged at it.

This fixes the date of the decision as Monday, 8th March (not 10th March as has been stated), and it would seem that at first Nicolson attached no special significance to one more exhibition of Royal eccentricity and irritability. But a week later he reverts to the topic in a full report because of certain consequences which had ensued.

> In my last I advertised you how the King discharged Mr Robert Bruce of his stipend being 14 chalders of victuals given him by the King and the commissioners of platt in the surest form accustomed in those behalfs, and that Mr Robert, suing and recovering it before the Lords in the King's presence, the King was wonderfully angry at it. Which matter having now other matters proceeding upon it, I set down at this length.
>
> The King came in person to the Tolbooth and persuaded the voting against Mr Robert, and in a manner commanded it. The President stood up thereupon, said to the King he was President and had first place to speak ; and therefore he said to the King that He was their King and they His subjects, bound to obey Him in all humility, which they all would do in all things for their lives, lands and geir ; but in that matter of law and conscience, being sworn to justice, they would do as their consciences led them unless He commanded them to the contrary ; in which case he said that he would not vote at all nor no honest man there ; protesting he did it not for Mr Robert's sake, being of little acquaintance with him, and yet he said he heard and kenned that he was an honest man.
>
> The Lord of Newbottle (Newbattle) then also stood up and said to the King that it was said in the town, to His slander and theirs, that they durst

---

[1] I am indebted for this clue to the Historiographer Royal, and to H.M. Register House for a copy of the correspondence which soon, it is hoped, will be published in full.

not do justice but as the King commanded them ; which he said should be seen to the contrary, for they would vote against Him in the right in His own presence.

The King reasoned much and very earnestly, sometimes persuading, sometimes taunting and chiding ; and the Treasurer in the time of the reasoning of it wrote some few lines and sent it to Mr Robert's lawyer, to be resolved whether that clause was contained in Mr Robert's grant or no, as a matter of most moment for the grounding of his vote upon.

After it was fully reasoned, the Lords all (saving Mr David Magill and the Secretary who was absent for the nonce) voted with Mr Robert.

Whereat the King raged marvellously and is in great anger with the Lords of Session.

So ends Nicolson's account of the case, which reads like the report of an encounter between Elijah and Ahab. Before proceeding to the sequel, let us identify the protagonists.

Mr Robert Bruce was the famous Edinburgh minister whose relations with the King fill many pages in the records of the period. The President was Alexander Seton, Prior of Pluscarden, who successively bore the titles of Lord Urquhart, Lord Fyvie, and Earl of Dunfermline. He was President from 1593 until 1604, and later became Chancellor. The Lord of Newbottle was Mark Ker, afterwards Earl of Lothian, who was created an extraordinary lord in 1584 and was probably the senior judge in 1599. Mr David Magill who (in the contemptuous words of Calderwood) " for feare durst not vote for Mr Robert," was the undistinguished son of the celebrated Lord Advocate McGill. He was appointed a judge in 1597, doubtless because he was his father's son, and resigned a few years later on the plea of ill-health. The Secretary was James Elphinstone, afterwards Lord Balmerino, who succeeded Seton as President. The Treasurer was Walter Stewart, Lord Blantyre, who had been raised to the bench in 1593. His indiscretion in communicating privately with Bruce's counsel during the hearing brought drastic retribution, as Nicolson proceeds to explain :—

That day after He was gone away and the Lords risen, the King was told of the Treasurer's note, whereon He sent for Sanders Douglas that carried it and Mr Jo. Russel (Mr Robert's lawyer), and discovered the note urging it was sent him as counsel how to reason the matter. And entering into a great rage against the Treasurer, He came to the Tolbooth the 13 hereof, openly charging the Treasurer to have given partial counsel by the note, and commanding him to enter into ward in the Castle here that day before 4 of the clock, which he did very dutifully.

We need not pursue the fortunes of the Treasurer, except to observe that, in addition to being imprisoned, he lost his position but was later restored to favour. The climax of the story is in Nicolson's concluding sentences :—

The King swears He will have Mr Robert Bruce's cause reversed, which the President understanding says he will pen in Latin, French and Greek to be sent to all the judges in the world to be approved, and that by his vote it shall never be reversed. And so say the whole Session.

One can almost hear the crash of Seton's fist as he struck the desk in front of him. Calderwood tells us that nine months later James did order the process to be wakened and forbade the entire Faculty of Advocates to appear for Bruce. But the judgment never was reversed. If James had pursued his preposterous tactics a little further, the tragedy of 1649 might have been antedated by fifty years. But he never crossed swords with Seton again.

Before turning to the prosaic official record of the case, there is a curious point to note. Tytler, though only citing Nicolson's letter, attributes to Seton the following speech :—

My liege, it is my part to speak first in this Court of which Your Highness has made me head. You are our King : we your subjects, bound and ready to obey you from the heart and with all devotion to serve you with our lives and substance : but this is a matter of law in which we are sworn to do justice according to our conscience and the statutes of the realm. Your Majesty may indeed command us to the contrary, in which case I and every honest man will either vote according to his conscience or resign and not vote at all.

To Lord Newbottle Tytler ascribes the following :—

It had been spoken in the city, to His Majesty's great slander and theirs who were His judges, that they dared not do justice to all classes but were compelled to vote as the King commanded : a foul imputation to which the lie would that day be given, for they would now deliver a unanimous opinion against the Crown.

Lord Birkenhead produced yet another version of the speech of Seton :—

Your Majesty, we who sit here are your servants. We have sworn on oath to be loyal to you and to maintain your dynasty and line. But we have sworn another oath, and that is that we will safeguard and protect the customs and statutes of this realm ; and that which you have asked us to do is contrary to and subversive of the statute law of this realm. You may deprive us of the offices we hold. We may cease to be the King's servants. But while we sit here we administer the King's law, and we decide and rule that this man has suffered wrong, and so ordain.

If these alternative versions or any of them rest upon any authority I have failed to discover it. As we shall see, they slightly misrepresent the position. In style and phraseology they strongly suggest rhetorical paraphrases of the sixteenth century original, and most of us prefer to remove Victorian paint and Georgian varnish from genuine Jacobean oak.

To the constitutional historian the interest and importance of the case are obvious. But the lawyers have put it to a dubious use, for it has been cited as bearing upon the liability of the Crown for delict and the applicability in Scotland of that curious maxim that " the King can do no wrong." It was for this purpose that it was used in argument in *Macgregor* v. *Lord Advocate*, 1921 S.C. 847—though without apparent effect —and in the same context it is referred to in articles on *Rex non potest peccare* (*Sc. Law Rev.*, vol. lv. pp. 1 and 40) and in the *Encyclopædia*, s.v. " Crown," vol. v. p. 335. But an examination of the elaborate interlocutor (*Acts and Decrees*, vol. 178, fo. 291) shows that the action was truly of quite a different character, and no reference is made to the case or to the King's intervention in the Books of Sederunt.

The background of the litigation is to be found in that confused and barely intelligible chapter of the law of Teinds which describes the various attempts which were made after the Reformation to deal with Church endowments and to make provision for the support of the clergy. On 15th October 1589 a grant was made under the privy seal to Mr Robert Bruce of a life stipend of £170 out of the " third " of the revenues of the Abbey of Arbroath, and on 6th November

1589 decree conform to this gift was obtained from the Lords of Council against the Collector General and the heritors and others liable in the payment.[1]   Payment was duly made to Mr Bruce for eight years until 1597 ; but, for the crop and year of 1598, conflicting claims were advanced against the heritors by Mr Bruce and by Lord Hamilton, Commendator of Arbroath, and double charges for payment were made. In that situation of " double distress " fourteen Angus heritors raised an action of multiplepoinding as real raisers, calling Bruce and Hamilton as defenders, and alleging (as all real raisers do) that they were ready and willing to pay once to the party having best right, but that they were not willing to pay twice.   Being merely in the position of stakeholders and having no interest in the real dispute, the pursuers were content with one counsel, Mr Henry Balfour, who was called in 1570.

Lord Hamilton, one of whose two counsel was William Oliphant, later Lord Advocate, founded simply on the fact that he was Commendator of Arbroath Abbey, and produced a decree of declarator dated 3rd March 1597 under which he was found liable to the ministers of the Abbey in payment of the third of the revenues as therein valued and quantified.[1]

Mr Bruce appeared by three counsel, of whom the senior was no less a person than Craig of Riccarton, the leading junior being John Russell, in whose hands the unfortunate note from Lord Blantyre was discovered by the King.   They founded upon the terms of their client's gift, which had been acted upon for eight years, and in particular upon a clause which it contained protecting the grantee against loss in the event of subsequent assignations being made to ministers. The clause runs as follows :—" Gif the said stipend be onywayis imparit be ressoun of ony uther assignatioun maid for the tyme or that suld thaireftir be maid to ministeris, than it suld be lesum to upsett the said stipend and to assigne alsmekill to the said Mr Robert furth of ony uther place as suld happin to be tane fra him be vertew of the saidis assignatiounes."   It was doubtless this clause that Lord Blantyre wished to verify

[1] These particulars are taken from the interlocutor.   I have not traced the originals.

when he sent the unlucky note to John Russell. Counsel further maintained that Lord Hamilton's claim was irrelevant in respect that he as commendator could have no right to the third assigned to the ministers. Finally they founded upon a bond by Lord Hamilton assuring Mr Robert in the enjoyment of his stipend. In reply, Lord Hamilton's counsel relied on the act of the Secret Council of 1573, and further argued that Mr Bruce's claim required for its validity a *yearly* assignation, and that there was no averment that such an assignation had been made for the year 1598.

The decision of the Lords was simply to allow a proof to Mr Bruce, assigning as a diet for this purpose 15th May with continuation of days.

It will be observed that the King was not a party to the action, and indeed that he had no legal interest whatever in the subject of dispute. Bruce had suffered no " wrong." There was no question of " delivering a unanimous opinion against the Crown." Nor is it evident how a decision against Bruce could have been "subversive of the statute law of this realm." The case has thus no bearing upon the question of the liability of the Crown to the jurisdiction of the Court, still less to the liability of the Crown for damages for delict. The issue was a straightforward issue of competing civil rights between Bruce and Hamilton, and the most that can be extracted from the judgment is that in the view of the court Bruce's claim was relevant and Hamilton's was not. It would seem that this decision must have rested mainly on a construction of Bruce's deed of gift. It follows that from a legal standpoint Nicolson's account of the proceedings squares with the official record, which is more than can be said for the embroidered versions of Tytler, Lord Birkenhead, and most of the historians. Doubtless James had strong motives for securing the defeat of Bruce, but it must have been as King, and not as a pleader, that he reasoned with the judges. His intervention was not as a party, nor as the self-constituted representative of a party, but merely in the assertion of his assumed prerogative right to dictate to the Court any decision which he wished to hear pronounced.

Bruce v. *Hamilton*—(or, as we should now design it, MP. *Auchterlonie & Others* v. *Bruce and Hamilton*)—has thus little, if any, significance as a legal precedent, and he would be a bold man who professed to say whether as a decision it was right or wrong. But it remains a leading case for the constitutional historian, for its attendant circumstances fully warrant Lord Birkenhead's description of it as " the culminating incident " in the vindication of civil liberty in Scotland. Considering that all these judges—in hard fact if not in constitutional theory—held their positions and enjoyed their personal liberty at the whim of the sovereign, and that Seton himself was under the added peril of being suspected of being a Catholic, their firm stand commands the deepest respect, and is all the more astonishing in view of the many allegations of corruption which have been brought against the judges of that time. James was no stranger to them, nor they to James, for Professor Hannay has told us that the King was then in the habit of attending in court as often as twenty-five days every year (*College of Justice*, p. 119). There were other occasions both in Scotland and later in England on which he sought to apply in practice his extreme views of the *Jus Regium*, but there was none on which he met with so decisive and humiliating a rebuff—not even at the hands of Coke.

The case must have created a prodigious stir amongst the denizens of the old Tolbooth, one of whom would be Sir Thomas Hope of Craighall, who in 1599 was " devilling " to an advocate (*op. cit.*, p. xv). Yet it was this same Sir Thomas Hope who, as Lord Advocate to Charles I, found it possible with the *Bruce* case within his recollection to propound this remarkable doctrine : " No judge hes anie power quhere the king is present : bot they all lose their light like starrs quhen the sunne shines, and their power (quhich they have from him onlie) is suspendit " (*Major Practicks*, vol. i. p. 13).

If the descendants of Mr David Magill found any consolation in this retrospective vindication of their ancestor, it is certain that both Seton and Newbottle must have turned in their graves.

1946

Frustration of Contract in Scots Law

As clearly appears from the latest Scottish appeal,[1] the doctrine of frustration of contract is common to the jurisprudence of both Scotland and England. Its later refinements and developments, dating from the First World War, have proceeded on parallel lines on each side of the Border. With certain important exceptions to be noted below, the expositions contained in the numerous decisions of the House of Lords in English appeals and of the Judicial Committee of the Privy Council would in the main be accepted in Scotland.

But the process of assimilation is not complete and it will never be complete ; for the juridicial principles on which the maturing doctrine now rests have been approached in Scotland from an individual standpoint and have been evolved by a different process of reasoning against a different legal background. Though two streams of thought have now in large measure coalesced, their sources lie far apart and each has flowed through its own juristic channel.

The key to the Scottish treatment of this problem (as of so many others) is to be found in four cardinal features of Scots Law. (*a*) With us law and equity have never been separated, and equity has tended to predominate. (*b*) We buried our forms of action in the Middle Ages, and have never allowed them to " rule us from their graves." (*c*) The doctrine of consideration, as understood in the Anglo-American law of contract, has no part in our system. (*d*) During the formative period of modern Scots Law the chief source of inspiration was found in the Roman Law of the later Commentators—a model which was rarely slavishly copied, but which has left a deep and permanent mark on many chapters of our law.

[1] *Denny, Mott & Dickson*, [1945] A.C. 265.

In any scientific account of the developed doctrine of frustration the subject would almost inevitably be treated as one of the methods by which contractual obligations are discharged. Paradoxical as it may appear, it was never from this angle that the subject was approached in Scots Law. The germinal ideas of frustration appeared in Scotland not in answer to the question whether a contract should be dissolved by operation of law by reason of certain supervening changes of circumstances, but in answer to the far wider question how the relations of two parties should be equitably readjusted by the Court when the one had been unintentionally enriched at the expense of the other. Frustration of contract was thus a by-product of a process directed to a different end. It seems to have been assumed, rather than asserted, that certain supervening changes in circumstances must necessarily sever the initial contractual tie, and attention was concentrated upon the substitute rights and obligations which on that event would emerge. It is necessary to refer briefly to the history of the law, not for its intrinsic interest but on account of its persisting influence upon later developments.

The idea of frustration was first foreshadowed in Scotland by Craig of Riccarton at the beginning of the seventeenth century [1] when he applied what is in essence the modern principle in an unexpected but revealing context—the forfeiture of a feu by a delinquent vassal—and justified his reasoning by invoking the Roman *condictio causa data causa non secuta* and *naturalis æquitas*. The same indirect approach was chosen by Stair in the famous passage [2] which was subjected to such close scrutiny in the *Cantiare San Rocco* appeal. [3] This passage occurs in a title devoted to the exposition of what Stair calls "the natural or obediential obligation of restitution"; and one of the many cases to which he applies that obligation is where "the purpose contemplated has failed." It is in the same juridical context that the rules are formulated in embryo form by Bankton, Erskine and Bell. [4] In all these statements the underlying conception, which seems to have

---

[1] *Jus Feudale.*, III. v. 23.   [2] *Inst.*, I. vii. 7.   [3] [1924] A.C. 226.
[4] *Bankton*, I. viii. 23 ; *Ersk. Inst.*, III. i. 10 ; *Bell Princs.*, s. 530.

been taken for granted, was that the original contract obligations were extinguished by a species of novation and replaced
by the substitute obligation of restitution, the occasion of the
transformation being failure of the consideration, in the sense
of the Roman *causa*.

Concurrently with this growth of legal theory a mass of
decisions accumulated from the seventeenth century onwards
dealing with the commonest type of supervening change of
circumstance by which a contract can be rendered incapable
of exact performance—the destruction, total or partial, actual
or constructive, of some specific thing essential to its performance. These cases introduced into many chapters of our
law a well-worn technical term, *rei interitus*. Associated with
rei interitus in its proper sense was the parallel idea of the death
or incapacity of the obligant in a contract involving *delectus
personæ*. The concept of *rei interitus* was exhaustively worked
out in relation to many different kinds of contract—lease, sale
and *locatio operis* in particular—but the rules were not systematised as part of the general law of contract. Indeed, the
tendency during the eighteenth century and even later was to
examine such cases more from the standpoint of the law of
property than from the standpoint of the law of contract.
Res perit domino was the brocard to which appeal was often
made ; and when the early decisions were collected in
Morison's *Dictionary* in 1801, the general heading under which
he assembled most of them was " *Periculum*," for the question
which the courts were in use to put to themselves was—On
whom should the risk of this casualty fall ? [1]

It was around these two fruitful ideas—Restitution and *Rei
Interitus*—that Scots Law had collected by the nineteenth
century a large volume of opportunist doctrine mainly of
Roman origin or inspiration. But little or no attempt had
been made to rationalise the rules in a generalised theory,
nor to correlate them to the principles of the law of contract.
Even when Bell, the last of our institutional writers and the
architect of our mercantile law, laid down his pen, he had only
reached the stage of formulating one part of the doctrine in his

[1] Cf. *Gloag on Contract*, 2nd ed. 351.

general theory of contract by reference to the principle of *rei interitus* [1] and another part in a different portion of his work dealing with Restitution.[2] As Lord Macmillan has pointed out,[3] it is in the posthumous editions of the *Principles* that the doctrine first begins to assume its modern shape in the crisp formula that " when by the nature of the contract its performance depends . . . on the existence of a particular state of things the failure . . . of that state of things liberates both parties." It is certainly to the credit of the editor that this generalisation appeared so early as 1885, but it is a little odd that its theoretical justification was then found in an implied term of the contract.[4]

From this summary review it follows that well before the beginning of the present century the common law of Scotland had amassed most of the raw materials required for the construction of the modern doctrine of frustration, and that Scottish lawyers were habituated by long experience to the task of solving the consequential problems to which such an event gives rise. The question had been attacked upon a narrow front and from an unusual angle, and the effort had been directed to the practical issue of deciding specific cases rather than to the theoretical problem of integrating the solutions in a generalised system. But it is just such differences in method of approach and process of reasoning that impart to Comparative Law its peculiar value and help to explain the ultimate divergences in detail.

The distinctive features of Scots Law can best be examined by considering the ascertained and potential divergences from English Law ; but the subject is obviously one for cautious handling, for the doctrine is still in process of development and the future course of judicial refinements cannot be predicted with certainty.

The outstanding instance is afforded by the rejection in Scotland of the rule in *Chandler* v. *Webster* that on the occurrence of frustration of a contract the loss lies where it falls. As we have seen, the Scottish solution of restitution goes

---

[1] *Princs.*, s. 29. [2] *Ibid.*, s. 530.
[3] [1944] A.C. at 272. [4] 8th ed. by Sheriff Guthrie, s. 29.

back for centuries. It was justified by Lord President Inglis in a leading case in 1871,[1] and was authoritatively confirmed by the House of Lords in *Cantiare San Rocco* in 1924.[2] For nearly twenty years the two systems continued to part company in this respect until as a result of the *Fibrosa* case [3] restitution, or something very like it, became part of English Law. But the reconciliation was shortlived, for in the following year the Law Reform (Frustrated Contracts) Act was applied to contracts governed by English Law, and the English Courts were thereby empowered to effect sundry adjustments of the rights and liabilities of parties to a frustrated contract. From the *dicta* of certain of the Law Lords who decided the *Fibrosa* appeal it would seem that differing views were held as to whether similar adjustments could, where necessary, be made by Scottish Courts in applying the doctrine of restitution, the doubts arising from the limited terms of Lord President Inglis's formulation in *Watson* v. *Shankland*.[1] The point has never been decided. It was deliberately kept open by the terms of the interlocutor pronounced by the Court of Session in *Denny, Mott & Dickson*,[4] and it was not before the House of Lords in the appeal in that case. The opinion may be hazarded that the Scottish courts have all the requisite powers. It would surely be very odd if a doctrine, which is rooted and grounded in equity of the widest type and which has already displayed its remarkable adaptability, were incapable of the development required to enable it to deal equitably not only with the contingencies to which the Act of 1943 applies but also with many others which could be figured. It is significant, moreover, that the Act of 1943 was not applied to Scotland.

The mention of *Chandler* v. *Webster* suggests another possible point of difference between Scotland and England, viz. : whether " the Coronation cases " would be followed in Scotland in so far as they hold that the non-occurrence of an unexpected event *per se* frustrates any contract which is based on the assumption that the event will occur. The case of *Trevalion*

---

[1] *Watson & Co.* v. *Shankland*, 10 Macph. 142.
[2] [1924] A.C. 226. [3] [1943] A.C. 32.
[4] 1943 S.C. at 316.

v. *Blanche* [1] and the high authority of the late Professor Gloag [2]
can be cited in support of the view that this is not in all circumstances Scots Law.   Time alone will show.

The contrast between the Scottish and English methods of
approach is further illustrated by the anxiety with which in
some of the English cases attention is devoted to the characteristics of the " action for money had and received " and " the
writ of *indebitatus assumpsit.*"   In the *Fibrosa* case, for instance,
this bulked largely in the discussion.   To a Scottish lawyer
such considerations are not only irrelevant but positively
distracting ; for with us a right never depends on the existence
of a remedy, but the remedy depends on the existence of a
right.   Of all the distinctions between the two systems this,
as Lord Dunedin pithily observed, [3] is the one most difficult to
bring home to a Scottish lawyer ; and if we may judge from
his Lordship's speech in *Sinclair* v. *Brougham,* [4] he did not find
it any easier to bring the distinction home to his English
colleagues.

In our latest book on Contract [5]—a work which has justly
acquired the highest repute but which is no longer abreast
of the latest developments—the attempt is made to divide contracts into those to which frustration is applicable and those
to which it is not.   Such a method of statement recalls the
early stage in the history of frustration of contract when the
doctrine had accidentally acquired a " definitely maritime
flavour " [6] simply because its principal illustrations were in
cases dealing with ships and charter-parties.   It is doubtful
whether Professor Gloag would have repeated that passage
to-day ; for the mature doctrine of frustration cannot be imprisoned within the formal categories into which contracts have
been divided since the days of Gaius, and the question whether
any given contract has been frustrated depends in Scotland
upon whether the conditions of frustration have been satisfied,
and not upon the particular species of the genus contract in
regard to which the point arises.   The pity is that in Scotland

---

[1] 1919 S.C. 617.   [2] *Contract*, 2nd ed., 353-4.
[3] *Encycl. of Scots Law*, 1926, i. p. vi.   [4] [1914] A.C. 398.
[5] *Gloag on Contract*, 2nd ed., 357.
[6] McNair, *Legal Effects of War*, 1944, p. 142.

the individual cases raising the issue are neither numerous enough nor varied enough to admit of the full development of our native principles, and there is an ever-present risk that, with the much larger flow of English decisions, these native principles may be inadvertently forced into alien moulds, regardless of the resulting strains and distortions.

A conspicuous instance of a cleavage where this risk has so far been successfully averted is offered by the question of the applicability of frustration to a lease. In England this matter has come up in a number of decisions which Scottish lawyers found very troublesome ; and these have now culminated in the *Cricklewood* appeal,[1] which discloses a sharp difference of judicial opinion based upon the fact that in England a lease is not only a contract but a demise of land creating a new estate. Such a distinction has no meaning in Scotland, whose law of heritable rights differs fundamentally from English real property law and does not recognise the doctrine of estates. It was in relation to leases that in Scotland the early developments of the concept of *rei interitus* found their principal illustrations, and the rule was soon settled that the accidental destruction of the subject of a lease, or its supervening sterility as a result of *damnum fatale*, liberates both landlord and tenant. Even more significant as a pointer to probable future expansions of the Scottish doctrine of frustration are the many decisions dealing with partial *rei interitus* ; for the question was treated as one of degree to be solved by reference to the equitable rule of *plus quam tolerabile*, and it was early recognised that a tenant was normally entitled at least to an abatement of rent proportionate to the extent of his eviction.[2] Against such a doctrinal background it is easy to understand why in 1929 a Scottish court had no difficulty in holding that, where a fishery had been rendered incapable of beneficial possession as a result of Air Ministry bye-laws converting part of the area into a danger zone for bombing practice, the tenant was entitled to abandon the unexpired portion of a nineteen-year lease.[3] A like conclusion was reached during the recent war

---

[1] [1945] A.C. 221.   [2] *Rankine on Leases*, 3rd ed., 225 ff.
[3] *Tay Salmon Fisheries* v. *Speedie*, 1929 S.C. 593.

when a furnished house had been requisitioned by the military authorities and so rendered indefinitely unavailable to the tenant.[1] The best comments on these cases—and they have a much wider validity—were made by Lord Wright, who said : " The Scotch authorities afford no analogy applicable to English law, because they proceed, it seems, on a different view of the contract and of the legal background," [2] and by Lord Normand, who spoke with greater emphasis : " In the chapter of leases, and I think also in the chapter of *rei interitus*, our law is by no means the same as the law of England, and, to quote Lord Justice-Clerk Hope, if we were to attempt to apply that law in these cases, we should run the greatest risk of spoiling our own by mistaking theirs." [3]

No inference can safely be drawn regarding the common law of Scotland from the terms of the emergency legislation passed at the outbreak of the recent war. For instance, the War Damage to Land (Scotland) Act, 1939,[4] conferred new powers on the courts to modify, and even to cancel, leases, dispositions or heritable securities affecting subjects destroyed in whole or in part by war damage. It is thought that to a large extent such powers already existed ; and it does not follow that they did not merely because Parliament saw fit in anticipation of an unprecedented situation to provide expressly and by a shorthand procedure for dealing with the emergency. It sometimes happens—*experto crede*—that an Act has to be applied to Scotland simply because a like Act has already been applied to England ; and, as we have been reminded in the pages of this *Journal*,[5] Bills nowadays made to pass as razors are made to sell.

To summarise, the principles of frustration now applied in Scotland harmonise in most essentials with those of Anglo-American Law. In the application of the doctrine to individual cases the different legal background of Scots Law has produced, and will yet produce, different results. Owing to its origin

---

[1] *Mackeson* v. *Boyd*, 1942 S.C. 56.   [2] [1945] A.C. at 239.
[3] 1942 S.C. at 63.   [4] 2 and 3 Geo. 6, c. 80.
[5] *Journal of Comparative Legislation and International Law*, 3rd series, vol. xxviii, p. xxvi.

in Roman equity and its freedom from the restraints imposed by the history of English common law, Scots Law in its application to this subject possesses a high degree of flexibility and adaptability, which may well lead to further incursions into areas closed to English rules.

It has not proved necessary for the Scottish courts to join in the search for philosophic explanations of the principles of frustration such as has for long engaged the attention of so many eminent English judges and jurists. But it is of peculiar interest to the Scottish lawyer to note that the latest writer on this subject, after reviewing the bewildering assortment of suggestions offered to explain the foundations of the doctrine, concludes with Lord Wright that " the time has come to shed the fiction of implied contract and to regard the doctrine as a mode by which upon the facts of a case the court itself does justice in circumstances for which the parties never provided." [1]   This in essence has been the Scottish view for more than three hundred years, and we need nothing better.

1946

[1] Webber, *Effect of War on Contracts*, 2nd ed., 414.

The Numbers and the Distribution of the Population of Medieval Scotland

THE close of the thirteenth century marks the end of a long period of relatively settled conditions during which the natural trends of population growth in Scotland cannot have been deeply affected by migration, pestilence or war. To the student of this fascinating period it would be valuable to know the numbers and distribution of the population which then inhabited the area which corresponds to modern Scotland, but this is a subject upon which little light has been shed. The problem is one for a vital statistician well versed in medieval history, or for a medievalist well versed in vital statistics. But such hybrids do not occur in nature ; and even if they did, they would probably recoil from a question for the solution of which the data are so scanty and so imperfectly vouched. In these circumstances one who is qualified in neither respect may be pardoned for rushing in where Registrars General have feared to tread, by throwing out certain suggestions with the object rather of eliciting than of imparting information.

To begin with a truism, the figure for which we are in search must be very small by comparison with the present figure. Taking Western Europe under a single survey it is clear that the population trend suffered a violent transformation during the eighteenth century, for about that time the curves suddenly began to climb very steeply, and they are only now flattening out at levels far above the starting point. This fact does not need to be vouched. In England an eight-fold increase occurred between about 1700 and 1900, and over Europe as a whole it has been estimated that there has been a five-fold increase since the beginning of the seventeenth century.[1]

[1] H. A. L. Fisher, *History of Europe,* 791 note.

Next, if we concentrate upon the censuses and the tolerably reliable figures for the last 200 years or so, we find that the recent expansion has taken place in Scotland at a notably slower rate than in England, the reasons being for present purposes irrelevant. To-day the ratio of England to Scotland is about 8 to 1. In 1881 it was 7 to 1. In 1851 it was 6 to 1. Such estimates as have been given for the eighteenth century indicate that it was then little over 5 to 1 and that the curves for the two countries were already diverging. The suggested inference is that during the static period which preceded the recent great expansion of population the ratio of England to Scotland was of the order of 5 to 1.

It may be a pure coincidence but it is an odd fact that Bishop Halton's assessment of the revenues of the Scottish Church in 1291 was about £40,000 and that the corresponding figure for England was £210,000, or roughly five times as much. Professor Tout found this difficult to believe [1] but he does not justify his scepticism.

The next question is whether any causes were at work during the four centuries which separate 1300 from 1700 which would materially affect the relative populations of England and Scotland. It is thought not. The chronic impoverishment of a large part of Scotland from the fourteenth century onwards and the disturbed conditions of the Borders would adversely affect the trend of the Scottish population ; but the northern counties of England had their share of disturbances too, and the indications are that in the earlier part of the period the Black Death wrought considerably more havoc in England than in Scotland. Temporary fluctuations apart, it seems unlikely that there was any notable departure from the 5 to 1 ratio.

If then we knew the population of England in 1300, one-fifth of that figure would give a first approximation to the population of contemporary Scotland. As it happens we do not know the English figure with anything approaching to exactitude, but there is a large measure of agreement in the estimates made or accepted by many English historians of

[1] *Reg. òf John de Halton* (Cant. & York Soc., vol. xii), xv.

the past population of their country, the figures being of the following order :—In 1600, 4,000,000 ; in the later fourteenth century, 2,500,000 ; and at the period of Doomsday Book, 1,250,000 to 1,500,000. Let us now plot the population curves of the two countries backwards from 1900. In so far as based upon the census or other more or less authentic figures, the converging curves fade out about 1700 with Scotland at something over 1,000,000 and England about 5,500,000. The English curve is already on a marked gradient, but the Scottish curve is not far from the horizontal. If we extrapolate the curves backwards for 400 years, the estimates of the English historians fit well into the assumed curve for England, and on the 5 to 1 ratio Scotland's figure for 1300 is about 400,000.

This is not an occasion for concluding the computation with the triumphant cypher Q.E.D. ; but it may not be unfair to invite anyone who can do so to justify a closer approximation to the true figure than 400,000 *plus* or *minus*, say 50,000. 400,000 was the figure suggested by Dr Barron,[1] and the one source of anxiety is due to Sinclair's estimate of 600,000 as at 1250.[2] No aid can be derived from the numbers engaged in the battles of the period, partly because the estimates are not reliable, and mainly because there is no known method of equating the armed array of a medieval army to the total population of the belligerent state.

If then there were some 400,000 people in Scotland in 1300, where did they live ? Once again let us begin with a wide generalisation, that population is a function of food supply, and that, except in highly developed industrialised communities, the bulk of the people live on or near lands that can be farmed or coasts that can be fished. It would be a mistake to press this too far in dealing with thirteenth century Scotland, for it was, according to the standards of the day, a rich country, and there is a surprising amount of evidence of foreign trade, industry and merchant commerce. For instance,

---

[1] *Scottish War of Independence*, 430.
[2] *Analysis of the Statistical Account of Scotland*, i. 148-9 ; see also Mr J. G. Kyd's paper in *Royal Phil. Soc. of Glasgow*, Procs., 1944.

enough has survived in the records to show that the menus in many a monastic refectory and noble hall or royal castle were on a scale which to-day would probably entail a summary prosecution, and that the well-to-do were accustomed to the use of a great variety of luxury articles which must have been brought from a distance and often from overseas.[1] But large localised populations cannot exist without an organised distributive trade which depends on facilities for communications, and in those days such facilities existed only in elementary form.   After making due allowance for all the crumbs which fell from the rich men's tables, it is safe to conclude that the mass of the population depended mainly on the local farmers and fishermen.   Dr Coulton has told us that in the fourteenth century 90 per cent. of the people of Europe were peasants,[2] and even of fifteenth century England and of the days of Queen Elizabeth Dr Trevelyan has much the same tale to tell.[3]

If this is the true view, the great mass of the mainland population of Scotland must have been settled in the Lowlands and on the eastern and south-western littorals, with penetrations up the larger river valleys.   This is precisely the conclusion to be derived from the sites of the monasteries and parish churches in existence at this date, for these indicate that in Scotland proper the population was concentrated along the shores of the Moray Firth and in Aberdeenshire, Angus, Fife and Strathearn, and that it was very evenly distributed throughout the Lowlands, but with notable concentrations in the Tweed valley and along the coasts of the Solway Firth, and with two thin areas in the Galloway uplands and the remoter Border dales.

Upon the assumption, which appears to be amply justified, that the density of the population would vary directly with the value of the land in each district, it is permissible to attempt yet another cross-bearing by using the early valuations made for the purposes of Papal and national taxation.   With the

---

[1] *Exch. Rolls*, vol. i., *passim*.
[2] *Great Events in History* (1934), 231.
[3] *Social History*, viii, 141.

aid of the chartularies of St Andrews, Moray, Arbroath and
Dunfermline, and the records of Bagimond's Roll and Bishop
Halton's assessment, it is possible to analyse the *antiqua taxacio*
as given in the legislation of 1366, and to piece together the
relative values of the eleven Scottish dioceses. A margin of
error must be allowed for to cover the fact that a monastery
in one diocese frequently drew some of its revenue from lands
or churches in another, and also for the lack of precise delimi-
tation of the diocesan boundaries. The total is about £16,000,
of which Glasgow and St Andrews contributed nearly two-
thirds. We can even go a step further, for, in addition to the
antiqua taxacio of Church property and endowments, we have
in the legislation of 1366 a return under 21 sheriffdoms of the
terre et redditus vicecomitatum, totalling about £50,000. Once
again the computation is precarious owing to the omission
of certain remoter areas and the uncertainty of the boundaries
of the sheriffdoms. But by combining all these figures and
resorting to judicious averaging so as to eliminate probable
errors, it is possible to reconstruct a thirteenth century Valuation Roll for all the lands, spiritual as well as temporal, in the
eleven dioceses, in so far as subjected to taxation ; and though
the figures afford little guide to absolute values, their indication
of the relative values cannot be far out. The following is
the result :—

				£	Per cent.
Glasgow	.	.	.	20,320	31·1
St Andrews		.	.	16,680	25·1
Aberdeen		.	.	6,500	9·9
Dunkeld	.	.	.	6,200	9·5
Dunblane	.	.	.	3,700	5·5
Argyll	.	.	.	3,600	5·4
Moray	.	.	.	3,500	5·3
Whithorn	.	.	.	2,000	3·0
Brechin	.	.	.	1,850	2·7
Ross	.	.	.	850	1·3
Caithness	.	.	.	800	1·2
				66,000	100·0

But these figures only cover what may be described as developed Scotland—the areas which had been brought within the sphere of organised civil administration and the parochial system.   Doubtless the mass of the 400,000 lived within these areas, but there must have been an appreciable proportion outside in the Highlands and Islands and the remoter districts which at that time were only nominally parts of Scotland.   How many must be allowed for in these areas is a matter for conjecture.   It would be a mistake to argue backwards from the present day when so large a part of the north and west is very sparsely populated ; since Webster's census of 1755 disclosed over 216,000 people in Caithness, Sutherland, Ross, Inverness and Argyll, and as recently as 1831 the five Highland counties supported a population of 388,000 or 17 per cent. of the then population of Scotland.   This was done under conditions of a rural economy which cannot have differed substantially from those of the Middle Ages, so far at least as the bare support of the resident population is concerned. Moreover, the natural resources of these distant places were supplemented in the thirteenth century by the exercise of what Tytler calls " the honourable profession " of piracy, from which many a Hebridean chief must have amassed great wealth. Finally the Norse records of King Hakon's expedition of 1263 surprise us by showing that places like Skye, Mull and Islay were worth plundering, and could provision an invading fleet, and be subjected to penalties running into hundreds of heads of cattle.   Even in the lonely fastnesses around Cape Wrath there were evidently enough able-bodied men on the spot to cause trouble to an anchored Norwegian ship of war.[1] On the other hand, the parish churches in central and western Sutherland and Ross (an area of 3000 square miles) which are known to have existed in 1300 number only 8 as compared with nearly 70 in both Fife and Dumfriesshire.

There the matter must be left.   On *a priori* grounds it seems unlikely that more than 50,000 people could have been supported in the outlying districts, leaving 350,000 for the developed areas.   Upon this view an application of the

[1] A O. Anderson, *Early Sources of Scottish History, passim.*

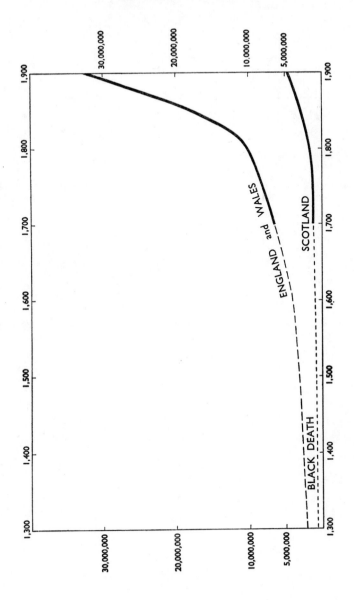

valuation percentages would give the following approximate diocesan populations :—

Glasgow	.	. .	107,000
St Andrews	.	. .	88,000
Aberdeen	.	. .	35,000
Dunkeld	.	. .	34,000
Dunblane	.	. .	20,000
Argyll	.	. .	18,000
Moray	.	. .	18,000
Whithorn	.	. .	11,000
Brechin	.	. .	10,000
Ross	.	. .	5,000
Caithness	.	. .	4,000
			350,000
Outlying Areas	.	.	50,000
			400,000

These figures are not claimed to be more than more or less intelligent conjectures based on the most slender of data. But they are inherently probable enough, and the methods by which they have been reached may suggest other and better lines of enquiry.

A graph of the population curves and a sketch map of Scotland showing the diocesan areas are appended, but the boundaries shown are only approximate.

1947

The Importance of Comparative Law in Scotland

THE UNIVERSITY OF ABERDEEN has to-day made history by inaugurating the first lectureship in Scotland for the teaching of Comparative Law. May I be permitted in the name of the legal profession to commend most warmly the initiative of those who have brought this to pass, and to convey our sincere good wishes to the lecturer and his future students for the success of this notable experiment?

The subject is one which has been seriously neglected in the United Kingdom as a matter of organised academic instruction. With us, the practitioner who aims at professional success can hardly become known as a legal theorist without imperilling his prospects ; and while, as I hope to show, the comparative study of law can be severely practical and conspicuously useful to Scotland, it still retains for the average lawyer and his client a suspiciously doctrinaire flavour. South of the Border the neglect of Comparative Law may be due to the fact that our friends there have long regarded it as axiomatic that English Law is the best of all possible laws ; and in this they may, or may not, be right. But we in Scotland have no excuse for the cavalier attitude which we have latterly adopted. For five hundred years Scotland was *par excellence* the home of Comparative Law. From the earliest days when we can first descry him the Scottish lawyer has been first and foremost an eclectic philosopher, eagerly but critically examining every alien system with which he has been brought into contact, and quick to adopt and adapt any good idea in principle or in practice which he thought could usefully be appropriated, irrespective of its source. In the thirteenth century he took what he wanted, but only what he wanted, from the first phase of Anglo-Norman Law and from the ubiquitous Canon Law, and adapted it to suit national needs and local tradition. Then—for reasons which were more political than juristic—he slowly discarded most of the English ingredients until there was pitifully little law of any kind left. In the sixteenth and seventeenth centuries he made a fresh start, and this time he selected what he wanted, but only what he wanted, from the civilians of France and the Low Countries, and on that foundation and by using the serviceable relics of the old tradition he erected the temple of Themis anew. In the eighteenth and early nineteenth century he appropriated a good deal of the Law Merchant as developed by Lord Mansfield and other English judges, and wrought it into the fabric of Scots Law. In recent times, the only significant external influence has come from England, but a good deal from that source has come to us not by *our* voluntary borrowings, but as a result of *their* forced loans. All through its formative period Scots Law has never lacked these fertilising foreign contacts, and until last century they were established and maintained not through mere book-learning but by the industry and enterprise of the " Scot abroad " ; for in those days the Scot who went abroad to study or to work came home to stay, bringing his knowledge and experience with him. With their aid he has fashioned not an unrelated anthology of borrowed rules but a coherent and distinctive legal philosophy, which has made no mean contribution to the jurisprudence of the modern world, and can do so again.

Has it ever occurred to you how little there is in Scots Law which could justly be described as aboriginal and indigenous, and how much that can be traced with certainty to an alien source ? It was not in the invention of new doctrines or procedural methods that the genius of the architects of our system was displayed, but in the creation of a synthesis of philosophical jurisprudence, marked by the deduction of the largest possible range of consequences from the smallest possible number of guiding principles. It is to this that we owe the breadth and flexibility of Scots Law, its fusion of law and equity with equity predominating, and its emancipation from artificial technicalities ; and these results would have been impossible without the comparative study of law and the repeated fruitful contacts which were maintained with selected foreign legal systems.   If these influences and the spirit which inspired their utilisation cease to flourish, Scots Law as an independent system will assuredly perish.

Well, someone may ask, why not?—though I should be deeply shocked if such a question were asked in the City of Aberdeen.   Let me digress to offer two answers out of many. For one thing, nothing would more effectively contribute to the swift obliteration of the individuality of the Scottish people than the loss of the legal system under which we have lived since the dawn of history ; and having said that, I have probably said enough.   But apart from that, the disappearance of Scots Law would be an unqualified loss to jurisprudence. Tested by the most exacting standards, the classical law of Stair, Erskine and Bell need fear comparison with no modern system, for it has proved as successful as any in meeting the needs of a fundamentally transformed society which its creators never beheld, even in a vision.   Again and again in recent times we have had the satisfaction of witnessing the introduction into English Law by legislative action of reforms which did little more than echo ideas with which we had been familiar in some instances for centuries.   In the caustic words of Lord Cockburn written just 100 years ago : " Not being able to reject what was right merely because it was Scotch, the English reformers have been driven to do from necessity what we have been long doing from choice."   Our modernised system of criminal law and procedure is openly envied.   So recently as 1912, when Lord Loreburn was consulted as to the drafting of the Federal Equity Rules, his advice to the American jurists was to " consider the Scottish method of pleading which in my opinion is the best."

It is right to recall that we are heirs to a goodly tradition, but in that very fact has lain our real danger.   For several generations we have been yielding in Scotland to the lawyers' besetting sin of insularity or isolationism.   Others laboured and we have been content to enter into their labours and to live on the inherited capital of ready-made ideas and on only one foreign contact, and that a very unwholesome one for us when operating in isolation—English Law.   Historically and doctrinally, Scots Law since the days of Stair at any rate has had no affinity whatever with English Common Law or Equity. Our affinities are with Roman Law and with its modern offshoots and developments which are now competing with Anglo-American Law for the allegiance of the civilised world— the Continental or Franco-German system, as exemplified in the long series of codes beginning with the Code Napoleon and continuing through such later codes as those of Germany, France, Austria, various South American States, Turkey and Japan. If Scots Law is not merely to survive but to thrive, we must renew and deepen our contacts with these kindred legal systems, and draw from them the inspiration for the task of perfecting Scots Law as an instrument for the service of our people in the days ahead.

But that may not be the only task which lies before Scots Law or the only service which it may be called upon to render to jurisprudence. One of the shrewdest and most penetrating judgments with regard to Scots Law ever uttered was pronounced over twenty years ago by an eminent Continental jurist, Professor Lévy Ullmann of the Sorbonne, and it is well to see ourselves as others see us. " Scots Law," he said, " gives us a picture of what will be some day the law of the civilised nations, namely a combination between the Anglo-Saxon and the Continental system." There is a profound truth in that observation. Our system still is in a very real sense the mid-couple connecting the two great rival systems, and partaking of a good many elements of both. If we can hold the middle course which our forefathers steadily followed for centuries, if we can preserve the integrity of our individual and independent attitude to the rival methods of thought while at the same time improving and modernising our system by judicious borrowings from both, a future generation of Scots lawyers may be able to point the way to the final solution of the problem of all jurisprudence by providing in Scotland a successful working model of world law.

These are distant ideals, and he would be a bold man who would hazard a guess as to whether and when Professor Lévy Ullmann's prophecy will be fulfilled. But whether we look

K

to the distant horizons or to the more immediate tasks which
lie ready to our hand, the revival of the comparative study
of law is for Scotland an urgent necessity, and the practical
issue is what can immediately be done to further that end.

The task may be tackled in many useful ways. I should
like to see, for example, a revival by means of travelling
scholarships of the good educative system under which the law
student spent part of his student days in a foreign law school.
That would be a far more useful outlet for the private endowments and public money now lavished on educational projects
than some of the purposes to which they are at present devoted.
I should like to see, here and elsewhere, worthy libraries of
foreign law. I should like to see more handbooks like Amos
and Walton's *Introduction to French Law*. Above all I should
like to see—what Aberdeen now has—organised academic
instruction in the comparative study of law.

Now I do not know how your new lecturer proposes to
teach his subject nor what aims or ideals he cherishes, and it
would be impertinent for me even to appear to instruct him
on that matter. But from my own standpoint, as one concerned
with the day-to-day application and development of Scots
Law, may I be allowed to throw out for your consideration a
few suggestions as to the practical use to which Comparative
Law might now be put in Scotland by Scots Lawyers?

Let me begin with a number of aspects of the subject which
I should relegate to a secondary position. The study of
Comparative Law is being advocated in many quarters as a
means of achieving a more or less world-wide unification in
the law of modern states—a legal Esperanto in which the
lawyers' Tower of Babel will soon sink into oblivion. Now I
admit that there are certain limited areas in which that can
with benefit be done. Indeed there are several chapters of
commercial law in which it has already been done—collisions
at sea, negotiable instruments, carriage by air and one or two
others. Further, it is high time that an attack on these lines
were made on International Private Law and Jurisdiction,
which, especially in relation to divorce, is chaotic, and not least
so in some of the American states. There are the fields in

which bodies like U.N.E.S.C.O. could achieve something really worth while ; but after all they are very limited fields, and I have little faith in the academic pursuit of Utopian ideals on a universal basis. With all respect to the enthusiasm of some recent organisations I feel convinced that efficiency and above all, vitality and growth, are much more likely to be found in freely developing state individualism with due regard to national and local tradition than in the dead levels of an insipid internationalism imposed from without. International codification has its place but I should give it a secondary place, especially in Scotland ; for we are too small a nation to play a major part in world movements and the work is in any event work for specialists and not for students.

Again, Comparative Law has occasionally been advocated as a means of enabling the lawyers of one country to understand and advise upon the law of another. This I venture to describe, without intending offence, as the beginner's view. It is as rare an accomplishment to be competently acquainted as a practitioner with two different legal systems as to be perfectly bi-lingual. Any practitioner who claimed such an accomplishment would on that very account be suspect. No Scottish court dreams of taking foreign law on any specific case from a book, for you are only half-way to knowing what the law is when you have found a text-book formulation of a legal rule. You must further know the exact sense in which terms are used, the canons of interpretation which are employed, and the historical and doctrinal background against which the rule must be examined. That is why when we require to know French Law or Brazilian Law on any given matter, we ask the opinion of a French or a Brazilian lawyer. By all means let us strive to discover the different principles which different states have applied to the solution of the same problems, for there is no better method of acquiring breadth of outlook and a just perspective in the study of legal problems. By all means let us strive to learn enough of any foreign legal system and of its technical vocabulary to enable us to understand what the foreign lawyer is trying to tell us or what we are trying to tell him. But the practical legal shoemaker must stick to his last, at which he will find occupation enough for a lifetime. And let no Scots lawyer study foreign law with a view to practising in two or more legal systems. It cannot be done.

These are negative suggestions, and I pass on to more positive and constructive ideas. Every practising lawyer knows only too well that there are chapters of his legal system which are in need of being re-written, and that entirely new problems are always being thrown up by the changing conditions of a rapidly changing world to which his legal system offers no answer, or no satisfactory answer. These are the topics on which the Scots lawyer should specially concentrate in his study of Comparative Law. In judging of the adequacy of an existing legal principle or method of practice the pragmatic test of whether it works is no bad test, provided the test is applied not merely by reference to the convenience of the lawyer and the law courts but also by reference to the satisfaction of the client. If that test is so applied in Scotland to-day, it will reveal that there are a good many parts of our legal machine which are emitting ominous creaks and groans indicative of excessive wear and tear and maladjustment.

Up to a point such symptoms need cause no serious anxiety, and their presence within limits is a criticism neither of Parliament nor of the courts. It is an inherent condition of the problem of government that there should be a time-lag between public opinion and the needs of society on the one hand and the production of an efficiently working rule of domestic law on the other hand. A legal system without critics and incapable of improvement has never been invented, and I should hate the dull task of administering such a system, upon the view that a certain amount of fleas is good for a dog. But the fleas must not be allowed to get the upper hand, and here and there they certainly have.

I cannot cover the field, but I shall single out a few subjects on which the Comparative lawyer could be of help in reconditioning the Scottish legal machine.

I take first an example where a great deal of the work has already been done, because it offers a good instance of an experiment in Comparative Law on the factory scale. It is the developed doctrine of Frustration of Contract ; and you will find ready to your hands in the current numbers of the *Journal of Comparative Legislation* a symposium of papers written by lawyers of many different states and explaining how this new problem, which only rose to prominence during the two world wars, has been handled under different systems. By a happy coincidence the first paper deals with Scots Law, and happens to have been written by myself on the invitation of Sir Arnold McNair. I commend these papers to your study not on that account but because they reveal two things which are apt to be overlooked by the beginner in Comparative Law—(first) the infinitude of subtle yet crucial differences which emerge when different systems with their different methods of approach attack the identical problem ; and (second) the extent to which these differences are deeply rooted in the juristic traditions of the distant past. These papers show that the task of the Comparative lawyer is akin to that of the scholar who seeks to translate a literary classic of one nation into the language and thought of another ; and, if it is to be adequately performed, that is of course an exceedingly difficult task. Whenever, as in these papers, the examination of even a single restricted subject is more than superficial, the student will learn a great deal not only about that restricted subject but also about the background, history and outlook of the several systems to which the enquiry extends.

Another subject which I should like to see treated on similar lines is contributory negligence. In Anglo-American law that subject has latterly degenerated into a branch of scholastic metaphysics, the esoteric mysteries of which will defy comprehension by any jury when juries come back, as they soon will. I hope that Scotland will be able in this respect to lead the way back to our old commonsense simplicity and intelligibility, and that the recent statute introducing generally the Admiralty rule of apportioning liability will sound the death knell of the later pseudo-scientific over-refinements. But we must find out how they manage these things elsewhere than in Britain and America, and the Comparative lawyer will be able to tell us.

Turn now to a different field. For centuries Scotland led the world in the matter of registration of conveyances of land, and our Register of Sasines has served us well since it was established more than 300 years ago. But long before the war our methods were already obsolescent by comparison with the modernised cadastral systems which had been established in many parts of Europe—whether they are still operating I cannot tell, but the machine was admirably finished and equipped—and it would only be appropriate if Scotland, which holds the master patent, were now to embark upon a close study of the newer methods with a view to taking the lead for a second time.

Next I take our law of intestate succession, which literally clamours for restatement. We have clung in Scotland far too long to feudal ideas patched up with bits and pieces of sporadic statutory amendments, but still resting foursquare on the antiquated distinction between heritable and moveable property and the equally antiquated notion that the former is more common and more important than the latter, which it is not. Much of our law on this topic is not only disgracefully untidy but utterly out of touch with reality. No sane testator would to-day dream of doing some of the things which, if he dies intestate, the law does for him. With the Birkenhead reforms in mind I had hoped when Lord Advocate to achieve some reform in this matter, but the foreign situation from 1938 onwards put an end to all that. Here is a subject peculiarly fit for comparative investigation.

Last of my chosen examples is a subject which in this country is now desperately in need of scientific formulation and of which some foreign systems could teach us much—the *droit administratif*. We have the thing, but it is so alien to our traditions that we do not even have a name for it in the English language. For weal or for woe a substantial part of the judicial function has latterly been taken out of the hands of the permanent trained judiciary and confided to all kinds of *ad hoc* tribunals and branches of the executive, who are being left to dispense amateur justice with little or no guidance from constitutional theory or legal principle, and often without legal aid. The process by which justice has come to be administered in the third floor back of a government department is one which a lawyer dislikes but is powerless to arrest ; and I have noted that some of my judicial colleagues have recently been lifting up their voices in the wilderness on this subject. The person who will chiefly suffer will be not the lawyer but the ordinary citizen, and the least we can do is to urge that, if this country is not to drift into an arbitrary totalitarianism in which the Rule of Law will be finally submerged, we should define and control on scientific principles the operations and the methods of this expanding innovation upon our established institutions.

I might pursue my search a good deal further—instancing, for example, the rule in *Rylands* v. *Fletcher*, the rule in *Bradford* v. *Pickles*, and desertion as a ground for separation or divorce, though in taking this last example I am differing from many who think that the law of family relations is outside the limits of comparative study. But we have re-written the law on this subject in a modern statute, and have evidently done that so badly that we have already had a Whole Court case and two House of Lords appeals revealing every possible permutation and combination of judicial opinion, while a third case is at this moment, I believe, on its way to the House of Lords. But I have said enough to indicate my conception of Comparative Law as a most useful and practical contribution to the development and improvement of the law of Scotland. My position might be summarised thus :—(1) The study of Comparative Law can only be pursued to best advantage by those who already possess a competent acquaintance with their own system. It is rather a subject for the postgraduate or honours student than for the tiro. (2) The study can best be pursued in relation to selected topics in which the need for reform is already felt, or on which it can be shown that we have lagged behind other systems in the adoption of new ideas or methods of approach ; (3) The outlook of comparative study, while necessarily embracing Anglo-American Law, should always be expanded to include the rival systems with which we have closer kinship. It is so easy to use Pollock to supplement Gloag, and Winfield to fill in the gaps in Glegg, or Jarman to answer the questions which McLaren left unsolved. But such methods have too often led to our native principles being forced into alien moulds, regardless of the resulting strains and distortions and their habitual use can only end in the slow suffocation of Scots Law as an independent system of jurisprudence.

To those of you who are looking forward to embarking on this new course of study I would say :—Do not think of Comparative Law as a soft option or a mere ornamental addition to the inescapable seven subjects of the legal curriculum. It is something quite different from that. The late Lord Shaw complained that in his student days " law was taught as a trade and learned as a trade " ; and that risk is always present. We dare no longer proceed on such lines nor rest content with narrow horizons. A richer cultural background, a deeper and more exact appreciation of the merits and defects of your own system, and the chance of acquiring the intellectual equipment to enable you to resume the age-old task of adjusting Scots Law to meet the changing needs of changing times, these are the prizes which are offered to the rising generation of lawyers and law students by the study of Comparative Law, and in their pursuit I envy you, and cordially wish you well.

1947

The Future of the Legal Profession

THIS is an age of transition. There is nothing original in that remark, for every age is an age of transition. Nevertheless it is incontrovertible that more has happened to affect the foundations of British life and thought in my own lifetime than had happened during the previous five hundred years. I therefore repeat, this is emphatically an age of transition. I can see the professional road over which I have travelled, but as I look up the hill at the road you will have to pursue, I am reminded of an incident which occurred the other day in an Irish court when a barrister paused in the breathless pursuit of a difficult argument to enquire : " Does your Lordship follow me ? " to which the judge sorrowfully rejoined : " I am following you closely, Mr Sullivan : but, tell me, where are we going ? "

The mantle of the prophet sits uneasily on my shoulders but I have deliberately assumed it in the hope that my audience will be more critical than appreciative. However obscure the omens, the time is ripe for an appraisal of the forces now at work in moulding our profession's future. As a lawyer of to-day, and perhaps of yesterday, I wish to present a few provocative ideas to a gathering of lawyers of tomorrow. Where are we going ?

Note that my subject is not the future of law but the future of the legal profession. These two things, though intimately associated, and to us virtually inseparable, are not identical. Let us begin by asking what is involved in describing the practice of the law as a profession.

It means, I suggest, that the lawyer has adopted as his lifework a vocation, entrance to which is guarded by prescribed standards of scholarship and experience, membership of which confers privileges which are held in public trust, and the pursuit of which entails that the lawyer's duty to his client is always subordinated to his paramount allegiance to the law. The purer the form in which this professional ideal is realised, the closer does membership of our profession approach to priesthood in the temple of Themis, and the further does it recede from every taint of commercialism. Every lawyer, from the youngest intrant to the Lord Chancellor of Great Britain, has devoted himself to the performance of that single function which Bacon happily epitomised in two Latin words, *jus dicere*.

That is the ideal which inspires the legal profession as we know it. Its basis in dogma, unspoken and assumed rather than asserted, is that there exists as the foundation of society and of government a residual framework of law, a *corpus juris*, which it is the lawyer's business to learn and to declare to his fellows in all its infinite applications to daily life and inter-course. That was true in the days of Ulpian and Papinian. It was true when the English Justices fashioned the Common Law and when Stair wrote his Institutions. It was true when the modern Franco-German codes were drafted. It has found its most significant expression in the classic principle which distinguishes a free country from a country subject to arbitrary government—the Rule of Law—which means that all govern-ment is conducted, and all coercive power is applied, only in obedience to pre-established rules fixed and announced beforehand, the effect of which in any given situation is capable, at least in theory, of exact prediction.

That ideal and its complementary dogma are indispensable to a legal profession and to any system of jurisprudence worthy of the name. They held until the other day. Do they still hold?

I must now exhibit to you the skeleton in our professional cupboard. It has always been there, but latterly it has been rattling its bones in a very aggressive fashion. It has shown itself in two ways. The courts of justice have recently been losing a great many customers who have preferred informal arbitration, often before a non-legal arbiter, to litigation in an ordinary court. They would rather hire a room in a hotel and pay fees to an arbiter and his clerk than avail themselves of the facilities provided in the courts at the public expense.

Even when we invent a specially expeditious, informal and inexpensive form of process indistinguishable from a common law arbitration, most of them still prefer to arbitrate. Simultaneously lawyers as a class have in my own time lost a great deal of the authority and esteem in which not long ago they were held in the public mind. Every lawyer who seeks to enter public life has first to overcome the handicap of being a lawyer. Parliamentary success by a lawyer, though not impossible, is hailed when it occurs as veritable triumph of mind over matter and evokes the same kind of admiration which we bestow on a dog which can walk on its hind legs. We are all supposed to be suffering from that incipient ossification of the brain which is politely referred to as the legal mind, and, until the contrary is proved, we are assumed to have an incurable proneness to chicanery.

In the good old days, if I may so describe them, we could have laughed all that off, for our faith and our dogma were never challenged. But the cosmic forces of social and political change, immensely accelerated by the two wars, have transformed a good-humoured suspicion of the law and the legal profession into an undisguised attack upon both. Observe what has been happening.

The statute book, and still more the Statutory Rules and Orders, contain more and more provisions which are incompatible with the Rule of Law. In widening areas of human intercourse law has come to mean specific edicts officially promulgated and applied as instruments of policy. Those concerned in carrying policy into effect have little use for lawyers and have not scrupled to say so. More and more matters affecting the private rights of the subject are being committed to the unexaminable discretion of the executive or the oracular pronouncements of *ad hoc* tribunals, before whom in some cases lawyers are actually forbidden to appear. The permanent judicature is being elbowed out. Law and lawyers are in eclipse.

Do not imagine that this new tendency is associated with the present administration. It is much older than that, and is unconnected with political or economic theory. It has been a feature of the second, third and fourth decades of this century that large and increasing areas of the life of the citizen have been lost to the lawyers and have been occupied by informal tribunals and the bureaucracy. Why? How far have we ourselves to blame? Can we mend our ways?

I have come to think that the root cause of our recent loss of prestige is that we have been making law an end in itself instead of a means to an end, and that the system which we have laboriously constructed is so excessively elaborate that it is breaking down under its own weight. We have fallen victims to our own professional enthusiasm. We have forgotten that the law was made for the citizen, not the citizen for the law.

Eighty or a hundred years ago the typical judicial opinion consisted of a concise formulation of a juristic principle and its logical application to the facts of the case. To-day every other case requires prodigious research and prolonged debate upon the authorities before a court dare commit itself to a decision ; and the moment the decision is pronounced, it is taken down, printed, bound in full calf, and added to the enormous load which burdens our groaning shelves. Our theory is that every decision must be integrated with all that has gone before. Our procedural methods are admirably adapted to that end, and, provided that time and expense are no object, they produce in skilled hands as perfect a result as ingenuity and toil can devise. So far, so good. But are we giving the public what they want? If the customer's purpose can be achieved by using a bicycle or a wheelbarrow, is it wise to tell him that we only deal in post-war Rolls Royces? Or if he wishes to cross from Granton to Burntisland, must we offer to charter a Cunard liner for his use?

Take one example out of many. The Workmen's Compensation Acts provide certain payments to a workman who has been injured by accident arising out of and in the course of his employment. Around that simple provision there have accumulated 3400 reported decisions which are still alive, many of them decisions by the House of Lords. At a moderate estimate they must have cost over £1,000,000 in legal expenses. They reveal incredible refinements, microscopic distinctions, not to mention a good many irreconcilable contradictions, with the result that there are few questions which still arise on which it is not possible for counsel to cite half a dozen seemingly apt precedents on both sides. Is it to be wondered at that under the new legislation which supersedes these Acts the courts have been left out in the cold ?

That instance will indicate what I mean by saying that we have made law an end in itself. We are being slowly suffocated by the doctrine of precedent. Like western civilisation itself law and the legal profession are dying of over-elaboration. With western civilisation the law and the legal profession may be forced to purchase survival at the cost of much simpler ways of life and thought.

These are hard sayings and I tremble at their implications. In large measure we may have to discard the best in favour of the second-best. If the area of our enterprise is much further curtailed and if the market for our products is further restricted, there may be nothing for it but to offer the public mass-produced utility law and risk the consequences.

I gravely fear that some such result will soon ensue on the adoption of the Rushcliffe proposals for making litigation a state service, free or heavily subsidised. But we as a profession must spare no effort to save law and the Rule of Law, and the question is what is to be done to that end ?

My first suggestion is not by any means a new one but it seems to me to be becoming every year more pressing and inevitable. It is the old proposal of codification. All the countries which escaped the influence of English Common Law—and that means half the civilised world—have done it already. They are at work at it even in the United States in their privately sponsored Restatement of the Law. Stair and Erskine and Bell showed us how it could be done for Scots Law before Scots Law had become anglicised. I know the difficulties of this stupendous task. Professor Campbell will tell you all the classical objections to codification and all the advantages in flexibility of judge-made law. But the relentless pressure of circumstances and the threat of strangulation which hangs over the head of our profession puts these objections in their true perspective. All we need is a Scottish Bentham. Perhaps he or she is in this room to-night. Note well, I say a Scottish Bentham. This scheme has nothing to do with English Law and must not be postponed to await leadership from Whitehall or Westminster. It is our own task. We dare not shirk it.

My second suggestion is that we must largely discard our pyramidal structure of courts with successive rights of appeal. A case normally begins in the Sheriff Court or before a Lord Ordinary, thence passes to the Inner House of the Court of Session, and thence perhaps to the House of Lords. It is not unknown for each judgment to be reversed in turn, sometimes by a majority, and for more judicial votes to be cast for the view which ultimately failed than for that which ultimately succeeded. *Victrix causa deis placuit sed victa Catoni.* That type of thing is not a good advertisement for our system ; and the worst of it is that it makes the cost of litigation unpredictable and so deters many a litigant from bringing a good case by the fear of unlimited liability. Such methods are all very well for the important test case or where the parties are agreed from the outset to fight to a finish : but in the ordinary run of cases I should be prepared to take the risk of leaving the judge of first instance final on questions of fact, allowing only a limited appeal on questions of law, and abolishing appeal to the House of Lords except by leave of the Court.

Next, we must get down to the task of formulating a British *droit administratif.* A large area of the field of rights and duties has gone for ever and will never come back to the courts of law. Rightly so, I am inclined to think, for the issues are not truly justiciable issues but more appropriate to ministerial discretion or specialist tribunals. But that does not mean that the Rule of Law and the function of the legal profession are permanently excluded from that field. If we are to steer a safe course for society between despotism and anarchy, we must aim at the acceptance of a code of rules based on the essentials of natural justice which will define the minimum conditions under which the rights and duties of the citizen can be determined otherwise than in an ordinary court.   The decisions may be unexaminable on their merits. The conditions under which the decisions are reached must remain in the independent hands of the courts.

These three tasks, amongst others, will fall to be tackled by the legal profession of Scotland in your time, if not in mine ; and there is one invaluable preparation for their study which I would commend to your attention, and that is the science of Comparative Law.   The besetting sin of the legal profession is insularity, and in Scotland and England that disease has become epidemic.   The English legal profession will doubtless die true to the central article of its creed that the Common Law of England is incomparable.   We in Scotland have nothing to do with that, for the Scottish lawyer has been first and foremost a comparative lawyer since the thirteenth century, and when he ceases to be a comparative lawyer Scots Law will die.   Other legal systems than Scots Law and English Law have faced and solved in different ways the problems which confront us, and we have much to learn both from the mistakes they made and the fruitful expedients they devised. In Aberdeen they have recently established a lectureship on Comparative Law, and it is high time that Edinburgh and Glasgow followed suit.   The subject is one which is barely capable of being studied in books, because they are so few and because each system of law thinks its own thoughts and speaks its own language, so that the interpretation of one to another is extraordinarily hard.   But the difficulties must be overcome for we dare not evade or shirk them any longer.

These, it seems to me, are some of the tasks that lie nearest to your hand.   If you ask me for a distant forecast I answer that, if civilisation as we have known it survives, the law and the legal profession will assuredly resume throughout the whole of the old area its traditional function of *jus dicere.* In so saying I am not thinking of the selfish interests of the profession, for any profession which was actuated by such interests would be doomed.   I am thinking rather of that service which the legal profession alone can render to society, a service which, in the words of Lord Clyde " every human community craves, without which no human community can hold together, and on the well or ill performance of which every human community depends." And so I end where I began by insisting that even in these difficult days you, who are at the threshold of a professional career in law, may stand firmly by the old professional ideal and rest securely upon its traditional creed.

1947

The Authorship of the Berne MS.

IN A NOTE contributed to the Edinburgh Bibliographical Transactions [1] the writer drew attention to certain suggestive features of the Berne MS. ; and further study has enabled him to amplify and correct the evidence and to deduce from it guarded conclusions as to the origin and authorship of the collection.

The Berne MS. contains the earliest written record of any considerable body of Scots Law. To it we owe many of the statutes of William and Alexander II, the Laws of the Brets and Scots, and part of the Laws of the Four Burghs ; and originally there must have been a good deal more, for the record breaks off abruptly in the middle of a paragraph, the remaining leaves having been torn off.

The MS., as we have it, extends to 63 folios ; and if it had ended at folio 59, it would probably never have been heard of, and would certainly never have reached H.M. Register House. These 59 folios contain nothing but a typical compendium of English legal material, similar in scope to many like collections which have survived in the South—a text of Glanvill, a list of English Kings and Dukes of Normandy, the Statute of Marlborough, the Laws of the Marches of 1249, and a Register of Writs. In the words of Maitland [2] such collections were " the property of some lawyer or religious house . . . lent by lawyer to lawyer, by abbey to abbey, for the purpose of being copied." We have our own counterparts in the Ayr, Bute and Cromertie MSS. and perhaps in Regiam Majestatem. These collections were the medieval equivalent of the modern office library, into which the lawyer put everything likely to be useful in his daily work ; and each tells us something of the background and experience of its compiler,

[1] Vol. ii. (1938-45), 379.   [2] *Collected Papers*, ii. 110.

though it usually extends to only one-tenth as many pages as
the modern lawyer needs in stout calf volumes.

But the Berne MS. does not stop at folio 59. It is there that
the English Law ends, but the compiler immediately proceeds
with a second part, introduced by the words " Incipiunt leges
scocie." So far as is known this is the only composite collection
containing the laws of more than one system. In the blank
space separating the English from the Scots Law there is drawn
an amphisbaena, or two-headed lizard, gazing with rapt
amazement at the " leges scocie " : and the reader must
apply his own interpretation to this mystic symbol.

The compilation of the Berne MS. can be dated with confidence about 1272. The contents are typical of the later years
of Henry III, but a few marginal additions and interlineations
in a different hand, carry us over into the reign of Edward I.
At that date it is impossible to suppose that an incursion across
the Border would be inspired by an academic interest in
comparative jurisprudence. Moreover the collection is manifestly a *vade mecum* for a practitioner, and not a source book for
a jurist. The question is—How did it come about that an
English lawyer in 1272 thought it worth his while to equip
himself with a Scottish law library ?

Cosmo Innes has told us all that is known about the later
history of the Berne MS.[1] but neither here nor anywhere else
shall we discover any extrinsic evidence bearing upon our
problem. Any light that can be gained must be found in a
study of the intrinsic evidence which the collection itself
affords. The one chapter in the collection which promises
aid in our search is the Register of Writs. It is a very large
register for the period, extending to 323 writs, most of which
are " original " writs. Lawyers have not changed much
through the centuries, and every enterprising lawyer when
making his own collection of styles is rarely content with the
standard forms, but usually retains, from professional interest
and on the off-chance that they may be useful, any odd or
interesting styles which he has encountered in his own practice.
The compiler of the Berne MS. seems to have been a person of

[1] *Acts Parl. Scot.*, i. 177-8.

this type. When transcribing his text of Glanvill—and a very good text it seems to be, though Professor Woodbine did not use it—he was perforce obliged to copy into his compendium the 80 impersonal styles which Glanvill used to illustrate his exposition of procedure ; and, when he came to construct his own collection of " Brevia originalia de cancelaria," he evidently made up his mind to enliven his register by interspersing amongst the abbreviated and impersonal forms a liberal selection from the processes in his own pigeonholes or from the forms which he had copied from the papers of other lawyers. Anyhow we find in this register some 60 writs of which it is possible to assert that some of them undoubtedly were, and the balance almost certainly were, employed in real litigations. Whether the compiler had been engaged as pleader or attorney in all these cases, or whether he had only availed himself of the chance of taking a copy of the writs, we cannot be sure ; but an analysis of the contents of these writs, in so far as the particulars are given with sufficient fullness to enable the persons and places to be identified, leads to some interesting results.

The High Court cases introduce us to most of the famous judges of the day, and it is doubtless a mere coincidence that Gilbert Preston and Richard Middleton are by far the commonest names, and that Westminster, and not an assise town, is by far the commonest venue. But when we pass to the County Court we get our first clue. Of 18 writs addressed to the Sheriff by his full title, 7 are addressed to the Sheriff of York ; 5 to the Sheriff of Northumberland ; 2 to the Sheriff at Norwich ; and 1 each to the Sheriffs of Westmoreland, Northampton, Huntingdon and Oxford. There is also an incidental invocation of the Sheriff of Wiltshire.

The same unequal local distribution is evident in the ecclesiastical group of writs, which contain 3 references to the Archbishop of York, 2 to the Bishop of Lincoln, and 1 to the Bishop of Carlisle, but none to any other prelate. There is also an appointment of an attorney to a Bishop of Winchester.

The writs contain about 50 place names of which 41 are identifiable with some confidence, though not with certainty.

They are shown on the accompanying sketch map. It will be noted that 26 are in Yorkshire or farther north, 11 in East Anglia, and only 4 in the remainder of England and Wales, the outlying places being Oxford, Kidderminster, Harlech and Kingston Deverell (Wiltshire).

From these facts it is plain that the compiler's predominating interest was in the Northern counties, and to a lesser extent in East Anglia or the Fen districts of England. But when we pass from places to persons, the analysis presents greater difficulty ; and the analyser who, without a competent knowledge of the records of thirteenth-century England, engages in a foray across the Border is soon made painfully aware of his limitations. We find amongst the plaintiffs and defendants upwards of 70 different individuals and 11 ecclesiastical houses. With only a few exceptions, the names of the individuals occur only once, and (apart from one or two instances) they appear to be undistinguished people—small landowners or tenants evicted from their possessions, widows of such persons, people complaining of sundry trespasses or seeking to recover debts or to establish their right to succeed to an ancestor. Others better qualified than the writer might well be able to trace relationships between the members of this motley assortment of litigants. In the great majority of instances the writer can find no point of contact except the fact that the papers in their cases somehow passed through the hands of the compiler of the Berne MS. In particular there is nothing to suggest that we are dealing with a selection from the muniments of noble houses, subject to one important exception to be later examined. Similarly the list of ecclesiastical litigants is uninformative. They never litigate with each other but always with a private individual, and they are curiously assorted. They include the Abbot of St Peter's, Westminster ; the Dean and Chapter of St Paul's, London ; the Dean and Chapter of St Peter's, Lisieux ; the Abbot of Ramsey ; the Abbot of Selby ; the Abbot of Cerne ; the Abbot of Sibton ; the Master of St Giles of Beverley ; and an unnamed Abbot with lands in Westmorland.

Let us now consider the few cases in which the same

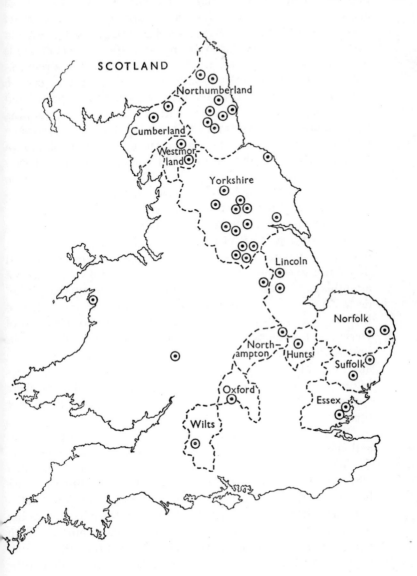

persons appear on more than one occasion.　Nos. 66 and 68 are two writs by which William de Grantcourt sought relief from various parties from the services sought to be exacted from him by Warren, Earl of Surrey, in respect of certain lands in Norfolk.　Nos. 199 and 322 relate to two stages in a remarkable action by the widow, Agnes de Vesa, against certain " homines " of the Abbey of Whitby who had misappropriated a cargo of wax and other commodities which she was shipping from Flanders.　Nos. 30 and 258 are two actions at the instance of Lisieux Cathedral, the one relating to their manor of Kingston Deverell, and the other for enforcement of a security obligation against R. de Vernon.　The next example (Nos. 269, 64, 65 and 270) is the most significant, for it suggests a point of contact with Scotland and with the Baliol family.

No. 269 is a multiple judicial writ dealing with the appointment of attorneys to Robert de Vipont, he being *languidus*.　In one of the actions narrated in this writ, de Vipont is opposed in a claim to certain manors in Westmoreland by a formidable assemblage of notabilities—John Baliol and Devorguilla ;　Alan de la Zouche and his wife, Elena ;　Alexander Comyn, Earl of Buchan, and his Countess Isabella ;　and Margaret, Countess of Derby.　The identical writ appears in the Coram Rege Rolls under date 29th April 1263, and is calendared by Bain [1] ; and from a later entry in Bain [2] we discover that the four ladies in question claimed descent from Hugo de Moreville and were engaged as heirs-portioners in a leisurely campaign to recover the ancestral estates.

Next we have in Nos. 64 and 65 two writs relating to an action by the Abbot of Ramsey claiming from Devorguilla the fishings in the River Elton in Huntingdon.　No. 64 is dated 26th October 1269.　Here too the reality of the litigation can be independently vouched.　Many years before John Baliol had evicted the monks *vi et potestate*, and when the Abbot retorted with a writ of right Baliol offered combat.[3]　Both parties named their champions, but it seems that the combat never took place, the Abbot's view doubtless being that, if he

[1] *Calendar*, i. No. 2333.　　　[2] *Calendar*, ii. No. 169.
[3] *Ramsey Cartulary*, i. 490 ;　Bain's *Calendar*, i. No. 230.

could bide his time till the old man died, he would find the widow easier to deal with. If that is what he thought, he was wrong. No. 65 must have been prepared and executed immediately after Baliol's death, but it was not until nineteen years later, and when a new Abbot reigned at Ramsey, that the action was settled by a final concord before the Justices at Westminster.[1] At this settlement appearance was made for Devorguilla by her seneschal, Richard Foxstone.

Finally, No. 270 is a writ appointing attorneys to Eustace Baliol to act for him during his absence overseas. This writ must have been issued about sixty years earlier.

The effort must now be made with the aid of this very miscellaneous mass of information to narrow the possibilities bearing upon the authorship of the Berne MS. and to account for its characteristics. We can be tolerably certain that the compiler of this register of writs was not permanently attached to a cathedral chapter or conventual house as their man of business, for there is an absence of the types of writ which would be most familiar to a man of that class, and the vast majority of the cases from which he draws his examples are litigations between two or more laymen. He may have been a cleric, and quite probably was. He may even have spent part of his life in a religious house. But the experience gained by the collector of these 323 styles was not acquired in a cloister.

Was he then the steward or seneschal of a noble house, or of several noble houses in succession, performing the duties described in Dr Denholm-Young's *Seignorial Administration in England*? The suggested answer is that he must at some time have been attached to the Baliol household, and possibly to some others, but that his professional interests and outlook were much wider than would be expected in a full-time professional servant of this type. As he had access to the papers in one case in which John Baliol and Devorguilla were plaintiffs, and in another case six years later in which Devorguilla was defendant, and as he also had examined the old writ granted two generations previously to Baliol's grandfather, it is almost certain that he was familiar with the Baliol charter chest

[1] *Ramsey Cartulary*, ii. 361.

and muniment room at Barnard Castle or elsewhere. Incidentally Barnard Castle is in the heart of the area in which most of the places mentioned in the Berne MS. are found.

But if a Baliol connection will explain much in the Berne MS. it will not explain everything. We have still to account for the compiler's apparent interests in Lincoln, Norfolk and Suffolk, and his wide contacts with some at least of the 70 individual litigants and 11 ecclesiastical litigants. There is of course no proof that he advised or acted for any of these parties, the possibility being that, having somehow contrived to obtain possession of the writs, he merely copied them into his book, gleaning from harvests that others had reaped. But surely this is to allow scepticism to run riot, and to ask too much of sheer coincidence ? In many of the writs which are set out at length with particulars of the persons and places, there is nothing in the style as such which could not equally well have been recorded as a dispute between *talis* and *talem* regarding lands in *tali villa*, or (after the fashion of Glanvill) by the use of alphabetical letters. When in these 60 odd instances the compiler takes the trouble to record the particulars in full, the high probability is that he did so because in some capacity he had been interested in the case. In particular it is difficult to suppose that, if he was a casual anthologist, he would have hit upon several instances in which the same plaintiffs recur. It is much more likely that de Grantcourt, the widow de Vesa, and Lisieux Cathedral were his own clients—and if they and the Baliols were, why not some at least of the others ?

Upon this view the theory which would best account for the features of the Berne MS. would be this. The compiler, after serving his apprenticeship to the law in Holy Orders and perhaps in some conventual house, began his working life in the neighbourhood of Norwich, doubtless as a steward in the household of some important family. He was allowed to act as pleader or attorney for various persons in East Anglia and elsewhere, and acquired an extensive connection and a reputation, which led to his services being given as " local solicitor " to distant abbeys and even to a Norman cathedral. He may have transferred for a time to Wiltshire or Hampshire ; but later he moved north and settled in Yorkshire, probably in the service of the Baliol family, and there extended his general practice to cover a large part of the Northern counties. We may even pursue a little further a very slender clue. In 1274 Devorguilla, as her husband's executrix, was employing Richard Foxstone to wind up the deceased's estate.[1] In 1286, when she paid a long visit to Scotland, she left her affairs in the hands of two attorneys, Richard Foxstone and Thomas de la More.[2] In 1288, as we have seen, Richard Foxstone was conducting the Ramsey litigation at Westminster on behalf of Devorguilla. In 1289 Thomas de la More was called along with Devorguilla as joint defendant in an action.[3] Devorguilla died early in 1290 and Thomas de la More was appointed her executor.[4] In the following year Thomas de la More, as such executor, appointed Richard Foxstone as his attorney for three years.[5] In 1293 Thomas de la More appears as attorney for the younger John Baliol, then King of Scotland.[6] The Berne MS. *might* have been compiled in the office of Foxstone and de la More and it *must* have been compiled by some person who at some stage in his career occupied a position similar to that held by these men.

This does not mean that, if there had been a Law List in the thirteenth century, it would have contained in leaded type an entry relating to the firm of " Foxstone, de la More and Company, Solicitors, York, formerly of Norwich." But the evidence is accumulating to suggest that it is no anachronism to maintain that even in those days someone very like the modern practising solicitor had already made his appearance, and that the lawyer was not always and exclusively the full-time servant of a monastery or the full-time member of a noble household. It must have been so. The ordinary persons whom we find litigating by the thousand in the Royal Courts could not possibly grapple with the incredible intricacies of Bractonian law and procedure without skilled aid. How exactly things were managed is not yet clear, but we have

---

[1] Bain's *Calendar*, ii. No. 13.
[2] *Ibid.*, ii. No. 274.
[3] Stevenson, *Hist. Doc. Scot.*, i. 93.
[4] Bain's *Calendar*, ii. No. 535.
[5] Stevenson, *op. cit.*, i. 215.
[6] Bain's *Calendar*, ii. No. 681.

many glimpses of the thirteenth-century attorney and pleader at work,[1] and even in Scotland, where procedure was simpler, Adam Urri was incurring censure in 1283 for turning his knowledge of law to account by accepting fees from clients.[2] The only explanation which will fully account for all the characteristics of the Berne MS. is that it was compiled for the office use of such a person who, in addition to acting at different times for one or more seignorial households or religious houses on a quasi-permanent basis, also engaged widely in what might be called general practice.

If this is the true view we can watch the Berne MS. growing page by page. In his early days in Norfolk the compiler's needs would be met by Glanvill and the other purely English material. But when in later years he moved to Yorkshire and fell in with the Baliols and their Scottish connections, and still more when his professional interests affected lands and landowners in Northumberland and Cumberland, the latest edition of the Laws of the Marches would be an obvious acquisition. Some of the actions relating to places around Alnwick would bring him within measurable distance of Berwick and Roxburgh where the Laws of the Four Burghs prevailed and where he would also learn of the leading Scottish statutes. Unable perhaps to procure a reliable " Scottish correspondent," or imagining (as some of his twentieth-century successors still fondly imagine) that it is possible for a lawyer of one country to practise in another, he would acquire copies of these Scottish provisions to aid him in advising clients with Scottish possessions. His visits to Carlisle and Stapleton would bring him close to the areas where the Laws of the Brets and Scots still prevailed, and it is significant that his copy of these laws is in Norman French.

In all this there is a good deal of imaginative conjecture, incapable of verification and at points liable to refutation. The writer is fully conscious of the fact that he has not squeezed the orange dry, and that any English medievalist, if he could

---

[1] Pollock and Maitland, *History of English Law*, i. 191 ; Holdsworth, *History of English Law*, ii. 315 ; *Introd. to the Curia Regis Rolls* (Selden Soc.), 405 ff.

[2] *Chron. Lanercost*, s. a. 1283.

be induced to spend a few hours on this register of writs, would doubtless discover much that eludes everyone but the specialist. The reader will judge whether the suggested line of enquiry is a fruitful one, and whether these provisional conclusions offer a plausible answer to the question that was posed.

1948

The Scottish Legal Tradition

I. Introductory

FOR a lawyer to write about law for the benefit of laymen may not seem a very hopeful project, and it is certainly not an easy one. But one of the declared objects of the Saltire Society is to make Scotland conscious of her heritage ; and of all the items which add up to make the sum total of that heritage none is more distinctive than Scotland's contribution to law. If the present series is to attain its purpose of disseminating knowledge of our record in order that this generation may draw inspiration from the past for further advances in the future, then assuredly it is impossible to dispense with a pamphlet devoted to the Scottish Legal Tradition.

The reader need not be afraid of being immersed in the pages which follow in any detailed exposition of the technicalities of legal doctrine or practice. The aim is a different one. It is to outline some special characteristics of our system, and to indicate how it came into being, its peculiar excellences and defects, and the prospects for the future. It will of course be necessary to paint with a broad brush and to generalise widely, ignoring the qualifications and explanations which would be indispensable in a legal treatise, which this is not.

An enquiry on such lines should suggest fruitful ideas, for Scots Law is in a special sense the mirror of Scotland's history and traditions and a typical product of the national character, and it is just as truly a part of our national inheritance as our language or literature or religion. But the enquiry has more than a general cultural value. It has a present practical significance because it touches a matter which might at any time develop into a live political and social issue. This point requires a word of explanation.

If we exclude Russia, regarding which our information is still regrettably imperfect, two schools of legal thought have latterly been competing for the allegiance of the modern world —the Anglo-American and the Continental or Franco-German—the first founded upon English common law and equity and therefore predominantly inductive and empirical, and the second founded on the law of Rome and its modern offshoots in many recent codifications, and therefore predominantly systematic and deductive. Each of these schools can number its adherents in populations of hundreds of millions. Each has extended its sphere of influence far beyond the countries of its origin, initially as a result of conquest or colonisation, and latterly through voluntary adoption or imitation. Both systems are original : both can point to unbroken development from the distant past : and they are fundamentally different. Broadly speaking, every system of law now in use by the advanced civilisations of the present day belongs either to the one school or to the other, and the single effective choice which is available to-day to any state in search of a new code of law is to seek inspiration either in Anglo-American law or in Franco-German law. In every state, of course, the legal system always presents many local characteristics, and carries forward from its past a substantial element of national custom and tradition. But the moment we penetrate beneath the surface the dualism of modern law becomes unmistakable. It is as if the lawyers of the world spoke only in one or other of two languages and reasoned only in obedience to one or other of two methods of thought.

From this cosmic conflict in the field of law Scotland stands apart, content with a system of her own devising, which, as we shall see, now occupies a position somewhere midway between the two great opposing schools. And yet the citizens who look to Edinburgh for their supreme courts number only five millions. Scots Law has never been imposed, adopted or imitated *as a system* beyond the boundaries of Scotland. And when a Scot settles abroad, as so many do, he does not carry his native law with him.

In these remarkable circumstances the question which arises, and may at any time be pressed, is—How do we justify the retention in so small a country of an independent legal system ? This pamphlet may supply some material for an answer.

One further introductory caution may not be amiss. The lay reader who derives his impressions from the public press may be excused for imagining that the chief concern of the lawyer is with sensational murder trials and the latest regulations of the Ministry of Food. Similar misplaced emphasis would classify the works of Edgar Wallace and the Telephone Directory as masterpieces of English literature. A few hours spent in the Parliament House would correct such misconceptions. The law relating to murder and other major crimes is of considerable interest to practitioners in the Court of Justiciary—and to the accused—but it has little or no practical importance for the great mass of law-abiding citizens, and most lawyers contrive to lead a busy and useful professional life without once being involved in a *cause célèbre*. Similarly, we are all imprisoned in the network of modern departmental regulations, but these administrative directions have no better title to be recognised as an integral part of our system of jurisprudence than the current issue of the railway timetable. Accordingly, when we speak of a legal system let us think rather of the body of principles and doctrines which determine personal status and relations, which regulate the acquisition and enjoyment of property and its transfer between the living or its transmission from the dead, which define and control contractual and other obligations, and which provide for the enforcement of rights and the remedying of wrongs. These are the matters which inevitably touch the lives of all citizens at many points from the cradle to the grave, and their regulation is a function of government with which no civilised community can dispense and on the due administration of which the well-being of every society depends.

If you would know what a thing is, you must know how it came to be what it is : and if we are to acquire a just perspective for a brief survey of the modern law, we must consider first the pedigree of its leading doctrines. Let us therefore begin with the historical background.

II. The Historical Background

By contrast with the Anglo-American and Continental systems Scots Law is a comparative novelty. Though many of its roots extend far back into history, it is substantially true to say that our modern system of law only came into being in the later seventeenth century, and that it owed its birth to the synthetic genius of Viscount Stair, the author of our earliest institutional work, who fashioned out of a mass of partially digested raw material a coherent system of jurisprudence. For present purposes we cannot ignore pre-Stair law, but we need not linger beside it.

When Scots Law first emerges above the horizons of reliable history in the twelfth and thirteenth centuries, it is in the main Anglo-Norman law—with a difference. These were the days when England led the world of law, and it was only natural that under the prevalent Norman influences Scotland should borrow from England many of the ingenious and novel institutions and devices which were being successfully tried out in the South ; and these were superimposed upon a stratum of local customary law and a certain amount of Canon and Roman Law, which we owed to the ubiquitous and omnicompetent ecclesiastical organisation of Innocent III and his successors. But there was no slavish copying. Even in those early days the Scottish mind evidently recoiled from excessive intricacy and artificiality, such as disfigured the English Law of Edward I, and it was not a case of wholesale and indiscriminate borrowing but of critical picking and choosing, simplifying, adapting and rationalising. Before the end of the thirteenth century Scots Law and English Law were already recognisably different, though bearing many marks of close relationship.

Then came the Wars of Independence, the greatest line of cleavage in all Scottish history, and the initial phase of Scottish legal development came to an abrupt end. We carried forward from the initial phase into the later law something of the grammar and even the idiom of Roman and Canon Law and not a little local custom, but of English Law not a trace. Of course Feudal Law persisted (and persists to this day) but it was not in England that Feudalism was invented. For four hundred years Scots lawyers resolutely turned their backs upon England and English Law ; and the law students from Scotland who had begun to flock to the University of Oxford later found in Bologna and Pisa, then in Paris and Orleans, and finally in Leyden and Utrecht, a more congenial atmosphere for study and a powerful source of inspiration for constructive work.

The political strife and economic troubles of the fourteenth and fifteenth centuries were hardly compatible with the development of private law, and this is the Dark Age of our legal history, only fitfully illuminated by a number of remarkable " statutes," which are still pivots of our law and which show that, despite the difficulties of their task, the lawyers had never laid their work aside. In process of time the French alliance and the steady pressure of Continental influences bore fruit in the gradual incorporation into Scots Law of a great mass of the Roman Law as taught by the French and Dutch civilians, which made an irresistible appeal to the Scottish mind. Once again the appropriation was not indiscriminate but carefully selective, the choice being confined to broad principles and praetorian equity, by recourse to which the gaps in our infant philosophy of law were repaired and its imperfections cured.

With the establishment of the Court of Session in 1532 the stage seemed to be set for an immediate and notable legal advance, but the religious and political controversies of the sixteenth and early seventeenth centuries were unpropitious for the arts of peace and distracted the lawyers from their long-term programme. Remarkable developments took place in certain directions, especially in relation to the land laws, but on the whole the advance was haphazard and unsystematic. In the Commonwealth period there occurred a complete but temporary break in Scottish legal administration when the Court of Session was superseded for some years by Cromwell's nominees. But when the " English Judges " disappeared at the Restoration, their work and influence vanished with them,

and the broken threads were picked up and united once
again.

Then came Stair. The publication of his *Institutions* in
1681 marked the creation of Scots Law as we have since known
it—an original amalgam of Roman Law, Feudal Law and
native customary law, systematised by resort to the law of
nature and the Bible, and illuminated by many flashes of ideal
metaphysic. To this work and its author every Scots lawyer
has since paid a tribute of almost superstitious reverence, and
the resort still occasionally made to Stair in the House of Lords
and the Privy Council suggests that it is not only in the estimation of his fellow-countrymen that he falls to be ranked amongst
the great jurists of all time.

Throughout the eighteenth century development proceeded
at a steadily increasing pace with continued reliance upon the
law of Rome and with a revival of interest in Feudal Law as a
consequence of the forfeitures and redistribution of lands
following upon the Jacobite rebellions. The position was
strongly consolidated by the posthumous publication in 1773
of the second of our great institutional works, Erskine's
Institute—not an original creation like Stair's unique work, but
a comprehensive re-statement of the law of unchallenged
authority, descriptive of the system as it had developed to
meet the changed circumstances of the writer's age.

Meantime commerce had come to occupy a more important
place in the affairs of men, and the international contacts to
which it gave rise attracted increasing attention to the Law
Merchant as it was being developed in England and elsewhere.
For the third time in three successive centuries a Scottish
jurist of world fame was ready to supply the need, and with
the appearance early in the nineteenth century of his *Commentaries* and *Principles* George Joseph Bell took his well-
merited place alongside Stair and Erskine as the third member
of the Scottish legal trinity.

Let us pause to single out some salient features of this
abbreviated retrospect.

(1) For long the story of Scots Law is simply a record of
false starts and rejected experiments. This was not the fault

M

of our lawyers but their misfortune, for the interruptions in
their work were due to the disasters which successively over-
whelmed their country, and their successive changes of outlook
faithfully reflect the vicissitudes of their distracted fellow-
citizens.

(2) Throughout the bulk of the formative period Scotland
was too small and her executive government was far too weak
to admit of the evolution of an entirely original legal system.
There has never been much in Scots law which is indigenous
to Scotland. Our lawmakers wisely preferred to exercise
their originality in selecting what they thought best in the
systems which they saw around them and in avoiding the
mistakes into which they considered that other systems had
fallen. Twice over—first in the thirteenth and then in the
seventeenth century—Scotland constructed a legal system out
of imported ideas, and on both occasions the work was done
with a sturdy independence of outlook. From first to last the
effort was to attain simplicity, flexibility and directness, and to
attain these things systematically.

(3) The Fates, who so relentlessly deferred and frustrated
the construction of our legal system, and even despoiled us of
our legal records—once by the hands of Edward I and a
second time by the hands of Oliver Cromwell—made handsome reparation when they eventually sent us the three jurists
whose masterpieces have done so much to create and to preserve
the rational simplicity of Scots Law.

(4) In the eighteenth century Scots Law came within an
ace of sinking its identity in the Franco-German school, and
only failed to do so because of the growing power of the
political forces introduced by the Union of 1707. To this day
our legal affinities are markedly closer with this school than
with Anglo-American Law, though we have latterly moved—
or drifted—to an intermediate position.

It has been well said that the fabric of mature Scots Law
is as variegated as a tartan. But it is possible to overstress the
vicissitudes through which our law has passed and the lack of
real continuity in its development. The forgotten architects
of our system, who toiled over a heart-breaking task for

hundreds of years, were all possessed of the same qualities—self-reliant, severely practical, invincibly logical and with a metaphysical bent—and they had something within them correspondent to the spirit of the supreme achievements of Roman jurisprudence. When at long last they had completed their task in the early nineteenth century, they had furnished Scotland with what most comparative lawyers will agree was an admirably finished philosophical system, well in advance of its times. That result was attained by the persevering application of the same technique—the contriving of the fewest possible number of tools capable of performing the largest possible number of different jobs, and the deduction of the widest possible range of consequences from the smallest possible number of carefully chosen general principles. These men may not have been creative artists in law, but they were supremely successful craftsmen.

III. The Present Position

It was of set purpose that in our historical survey the line was drawn about 1820. That may seem a long time ago, but the purpose of history is not to chronicle events but to isolate and interpret controlling tendencies ; and we are still too near the trees of the nineteenth century to see the wood. In law the last one hundred and twenty years belong to the dynamic present rather than to the historic past.

It is now convenient to introduce one technical term, beloved of British lawyers, and used by them in so many different senses as sorely to mystify the Continental school of jurisprudence—the Common Law. Let us define it as meaning the whole of our legal rules and doctrines which are not derived from enactments of the United Kingdom Parliament. In this sense the great bulk of the law of Scotland in 1820 was Common Law, owing its origin to Roman Law, Feudal Law and ancient customs, as developed, interpreted and applied by the courts and expounded by the institutional writers. The first leading characteristic of the period since 1820 has been the

steady encroachment of modern statute upon the Common
Law, mainly as the fruit of conscious efforts at law reform, but
sometimes as the by-product of political and social theory. The
formidable and still rising torrent of Acts, Regulations and
Orders has been the subject of many an unavailing protest by
lawyers and laymen alike, and the rule to which we still pay
lip service that every citizen is presumed to know the law has
long since degenerated into a pious fiction. Indeed there are
now vast tracts of so-called " law " the mastery of each of
which is the lifework of a specialist—Income Tax, Social
Insurance, Local Government and many others—and, although
the interpretation and application of the positive rules which
deal with such matters now engage much of the time and
attention of the courts, none of them contains more than a
faint tincture of juristic principle. The attitude of the normal
lawyer to the provisions which define and regulate these sub-
legal matters is that of the mathematician to the table of
logarithms. He consults them when required, and then
dismisses them from his mind. The important point for the
layman to grasp is that, despite this enormous accretion of the
indispensable apparatus of the complicated modern state, it
is still the Common Law of Scotland that regulates and defines
all the main rights and duties of the Scottish citizen. In 1948
as in 1820 the great bulk of the law of Scotland is still Common
Law—improved, simplified and modified in details, but in
essence the same.

The second leading characteristic of the period since 1820
has been the revival of English influence, not as in the thirteenth
century through the conscious pursuit by Scots lawyers of a
desirable foreign contact, but unsought and indirect. It has
made itself felt increasingly through two different channels,
each of which merits examination.

The first is the legislative practice adopted at Westminster
through pressure of work whereby statutes are normally
drafted by English lawyers for England, and then applied with
the minimum of " adaptation " to Scotland, the tacit assumption being that whatever England wants must be good enough
for Scotland, and that statutes should always conform as

closely as possible to a uniform pattern, capable of being understood and applied from London by one set of officials. In the
purely administrative and governmental sphere this legislative
technique is an intelligible consequence of the political union
between the two countries, and often does no harm. But in
the last fifty years the statute book will reveal not a few
instances of the forcible compression of Scottish legal principles into English moulds without much regard for the
resulting strains and distortions. Every translator knows that
there are many terms in one language which have no exact
equivalent in another ; and what is true of language is also true
of law.

The second channel of English influence is the House of
Lords, the final court of appeal for Scotland in civil (but not in
criminal) cases. We are habituated in these islands to constitutional usages which defy logical justification but which
nevertheless work ; and that is probably why we see nothing
anomalous in confiding the last word on a Roman system of
law to a court whose members are drawn predominantly from
the opposite camp of Anglo-American Law. As was observed
of Newman's conversion, the matter has been apologised for
but never explained. No difficulty arises when the case
relates, as so many appeals do, to some problem in fiscal or other
modern legislation common to the United Kingdom. But
when the matter in issue is some narrowly balanced problem
of Scots Common Law, it is only natural that an English
lawyer's search for a solution should be from the angle of
English Common Law and equity and that his logical processes
should be inductive and empirical. As a result it has happened
that there have been authoritatively imposed upon our
Common Law more than one complete innovation for which
Scottish lawyers have not been enthusiastic in their acknowledgments, and one of which has recently had to be excised by
the surgical operation of an amending Act. Even in our own
courts cases have occurred to which our own law provided no
explicit answer but English law did, or appeared to do ; and
in such cases it is very tempting to adopt the ready-made
English solution and to justify the adoption by the assertion

that in regard to the matter in hand the two systems are the same. They rarely are. The resemblance is usually superficial.

The academic lawyers of many countries are widely discussing to-day the ideal of the eventual fusion of the Roman and the Anglo-American schools of legal thought in a super-system, so rational in its conceptions and so compelling in its equity as to command universal assent. Such an ideal, assuming it to be desirable and practicable, would be better achieved by mutual co-operation between the two schools in a systematic attack upon the problem and in an effort to reconcile deduction and empiricism rather than by the haphazard inoculation of one system with ideas taken from another.

Be that as it may, the fact is that Scots Law and English Law are to-day much closer to each other than when Bell wrote his *Principles*, and Scots Law has correspondingly drifted further away from the Continental school of thought. The traffic in ideas between Scotland and England has not been one-way traffic, for England has recently incorporated in her system a good deal that Scotland already possessed. The two outstanding matters in regard to which Scotland has latterly followed the English, and rejected the Continental, tradition are :—(i) in adopting, almost unconsciously, the English rule of the rigidly binding force of judicial precedents, and (ii) in rejecting large-scale codification, now almost invariable outside the Anglo-American camp, and leaving her Common Law as judge-made law. These things are now second nature to us, but they represent a significant departure from the Scottish tradition, and they still excite the comment of jurists of the Continental school. Codification, or something very like it, has of course been undertaken in special branches of modern mercantile law which transcends national boundaries ; but our old Common Law is still uncodified and likely to remain so, though Bell demonstrated long ago how it might be done.

But the anchors of the Common Law of Scotland have not yet dragged. We still retain, and are justified in retaining, in their pristine purity the mass of our classical principles. There are two special matters in respect of which we have always differed from Anglo-American Law, (i) in refusing to admit any distinction whatever between law and equity, and in having from the first merged the Chancery and the Common Law Courts in one ; and (ii) in subordinating the remedy to the right, and attaching no importance or value to forms of action as such. These distinctions may seem of small significance to a layman, and they are certainly much less important to-day than they were a generation or two ago. But they still vitally affect the processes of thought by which a Scots and an English lawyer respectively attack a legal problem, and the lines of approach adopted by the two systems in expanding and developing the law to meet the changing needs of a changing society.

Every allowance must be made for the partialities and prejudices created in every lawyer in the course of a professional lifetime devoted to the study and application of any one system ; but this assertion may be ventured that, tested by the standards of the modern philosophy of jurisprudence and by experience, the classical law of Stair, Erskine and Bell has proved to be eminently suited to Scottish needs and eminently capable of adaptation and adjustment to solve the new problems of a transformed social world, which its authors never beheld even in a vision.

Let us now descend from generalities to particulars by passing in review a few of the distinctive features of Scots Law. The limits imposed by this short study demand that this review should be highly selective ; but the broad outlines of the complete picture will sufficiently appear from a glance at the law of the family, the land laws, the law of succession, the law of contract, the law of reparation, the civil courts and procedure, and our system of criminal law and administration.

It is a painful confession to have to make, but all that follows is Lowland and not Highland law. The story of the clan system and its incidents, which persisted so late in Scotland's history, and of such special topics as the Udal Law of the Orkneys and Zetland, is outside the limits of any brief account of Scots Law, the harvest of which was gathered below the 500-foot contour line, and mainly south of the Forth.

A *The Law of the Family*

Marriage, divorce and the personal and property relations of husband and wife and of parent and child are common to all civilised societies, and the differences between one legal system and another, or between different ages of the same system, tend to be superficial. In Scotland, the basis of our law is immemorial custom and the religious tradition, considerably coloured by Canonist doctrine, traces of which still survive.

Until a few years ago Scots Law was unusual in allowing marriage to be constituted without either official formality or sacerdotal benediction. The old " irregular " Scottish marriage provided material for juristic disquisitions and plots for novels, written by authors who fondly imagined that it was not uncommon in Scotland for marriages to be contracted inadvertently and even unawares. But it was only when the abuse of the irregular marriage and its commercialisation at Gretna Green and elsewhere led to instances of hardship and complications in the vital statistics that it was deemed advisable to sweep it away. There were no mourners at the graveside. But it would be quite wrong to suppose that this change made much, if any, difference to the vast majority of prospective spouses, for a very large proportion of irregular marriages were immediately registered under a sheriff's warrant, the need for proof of married status being nowadays so vital for the purposes of many insurance and other official schemes. The alteration in the law has thus meant nothing to those who prefer a civil to a religious marriage except the substitution of a registrar for a sheriff as the functionary representing the interests of the state.

Some ten years ago England introduced far-reaching reforms in her law of divorce, and Scotland took advantage of the opportunity to make a few minor changes, the most notable being the introduction of divorce for insanity. The English controversy chiefly centred around divorce for desertion : but Scotland has had divorce for desertion since 1573, and numerous Scottish decisions have refined and developed every

aspect of this difficult remedy.   Scotland has never known the
provisional decree *nisi* of English divorce practice.

Our law of parent and child has been slightly modified by
modern legislation dealing with child welfare and related
topics, but in the main our Common Law principles still
stand and work well.   We still adhere to the Roman tradition
of drawing a dividing line at puberty between the pupil and
the minor instead of adopting the English rule of classifying
all who are not adults as infants.   An anomalous inroad upon
the Common Law was recently effected by the introduction
of the institution of adoption, the merits or demerits of which
are still an open question.

It is possible that future transformations of social habits
and religious outlook may be reflected in a demand for changes
in this chapter of our law ; but short of that no substantial
alterations seem either probable or desirable.   The standard
treatises of the late Lord Fraser and the steady current of
decisions on fresh aspects of old questions will supply our
needs for a long time to come.

B   The Land Laws

This is the branch of Scots Law which is most distinctively
Scottish and which has been allowed to evolve without the
intrusion of alien influence for some eight hundred years.
Though the law has been simplified and clarified by amending
statutes again and again, its central doctrines are still purely
feudal, and, so far as known, it is at present the most feudal
of any system of land laws in the world.   This is at once its
peculiar merit and its defect.

In the seventeenth and eighteenth centuries, and even
earlier, our classical system of conveyancing and heritable
rights was worked out to the last detail with a rigorous logic
and a felicitous ingenuity which it is a pleasure to study.   The
great Scottish lawyers of these days were pre-eminently
feudalists, and lavished their acumen and sagacity for generations on the task of perfecting the Scottish version of feudal
practice.   The law came to pivot upon the public registration

of deeds, and with the establishment in the seventeenth century (after much trial and error) of the Register of Sasines, substantially in the form in which it still exists, Scotland was recognised as having equipped herself with a very advanced code of land laws which for long was discussed with envy and admiration by the lawyers of foreign states. There were few of the innumerable problems which cropped up before the middle of the nineteenth century which proved incapable of elegant solution by application of, or deduction from, the finished principles which had been elaborated by the old feudalists, and the leading cases of the period contain many judgments which are models of philosophic law.

All this may be put to the credit side of the account, and an impressive total it makes. But there is also a debit side, and it has been steadily mounting. Lawyers still living had to learn in their youth much medieval lore about antiquated incidents of tenure, which still occasionally stir in their graves to the extreme discomfiture of the younger school ; for it is no disparagement to the present generation of Scots lawyers to say that Lord Dunedin was the last of the feudalists. A great deal of dead wood has been pruned away by the later conveyancing statutes, but a great deal still remains, and it is to be feared that we have lived a little too long upon our feudal reputation and have hardly kept abreast of a new world to which the very idea of vassalage, however theoretical, is repellent.

For instance, it is both easier and cheaper to acquire a marketable title to a Rolls Royce than to a shed in which to keep it, and much simpler to invest £100,000 in Stock Exchange shares or securities than £100 on a heritable bond. The preparation of deeds relating to land is the province of skilled experts, and the same is true of the examination of title deeds and the searching of the official records : and every time a property changes hands the whole process may have to be undertaken anew. Meantime younger countries in Europe and America, unencumbered by long tradition and able to start with a more or less clean slate, have set up various types of registration of title by means of which rights to land can be transferred at trifling cost, usually with a state guarantee of the title, which is investigated once and for all under official auspices. In an old country like Scotland a change-over from the old to a new system would be far from easy, and there are many incidental complications arising from our local law of property—a notable example being the wide prevalence in Scottish burghs of tenements, subdivided both vertically and horizontally into separate premises, each of which is, or is capable of being, owned in fee simple by a different proprietor, who further enjoys a common interest along with his fellow-proprietors in the remainder of the building. To delineate such rights on a map or plan would tax the skill of any draftsman, and their compendious description on a card-index might be very difficult. Whether the administrative changes required to give Scotland a modern system of registration of title would be feasible, and how far it might be necessary to preface them by recasting our land laws as England did by the Birkenhead reforms of twenty years ago, are large questions to which a Committee presided over by Lord Macmillan is at present seeking an answer. The problems are not new and drastic answers have been proposed in the past : for it is on record that an iconoclastic Lord Advocate once drafted a one-clause Bill with the single provision :—" The Feudal System is hereby abolished " !

Scotland is rich in her legal literature relating to heritable rights, beginning with Craig's historic *De Feudis* and extending downwards through a long succession of valuable treatises and published lectures, written by feudalists and modern conveyancers of high authority. We need these works ; for the many conveyancing statutes have never been codified and it is still on occasions necessary for the conveyancer to know not only what the law now is but what it was at some date in the past.

C   The Law of Succession

The rules which in Scotland regulate the transmission of property from the dead to the living, whether by will or on intestacy, have not been deeply affected by statute, their chief continuing source being Roman Law, Canon Law, and native customary law, now heavily overlaid and refined by an embarrassingly large mass of decisions.

The basic principles of the law of wills, trusts and settlements of all kinds are adequate and distinct ; but it is impossible to set a limit to the speculative benevolence of testators or to the ingenuity or wrong-headedness of their advisers, with the result that the stream of litigation shows little signs of abating. The title of " Succession " is still much the largest in our digests of cases, and no branch of our law reveals narrower distinctions or more subtle refinements of interpretation. This is probably inevitable, and the difficulty is by no means confined to Scotland. But it is always a pity to have to credit ordinary people with metaphysical conceptions which it is certain that they never harboured, and which they were probably quite incapable of apprehending. No lawyer would relish the task of expounding to an intelligent layman the doctrine of " vesting subject to defeasance."

A distinctive and salutary rule of Scots Law which dates from the earliest times is that which prohibits a husband (and latterly a wife) from disinheriting his (or her) spouse, and a parent from disinheriting his children, by guaranteeing to the surviving spouse or children certain " legal rights " in the estate of the deceased. Another speciality of our law is the acceptance as sufficiently authenticated of the " holograph " will, written in the testator's own hand and signed by him but without further solemnities of execution. We have also elaborated through long tracts of decisions a variety of canons of interpretation, dealing with the effect to be assigned to the expressions most commonly used in testamentary documents, and the consequences to be attributed to common contingencies, such as the birth of a child to a testator after the execution of his will, or the predecease of a legatee leaving issue. On the whole, and for all its unavoidable elaboration, our law of testate succession works well, and the capacity of its foundation doctrines for expansion and adaptation is by no means exhausted.

When we pass from testate to intestate succession any cause for complacency vanishes. Our rules are redolent of the eighteenth century when land and interests in land were the wealth of the community. This is pre-eminently the chapter of our law which cries aloud to be re-written, for it is out of touch with present-day realities and ought to be discarded as obsolete and outworn. No sane testator would dream of making the distribution of his estate which, if he dies without making a will, our law will make for him. Twenty years ago the Birkenhead reforms in England effected the corresponding changes in the law which were required there, and a like reform in Scotland is long overdue. Proposals to that end, mooted before the last war, were deferred as a result of the international situation, but they are bound to be revived, and the sooner the better.

In addition to the institutional writers and a huge corpus of decisions we are well served in this branch of our law by Lord McLaren's monumental treatise on *Wills and Succession* and by a number of valuable modern text-books. But it is on our decisions that we chiefly rely.

D   The Law of Contract

Many chapters of the law of contract which specially affect the mercantile community—charter-parties, bills of lading, bills of exchange, sale of goods and marine insurance, for example—have largely passed from the control of individual national systems of law and in the main are now international in character. Local features still persist, but future development in this field is likely to be a matter for international convention. It is with the general law of contract that we are now concerned, and this is a subject which has been successfully developed in Scots Law on Roman foundations and in general conformity to the Franco-German pattern. Without breach of the initial promise not to enter into technical details it would be impossible to discuss the features which differentiate Scots Law from Anglo-American, but it may be permissible to observe that the cardinal English doctrine of " consideration," which so deeply affects their law of contract, has no part in Scots Law, and that in recent times the tendency has been for English Law to be brought into conformity with the principles which have long prevailed in Scotland and which originated in Roman Law.

The reader may be surprised at this repeated invocation of Roman Law, but it requires no apology. In certain types of human enterprise, of which the formation of obligations is one, the essence of the transaction—the intention of parties, their mutual consent, the factors which may exclude such consent and many other elements—has stood, and must continue to stand, unaltered through the ages. In relation to such matters the conclusions wrought out by generations of jurists, belonging to a race whose genius for jurisprudence is unexampled in history, are imperishable, incapable of being abolished, and in many respects incapable of being improved upon. Their collective wisdom has furnished the groundwork for the municipal law for half the world, and it is not from blind traditionalism, but from recognition of the supreme merits of its model, that the Scots Law of Contract has always been, and will remain, Roman in principle.

Our chief authority on the law of contract is George Joseph Bell, along with whose famous works it is not wholly inappropriate to mention the outstanding modern treatise of the late Professor Gloag of Glasgow University.

E   The Law of Reparation

What the Scots lawyer calls a " delict " and the English lawyer a " tort " might be popularly defined as an actionable wrong for which the common remedy is an award of damages. Its categories are already legion, and they continue to expand in numbers and variety. The subject is hardly known to early law : it was confined within narrow limits when our institutional writers lived and worked ; and it has only been within the last two generations that the full flood has burst upon us.

On this topic (as on nearly every other) Scots Law was true to type by laying down, while the subject was still fluid and adaptable, a few cardinal principles from which a very wide range of consequences could be deduced. Chief amongst these was the principle that liability for reparation cannot exist without fault or breach of duty—a rule which stands in vivid contrast to the original basis in principle of the English law of tort, which imposed liability in many cases where there was no fault. In more recent times this point and other vital distinctions in principle have been progressively obscured in the wilderness of single instances, and in certain restricted but important types of case the indiscriminate citation of English precedents in Scottish cases and the facile assumption that the law must be the same on both sides of the Border have threatened to produce in Scotland rather unsystematic and illogical results. The law both here and in England is still in active development, and with no strong lead from our institutional writers and with Anglo-American influence at its highest, it is to be feared that in process of time the rational simplicity of our law of delict will be submerged—not because it is inferior to, but because it is different from, English Law.

The subject is one on which in every country new problems are presenting themselves for solution every day. In the last resort it does not greatly matter what solutions are found, but it does greatly matter that in any given country the law should develop systematically and logically so that its future trend and application shall be capable of reasoned forecast. Either oil or water is preferable to the unsatisfactory emulsion which results from attempts to mix the two.

F   Civil Courts and Procedure

The Supreme Court, which sits in Edinburgh, consists of the Lord President, the Lord Justice-Clerk and twelve Senators of the College of Justice, and is divided into the Inner and the Outer House. The Inner House deals with appeals from the Outer House and from inferior courts, and also exercises an original jurisdiction in a number of special types of case. It sits in two Divisions, the full complement of each being four, the First Division presided over by the Lord President and the Second by the Lord Justice-Clerk. Owing to the demands of criminal circuits and other special duties, the services of Division judges are frequently required elsewhere, and the Divisions often sit with their minimum quorum of three judges. The Outer House consists of the remaining six judges each of whom sits alone as a judge of first instance. When, exceptionally, issues of high principle and difficulty are raised involving the consideration of conflicting authorities, the two Divisions may sit together as a Court of Seven Judges with authority to overrule prior Division judgments ; and still more exceptionally a case can be referred to the Whole Court. In these expedients Scotland retains the last safeguard against the excessive rigidity of precedent. Normally the decisions of each Division are binding on both, and on the Outer House and inferior courts. Considerations of convenience lead to the appropriation of some types of case to one Division or to one Outer House judge ; but every judge is assumedly capable of dealing with every type of case, and there is no subdivision of the Court as in England into branches, each dealing only with specified classes of judicial work.

Throughout the whole of Scotland from Shetland to Wigtown there are distributed some fifty locally resident Sheriff-Substitutes who are full-time professional judges, roughly corresponding to the English County Court judge, but with a wider civil jurisdiction and extensive criminal duties. The sheriff as a judicial and administrative officer dates from the twelfth century and is thus much older than the Court of Session and by reason of the multiplicity of his functions he has always occupied a very important place in the Scottish governmental scheme. In civil cases an appeal lies from the Sheriff-Substitute either to the Sheriff-Principal, of whom there are now twelve, or to the Court of Session ; and there is also an appeal from the Sheriff-Principal to the Court of Session. In criminal cases, the Sheriff in Scotland discharges the great bulk of the work which in England is entrusted to lay justices in petty or quarter sessions ; for the Justice of the Peace is not indigenous to Scotland but is a comparatively late importation, and he has never played more than a very minor part in the

judicial administration of Scotland and in many parts of the
country does not function judicially at all.

The procedure of the Court of Session was overhauled in
1934, and minor improvements were effected in the present
year. It retains of set purpose a special feature which has
characterised its written pleadings for centuries, viz. the
requirement that the essential facts underlying both the demand
for a remedy and the defence to that demand should be sufficiently set out in an articulate " condescendence," and that
the legal basis of both the claim and the defence should be
formulated in a series of " pleas in law " or legal propositions
related to the facts set out. When the pleadings have been
adjusted, the case in fact and in law advanced for both the
parties is, or ought to be, instantly discoverable. Neither will
be allowed at any later stage to trespass beyond the limits of
their adjusted pleadings, and if the facts averred provide an
insufficient legal basis for the claim or the defence, the action
or the defences may be dismissed as " irrelevant " without
further enquiry—a procedure analogous to the now discredited
English " demurrer." Great value is attached in Scotland to
this method of written pleading, which compels the parties at
the initial stages of a litigation to define with precision the
essence of their case, and which enables many a case to be
disposed of cheaply and quickly without the expense and
delay involved in an investigation into the facts. Lest it should
be supposed that Scottish lawyers are unreasonably prejudiced
in favour of their native methods, it is worth recording that,
when the United States Government was engaged in 1912 in
drafting what became the Federal Equity Rules, they applied
for advice to Lord Chancellor Loreburn, who suggested that
it would be worth their while to consider the Scottish method
of pleading " which in my opinion is the best." Coming
from so authoritative and independent a source, this is indeed
high praise.

Trial by jury in civil cases has had a curious history in
Scotland. When the early Anglo-Norman influence had
evaporated, the civil jury disappeared from our midst and had
been completely forgotten long before the early years of the

N

nineteenth century when it was re-introduced from England. For long it did not work well, and there was much controversy on the question what types of case were, and what were not, appropriate for trial by jury. Gradually we became habituated to the innovation but are not yet resigned to its acceptance. Numerically the vast majority of jury trials now relate to traffic accidents, and the institution has become an accessory of the internal combustion engine. It has never been explained why twelve casually chosen ladies and gentlemen should be assumed to be better qualified to determine whether John Smith sounded his horn or passed a traffic signal " on the red " than a highly trained judge, familiar with the rules of evidence and accustomed to its appraisal. Moreover as all civil jury trials take place in the Court of Session, what we enjoy in Scotland is not trial by jury but trial by Edinburgh citizens. For six years during the recent war jury trials in civil cases were suspended, and the work was taken by the judges in their stride. But now jury trials are back again. These facts are worth pondering by those who justify the civil jury in Scotland by a vague and mistaken reference to Magna Carta or the Treaty of Union. At a time of such economic difficulty it is odd that we can tolerate the waste of manpower involved in taking so many people from their work, often for days at a time, in order that they may settle the quarrels of other people.

This part of the picture would be incomplete without a word regarding the organisation of the legal profession. The solicitors have formed a large number of central and local societies, recently loosely federated under a General Council, the premier society being that of the Writers to the Signet. There is nothing corresponding to the Inns of Court, but the Faculty of Advocates is a corporation of historic dignity with an amazing record of public service, and a unique cultural tradition, its members having included during the last two hundred years the majority of the outstanding figures in the Scottish annals of law, literature and public life.

G   Criminal Law and Administration

This is a branch of our legal system in which Scotland may justly take pride, and which has been maintained at a high pitch of efficiency. The substantive criminal law is indigenous to Scotland, and it is almost entirely Common Law with only trifling statutory ingredients. In the main it is the product of native custom, elaborated and developed by judicial decision ; and in this respect it enjoys a flexibility and a capacity for expansion which are denied to many countries, of which England is one, in which nearly every crime or offence has to be found in the provisions of a statute. Scotland has been fortunate in a succession of notable treatises on the law of crime, commencing with the famous *Commentaries* of Baron David Hume, published in 1797, which has all but attained the dignity of an institutional work, and richly merits the high authority in which it is held.

Whatever the position may have been in days gone by— and if Scotland had her Braxfield, England had her Jeffreys— the Scottish law of crime and especially of criminal evidence has latterly been exceedingly scrupulous in guaranteeing fairness to the accused, preferring to allow the guilty to escape rather than incur any risk of convicting the innocent. Notable instances of this attitude are afforded by our refusal of an opening statement to the prosecutor and our concession to the accused of the last word to the jury ; by the very sparing admissions of confessions or incriminating statements by the accused ; and by the cardinal rule that (apart from a few statutory exceptions), no person can be convicted unless there is evidence of at least two witnesses implicating the accused in the commission of the crime charged. The chief search in most prosecutions is thus for sufficient corroboration, in the absence of which a conviction cannot take place, or, if obtained, cannot stand, however credible the principal witness may be.

Another outstanding feature of our criminal law is the exclusion of private prosecutions, and the concentration in the hands of the Lord Advocate, acting through his Deputies in the Crown Office, and his local officers in each sheriffdom, (the procurators fiscal), of the sole right to prosecute all crimes, exclusive of petty offences which are dealt with in police and minor courts. By this method Scotland avoids the prejudicial publicity in the earlier stages of a criminal prosecution which arises from coroner's inquests and proceedings before magistrates, and secures that the jurors empanelled to try an accused person know substantially nothing of the case until they hear the evidence from the lips of the witnesses at the actual trial. This feature of our system, which involves that all preliminary enquiries are conducted officially and confidentially, has worked extremely well, and, notwithstanding the very wide discretion which is vested in the Lord Advocate, it is over a century since a holder of that high office has been publicly called in question on the charge of abusing his powers. It is another prerogative of the Lord Advocate that he, and he alone, determines by his estimate of the gravity of the alleged crime, whether the prosecution shall take place in the High Court with a jury, or in the Sheriff Court with a jury, or before a sheriff sitting without a jury. The sheriff's powers of imposing punishment are limited, and major cases cannot be taken in the sheriff court ; but once a case has been sent to a sheriff to be tried summarily without a jury, the accused has no right to demand a jury.

Since 1926 Scotland has had a Court of Criminal Appeal from which no appeal lies to the House of Lords, so that in the whole field of criminal administration Scotland still enjoys self-determination. Our native principles have served us well and have proved capable in more than one recent decision of being expanded to cover situations of a novel type. The process of detailed improvement of the law and procedure to meet new needs is constantly in progress ; but taken as a whole this branch of our law is one with which the Scottish people may feel well satisfied, and which will challenge comparison with any criminal system in the world.

The Lord President of the Court of Session, the Lord Justice-Clerk and the remaining Senators of the College of Justice occupy automatically the positions of Lord Justice-General, Lord Justice-Clerk and Lords Commissioners of

Justiciary ; and, wearing different robes, conduct the major trials not only in Edinburgh but in various Circuit towns in Scotland, and dispose of the criminal appeals in Edinburgh.

In conclusion mention should be made of a feature of our criminal law which attracts more public notice than it deserves —the verdict of Not Proven. Historically the Not Proven verdict is an accident, if not a mistake. Logically it may be difficult to justify. Practically, it works, and its abolition might have unintended consequences. However plainly a presiding judge may explain that an accused is presumed to be innocent until he is proved guilty, that he is entitled to the benefit of every reasonable doubt, and that the burden of proof is on the prosecution, the hard-headed Scots juror will nevertheless draw a common-sense distinction between the person who is entitled to leave the court without a stain on his character, and the person whose guilt is beyond moral doubt but who luckily escapes by the skin of his teeth for lack of some element of corroboration, or on some other narrow ground. The question is an open one, but those who complain of the stigma supposed to attach to an acquittal on a Not Proven verdict should consider whether, if there were no such verdict, the result in a narrow case might be not an acquittal but a conviction. There are occasions when sheer logic may not be the safest guide. It only remains to add that we accept a verdict by a majority and do not insist on unanimity ; and long experience has not given rise to any demand for a change, either from the public or from the legal profession.

IV. The Prospects for the Future

The safest method of supplying the contents of this section would be to leave a blank page. But this is no time to play for safety. Let us ignore the enigmas of the present situation and endeavour to apply with courage and cool detachment the lessons to be learnt from the preceding pages.

The Scottish legal tradition is a thing to be prized both in Scotland and beyond its Borders, and the public of Scotland should be more conscious of the fact. It is in a very real sense a typical product of the Scottish ethos, and has attracted to its enthusiastic service some of the greatest figures in our country's history. There are not many legal systems which can number amongst their modern exponents three such universally respected lawyers as Lord President Inglis, Lord Watson and Lord Dunedin, whose work is known the world over. We need not be afraid to submit Scots Law to the scrutiny of comparative jurists or to the test of its capacity to meet present-day needs. As has been shown, there are certain parts which are due for reconditioning and overhaul, having worn out through long service ; but there is no legal system of which the like cannot be said, and against the deficiencies we can set many conspicuous successes. But it is possible to go further and to consider Scots Law from a wider standpoint than the merely local and domestic. In respect of the intermediate position which it now occupies between the two great schools of legal thought Scots Law is at the moment unique. A very eminent and detached critic, Professor Levy Ullmann of Paris, has ventured the assertion that " Scots Law as it stands gives us a picture of what will some day be the law of the civilised nations—namely, a combination between the Anglo-Saxon system and the Continental system." Whether we agree with that forecast or not, it is a striking appraisal of what Scotland has achieved, and might yet achieve.

The difficulty is that times are hard and Scotland is small, and this is not the day of small things. Even the overhead cost of the production of reports and legal works, without which any legal system must rapidly wither, is becoming a serious matter for a country where the turnover is necessarily restricted. For many practitioners the *res angusta domi* compels increasingly close application to the daily task and oblivion to the wider horizons. The fertilising foreign contacts, upon which Scots Law has thrived for ages, can only with difficulty be maintained, and there is a visible risk that the old breadth of vision may be succeeded by an insular parochialism and a disposition to rest content with our inherited capital of ideas. The dangers of these tendencies are appreciated within the legal profession, and they can and will be resisted. If they were not, the future of Scots Law would soon lie behind it.

But this pamphlet is addressed not to the legal profession but to the lay citizen of Scotland, for he has an interest at stake and a part to play. Let us be frank. For some time past law and lawyers have declined in popular estimation, having become associated in the public mind with the merely traditional and reactionary. Perhaps we lawyers are in some measure to blame, in so far as we have yielded to the temptation to make law an end in itself instead of an instrument for the service of society. But the main danger to Scots Law is a different one. The spirit of the age has manifested itself in one of those recurrent crazes for the sinking of differences, the obliteration of individual characteristics, and the absorption of small units in ever larger amalgamations, as if a special virtue resided in mere size. To this there has been added an epidemic outbreak of the itch for change—what Hale described long ago as " a certain restlessness and nauseousness in what we have and a giddy humour after somewhat which is new." There are fields of human enterprise in which such tendencies may be allowed full play in the knowledge that they will surely issue in salutary reforms ; but private law is not one of them. Their wholesale application to Scots Law could only mean its fusion with Anglo-American Law, and this would involve the swift annihilation of what is left of Scotland's independent life and culture. Is that what Scotland wants ? No one imagines that there exists amongst English lawyers any conscious desire to interfere with Scots Law ; for the first article of the English lawyer's creed is that English Law is so incomparably superior to other systems that the others are hardly worth a glance, and there are few subjects on which England is so contentedly ignorant as Scotland and her institutions. The truth is that law is the reflection of the spirit of a people, and so long as the Scots are conscious that they are a people, they must preserve their law.

It is possible to take a higher and more universal ground. In these anxious times the sole remaining guarantee of the liberty of the subject and the freedom of a nation is the Rule of

Law—that all government should be conducted, and all coercive power applied, only in obedience to pre-established principles, fixed and announced beforehand, the application of which to any given situation is capable of prediction. Unless a system of law and legal administration is maintained in a state of high efficiency and allowed to develop freely in harmony with its own distinctive principles and methods, the Rule of Law in that country will inevitably languish, and it will be the ordinary citizen who will be the victim.

The Scottish people have thus good cause to place supreme value upon their system of jurisprudence, and to promote by their interest and support every effort to preserve its unique individuality and to perfect it in its future service of the common purposes of Scottish society.

1949

The Common and the Civil Law—
A Scot's View [1]

ONE of the many debts which we owe to the German school of jurists of the nineteenth century is the distinction between lawyers' law and professors' law. The terms are self-explanatory. They express a difference as old as that which distinguishes *jus* from *lex*. Since it is in active practice that my experience has been gained, it is from the standpoint of lawyers' law that I propose to discuss my subject : the influence of Roman and Canon Law in the modern world. The legal system which it has fallen to my lot to administer—the law of Scotland—occupies a special position amongst the legal systems of the modern world. These systems, as is well known, tend to fall into one or the other of two great categories, (*a*) the Anglo-American or common law systems, and (*b*) the Roman, civilian or Franco-German systems. But Scots Law sits on the fence, Roman in origin, doctrine and method, but now largely infiltrated and overlaid by the later developments of Anglo-American Law and by statutory changes enacted by a legislature predominantly English. It has been well said that Scotland has never yet been successfully invaded except by Christianity and Roman Law ; but in these later days Scots Law, like the law of Quebec and Louisiana and the Roman-Dutch systems of South Africa and Ceylon, has tended to become a hybrid system.

A seat on a fence may not be a very secure seat, but it offers the conspicuous advantage of a view on both sides of the fence. Half a civilian and a half a common lawyer, accustomed to thinking of law functionally as an applied science and not dogmatically as an aspect of sociology or of political philosophy

[1] Translated into Italian by Mrs Roberg de Laurentiis of Chicago, and published in the Italian legal journal *Jus*, in March 1956.

or of the history of human culture and institutions, the practising Scots lawyer ought to be able to form some estimate of the comparative excellences of the two great rival juristic schools of thought and their adaptability to the needs of a changed and changing world.

When we speak of a continuing influence being exerted in the modern world by the Romanist and Canonist legal tradition, what precisely is the nature of that influence? It is best to begin by stating what that influence is not. The truly significant part of that influence no longer resides in the conscious appropriation by Romanist systems of detailed doctrines or remedies borrowed from the *Corpus Juris Civilis* or the *Corpus Juris Canonici*. There was a time—and it lasted for centuries—when it was second nature to the lawyers of Scotland and of other countries which followed the civilian tradition to turn to Roman Law (or what they thought was Roman Law) for an answer to every question which their own system left unsolved. But that time has passed. Borrowing still goes on ; but under the impact of the new interest in comparative jurisprudence the lawyer in search of new ideas has now the civilised world at his disposal and is not confined to Justinian or Gregory IX. It is no longer in the provision of ready-made rules and doctrines to fill the gaps in an imperfect legal system that the continuing and abiding influence of Roman and Canon Law is to be found.

There are two points bearing upon this matter which are worthy of a brief digression. The first is that Roman and Canon Law have latterly shifted from the domain of lawyers' law to that of professors' law. As a result of the researches of modern scholars it is now known that few of the distinctive principles of Roman Law were not fundamentally transformed during the centuries throughout which the law of Rome was slowly evolving, and many of them have substantially changed their accepted content within living memory. If we take as an example the Roman Law of sale, it is a solemn reflection that the works by Mackintosh and Moyle on *emptio-venditio*, which were studied at British Universities by the present generation of lawyers, have had to be replaced by yet a third work on the same subject recently published by Professor Zulueta. These and other admirable specimens of professors' law have had the unintended consequence of depriving Roman Law for the working lawyer of much of its splendid isolation, and of converting it into little more than one chapter in the history of comparative jurisprudence, suitable like Greek Law, Hindoo Law, and the oriental systems as a subject of research by specialists, but exhaling an atmosphere too rarefied for the ordinary practitioner.

The second point is related to the first. The Roman Law which deeply affected the Romanist systems during their formative period was not the Roman Law of Mackintosh or Moyle or Zulueta, nor even the Roman Law of Justinian. It was Roman Law as our forefathers accepted it at second or third hand from the civilian commentators of the seventeenth and eighteenth centuries, and the Civil Law as taught by them was conceptual in a sense that the law of Rome never was. Here in Scotland we took our Roman Law less from the fountainhead than from such French lawyers as Cujacius, later from Voet, Vinnius, and others of the Bartolist tradition, and finally from the French Pothier ; and these names bulk far larger in our early works and reports than that of Justinian. Similarly with Canon Law. The Canon Law which has left its mark upon the law of Scotland and other kindred systems is not the developed law of the Roman Catholic Church, but the twelfth and thirteenth century law of Gratian's *Decretum* and Gregory's *Decretals* and the practice of the Curia Romana and its " judges delegate " in the halcyon days of Pope Innocent III.

This attitude is not so painfully unscientific as would at first sight appear. When the architects of a legal system are looking around for new material with which to fill in the blanks in their native legal philosophy, it matters little where the chosen principles originated, provided they are capable of being usefully adapted to meet the needs of the situation. The lawyer who wishes to learn Civil Law, as distinguished from the student who wishes to learn Roman Law, would accordingly do well to concentrate chiefly on the later civilians, who reminted the coinage of classical Roman Law and gave it in its new form an almost world-wide currency.

What then is the real essence of the contribution which has been made, and is still being made, to modern law by the civil and Canon Law? In the last analysis it is nothing more and nothing else than an idiom of legal thought and a guiding habit of mind—what Lord Macmillan once called " one of two ways of legal thinking "—and not merely of legal thinking but of philosophic thinking and scientific thinking as well. The distinction may be put in many ways. A civilian system differs from a Common Law system much as rationalism differs from empiricism or deduction from induction. The civilian naturally reasons from principles to instances, the common lawyer from instances to principles. The civilian puts his faith in syllogisms, the common lawyer in precedents ; the first silently asking himself as each new problem arises, " What should we do this time? " and the second asking aloud in the same situation, " What did we do last time? " The civilian thinks in terms of rights and duties, the common lawyer in terms of remedies. The civilian is chiefly concerned with the policy and rationale of a rule of law, the common lawyer with its pedigree. The instinct of the civilian is to systematise. The working rule of the common lawyer is *solvitur ambulando*.

The above is, of course, a deliberate overstatement of the position, in which the shadows have been deepened and the high lights sharpened with the object of throwing an elusive object into high relief ; and in the best traditions of the old scholastic dialectic many necessary qualifications have been temporarily ignored. But in the eyes of those who are in working contact with both the civilian and the Common Law tradition, the difference is unmistakable and persists strongly to this day, making itself felt not only in the fashioning of new law but in the day-to-day work of the courts, though the gulf which separates the two juristic methods has notably narrowed in the last half century.

Eminent representatives of the Common Law systems have recently laboured to minimise, if not to efface, the root distinctions between the civilian and the Common Law traditions by cataloguing the similarities in result which have been achieved by the two schools of legal thought in certain chapters of law. Whether it be that the seat on the fence offers a better view or whether (as is equally likely) we in Scotland are simply wrong, it is for others to judge ; but I can only record the personal conviction that the differences in method are fundamental and far more significant than the apparent similarity of the end products of widely different processes of thought. No doubt the similarities prevail once you get back to the basic concepts common to all mature jurisprudence. But that is professors' law ; and those who labour in the humbler field of lawyers' law become very sensitive to the difference in the legal climates which prevail in a civilian and in a Common Law state.

The most important and widespread product of the civilian legal tradition is, of course, codification. The Anglo-Saxon is instinctively hostile to codification. The Latin is instinctively enthusiastic for codification. The Germanic and Slav races began by being suspicious, but were soon won over to the Latin side. The effort to codify, so characteristic of Romanist systems, is not merely the result of the civilian lawyer's familiarity from his student days with the legislation of Justinian, and indirectly with the innumerable *Summæ* in law and in theology which appeared throughout the Middle Ages and later. It is the natural product of the civilian method of thought, which always aims at reason methodised and presented systematically and at the application of rationalistic science to law.

Whatever the abstract merits or demerits of codification, it is undeniable that it is the systems codified and applied on the civilian principle which have spread far and wide throughout the modern world as a result of voluntary imitation and free adoption, and they have carried with them the Roman idiom of thought into half the civilised world. Anglo-American Common Law by contrast has been imposed by conquest and has followed colonisation, but it has rarely or never been freely chosen by any modern state. Even in the United States, the domicil of choice of the Common Law, the civilian method of approach has recently found remarkable expression in the unofficial Restatement of the Law, in much of which Scots lawyers feel perfectly at home—far more so than in the Reports of the English Chancery Division.

Despite our powerful Romanist tradition we in Scotland have never yet codified, but we possess in our great institutional treatises by Stair, Erskine and Bell what are in substance codifications of the mass of our law as it was in the seventeenth, eighteenth and early nineteenth centuries respectively. These remain to this day authoritative and deeply respected formulations of our foundational legal principles, and occupy a position in Scottish legal thinking to which a code is the nearest parallel. For us complete codification would present no insuperable difficulty ; and, but for the political and economic consequences of the Union with England in 1707, we should unquestionably have codified long ago.

On the other hand, the most distinctive practical manifestation of the Common Law tradition is the doctrine of the individually binding precedent, still conspicuous in its most rigid form in England, but looked at askance by the Romanist school of legal thought. The doctrine formed no part of the classical law of Scotland but crept in unobserved some 150 years ago, and we are now helpless in its suffocating grip. Up to a point we can still mitigate its rigour by submitting doubtful decisions for reconsideration by a court of seven or even thirteen judges ; but that expedient is of no avail if the case is carried to the House of Lords, our final court of appeal in civil cases.

Everyone will freely admit that in judicial administration a very large measure of consistency must be secured in order that the law affecting any given situation may be reasonably predictable. The utmost respect will always be conceded to a tract of similar decisions, or the settled opinion of jurists of weight, or the accepted practice and understanding of the profession. But such principles are far apart from the superstitious fetish of ancestor worship which inspires the rigid rule of the individually binding precedent. For practical reasons, if for no other, the rule is bound to be abandoned soon, because the crushing weight of centuries of law reports, digests, and indices has become all but overwhelming, and it is fast increasing every year. But, practical considerations apart, is there any answer to the protest of Holmes that it is revolting to act in blind imitation of the past and to magnify consistency at the expense of common sense ? Too often the imitation of the past is a " blind " imitation, for the parallelism between cases is much less common that we lawyers pretend. Very slight differences in the facts—and these are not always recorded fully in the reports—may easily turn the scale ; and even when the facts are to all appearances identical, the social, political and economic background may be entirely different if the cases are separated, as often happens, by a long period of time. As Mr Churchill has recently observed in a different connection : " Past experience carries with its advantages the drawback that things never happen the same way again. Otherwise I suppose life would be too easy." In the eyes of the civilian the common lawyer has tried to make his professional life too easy by excessive reliance upon precedent and the ascription of infallibility to hierarchies of judges down the ages. The attempt has failed, and its abandonment will be joyfully received in Scotland by those who are ashamed to have to decide cases upon grounds with which they disagree simply because their remote judicial ancestors have decided another case long ago upon a rationale which it is impossible to distinguish. All legal systems require a cement to bind them into a coherent whole ; and the question which the Common Law systems will very soon have to face is whether a better cement than rigid precedent cannot be found in more codification and in methodised reasoning from clear principles in accordance with the civilian tradition. The judge should not be the parties' oracle, but he must be something more than an animated index to the law reports.

An important question for every lawyer to-day is which of the two contrasted methods of legal thinking should dominate the future. Is the civilian tradition a spent force ? My belief is that the world of the future will be ruled to an increasing extent by codes administered on the civilian rationalistic principle, and that our successors will some day look back upon the great experiment of the Common Law as a brilliant improvisation, which served its day and generation and was then assigned an honoured niche in the Valhalla of governmental expedients.

The reason, I suggest, is tolerably clear, at least to those on this side of the Atlantic. In the spacious and leisurely days of the nineteenth century, when the dominant conception was the adjustment of private interests and not the regulation of state and social rights and obligations, it took judge-made Common Law all its time to keep abreast of the growing needs of a developing society. Remember Dicey's famous remark that in those days statute law reflected the public opinion of yesterday ; and judge-made law, the opinion of the day before. Even then the vaunted flexibility of the English Common Law made a poor showing by comparison with the European codes. But to-day, whether we like it or not, the old outlook has gone never to return, and the individualistic background of the past is being swiftly replaced by transformed conceptions of social functions and state interests, conceived from the angle either of the Right or of the Left. Britain is now a trading corporation. The age is one of association in vast units aiming at the mass production of social results. The individual citizen is losing his identity. Statute and regulation, once the exception, are now the rule. We in these islands are already in the twilight of landownership and the afternoon of private property. Private law is receding all along the line and public law is taking its place.

Fundamental transformations like this cannot be worked out empirically by the Anglo-Saxon method with its reliance upon slowly developing tracts of judicial decisions evolved with infinite caution by generations of elderly and timorous judges conditioned by Victorian ideals. Even if they could, many governments of the day have already made it plain that they have other ideas on the subject. Vast regions hitherto sacrosanct to the law courts have recently been taken out of their hands and entrusted to organs of the executive or administrative branches of government. We lawyers do not like it, but it must be so. Now that society is being forced by the pressure of relentless circumstances to assume a new look, it is inevitable that positive political and economic enactments should acquire increasing predominance in the definition and regulation of legal rights, and that the views of well-meaning judges, who lived and worked without dreaming of the situation which confronts us to-day, should be deprived of the verbal inspiration too often conceded to their casual utterances.

Under conditions such as these it is of supreme importance for the preservation of what remains of the last bulwark of individual freedom, the Rule of Law, that the transition should be accompanied by a conscious return to the civilian methods of legal thinking, if we are to avoid the ultimate disaster of witnessing our systems of law replaced by the opportunism of arbitrary dictatorships. This at least seems incontrovertible, that the lawyers of every modern state must recognise and take up the challenge presented to them by the social and economic revolution which is upon us and must not lag one inch behind the demands of a progressive society. What form these demands may yet take we cannot foresee, but they will certainly be demands for something different from what the legal profession has been supplying for generations. Public respect for law, without which law cannot exist and civilisation itself is threatened, depends upon the law's ability to satisfy the average man's feeling for common justice visibly done ; and we may have to forget a lot and discard much of our old legalism if we are to satisfy this test. The civilian will have to abate something of his worship of the Roman genius for jurisprudence, unexampled as that genius was ; and the common lawyer will have to recognise that his methods and their fruit are not necessarily the final perfection of human wisdom. We shall need both the civilian and the common lawyer to tide us over the great transition ; but if we are to preserve an even keel in the storms which are breaking, we shall need above all the ballast which only the civilian method of legal thinking can offer.

1949

o

The Profession of the Law To-day

THE ETHICAL IDEALS of the legal profession have provided the theme for many an address to a legal gathering, culminating in Lord Clyde's memorable lecture to the Juridical Society of Edinburgh in 1922. While all these addresses bear the distinctive imprint of their several distinguished authors, they are all variations on a single theme, framed on the same pattern, informed by the same spirit, and based upon the same principles.

The explanation of this substantial identity of treatment is plain enough. Ever since the practice of the law became the province of an organised profession until quite recent times, the course of development has been uniform and homogenous. The lawyer's function as a social agency has remained much the same. He has enjoyed—at different times in different degrees—a privileged status. At the lowest this privileged status was accorded to him as a member of an esoteric craft possessed of valuable knowledge which was not revealed to the common herd. At the highest it was accorded to him as the champion of the weak against their oppressors, and latterly because he had acquired—in the later nineteenth century in a conspicuous degree—the attributes once associated in popular esteem with " the scholar and the gentleman." Moreover, if we pass from the social background to legal and political theory, we can trace in all these expositions of the lawyer's faith a tacit acceptance of those foundation principles of civil government which persisted without essential change from Montesquieu to Dicey and Bagehot, and which the happenings of the last dozen years have done so much to invalidate.

From all this it naturally followed that the ethics of the legal profession hardened into a traditional orthodoxy, capable of receiving expression for generations in terms of one creed and a single confession of faith.   The law had unquestionably become the aristocrat of the learned professions, and its professional ideals remained susceptible of precise and eloquent formulation.

Of course the practice of the law has always had its seamy side, and there have never been lacking critics to pour well-merited scorn upon its delays and expense ; to impart a sinister meaning to that method of approach to a practical problem which is known as " the chancery view " ; and to diagnose that incipient ossification of the brain which laymen refer to as " the legal mind."   But these shafts were usually directed good-humouredly at limited targets ; and the profession as a whole could afford to smile and to bask in the sunshine of self-esteem.

So much for the past. As I turn to the present, need I say to an audience largely composed of the younger generation that, as we look out to-night upon the world of 1950, we look at a transformed society and one which is still in process of further transformation ?   The old outlook has vanished. We are further from 1914 to-night than 1914 was from the Reformation. The old values have gone never to return ; or if they do return, they will be a materially different thing, for the cycle of change follows a spiral curve and not a circle, and the spiral is not necessarily upwards.   " Humanity," said the late General Smuts, " has struck its tents and is once again on the march " ; and those of us who were born and bred under the old regime are tempted in moments of bewilderment to carry the metaphor one stage further and to say, with Omar Khayyam :

> The stars are setting, and the Caravan
> Starts for the Dawn of Nothing. Oh make haste.

Or, to descend to a lower plane, nearer the level of 1950, take the remark of an American judge the other day : " This old world in its writhings and twistings has turned completely upside down—a rather undignified posture, suggesting and provoking a good sound spanking."

But my purpose this evening is neither to welcome nor to

deplore these changes, still less to administer the good sound spanking which the situation may demand ; but simply to accept these cataclysmic changes realistically as conditions of the problem of defining anew the ethical ideals of our profession. I fear that this is a problem for to-morrow rather than a problem for to-day, and that its solution will be better formulated by the native denizens of the brave new world than by an astonished survivor of the Victorian era. But let us try.

To put the old traditional ideal in a nutshell, it was that the profession of the law is a vocation of exuberant trust, entrance to which is jealously guarded by prescribed standards of skill and experience ; the exercise of which is regulated by self-imposed requirements of integrity and professional honour ; and the pursuit of which always entails that the lawyer's duty to his client, and still more his regard for his own self-interest, must be rigorously subordinated to his paramount allegiance to the law. Such a faith, conscientiously held and applied, breathes the spirit of the old craft guilds, almost of priesthood in the Temple of Themis. It assumes that there exists as the foundation of all government a framework of pure law, a *corpus juris*, which it is the lawyer's privilege to master and to expound to his fellows in all its infinite applications to their daily walk and conversation. It requires that in the exercise of a function indispensable to civilised society, the lawyer should work in an atmosphere of objective detachment, free from influence or pressure from any quarter, and resolved to do his duty as he sees it without fear or favour, affection or ill-will. Over it all there hovers the conception of an imperious and transcendent Rule of Law. Beneath it all stand the classical doctrines of liberty and individualism in the best senses of these rather ambiguous terms.

These were the texts on which the old sermons were preached. Now let us take a few brute facts ; and in the best traditions of the old scholastic dialectic I shall state them brutally and without the necessary qualifications.

Privileged status, once widely respected, is now as widely despised. Scholarship, except in the dubious form of technological aptitude, is struggling for survival. Egalitarianism persists in asking the old question :

> When Adam delved and Eve span
> Who was then the gentleman ?

—and it now asks it even if Adam does not delve and Eve has never learned to spin. The realisation of current conceptions of social justice has been elevated to the highest place in the basic values of society. Individual liberty threatens to become a synonym for selfish exploitation. In some quarters the legal profession has come to be regarded as the obsequious lackey of the *ancien régime*, chiefly engaged in helping property and privilege to rescue what little is left to them of their ancestral possessions.

In these deliberately exaggerated epigrams you will sense a change of climate in public opinion in which, to put it mildly, the nineteenth century conceptions of the learned professions do not thrive.

Next, we must admit that the profession of the law has latterly suffered a tremendous decline in relative stature amongst the gainful occupations of the modern world. A generation ago, as I said, law was the aristocrat of the three professions of law, medicine and the Church. To-day there are 41 professional bodies incorporated by Royal Charter or Act of Parliament, and many more well on the way to the acquisition of similar professional status. The very connotation of the term " profession " is no longer susceptible of definition. All this is the product of the expansion of education and the growth of occupational specialisation, and the community at large has benefited greatly. But, when the lawyers of the old school recall their former position of splendid isolation and elbow their way through the milling crowd of modern professions, they will, I hope, be exonerated from the charge of snobbery if they mutter with the Red Queen : " I could show you hills in comparison with which you'd call *that* a valley."

These are weighty factors in our problem, but there is yet another. In these islands and elsewhere the whole theory of law and civil government has undergone a change. The classical theory of the separation of powers of the legislature, the executive and the judicature—and I have had the privilege at different times of belonging to all three—guaranteed to the lawyers a sphere of exclusive activity in which they were sovereign. But the dogma of the separation of powers has been replaced by the convention of the balance of powers, which may mean anything or nothing. The executive is now supreme ; and its subordinate agencies already encroach very heavily both on the traditional province of the legislature, through the medium of delegated legislation, and also on the province of the judiciary, through the medium of departmental and *ad hoc* tribunals, still completely unregulated by any coherent system of administrative law. If you ask me to define with precision the exact function of the judiciary under these revised constitutional principles, I cannot do it. What I do know is that Private Law has declined very markedly in our time as compared with Public Law ; that the territory still in the lawyer's occupation has been seriously narrowed ; and that the function of Private Law and of the legal profession as social agencies is less significant to-day than at any time since the establishment of Parliamentary democracy.

Once again let me remind you that I neither applaud nor deplore these tendencies. I am not arguing with you ; I am telling you. I have learned, in whatsoever state I am, therein to seem content. As lawyers we must strive to adapt ourselves and our ideals to these altered conditions.

To come a little closer to our own domestic situation as professional men, it is plain enough that in the last quarter of a century we have lost a great many customers for good. Further, in an impoverished land beset on every hand by the *res angusta domi*, it is impossible without impertinence to talk as our fathers did to the white-collared workers of the legal profession about the " taint of commercialism." The advent of Legal Aid has itself made a serious inroad on our traditional outlook ; and in the Law Society of Scotland we have something more nearly approaching to a Trade Union than any of the professional associations whom the Society will in some measure supersede.   Finally, there is less need to-day for training in juristic reasoning from principle than for the all-embracing memory and the capacious card-indexes which enable the social worker to peddle the latest departmental fiat over the counter of a Citizens' Advice Bureau.

So much for the past and the present.   As I turn to the future I feel the mantle of the prophet sitting uneasily on my shoulders ; but we have a duty to look ahead.

I think that we should all remind ourselves of what Acton described as the most profound lesson of all history, that every institution, every movement, carries within itself the seeds of its own decay and ultimately contributes to the success of its most hated rival.   There is a tide in the affairs of men, a rhythmical swing of the pendulum, whose slow operation can be observed in politics, economics, philosophy and religion from the dawn of civilisation until now.   Just as the occult phenomenon of " spin " seems to pervade the physical universe from the electron to the furthest nebula, so the swing of the pendulum pervades human society, manifesting in a thousand forms the eternal and irreconcilable conflict between the individual and the group.   It is with the individual and not with the group that law as we know it finds its chief concern, and latterly the pendulum has swung far from the individual towards the group.   To-morrow that swing may be arrested, or even reversed.   Do not mistake the surface ripple for the flowing tide.   Do not forget that, even if the present swing is not arrested in our day, the age-old conflict between the individual and the group will persist to the last syllable of recorded time, and that there will always be a place in the body politic for justice and equity as between man and man and man and group, whatever may be the agency entrusted with their application.

It seems to me that the immediate future holds two possibilities.   The swing towards the group may continue until the single function of the lawyer will be to act as the salaried servant of the State, helping to carry into detailed operation a public law which will simply be another name for the planned policy of the party in power.   In that event the lawyers will have to fashion for themselves an entirely new ethic, similar to that which now inspires the higher ranks of the Civil Service. That is one possibility ; but I do not think that it will happen yet awhile. In a country like ours, with its genius for compromise and the *via media*, however illogical, I apprehend that the swing towards the group will be arrested and that a new frontier will be delimited between public law and private law. Behind a shortened line and within an area contracted within narrower boundaries, the profession of the law will still be needed—perhaps desperately needed— to cultivate and apply the *constans et perpetua voluntas jus suum cuique tribuendi.*

Constans et perpetua—yes, however contracted the sphere of activity, there will be redoubled need for reaffirming in its highest form the old professional ideals—not a muffled or attenuated version but in their purest form, suitable for a profession which relies no longer on inherited traditional privilege, but on worthy service to society, worthily rendered, and on the faithful discharge of a function with which society cannot dispense.

Consider this. The Rule of Law, to which the legal profession has given absolute allegiance for centuries, may take more than one form. Until recently the Rule of Law in this land was in the last analysis the rule of judges, interpreting and applying Acts of Parliament, and declaring the Common Law—often doing so in such fashion as to make new law. That aspect of the judicial function has been notably reduced, and the Rule of Law is tending to become more than ever before the rule of a Parliamentary majority, or of the executive organs to whom they have delegated functions. But the Rule of Law remains ; and so long as the democratic ideal survives, even as a pious fiction, there *must* be a residuum of protected individual rights and an impartial judicial authority to enforce and safeguard them. I do not pause to enquire whether that authority will be found in the ordinary courts or in administrative tribunals or partly in the one and partly in the other. Wherever it may be found, the ultimate and abiding task of the legal profession will remain what it always has been—

to enforce the Rule of Law, to spare no effort regardless of consequences to ensure that justice is done as between man and man and as between the individual and the group, and above all to see to it that justice is *visibly* done. The resolute pursuit of that end with utter courage and detachment will provide us in the future, as it has provided us in the past, with inspiration enough.

Innate ideas have been common to civilised humanity in all the ages, and they should be allowed full play and a commanding influence in social and governmental relations. The *epieikeia* of the Greeks, the *jus naturale* of the Romans, and our own sense of " fair play " according to " the rules of the game," are in essence one and the same, and they can be recognised by an instinct which is unerring. In the international field a great world effort is in progress to-day to protect human rights against the misuse of arbitrary power. That is the task of statesmen, and on their successful discharge of that task the very existence of civilisation may depend. Within the domestic sphere the comparable task of protecting human rights against the corruption of power and the arbitrary exercise of authority is the task of the legal profession, and in this phase of transition its due performance will demand from the lawyers what Lord Clyde called the " favourable conjunction of trained intellect and courageous character." The trained intellect can be left to look after itself. The emphasis to-day must be on the courage and the character— such high character as is expected from every American lawyer, who takes an oath on admission that he will " demean himself uprightly," and the high character which scorns slipshod work and shrinks from the suspicion of sharp practice as from a mortal wound ; and the courage to pursue in face of every obstacle and defiant of pressure or influence every worthy professional target at which the lawyer aims.

And so I would say that the old ideal, shorn of a few unworthy excrescences which dimmed its original lustre, still persists as the guiding light of the lawyer of to-day and of to-morrow. The old texts are still true, and the old sermons can still be read with profit.

Let me conclude with a parable, drawn against a very different background, but still conveying a message for to-day. It is an old story and a true story. On Monday, 10th March 1599, the Court of Session were engaged in the Old Tolbooth in Edinburgh in hearing counsel in a multiplepoinding— *Auchterlonie and Others* v. *Bruce and Hamilton*. The debate was interrupted by the arrival of the King, James VI, who took his seat on the Bench and after listening for a short time " commanded " the Court to decide in favour of the pursuers. The scene lives again in the account of an onlooker. The Lord President Seton rose and addressed the King.

I am President, he said, and have the first place to speak. You are our King, and we are your Majesty's subjects, sworn to obey you in all humility, which we shall do with our lands, with our gear and with our lives. But in this matter of law conscience, being sworn to do justice, we shall do as our consciences lead us ; unless your Majesty command us to the contrary, in which case I shall not vote at all nor any honest man present.

There was a painful scene, but the King withdrew. Let me continue in the words of the old record :

The King swears that he will have the case reversed, which the President understanding says that he will pen it in Latin, French and Greek to be sent to all the judges in the world, and that by his vote it shall never be reversed. And so say the whole Session.

Will you join with me in adding, 350 years later : " *And so say all of us.*"

1950

The Dark Age of Scottish Legal History, 1350-1650

As I looked back over the list of eminent scholars who have lectured under this foundation during the last twenty years, I was consoled for my sense of unworthiness to be included in such a company by the reflection that, unlike nearly all of them, I knew Dr David Murray. To us, his younger professional colleagues, Dr Murray was the living embodiment of the lawyer's ideal of supreme business capacity united to accomplished scholarship, both wide and deep. In these days of whole-time specialisation in ever-narrowing fields it is fitting to recall that a single generation of busy Glasgow legal practitioners produced three men—Dr Neilson, Dr David Murray and Dr Baird Smith—whose native ability and tireless industry enabled them by spare-time research to win honoured positions in the world of pure scholarship, and by so doing to add lustre in public esteem to the profession of which they were distinguished ornaments. Of the three Dr Murray stood out by reason of the wide range of his interests and the versatility of his genius ; and any Scottish lawyer would count it a privilege, as I most assuredly do, to add yet another stone to the memorial cairn which is rising in his honour within the University which he served so long and so well.

I have chosen my subject from Scottish Legal History because Dr Murray was among the first of the modern school to penetrate far into that little explored territory, and because I gratefully acknowledge the inspiration I have derived from the study of his published works on different aspects of the subject. My title—The Dark Age of Scottish Legal History— requires a word of explanation.

The period of our country's history on which I invite you to concentrate for a little this afternoon began about the middle of the fourteenth century and ended about the middle of the seventeenth. There is a twilight period at both the beginning and the end of this prolonged eclipse, but for something like 250 years the student of Scottish Legal History has to grope his way in semi-darkness, which is rendered all the more oppressive by contrast with the growing light which now illuminates the thirteenth century and the high noon of the later seventeenth. Before the shadows fall we can identify most of the salient features of the legal landscape as it was in the days of Bruce ; and when we emerge again into the clear light of Restoration Scotland the stage is already set for the rapid creation of a distinctive system of jurisprudence which in its main essentials still persists. How far is it possible to penetrate the intervening gloom and to link up the medieval with the modern world in Scots Law ?

Openly envious of the wealth of material at the disposal of his English colleagues, the student of Scottish Legal History has long been accustomed to lament the loss or destruction or inaccessibility of our native records, and to throw up his hands in despair. For such an attitude there is much to be said in extenuation. It is depressing for us to note that in one recent history of English Law [1] the author was able to cite more than 400 reported decisions dating from before 1500 ; and that in another special study [2] the writer relied upon 192 published and unpublished Year Books covering the period from 31 Edward I to 27 Henry VIII. And in addition to Year Books, of course, Plea Rolls abound. By the middle of the thirteenth century the English Bench was administering centralised Royal justice, at Westminster and on circuit, according to a pattern of organisation which persisted without material change until the Judicature Act of 1873 ; and the law thus consistently administered by successions of skilled and (virtually) professional judges was already being systematised in text-books and abridgements, culminating in Littleton's famous treatise of 1475. In the fourteenth century the Temple had already become the headquarters of English Law ; and well before the

---

[1] Plucknett, *Concise History of the Common Law*, 4th ed. 1948.
[2] Kiralfy, *The Action on the Case*, 1951.

close of the fifteenth century an organised legal profession with
teaching facilities was centred in the Inns of Court.   Is it to be
wondered at that the scholars of England and America, confronted with such an embarrassment of riches, have already
provided a whole library of books devoted to the history of
the Common Law, and that their labours are by no means
complete ?

Now we in Scotland have nothing remotely resembling
that, and we never shall have, for with us events pursued a
very different course.   We must never forget that in this
wealth of historical sources English Law is unique, or equalled
only by its great rival, the law of Rome ; and that the feature
which specially impresses the foreign jurist when he looks
across the Channel is the extent to which modern English Law
is the product of an unbroken and traceable historical evolution, in which respect it differs from Scots, French, German,
Dutch and Italian Law.[1]   It would thus be quite inappropriate that we should approach our problem in the spirit
of a member of the Selden Society, whose chief difficulty is to
see the wood amongst the trees.   We must stand much further
back and take a wider sweep of the distant horizons before
we can hope to discern the controlling tendencies and trends of
development which were in operation during the transition
from medieval to modern Scots Law ; and we must take
comfort from Raleigh's pregnant warning that " whosoever
in writing a Historie shall follow truth too near the heels,
it may haply strike out his teeth."

Nor is the poverty of our Scottish sources so extreme as
we sometimes pretend.   Let us count our blessings, such as
they are.

First I place the general history of the institutions of
Western Europe during the period when the Middle Ages
were breaking up.   Amongst the peoples which then composed Western Europe there were local and racial differences
enough, as there still are : but their common origin in the
Roman Empire of the West and their common inheritance of thought, achievement and religion ensured that,

[1] René David, *Introduction a l'Étude du Droit Privé de l'Angleterre*, Paris, 1948.

governmentally, evolution should take place more or less according to a single pattern, and what that pattern was it is not unduly difficult to discover.[1]

Next I place the knowledge we now possess of the position as it was in Scotland in the days of Bruce,[2] and the infinitely fuller information we have long possessed as to the position as it had become by the later seventeenth century. At first sight the contrast between these two pictures is a little bewildering, but on narrower examination it is possible with some confidence to " extrapolate the curve " across the intervening areas where precise data are lacking.

Thirdly and lastly I take our own native sources for the fourteenth, fifteenth and sixteenth centuries. We part company with the detail of the early law in *Quoniam Attachiamenta* and in the fourteenth century Registers of Brieves ; but these can be considerably supplemented during the fourteenth and fifteenth centuries by numerous records imbedded in monastic cartularies and other charter collections, disjointed and imperfect though such records too often are.[3] From the time of James I onwards a mass of new information becomes available in the Statute Book, but caution is required in drawing inferences from numberless, and not wholly consistent, enacted aspirations after reforms, which may, or may not, have enjoyed more than a paper reality. Published records of the Lords Auditors and the Council and Session become available as from 1466, and will soon be more or less complete to 1532 ; but as these records consist only of abbreviated minutes of the proceedings and of formal orders of the courts, and rarely disclose the reasons for a decision, they are much less informative than one could have wished, and not comparable in

---

[1] H. A. L. Fisher, *History of Europe*, 1936, p. 6. The standard works of the several countries are conveniently accessible in the *Continental Legal History* series (London, 1912-28). See especially Brissaud, *Manuel d'histoire du droit français* ; Esmein, *Continental Criminal Procedure* (Eng. ed. 1913), and Olivier-Martin, *Précis d'histoire du droit français*, 1938.

[2] The sources are discussed in vols. 10 and 11 of the Stair Society Publications, entitled *Regiam Majestatem* and the *Register of Brieves*.

[3] Mr Hector McKechnie, K.C., has collected these sources in so far as dealing with the procedural brieves, and I am indebted to him for a perusal of the MS. of an article which it is hoped will soon be available in print.

value with the English Year Books.[1] For the early sixteenth
century the records of the Sheriff Courts of Aberdeenshire
and Fife and of the Barony Court of Carnwath are specially
valuable for the information they afford regarding the inferior
courts.[2] To the same period belongs the *St Andrews Formulare*,
which may be dated 1514-46, and which provides a rich selection of ecclesiastical and regality writs [3] ; and later in the
sixteenth century there were compiled several descriptive
treatises which contain much suggestive and authentic historical
material—the *Discours Particulier* of 1559,[4] Balfour's *Practicks*
of 1575,[5] Sir John Skene's notes to the " Auld Lawes " and his
De Verborum Significatione at the close of the sixteenth century,[6]
Craig's *Jus Feudale* [7] which, however, is European rather than
Scottish, and Bisset's *Rolment of Courtis*,[8] the last two belonging
to the early seventeenth century. For the criminal law and
practice we have also Pitcairn's *Criminal Trials*,[9] and much
valuable information on every phase of the earlier law may be
obtained from the last of the pre-Stair compilations, Hope's
Major Practicks.[10]

Let it be freely acknowledged that, both in quality and in
quantity, these sources make a poor showing as against the
abundance of authentic contemporary raw material on which

[1] *Acta Dominorum Auditorum* (1466-1494) ed. by Thomas Thomson, 1839 ;
Acta Dominorum Concilii (1478-1495) ed. by Thomas Thomson, 1839 ; *Acta Dominorum Concilii* (1496-1501) ed. by Neilson and Paton, 1918 ; *Acta Dominorum
Concilii* (1501-3) ed. by Lord Clyde for the Stair Society, 1943. A further volume
of this series in the Stair Society publications is in the press.

[2] *Aberdeenshire*, ed. by D. Littlejohn for the New Spalding Club, 1904-7 ;
Fife and *Carnwath*, ed. by Prof. Dickinson for the Scottish History Society, 1928
and 1936.

[3] Ed. by Donaldson and Macrae for the Stair Society, vols. vii and ix, 1942-44.

[4] By MacGill and Bellenden (Bannatyne Club Publications).

[5] *A System of the More Ancient Law of Scotland* by Sir James Balfour of Pettin-
dreich, published in 1754.

[6] *The Auld Lawes and Constitutions of Scotland* collected by Sir John Skene,
1609, 1613 and 1774.

[7] By Sir Thomas Craig of Riccarton, published 1655, Eng. translation by
Lord Clyde, 1934.

[8] By Habakkuk Bisset, ed. by Sir Philip Hamilton-Grierson for the Sc. Text
Soc., 1920-26.

[9] *Criminal Trials in Scotland*, 1488-1624, ed. by Robert Pitcairn for the Maitland
and Bannatyne Clubs, 1833.

[10] Ed. by Lord Clyde for the Stair Society, 1937-38.

the English legal historians are at work. Many questions can be asked with regard to this intermediate period of Scottish legal history which cannot be answered, and many of the propositions which are advanced rest upon the slender foundation of speculative inference. But as we are not watching in Scotland (as we are in England), the progressive organic evolution of a unique system of doctrine and practice, but only the successive tentative efforts of a state, under conditions of extreme difficulty, to construct a legal system which would command public confidence, most of the questions which have been asked and are being answered regarding early English Law are not worth asking as regards early Scots Law. Be that as it may, we have at least a foundation on which to build ; and while it would be impracticable within the limits of a lecture to pursue the investigation into any detail, let me try to summarise the general conclusions which seem justified from a study of the sources.

To begin, as we must, with the general background, the phase of development through which Scotland was passing during the period under review had its counterpart in all Western states. In different countries that phase began and ended at different times. It assumed several different forms ; and its end products varied widely. Its common characteristic was the decay of the political, economic and social bonds inherent in the feudal pattern of society, and the concentration of the effective power in fewer and larger units. In some countries—but not appreciably in Scotland—it was not accomplished without convulsive strains and stresses—witness the stories of Wat Tyler in England, and the Jacquerie in France and the Hussites in Bohemia. In England it rapidly resulted in the triumph of royal justice, and later in the supremacy of Parliament. In France power came to be concentrated in the monarchy, but legally the country we now know as France was for long all but split into two. In Germany the process shattered the country into fragments which were not reunited for centuries. And in Italy the transformation was obscured in parts of the country by the persisting influence of Roman and Canon Law and by a great revival of the former.

For present purposes we may single out two features of the old régime which was everywhere slowly dissolving. The first was the boundless authority as a source of law of old custom—the general custom of national tradition, the custom of the Books of the Feus, the local variants of that general custom, and even the custom of a manor or a barony or a vill. A rigid conservatism in the worst sense of the term was the guide of life, and the search in times of trouble was for the " good old law." [1] The second outstanding feature was the fragmentary dispersal of the judicial power and its consequent inefficacy.[2] The spirit of an age which was being reborn amid a maelstrom of new problems to which the " good old law " offered no real answer demanded justice with a sword in its hand. There were plenty of swords in those days, but rarely in the hand of justice.

With this broad picture in our minds let us now return to contemporary Scotland. With us—for reasons which belong to the political history of the period—the transformation was much later in its onset and much slower in its operation than elsewhere in Europe. As a result Scots Law still displayed even in the later sixteenth century a pronounced flavour of medievalism, as every reader of Balfour's *Practicks* can see for himself. It is most significant that the Scottish authorities, who were perfectly well aware of the weakness of the position, continued for centuries to grope for a solution in the " good old law " by setting up commission after commission to disinter and re-edit *Regiam Majestatem* and *Quoniam Attachiamenta*,[3] and were still pursuing this forlorn hope hundreds of years after Pope Urban II had exposed its futility.[4] It is always in a country's land law that medieval usages make a last-ditch stand for survival, and to this day the land law of Scotland is the most feudal of

---

[1] " Le système juridique du premier âge féodal réposait sur l'idée que ce qui a été a par là même le droit d'être. Marc Bloch, *La Société Féodale*, Paris, 1940, p. 179. Cf. also the same author's *Les caractères originaux de l'histoire rurale française*, 1931 ; and Fritz Kern, *Kingship and Law in the Middle Ages*, transl. by S. B. Chrimes (Oxford), 1939.

[2] " le prodigieux morcellement des pouvoirs judiciaires," Bloch, *op. cit.*, ii, 117.

[3] For an account of these efforts see Stair Soc., vol. i, 71 ff.

[4] " Scire debes Creatorem tuum dixisse—Ego sum veritas—non autem usus vel consuetudo," Migne, *Patr. Lat.*, vol. cli, 356.

P

all the systems of land law which exist.　But the persistence of legal medievalism in Scotland long after it had become outmoded there and elsewhere was not so much the conscious choice of the Scots of the fourteenth and fifteenth centuries as the inevitable consequence of their inability to provide the conditions under which alone something better might take its place, and in particular of their failure until well into the sixteenth century to set up a centralised supreme court worthy of the name.　For it has never yet proved possible to construct a first-class system of Common Law without a first-class system of judicial organisation and a skilled body of lawyers to work it.　It is possible to have a totalitarian legal system consisting of a prefabricated civil or religious code imposed from above.　But if instead of that you prefer to establish a Common Law system, you must accept an article which is practitioner-made, and slowly hammered out by the craftsmanship of generations of judges and pleaders.　This point merits deeper consideration.

The death of Bruce, even more truly than the death of Alexander III, marks the close of an epoch in Scottish history. By this time Scotland had created a system of Scoto-Norman law which, though initially modelled upon the Anglo-Norman law of the age of Glanvill, was developing along lines of its own and had diverged appreciably from the English Law of Edward I.[1]　If judicial machinery had been provided in Scotland in any way comparable to that which existed South of the Border, the evolution of Scots Law might well have proceeded without interruption (as the evolution of English law did) during the troublous centuries which ensued.　Indeed the prospects of rapid and successful development were even better in Scotland than in England, for we had already avoided the premature crystallisation of our law in a rigid technical framework,[2] and would never have required to force the barriers by the *consimilis casus*, the *querela sine brevi*, the action

---

[1] This theme is developed in the writer's introductions to the *Register of Brieves* and *Regiam Majestatem*, Stair Society publications, vols. x and xi.

[2] Cf. Plucknett, *Concise History of the Common Law*, 1948, 103 ; Holdsworth, *History of English Law*, ii, 591.

on the case, or a separate equity jurisdiction.[1]   But one indispensable condition for development, a powerful and skilled
central court, was lacking, and in its absence Scoto-Norman
law was a house built upon the sand.

This is not the place in which to trace the confusing story
of the many efforts which were made in Scotland between 1341
and 1532 to create out of the " Council " or the " Session "
or the " Parliament " or Committees of these bodies an ersatz
substitute for a supreme court.[2]   It is a story of patient trial
and error and of repeatedly rejected constitutional experiments.   That the public had little confidence in feudal courts
or sheriffs or baillies of burghs is plain enough.   They wanted
something better and they could not get it.   At the risk of
inviting the retort that there is nothing like leather, I make
bold to assert that the main source of the trouble was the
persistent policy of confiding the judicial function to an unpaid,
part-time, lay magistracy, masquerading as judges and
engaging casually in the discharge of judicial duties in intervals
snatched from their major preoccupations as territorial
magnates, or statesmen, or ecclesiastical dignitaries.   Doubtless
they did their best.   Doubtless a general acquaintance with
the materials of the law was widely diffused and some of the
clerics would of course be accomplished civilians and canonists.
But what could be expected of these casual committees ?
To take an instance at random, the court which sat on 19th
March 1482-83, consisted of sixteen persons, all of whom had
never sat together before and never sat together again—an
archbishop, three bishops, an archdeacon, a priest, three earls,
three barons, the chancellor and three nondescript persons—
truly an oddly constituted tribunal, capable of dispensing
rough justice, but quite incapable (especially in the absence of
reports) of making any coherent contribution to the orderly
exposition and development of Common Law.

To this single cause, explained but not altogether excused
by the political difficulties of the times, I think that we may

[1] See *Select Cases of Procedure without Writ* (Selden Soc., vol. lx) ; Kiralfy,
The Action on the Case, 1951.

[2] The literature on the subject is reviewed in Lord Clyde's Introduction to
Acta Dominorum Concilii, 1943, Stair Society, Vol. 8.

ascribe the ominous symptoms of decline and decay which become apparent in Scots Law and its administration during the later fourteenth, the fifteenth and the early sixteenth centuries, and nowhere more notably than in legal procedure. At the start of this period Scotland possessed as an inheritance from Norman Law an armoury of well defined remedies by way of brieves, the equivalent of the English writs—much less rigid and technical than the writs, and employed with greater flexibility and freedom, but still supplying early Scots Law with the indispensable skeleton to be clothed with the flesh and blood of legal doctrine. A number of these brieves (administrative brieves rather than contentious) continued in regular use into modern times ; but in ordinary contentious litigation outside the special spheres of the small number of brieves which survived, the effort at scientific precision in the choice of appropriate legal remedies was gradually relaxed and eventually abandoned, at least in the supreme court. In the Statute Book and the court records of this period there are numberless references, in Latin and in the vernacular, to " actions," " causes " and " complaints," and at least one [1] to the English technical term " *audita querela* " ; but, though we have thousands of specimens to examine, it is still impossible to determine in what respect, if any, an action differed from a complaint, or whether different forms were used for initiating the two types of process—if indeed written forms were usually employed.[2] Latterly the normal, and probably the invariable, written initial writ was the Summons and not the Brieve, the Summons being capable of adaptation so as to take the place of any pleadable brieve, and also to meet situations for which no brieve ever existed. Practically every action in Scotland thus came to be " an action on the case."

The infection of lax informality and lack of precision necessarily spread swiftly from the adjective to the substantive law. The records of the later fifteenth and early sixteenth centuries provide specimens of a very wide range of causes of action, some belonging to categories which had already

---

[1] In 1400, A.P.S. i, 576.

[2] Cf. Lord Clyde in Introduction to *Acta Dominorum Concilii (cit. supra)*, p. lii.

been labelled and pigeon-holed in the thirteenth century, but the majority entirely new. With insignificant exceptions one and all of them are envisaged simply as the infliction of a wrong by the defender upon the pursuer, as if the only chapter in the law of Scotland were one devoted to delicts or torts. Irrespective of whether the action is one for breach of contract, or for payment of a debt or the price of goods sold, or for damages, or for specific implement, or for delivery, or for warrandice of title, or for reduction of a challenged transaction, or for half a hundred other things, the pursuer simply takes objection to the " wrangous " detention and withholding of something, or the " wrangous " postponing to do something, or the " wrangous " occupation and labouring of certain lands, and so on ; and the common form of judgment is one which simply finds that the defender did " wrang," or did " na wrang," as the case may be. It is hardly an exaggeration to say that each pursuer eventually presented himself before the tribunal in the guise of " an infant crying in the night, And with no language but a cry," and that the whole of Scots Law had been compressed into a single commandment : " Thou shalt do na wrang ! "

This curious over-simplification is not of course peculiar to Scots Law but is characteristic of much early law, which exhibits a tendency " to conceive of *any* legal question as one of wrong-doing and its suppression." [1] As the contemporary Year Books show, English lawyers were also liable in argument to slip into the same methods of expression.[2] But the Scottish courts of our period seem to have adopted to an exceptional degree the primitive notion that the chief task of a civil tribunal is not to enforce a right so much as to avenge a wrong.

Such a reversion to patriarchal method and archaic ideas was of course incompatible with legal development. It involved turning back the hands of the clock to the early days when all civil actions were described as *placita de wrang et*

---

[1] See Professor Daube on " The Scales of Justice," *Jurid. Review*, lxiii, 124 ff.

[2] In the early days of the Action on the Case, " the action is not conceived of as making the Act wrongful but as providing a remedy for an existing wrong," Keralfy, *Action on the Case*, p. 9. This feature seems to have vanished in England by the late fifteenth century.

unlauch [1] and when legal principles were as yet undifferentiated. This was unquestionably the period when Scots Law, viewed as a science and a philosophy from the comparative standpoint, reached its low-water mark ; and it is not easy to see why it should have sunk so low unless the explanation is that the executive remained so impotent and the courts so inferior in capacity and efficiency for so prolonged a period that they gradually dragged the substantive law down to their own level. The odd thing is that from the fifteenth century onwards there was an insistent and persistent public demand from a growing population for better and stronger organised justice, and in those disorderly times there must have been many who had good cause to seek protection against oppression.[2] Not only so but we can be sure from independent evidence that there was plenty of good law in the background and plenty of lawyers to handle it with competent skill. Let me digress to examine this last point a little more fully.

Throughout the fourteenth and fifteenth centuries the Scottish charter records abound in transactions devised and executed with high legal ingenuity and an undoubted grasp of principle. There are also to be found sufficient detailed pleadings and legal opinions to show that familiarity with the classics of the Civil and Canon Law was by no means uncommon.[3] What else would one expect of the descendants of the skilled Canonists of the thirteenth century who were now being educated in Paris and Orleans and other famous Continental law schools ? [4] Still more significant and specific is the evidence of the Statute Book from 1449 onwards, for it contains a long succession of pivotal reforms around which whole chapters of Scots Law continued to revolve for centuries and many of which are still in force.[5] Had it not been for these

---

[1] See *Regiam Majestatem* (Stair Soc. vol. xi, p. 312).

[2] Reference may be made to the anonymous poem in the *Liber Pluscardensis* ; Dunbar's " Tidings from the Session " ; and many passages in Sir David Lyndsay's " Satyre of the Thrie Estaits."

[3] Notable instances are afforded by the appeal of John Crab, (*Reg. Episc. Aberd.* 143 ff.), and the *Chartulary of Lindores* (Sc. Hist. Soc. vol. xlii), Nos. cxlix and clx.

[4] Cf. the writer's *Select Scottish Cases of the Thirteenth Century*, Edinburgh, 1944.

[5] Notably 1449, c. 6 ; 1469, c. 4 ; 1469, c. 12 ; 1469, c. 36 ; 1573, c. 1 ; 1581, c. 24 ; 1594, c. 24 ; 1617, c. 12 and 1621, c. 18.

statutes, modern Scots Law would have been an entirely different thing in many respects, and their enactment is proof positive of the existence of legal statesmanship of a high order at the time when they were passed. It was during this period too that unknown lawyers of vision and experience brought to perfection our classic system of conveyancing, and devised after many experiments our distinctive system of registration of deeds. We only know these men by their work, but the legacy they bequeathed to later generations proves that, even during the Dark Age of Scottish Legal History, Scotland had conveyancers and academic lawyers of real merit. Nor must we overlook the part played throughout the whole of Scottish legal history by arbitration, though an arbitration requires in the contestants, from its inception to the execution of the award, a measure of mutual consent and sweet reasonableness too often absent during the centuries under review.

It may be objected however that it is not by chamber lawyers or legislators that the Common Law is developed, but in the clash of contested litigations and with the aid of skilled forensic practitioners ; and Lord Clyde has hazarded the view that during our period there was " a dearth of skilled practitioners before the Courts " and that it was (at least in part) to this fact that the the informality and amateurishness of judicial process was attributable.[1] I feel the force of this point, but I question whether it is nearly as strong as has been suggested. As early as 1455 it was considered appropriate to prescribe by statute a distinctive costume for pleaders.[2] From the time when the printed records of the supreme court become available, " procurators " are appearing regularly on behalf of their clients at important stages in the proceedings, though litigants were freely permitted to appear in person if they so desired. Between 1496 and 1501 it is possible to identify at least a dozen supreme court practitioners, some of them practising on a very extensive scale ; for, to take a few examples, Mr James Henryson, in addition to acting as King's Advocate in many litigations to which the Crown was a party, appeared in private practice on ninety-three occasions,

---

[1] *Acta Dominorum Concilii* (*cit. supra*), p. lvi.   [2] A.P.S. ii, 43.

Mr Thomas Allan on forty-three, and Mr David Balfour of Caraldstane on thirty-three.[1] A few years later four "forspekars" repeatedly appeared in different cases before the Sheriff Court of Aberdeenshire [2] ; and the Fife Sheriff Court records for 1515-22 reveal the existence of scores of procurators, some of whom appear for different persons on different occasions.[3] Many of these may have been, but all of them cannot have been, private friends of the litigants acting as unpaid amateurs. Finally, when allowance is made for the relative population, the numerical strength of the Faculty of Advocates in the sixteenth century was greater than it is to-day, 126 advocates having been admitted between 1532 and 1600, and fifty-two being in practice in 1586.[4]

From all these indications we may conclude that during this long intermediate period in our legal history there was plenty of law in Scotland and plenty of lawyers to apply it ; but unfortunately an absence of tribunals, adequately manned and equipped, in which the law could be effectively applied in contested litigation. Supreme courts before which one or both of the parties appeared as often as not in person and without skilled aid ; which often permitted the pleadings to be presented orally, and administered summary justice on the basis of a grievance informally aired [5] ; which regarded the appellate jurisdiction as a means of disciplining the court below and not as an opportunity for reviewing the judgment appealed against ; and which rarely preserved any record from which their *ratio decidendi* could be ascertained—such courts were largely useless for the purpose of working out legal principles by the only methods by which that process has ever been effected, or for providing solutions for the many new

---

[1] *Acts of the Lords of Council in Civil Causes*, ed. by Neilson and Paton, 1918. Comparable figures can be given for the years 1501-3.

[2] *Records of Aberdeenshire Sheriff Court* (New Spalding Club), 904.

[3] *Sheriff Court Book of Fife* (Sc. Hist. Soc.), 1928.

[4] Hope's *Major Practicks*, vii, 5 ; *Early History of the Scottish Signet*, R. K. Hannay, 50 ; *The Faculty of Advocates* (Scottish Record Soc.), by Sir Francis Grant, 1944 ; early Acts of Sederunt.

[5] " Les partyes sont constraintz de respondre et repliquer par vive parolle . . . les dits sieurs procedent en toutes leurs causes sommairement," *Discours Particulier* (*cit. supra*).

problems posed by an expanding society.   The lawyers of
Scotland seem to have silently acquiesced in a situation which
they were powerless to remedy, and to have sought an outlet
for their activities elsewhere than in the disappointing arena
of the Lords Auditors and the Lords of Council.   The contrast
with England in this respect is arresting.   " It is this curious
combination of legal development with political retrogression,"
said Holdsworth of contemporary England, " which is the
distinctive characteristic of these two centuries " [1] ;   and all
the English legal historians remark upon the fact that an era,
in other respects so unsettled and disjointed, left little or no
impression upon the singular and steady unity of England's
Private Law.   But in England the Common Law was already
firmly rooted before the storm fell, and the powerful organisation of efficient centralised courts provided the developing law
with an anchorage which never failed.   Such statements
cannot be made of contemporary Scotland, where legal
retrogression and political retrogression went hand in hand ;
and where law was driven underground into the studies of
the conveyancers and the chapter houses of abbeys and
cathedrals and into Continental law schools, until long afterwards and under very different administrative auspices the
entire structure was erected anew.

But it was not all loss.   When the architects of modern
Scots Law were at long last free to resume the forward march,
they were already habituated to thinking of law and equity
as indissolubly fused into a single medium suitable for administration by a single court.   Impatient of technicalities, scornful
of fictions and schooled in the civilian idiom of legal thinking,
what mattered to these men were rights and wrongs deduced
from principle, and not remedies as such : since every right
had to be enforced, and for every wrong there had to be
found a remedy.   Their thinking was deeply tinged by the
experiences of the generations of students who had frequented
the law schools of France and the Low Countries, and of
generations of churchmen steeped in Canonist lore.   Against so
rich and inspiring a background they were able to pick and

[1] *History of English Law*, ii, 406.

choose from civilian and Canonist Law and from the best from Scotland's legal past, including much that had been accomplished behind the scenes in the fifteenth and sixteenth centuries ; to avoid some of the errors into which others had fallen ; and in process of time to fashion that eclectic system, midway between the two great schools of Romanist and English Law, which represents Scotland's unique contribution to the jurisprudence of the world. But all this only became possible long after the creation of an efficient central court of trained judges, working in association with a trained legal profession.

So far I have been thinking of the civil law of Scotland, and if I have said very little about the criminal law, that is because there is very little that can usefully be said. Until modern times all criminal law resolved itself into little more than a method of avenging infringements of the sixth and eighth Commandments, and few significant differences emerge between one legal system and another except in the spirit in which the law is administered. In the Scotland of our period—and indeed until much later—the prevailing impression is one of a rather chaotic welter of ill-defined and over-lapping jurisdictions—the Justiciar, the Deputes for the Justiciar, Lords of Regality, the sheriffs and the barons, with the Council hovering in the background—all professing to administer rules which differed but little from the rules in " the auld lawes " and in the wonderfully advanced exposition in the Fourth Book of *Regiam Majestatem*, but for the most part administering it in the spirit to be expected in a land which was in a chronic state of disturbance, where life was cheap and relics of the blood feud still survived, and where everything within the Highland line was literally beyond the pale. Such being the general scene—and it is one from which a modern lawyer would rather avert his eyes—it is of special interest to note (at a time when a Royal Commission is engaged upon the problem of capital punishment) that, under French and Canonist influences, the Scottish lawyers of the fourteenth and fifteenth centuries were already anxiously drawing distinctions between the different degrees of homicide so as to secure that the wilful and premeditated murder should stand in a class apart.   Significantly enough the reforms in the law on this point were embodied in statutes, and owed nothing, so far as we know, to the criminal courts of the time.[1]

But there is another and very important chapter of the law which must be mentioned—that large part of the legal business of Scotland which was appropriated by the Church courts. The papal judges-delegate, who figured so conspicuously in the legal history of the thirteenth century, had lost most of their former importance, but the Courts Christian remained, and the Bishop, the Archdeacon and the Official were permitted, and almost encouraged, to exercise an exclusive jurisdiction in matrimonial cases, including questions of legitimacy and dowry, and in all matters affecting wills and moveable succession.   In Scotland their relations with the civil authorities seem to have been much more harmonious than in most other countries.   The law administered in the Courts Christian was of course the highly refined and fully formulated Canon Law which was being taught in practically every University in Europe, including in the fifteenth century St Andrews, Glasgow and Aberdeen,[2] and which possessed as two notable characteristics an elaborate system of written pleadings and an equally elaborate hierarchy of appeals. One of the puzzles to which this study gives rise is how it came about that the same Churchmen, who were handling this finished system of law and procedure in their own courts, who often acted as arbiters, and who were at the same time regularly sitting as members of one or other of the civil courts, found it possible in the latter capacity to rest content with methods so jejune, so informal and so relatively immature.

As we part with our subject may I suggest that the Dark Age of Scottish Legal History is not quite so dark as it has been painted, and that the prime defect which caused the darkness was a defect not in the law nor in the lawyers but in the judicial arrangements—the " inefficiency of an unprofessional judicature " ? [3]   And yet Lord Clyde, who coined

[1] See (in 1369) A.P.S. l. 509 and the Act of 1469, c. 35.   The subject is discussed in the notes to *Regiam Majestatem*, iv, 5 (Stair Soc. publications, vol. xi, p. 255).
[2] Dr Baird Smith in Stair Soc. Publications, vol. i, p. 186.
[3] *Acta Dominorum Concilii (cit. supra)*, p. xlv.

that phrase, himself suggested the doubt in the last letter he wrote to me that we might be doing these men less than justice ; that the imperfections of the records might conceal in them a competent knowledge at least of the materials of the law, and a conscious resort in each case to either customary or canonical or civil or feudal law, as the circumstances might dictate, with the overriding object of finding the *bonum et aequum.* To that doubt we shall never know the full answer ; but we may safely conclude that, though Scots Law as judicially administered in those days, seems strangely inchoate, inarticulate and amorphous, it was steadily maturing in the background, and that the work done in the background during the Dark Age of our legal history played a vital part in preparing the way for the ultimate culmination of modern Scots Law.

You may think that my conclusions regarding this period are disappointingly negative, and so they are. The legal historian must be both a historian and a lawyer, but he should be a lawyer first. In his capacity as a historian he sees in the story of Scots Law three chapters—the first recording the false start of the Scoto-Norman law ; the second devoted to a prolonged retrogression and decline ; and the third containing the story of a fresh start and the fashioning of a new system in the construction of which the old law was only one, and by no means the most important, of the ingredients. But in his capacity as a lawyer, the first two chapters will present themselves to the legal historian as a valuable introduction, but no more than an introduction, to chapter third, showing the sources of inspiration upon which the architects of the modern law drew and the raw materials, some of which they utilised and others of which they discarded. For it is only in the later seventeenth century and with the publication of Stair's *Institutions* that the history of Scots Law acquires for the first time supreme interest and value for the Scottish lawyer.

1951

Early Scottish Statutes Revisited

WHEN in 1861 Sir Henry Maine published his classic treatise on "Ancient Law," he founded a school of historical jurisprudence of permanent worth. But it is a long time since 1861 ; and in the interval archæologists, historians and anthropologists have assembled from every corner of the globe and from every era of human history masses of information as regards primitive law of which Maine excusably knew nothing. It is indeed a tribute to Maine's scholarly intuition that so many of his brilliant inductions have survived such a widening of the horizons of his subject; but the student of to-day, presented with all this new evidence, has a manifest duty to re-examine some of the old problems afresh.

To risk a few perilous generalisations, the conclusions which seem to be emerging from a study of the fresh data are these :— In every age and in every land the reactions to the advance of civilisation are very much the same. There is a single common reservoir of juristic ideas upon which every people draws instinctively when the need arises, applying the same solutions to the same problems, subject only to such variations as are imposed by racial, economic or climatic conditions, by foreign infiltration, or by wars of conquest or other like extraneous agencies. Viewed upon the cosmic scale the entire process is a standing illustration of the principle of relativity, for the phase reached in each community is not dependent upon the time factor but solely upon the stage of development which has been attained ; so that much the same stratum of legal institutions can be traced, say, in early Babylon of 2000 B.C., in Republican Rome, in Western Europe before the " age of Glanvill," and in some undeveloped parts of the world at the present day. The detailed differences are many, but they are submerged beneath substantial identity of content and of method.

If these views are well founded—and they are certainly supported by a volume of eloquent testimony—the legal historian must abandon the old insularity of outlook which confined attention to one system at a time and very rarely looked beyond the law of Rome and the law of England, and must be prepared to survey mankind from China to Peru throughout four millennia. Even if the new views are not wholly well founded (and it is still too soon to determine their exact validity), the student of early Scots Law has a great deal to learn from an examination of the many " books of the law," " codes " and other written legal compilations which have come to light—the Assyrian and Sumerian Laws, the Codes of Hammurabi and of the Hittites, the Laws of Gortyn and of the Greek States, the Hebrew Code, and the laws of the Germanic States, from the Salic Law to the Lex Burgundionum. He will find, for instance, that there is nothing new under the sun ; that conscious borrowing will not explain the repetition of the same ideas almost in the same words in several states widely separated in space and time ; that early codes and legal text-books tend to fall into several distinct categories, differing in source and in character ; and that " legislation " (in the sense of the deliberate enactment of positive rules of law and practice), may have played a more important part in legal history than has hitherto been supposed. He will also learn, if he does not know it already, that false ascriptions of laws to lawgivers are as abundant as spurious charters. Against this crowded and suggestive background let us again look at the " statutes " of David I, William the Lion and Alexander II, as these have been recorded for us in the first volume of the Record edition.

The period covered by the reigns of these three kings is 1151 to 1249. There have been ascribed to David thirty-five " statutes," to William forty-two, and to Alexander fifteen, making ninety-two in all. There are no contemporary or official records, and all that Thomas Thomson or Cosmo Innes could do was to reproduce the testimony of a number of MS. compilations, the earliest of which cannot be less than a generation later than the close of the period, and most of which

were written at least a century after the last of the matters
which they purport to record. Nor do the various MSS. speak
with one voice, either as to the text of the enactments or as to
their ascription to the several kings. It follows that, from the
point of view of direct authentication, matters could hardly
have been worse ; and the misgivings entertained by the
editors have been reinforced by the blunt criticisms of later
scholars. Here is a fair field for testing out new views of
primitive law.

Taking first the purely formal aspect of the three sets of
" statutes," it is easy to see that they fall into three distinct
classes :—

(1) There are three reports of judicial decisions (Will. cc.
22 and 23, and Alex. II, c. 3), and one report which is expanded
into a " statute " (Alex. II, c. 10) ;

(2) There are a number of " statutes," properly so called,
in the sense of formal records of an enactment bearing to have
been made at a stated time and place by the king, acting in the
presence, or with the advice or assent, of certain magnates
named or described ; and

(3) There is a large residue consisting of brief text-book
formulations of some rule of law or practice, which are not
ascribed to any specific source though occasionally introduced
in the fashion of the time by some such dubious phrase as
" dominus Rex statuit " or " statutum est." Most of these
reappear in *Regiam Majestatem* or *Quoniam Attachiamenta*.

The Assise of David contains no example of class (1) or
class (2), but examples of all three classes occur haphazardly
throughout the so-called legislation of William and Alexander.
Let us now examine more closely each of the three classes in
turn.

I. *Judicial Decisions.*—Will. cc. 22 and 23 bear to be decisions made by the " Judices Galwidie," whoever they may have
been. Both are directed to bringing Galloway into line with
the rest of Scotland. Both occur in the early Berne MS. There
is independent evidence that about 1175-76 William led an
army into Galloway to subdue Gilbert, the son of Fergus

(Lawrie, *Annals*, 205-6), and it is probable enough that these chapters record part of the efforts at settlement after the suppression of the disturbance. The substance of the decisions is repeated in Skene's *Regiam Majestatem* and in *Quoniam Attachiamenta*, c. 74. While, therefore, there seems to be no reason to doubt the authenticity of the decisions as records of important action taken in the reign of William, they are not " statutes " in the strict sense of the term, and it would be an anachronism to adopt at this period the later view of judicial decision as a source of law.

Alex. II, c. 3, is the " doom against Gillescop " pronounced at Edinburgh in 1228 by judges both of Galloway and of Scotland. The background is given by Fordun, and the record appears in part in the Berne MS. But it has no visible significance as part of the general law. None of these three chapters has any apparent claim to be included in a collection of " statutes."

Alex. II, c. 10, begins as a report of the decision in the action *Helen de Burneville* v. *Henry of Stirling*, which was discussed at some length in my *Select Scottish Cases of the Thirteenth Century* (pp. 52 ff.), and it ends as a general enactment designed to settle the principle for the future. While this chapter may fairly be described as a " statute," it is more than doubtful on intrinsic evidence whether it belongs to the reign of Alexander II and its meaning is still conjectural.

II. *Statutes, properly so called.*—Of these sixteen belong to the reign of William and six to the reign of Alexander II ; and if, as I suggest, chapters 30 to 35 of the Assise of William should be read as part of chapter 29, and chapters 37 to 42 as part of chapter 36, this category covers a large part of William's so-called legislation. Four of William's " statutes " and all of Alexander's are dated. In the Assise of William the introductory formulæ are vague and various, presenting a pretty problem for the constitutional historian, and raising a doubt as to their authenticity ; but in Alexander's statutes the trend is towards the detailed particulars of the testing clause of a contemporary charter, and there are no solecisms or incongruities to suggest forgery. Moreover, nearly all these enactments contain place names or other terms which are distinctively Scottish. The statutes of William are well represented in the Berne and Ayr MSS., though the latter consistently attributes them to David I ; but the manuscript authority for the statutes of Alexander II is relatively poor. As against that, many of Alexander's statutes are concerned with altering pre-existing law in a fashion which finds a congruous background in the mid-thirteenth century—the final stages of the trial by combat, the introduction as an alternative of the assise, the use of novel dissasine, the restriction of repledging, the employment of champions, the new indictment procedure, and other matters. The guarded conclusion is that all the chapters in this class are entitled to inclusion in a collection of statutes, that the chapters ascribed to Alexander II do in fact belong to his reign, and that those ascribed to William, except where sufficiently dated, may have been enacted either in his reign or in the reign of David I.

III. *The miscellaneous residue.*—Within this class I would include the whole of the Assise of David, eleven chapters of William, and four of Alexander II. In addition to sundry vague aspirations after equal justice, judgment by peers, protection to widows, and to the poor, strangers, and merchants, and other generalities, we find the familiar text-book rules about the punishment of theft ; the precautions to be taken to avoid an accusation of theft ; the thief caught red-handed ; haimsucken and other assaults ; burthinsak ; the harbouring of strangers ; the lordless man ; the precautions to be observed when travelling, especially by night ; the regulation of distraint ; the right of asylum ; the thief " habit and repute " ; the hue and cry ; and even the weregild. None of this is distinctive of Scotland, nor indeed of any country, for it is all part of the common stock of the primitive codes which have come to light and can be paralleled more or less exactly by provisions to be found in different ages throughout Europe and the Middle East in every community which reached the state of reducing to written form its embryo legal system. This category of the " statutes " belongs to an entirely different stratum from classes (1) and (2), and they do not all belong to the same stratum. They do not cover the whole field of law, civil and criminal, but only a small part, and many of them are visibly less mature than some of the very early codes of the Middle East, notably the Code of Hammurabi. They do not purport to change or correct the law, nor to introduce new provisions, but merely to declare either customary law or the effect of possible earlier enactments. A few can be traced to a probable source, their inclusion amongst the "statutes" being doubtless accidental. In the Assise of David, for example, chapter 3 echoes the Assise of Clarendon and chapter 5 Magna Carta ; while chapter 35, which bears to introduce the assises of mortancestor and novel dissasine, was manifestly never passed by David I. Chapter 8 of William, which also appears in *Regiam Majestatem*, is an extract from Glanvill's *Tractatus.*

When perusing these old rules, one is sometimes tempted to wonder whether some monkish practical joker did not have a hand in their compilation. Some such person it must have been who foisted upon the lawyers of Scotland the preposterous fable about the sheep, the horse and the mill, which was actually accepted by Balfour in his *Practicks* (p. 509) as a decision by David I, and by Sir John Skene and Sir David Carnegie as chapter 26 of David II, whereas it was in fact an extract from an earlier variant of the Faust legend contained in the *Gesta Romanorum*, remarkable only because in the original it recounts the only known specimen of a legal rubric composed by the Devil in person—and in elegiac couplets at that ! Take for instance chapter 33 of David I, by which this king is actually credited with having enacted that any man who killed a dog must for a year and a day discharge the duties of the deceased animal by keeping watch over its former owner's midden : or chapter 10 of William, which prescribes the gap to be kept in a stream by requiring that it must be wide enough to enable a well-fed three-year-old pig to turn himself about without either his snout or his tail touching the sides. If any of my readers has encountered a parallel to these provisions in any other legal system, ancient or modern, I hope that he will communicate with the editor and so rescue me from the suspicion that these provisions were invented by some medieval A. P. Herbert.

The conclusion is that, when the time comes—and it is surely overdue—for a new edition of the early Scottish statutes, only class (2) of these enactments will be included, sometimes with cautionary notes, in the statutes of the period, and that classes (1) and (3) will be relegated to an appendix of *Fragmenta Collecta*.

1952

Defects in the British Judicial Machine

WHEN in conversation some time ago with a very eminent legal authority, I alluded with admiration to a recent judgment of one of his colleagues who is noted for his independence of outlook, only to elicit the implied rebuke : " But he's a bit of a Bolshevik, you know."

If he is, so, I fear, am I. Not in the sense that either of us have so far incurred or deserved the displeasure of Senator McCarthy ; but in the sense that in these changed days we are finding it increasingly difficult reverently to accept the faith once delivered to our judicial fathers, and to base our daily exercise of the judicial function upon a cautious traditionalism of thought and of method, still less upon a pious *credo quia impossibile.*

Speaking as a practical lawyer, and only as a practical lawyer, whose experience, forensic and judicial, has been acquired mainly in Scotland, I welcome the opportunity of unburdening myself of some of my perplexities to an audience composed for the most part of academic lawyers, who enjoy the immeasurable advantage of being able to watch the frantic strife of the law courts from the comfort and security of ringside seats ; and I do so not merely to implore the passing tribute of a sigh, but to urge you in your writing and teaching to introduce into legal thinking another breath of the fresh air which I like to associate with the name of Jeremy Bentham.

My thesis is founded upon what to me at least is a glimpse of the obvious. It is this. The paramount duty of a court of law and of all who participate in its decisions is a duty owed not to the legal theorist, nor to the writer of text-books, nor to the legal profession, but to the litigant. The judicial function was well described by one of my predecessors in office as one " which every human community craves, without which no human community can hold together, and on the well or ill performance of which the well-being of every human community depends "—the function of *jus dicere*, the function of translating into prompt and effective action in a concrete case the *constans et perpetua voluntas jus suum cuique tribuendi*. It is true that that function cannot long be performed in any community without the gradual formation of a precipitate of principle and generalised doctrine which provides the raw material for the invaluable philosophic synthesis of the academic lawyer. But that precipitate is only an incidental by-product of a process the primary object of which is the rendering of a service to the community, represented in each case by the parties to the litigation. You may not wholly agree with this ; but if you had spent a lifetime face to face with live pursuers and defenders, petitioners and respondents, plaintiffs and defendants, I rather think that you would. The question is whether our Courts are discharging that primary function efficiently, or whether they have lagged behind the needs of an age which has witnessed social, economic, and political trans-formations as sweeping as any that have occurred since the Middle Ages. If that function still is being discharged effi-ciently, it must be little short of miraculous, for in basic essentials our civil courts are still operating the same judicial machine in much the same way as in the last quarter of the nineteenth century.

The rule that the customer is never wrong has its limitations; but it is always a good thing for servants of the public to see themselves as others see them. Whatever the causes, and they are doubtless manifold, it is unfortunately undeniable that the legal profession has rarely been more unpopular than it is to-day. To an increasing extent during the present century large areas of territory previously within the exclusive control of the Courts have been successively withdrawn from their jurisdiction. This process has been in part the result of specific Governmental action directed to the creation of *ad hoc* tribunals more or less completely freed from control by the Judiciary, a subject on which the Lord Chancellor was speaking in America the other day, and in part the result of the deliberate action of the litigants themselves.

As regards the first of these processes the lawyers began by protesting on high grounds of constitutional principle, and these protests were well warranted ; but when it became apparent that the process was not going to be relaxed and was by no means confined to these islands, the protests died away, we have withdrawn our lines to a 38th parallel, and the main effort is now directed towards the provision in the evacuated area of some kind of *droit administratif*. Take one example out of many. For half a century the Workmen's Compensation Acts, and in particular the famous formula " arising out of and in the course of the employment," provided British practitioners and the Courts (and incidentally Mr Willis and Messrs Butterworth) with a happy hunting ground, resulting in literally thousands of reported decisions, many of them in the House of Lords, and countless decisions which never reached the reports. The Table of Cases in the 34th edition of *Willis* extended to 135 pages of print—a veritable quarry in which ample authority could be found for practically any proposition which the ingenuity of counsel might devise. It has been estimated that the reported cases alone must have involved the industries and the trade unions of this country in costs of the order of £1,750,000. By a stroke of the legislative pen the entire subject was removed a few years ago from the jurisdiction of the Courts and placed in other hands ; and I question whether anyone will now be found to advocate in the public interest that that step should be retraced. To a lesser extent the same policy has already been applied to the fertile field of controversy associated with the Agricultural Holdings Acts, and it is probably only a matter of time until it is also applied to the Rent Restriction Acts, which at present seem to occupy so much of the time of the Court of Appeal.

So much for the Governmental attitude. What of the litigants themselves ? Throughout the entire field of mercantile law—insurance, charter parties, bills of exchange, building contracts, sale of goods and many other subjects—the widespread adoption in contracts of arbitration clauses has resulted in the withdrawal from the Courts of the great mass of the business ; for parties evidently prefer to pay for the services of an arbiter and a clerk and accommodation in which to hold the arbitration rather than to take advantage of such facilities virtually free of charge in an ordinary court. It cannot be that arbiters as a class are superior to judges as a class ; for the same persons whose services were in heavy demand as arbiters while they were still at the Bar are rarely given an opportunity of handling the identical type of case after their elevation to the Bench, even when we provide simplified machinery and exclude appeal.

To obviate misunderstanding it is necessary to interpose a cautionary note. Notwithstanding these withdrawals of large classes of work, there is so far no question of our Courts being under-employed. Far from it. The growth of population, the steady flow of new statutes and orders, and the infinite capacity for expansion displayed by what in Sheffield I shall call the law of torts, have taken care of that. Indeed in Scotland the number of actions annually initiated in our Supreme Courts is roughly twice what it was before the war, and the delay in the disposal of cases is at the moment a source of anxiety. Next, it is obvious that the concentration of function in the central government and various public corporations has given rise to many classes of contested issues of which it is at least arguable that they are unsuited for determination by normal judicial processes. Putting all that aside, the conclusion seems inevitable that the Courts are steadily losing popularity, that they are no longer being permitted to exercise their traditional functions as they once did, and that the area of their operations is now confined to only a diminishing part of the entire field. What is wrong ? Are we rendering the service which the community expects and demands ?

It is one thing to describe the symptoms and another to diagnose the cause and suggest a cure. All I can hope to do is to lay before you some of the weaknesses as they appear to a judge, and to leave you to draw your own conclusions. My conviction is that, by misplaced emphasis and excessive concentration upon the theoretical and doctrinal aspect of our task in developing the Common Law, to the neglect of our primary duty to determine concrete disputes with the maximum of expedition and economy, we have made law a luxury article and the judicial process so costly, so meticulous and so leisurely that the supply now exceeds the demand, and that we are no longer offering the type of service to the community which the community desires.   To put the matter in deliberately exaggerated form, solicitors, counsel and judges, when dealing with a case of any legal difficulty, are nowadays forced to think, or have habituated themselves to thinking, all the time, first, of the law reporters, second, of the House of Lords, and only lastly of the litigants.   Let us examine the difficulty a little more closely with reference to a few practical points.

In the Anglo-American legal systems, within whose orbit Scotland has been reluctantly drawn, the burden of judicial precedent has already become overwhelming and must soon by its sheer weight crush the life out of the law.   I am not for the moment concerned with the theory of *stare decisis*, to which several of you have made notable published contributions in recent times, but with the severely practical consideration of the snowball which threatens to assume the dimensions of an avalanche.   Year after year we have each to add many feet of shelving to our libraries.   In the last eight months alone the reported decisions in Scotland and in England, with which I must generally familiarise myself, and any of which I may have to scrutinise microscopically at any time, extend to over 2500 pages of print ; and I leave it to any of you with a head for figures to estimate what the position will be twenty-five years hence.   In every case of any weight counsel have to lay before the court for examination an ever-increasing mass of decisions, which must be patiently perused and discussed if justice is to be visibly done to the arguments submitted to us. All this materially prolongs the proceedings and increases the expense, for judicial costs are a function of the time absorbed. The result is—and it is demonstrable from our records—that to a rough approximation any given type of case in the 1870's occupied about one-third of the time, and involved only a fraction of the cost, which the same type of action occupies and involves to-day ; and the time factor is increasing in a geometrical progression.

As a Scottish lawyer, trained in a system of the Romanist tradition, and in the deductive method of legal reasoning from first principles, I am probably more sensitive to this danger than an English lawyer is ; but I know that my apprehensions on this score are more than shared by at least one Federal Judge of the United States, where the weight of precedent is already far greater than it is on this side of the Atlantic. Remember this : you for the most part are specialists and can within limits ignore whole chapters of law which lie outside your special interests and chosen sphere. To a judge such specialisation is very largely impossible, at least in Scotland, where we draw no dividing line between Common Law and equity, and have no separate division of the Court devoted to Probate, Divorce and Admiralty cases. The pressure of work at headquarters and on circuit requires that our judges should be interchangeable and omni-competent ; and if a judge is engaged more or less continuously, each term for eleven or twelve weeks on end hearing and deciding cases covering any and every branch of civil and criminal law, the task of simultaneously keeping abreast with the reported decisions of all the other courts of the United Kingdom and with the activities of Parliament and subordinate legislative authorities, already transcends human capacity and must soon reach a stage at which it will only be a legal fiction that any judge can be credited with a knowledge of law. And even if the lawyer's duty is restricted to knowing where to look for the law, the bare search already absorbs time and energy to an extent incompatible with the due despatch of business.

What can be done to meet the growing difficulty ? In the past, as you know, the problem has been solved, or at least prevented from getting out of hand within limited fields— Sale of Goods, Bills of Exchange and Partnership, for example —by the expedient of a skilful quasi-codification, which virtually closed the door to further examination of the earlier case law. Indeed the door was closed so effectually that some of these topics have very nearly ceased to be the subject of litigation altogether, in Scotland at any rate. For several reasons I see little hope of a solution along these lines in our time. You know the difficulties which were encountered and the time that was absorbed in the effort to codify, or rather consolidate, the law of Income Tax ; and the Imperial Parliament has far too much on its hands nowadays to give attention to purely legal subjects. Moreover, the topics on which the present difficulty mainly arises would present almost insuperable difficulties in codification, the conspicuous example being the law relating to negligence, the categories of which, we are authoritatively assured, are never closed, and which provides easily the most fertile field for argument in the work that is still left to the Courts. And so I regretfully rule out quasi-codification as a ready means of escape from our perplexities.

One criticism that I desire to voice is against the excessive number of cases that are reported, illustrative of every conceivable shade of difference in the facts, and too often uselessly duplicating and reduplicating each other so far as the basic principles are concerned. When it is remembered that every reported decision is capable of adding at least fifteen minutes to the length of the debate in the next case, the time has surely come for the exercise by the law reporters of a little self-denial and for a reduction in the number of different series of reports. Another criticism, directed against the judges, including myself, is against the practice of three or more full-dress opinions being delivered by different judges, too often with little apparent effort at co-ordination, with the result that much time and thought have to be expended by the reader in the effort to discover the common *ratio decidendi*, if there is one, and not seldom such a common *ratio decidendi* is incapable of discovery. I cannot understand, for instance, why the House of Lords, a final court of appeal, does not issue a single judgment as the Judicial Committee does, instead of compelling us to pore over 40 or 50 pages of print, embodying much repetition and often one or two dissenting opinions. Once again, if you compare 1870 with 1953, you will find that the average length of the judicial opinions has more than doubled. These may seem trifling suggestions, but their adoption would at least help to check the steady growth of the snowball.

Why is it, I ask, that English Law, and latterly, under the

influence of the House of Lords, Scots Law as well, attach such supreme value to tradition and precedent in judicial administration, and have even bowed to the amazing consequences of the rule in *London Street Tramways* v. *L.C.C.*? In the last analysis the only answer is—to enable all and sundry and in particular legal advisers, to be *certain* what the law on any given point is. There are other answers, but that is the popular pragmatic test, and it is the justification which was given to me only a short time ago by a very eminent English judge. I invite you who are experts in your several fields to tell me frankly whether that certainty has in fact been attained, and, in so far as it has, whether it has not been bought at far too dear a price. Think of the law of contributory negligence, beginning with *Davies* v. *Mann* and continuing through the long series of House of Lords decisions such as *The Volute.* Think of the antinomy between *Cavalier* v. *Pope* and *Donoghue* v. *Stevenson.* Think of the decisions, and their number is legion, which have been built upon *Indermaur* v. *Dames* and of the discussion now being revived as to the famous categories of invitee, licensee and trespasser. Think of the forty-one reported decisions within the last twenty years on the meaning of " charity." Think of the judicial explanations which have been offered of the rule of *respondeat superior,* contemptuously but not unfairly described in a standard work as " rhythmical inanities." Without multiplying instances I venture to assert, with the support of many of the text-books which have been written by some of your number, that on many subjects we are far farther from certainty than we were in the middle of the nineteenth century, and that far too many cases are presented daily in our Courts the result of which in the light of conflicting authorities is wholly unpredictable.

Pass to another point. In the old days the Courts could exert a fairly effective control over unjustifiable delays and improper use of process by the expedient of adverse awards of costs applicable to the whole or part of the litigation. It was not an ideal expedient, but up to a point it worked. One of the expected but undesired consequences of the introduction of Legal Aid is that the Courts have been left substantially powerless in this matter. If one of the parties to an action is an " assisted person " (and both of them quite commonly are), what can the Court do to prevent amendment of the pleadings after amendment, requests for continuations and postponements, and all the other expedients which increase the expense, gravely delay the despatch of business, dislocate the judicial arrangements, and are unquestionably inimical to the proper administration of justice ? Short of professional misconduct and a report to the Discipline Committee, we are literally powerless. I am far from suggesting that improper motives are consciously allowed to creep in, but the blunt truth is that under the new system the parties' advisers have a financial interest in making the litigation as slow and as complicated as possible ; and I find it difficult to believe that such considerations do not have some subconscious effect in producing the slowing down of litigation which is already marked, and which, together with the great rise in costs, and the risk of being dragged from court to court to the House of Lords, is undoubtedly acting as a deterrent to every litigant who cannot litigate as an " assisted person " on the basis of a nil contribution—in other words, who cannot litigate at your expense and mine.

The pyramid of appellate tribunals calls for a word of comment. In the upper stages of the pyramid—the Court of Appeal in England and the Inner House in Scotland and the House of Lords in both countries—the presentation of an appeal is normally impossible without the reproduction in print or some equivalent process of a mass of evidence and documents (unless of course the appeal is by way of stated case), and the cost of printing as you know has risen phenomenally. I have verified that to-day, in an average case involving a print of, say, 100 pages, a House of Lords appeal from Scotland involves in solicitor and client costs to both sides a total expenditure of the order of £1200 ; and the intermediate appeal to the Inner House in such a case will cost about £400, so that the expedient of the " leap frog " is of little use to us. The extra-judicial costs are incapable of exact estimate. Of course every case is not appealed ; but *any* case may be appealed. And the possibility of exposure to costs of such an order is tantamount in many cases to a denial of justice to the litigant who dare not take the risk, especially if his opponent is an assisted person. The truth is that justice of the best quality is available in this country to the very rich and to the poor. To the person of moderate means it is as inaccessible as a suite in Claridge's Hotel : and when you feel inclined, if you ever do, to wax lyrical about " the British way of life " and our superiority to lesser breeds without the law, may I beg you to remember this fact ? However politely you may describe the situation, the hard fact is that an impecunious opponent can virtually blackmail a person of means into buying off a litigation, and I have seen numerous cases where that has had to be done.

The notes for this address had already been prepared when there appeared the recent Report by Sir Raymond Evershed's Committee on certain aspects of the Supreme Court procedure. You will find in that Report, expressed with the moderation appropriate to a Command Paper, much criticism on the same lines as I have been pursuing. The identity of outlook between the Committee's observations on certain matters and my own views are not, let me assure you, evidence of plagiarism, but merely additional proof of the foundation principle, that great minds think alike. I am not qualified to comment upon the Committee's detailed proposals. But my feeling is that something a good deal more drastic will be required in Scotland to produce the " new approach." One thing seems clear that in both countries there is no hope that litigation as at present conducted will get any cheaper, for counsel and solicitors are certainly not overpaid for the work now expected of them.

The essence of Scottish procedural law—and the same, I believe, is also true of England—is that the initiative is left almost exclusively to the parties and their advisers, the role of the Court being the relatively passive one of determining by interlocutory or final judgments the various matters presented by the parties for determination, but only as and when these matters are so presented. Partly through the difficulties of the post-war world, partly through sheer dilatoriness, partly through lack of competent skill, the parties' advisers too often unduly defer the initiation of the action or the setting in motion of some piece of procedural machinery, or at least do these things so imperfectly, that the Court's decision is delayed or frustrated to the grave detriment of the interests of justice. The law's delays, on which the journalistic mind delights to expatiate, cannot in the main be laid at the door of the Courts. I freely admit that at the present time there is considerable delay due to the inability of the Courts for lack of judges or of court accommodation to cope with the recent spate of litigation in divorce and actions of damages largely due to Legal Aid. But that is a new feature, and I hope a passing feature, in judicial administration ; and on a survey of a period of years I make bold to say that, once an issue is ripe for presentation, there is very seldom any delay worth speaking about in securing its determination. It is in the preliminary stages that the time is lost—in the laborious adjustment and amendment of written pleadings, in the detailed working out of procedural rules and expedients, in the give and take between counsel and solicitors in according to each other facilities to avoid time limitations, and often in prolonged and abortive negotiations for a compromise generally deferred to the last possible moment. I see many ordinary actions of damages which are only brought to a head two, three or even four years after the accrual of the cause of action. Only the other day I encountered an action, admittedly unusual in character, in which the preliminaries had consumed over five years, and the proof will only take place next October. This is discreditable to us all ; but the blame does not lie with the Courts but with the law of procedure and the method in which it is worked.

I suggest accordingly that the time is ripe for a revision of the whole system of procedure by giving the Court effective powers to take active control of the litigation once it has been brought into court, and by greatly simplifying the preparatory stages, even at the risk of occasional prejudice to one or other of the parties. Let me throw out one illustrative proposal. A considerable part of the work now arises out of traffic or industrial accidents. In many such cases things begin with a criminal prosecution, under the Road Traffic Acts or the Factories Act, as the case may be, and until that stage has been completed the civil claims are set aside. After a full investigation in a criminal court ending, let us assume, in an acquittal, the civil action is commenced and the whole investigation has to be undertaken a second time long afterwards, when the recollection of the witnesses has been dimmed, when perhaps an essential witness has died or gone abroad, and when vital evidence has been lost. In France, I believe, the victims of the accident can be made parties to the criminal process and civil liabilities and damages can be assessed in that process. Why not ? I know of one recent case in Paris in which the cheque in payment of the damages was sent to the plaintiff within three months of the accident, the action having been fought out in the interval.

You may retort by enquiring why the Courts do not set their own house in order. The answer is that to a very large extent our procedure rests on statute, and requires amending statutes for its alteration. And this brings me to another point. I shrink instinctively from suggesting the creation of yet another Government Department, but is there not a powerful case for asking for a Ministry of Justice ? Law reform, whether affecting procedure or substantive law, is a heartbreaking enterprise. *Experto crede.* It has no vote-catching value, least of all when it is technical as it usually is, and it makes no appeal to either Government or Opposition. With infinite difficulty it may be possible to secure the appointment of a Committee ; but too often that Committee's report when at long last it appears is left to languish in a pigeon-hole to await that most elusive of all commodities—Parliamentary time. And Parliamentary time will rarely be allotted to such a subject except for an agreed measure, which means that one determined opponent can veto action. I am now trespassing on Constitutional Law, but I should like to see, at any rate for Scotland, a Minister of Justice, empowered to deal with such matters, with the approval if you like of a Select Committee containing a sufficient number of trained lawyers, and thus enabled to relieve the Imperial Parliament of matters with which it cannot or will not effectively deal. Of course, even a statute might not end the difficulty unless it was very strictly drawn, for we have to reckon with the inveterate conservatism of the legal profession. Several important reforms enacted in my own time have been virtually dead letters because the legal profession have simply declined to utilise them. We brought the horse to the water but he would not drink.

All this leads me to suggest for your consideration the need for intensive study by you not merely of our substantive law, for which academic lawyers have done so much, but also of our adjective law, with a view to exposing the weaknesses of the present system, forcing upon the attention of the public the best of the improved expedients which have been adopted in other countries, and inculcating into the legal profession a sense of urgency and a livelier spirit of responsibility in the discharge of a function, the sole *raison d'être* of which is the provision of an efficient service to society. I cannot claim familiarity with the curricula of all the law schools of this country, but I think that I am correct in saying that British universities, in contrast with the universities of the Continent and of America, have neglected the subject of Procedure as a matter for scientific study and teaching, and have left the embryo lawyer to pick up the rules of the game as part of his practical training. That is all very well if the tacit assumption is that the rules of the game are the best possible of all rules, and partake of the quality of the Laws of the Medes and Persians. But what is the value of a system of substantive law which is scientifically and philosophically perfect if the machinery for its practical application is obsolete and inefficient? *Ex occidente lux.* We have much to learn in this respect from the United States. Under the auspices of the National Conference of Judicial Councils there have been published within the last few years a magnificent series of volumes containing numerous reports by some of the most eminent judges and jurists of America, devoted to promoting improvements in the judicial system, and a great many of the suggested improvements have already been adopted with marked success in the leading States of the Union. One striking development out of many which I might instance is the widespread introduction of the " pre-trial hearing," of which the judges have already reported that it has resulted not only in great efficiency in the judicial process but in great economies in time and money for the courts, the litigants and the public. I freely admit that in certain respects some of the American States have evidently still a great deal to do ; but they have tackled the problem on a nation-wide basis and on the highest levels of practical experience and of academic scholarship, and have laid under contribution ideas borrowed from other systems in all parts of the world, including Scotland, in their search for improvements.

I sometimes wonder whether we lawyers should not take a leaf out of the book of the motor car manufacturers. It is no use in these days offering a hand-made Rolls Royce to a motoring public which wants a mass-produced utility article. That is a parable of what we judges are doing in the Supreme Courts of this country—trying to sell to the public what at its best is a magnificent article, on which infinite care is lavished and which inevitably consumes in its production a great deal of time and of money, time and money which are well spent if the quality of the product is to be maintained. But do our customers really want that ? Can our impoverished nation any longer afford the luxury article ? May we not be forced to make do with something much less ambitious in order to satisfy the demand for justice which will be swift and cheap ?

You will note that I have said nothing of criminal law and practice. Curiously enough, so far as Scotland is concerned, we have contrived to keep the criminal judicial machine in a condition of high efficiency, and we are constantly engaged in adjusting and improving it to avoid and cure the occasional defects which emerge in practice. It is the civil courts that inspire my apprehensions, and my plea to you is to undertake in the interests of us all a closer scientific study of the weaknesses to which I have ventured to draw your attention, and of the remedies which are capable of being applied with effect, before it is too late.

R

The justification for that plea is admirably put in the two propositions which are prefaced to the Final Report of the Evershed Committee. Let me quote them : " The shape and development of the substantive law of England have always been and, we think, always will be strongly influenced by matters of procedure." Unquestionably true of English law though not accurate when applied in Scotland, where, as Lord Dunedin never tired of emphasising, the right never depended upon the remedy but the remedy on the right. But the second proposition is universally valid and expressed the view which I have been pressing upon your attention. " It is," the Committee say, " from the practice and procedure of the Courts . . . that the ordinary citizen as a litigant, witness or even spectator obtains his experience of our judicial system ; and on that evidence he is likely to form his judgment on the claim commonly made by Englishmen to excellence in the administration of justice." Tried by that test, what does the ordinary citizen think of that claim to-day ?

Professor A. L. Goodhart, K.B.E., Q.C. (University of Oxford), began by congratulating Lord Cooper on one of the most interesting papers that had ever been read to this Society. It was also a most surprising one because he never suspected that a Scots lawyer might be interested in costs. He appreciated his kind references to the Evershed Committee, but would like to point out that he only committed himself to having received the report : he did not say that he had read it !

On the subject of arbitration, to which Lord Cooper referred, the Evershed Committee reached the conclusion that the increasing popularity of this informal method of settling disputes was not due primarily to the fact that it is less expensive than is the ordinary legal procedure, because in a certain number of cases it may prove to be even more expensive. The great advantage of arbitration from the business man's point of view is that the whole atmosphere is less formal and litigious. When a case gets into Court it is almost inevitable that a hostile spirit will develop between the parties, with the result that in the future there will be no further business relationship between them. An arbitration does not produce a similar result, as it is more friendly and less formal. It is also more convenient for the parties.

In his references to precedents in English law there was, he thought, a slightly critical tone in Lord Cooper's comments. This might be due in part to the recent *Glasgow Police Athletic Association* case, in which the House of Lords has held that the Scottish judges must be presumed to know and understand the English law relating to charities.

On the relationship between precedents and certainty he was, if he might say so, in complete agreement with Lord Cooper's view that the emphasis on certainty may be exaggerated. Lord Wright pointed out in a former address that it is difficult to justify the certainty of injustice. This is true in particular when the social and economic conditions of a country may be in a state of flux, for it then becomes desirable that the law should be able to adjust itself to them by making the necessary changes. There ought to be a balance between rigidity and flexibility.

On the other hand he had some hesitation in agreeing with Lord Cooper's suggestion that there ought to be only one judgment in the House of Lords as there is in the Privy Council. The multiplicity of judgments enables us sometimes to point out that the noble Lords were not in agreement with each other concerning the grounds on which they reached their conclusion, with the result that the force of a precedent may be diminished. It is due to this that we can explain away many of the *dicta* in *Bourhill* v. *Young*.

A similar point can be made concerning the steadily increasing number of precedents. It is true that it may take a considerable time to consult them, but, on the other hand, there is the great advantage that they may contradict each other. It is then possible to choose the one which, on further consideration, is found to be the most in accord with reason and convenience. He was inclined to think that the difficulties caused by a plethora of precedents have been exaggerated. It is largely a question of indexing. Although there are fifty times the number of precedents in the U.S.A. it is easier to find your relevant cases there, because Shepherd's *Citations* and other similar machinery can be worked with such ease.

The Evershed Committee has not made any radical recommendations, but, as a member of the Committee, he did not apologise for this. It was clear to the Committee that if the report was to prove successful they had to try to carry both branches of the legal profession with them. As Lord Cooper had pointed out, there is no good to be gained by putting a law in the Statute Book if it is not going to be enforced. He was not certain how successful they had been in persuading the Bar. Certainly the enthusiasm shown by certain members, especially of the Junior Bar, has not been of an exaggerated nature. The major criticism, which has been repeated in a number of published letters, would seem to block the possibility of any reform. It is said that as the legal profession is not as a whole overpaid— which is undoubtedly true—it therefore follows that there ought to be no reduction in any of the fees. That, he was convinced, is a fallacious argument. If certain fees are found to be too low and others are found to be too high it cannot be said that they cancel each other out with the result that we need not do anything in the matter. It is no comfort to litigant A, who believes that he has been forced to pay too high a fee, to be told that litigant B has paid too small a one. The much-criticised " two-thirds " rule, which the Committee have said ought to be altered in some respects cannot be defended on the ground that the fee for drafting a statement of claim may be too low.

Lord Cooper had referred to the pre-trial procedure which is to be found in certain of the American and the Canadian Courts. The Committee studied it at length and heard oral evidence from American and Canadian judges, and regretfully came to the conclusion that in its transatlantic form it would not prove successful here in reducing the cost of litigation. The Committee pinned their hopes to a robust summons for directions, which may be said to have been the progenitor of the pre-trial procedure. Unfortunately it was not found possible on practical grounds to recommend that the summons should be heard by a judge instead of by a master. The additional authority which a judge can exercise might have made all the difference between success and possible failure.

The most difficult problem faced by the Evershed Committee concerned the foundation on which the whole doctrine of costs ought to be based. The English system, unlike that in force in most other countries of the world, is based on the indemnity principle ; that is that the loser should pay to the winner all costs, including the fees of counsel and of solicitor, reasonably incurred by him. Theoretically there is much to be said for this principle, but it is subject to the great disadvantage that neither party can ever foretell what he may have to pay in costs if he loses. It also has a " snowball " effect, because if A engages a Queen's Counsel then it will probably be held by the Taxing Master that it was reasonable for B to take a similar step. In other countries, and especially in Canada, the costs which a loser will have to pay to the winner are more or less limited by the amount involved in the litigation. There is therefore no temptation to pile up heavy costs in a comparatively small case, which is the main weakness of the English system. It will be seen that in the Evershed Report some of the members expressed the view that if the present recommendations do not prove successful in reducing costs then it will be necessary to make a more radical change, probably along the Canadian lines.

With great respect he wished to express his strong agreement with Lord Cooper's suggestion that more attention should be paid in the university law schools to the study of practice and procedure. Our students know, or, at any rate, are supposed to know, a considerable amount concerning the medieval forms of action, and also *Bullen and Leake*, 3rd edition, but when it comes to the present-day practice they are woefully weak. Even that statement flatters their knowledge. Fortunately we are beginning to realise that it is a mistake to regard our procedure as nothing more than a collection of arbitrary rules unworthy of university study ; it is becoming clear that it does contain principles of great importance which are as interesting both from the theoretical and from the practical standpoint, as are those of the substantive law. Nothing will encourage the development of that study more than the delightful and stimulating address which Lord Cooper had given us that morning.

Dr C. d'O. Farran (University of Liverpool), welcomed Lord Cooper as a personal friend with remembrance of his kindness when he was studying Scots law. He also welcomed him as what he might call an " outside " opinion, coming from Scotland. In fact, he believed we have in Lord Cooper the most eminent possible outside opinion on English law. He enjoyed his paper very much and yet had a feeling of regret on hearing the title of it and finding that it did not deal with the subject of Scots law. As he once wrote : " the first article of an English lawyer's creed is that English law is so incomparably superior to other systems that the others are hardly worth a glance, and there are few subjects on which England is so contentedly ignorant as Scotland and her institutions." Many people here, knowing of his interest in Scots law, had asked him to tell them the correct title of Lord Cooper's office in Scotland—a proof that though there is no sea between our two countries there is a sea of ignorance between English and Scots lawyers.

There is a great need for simplification of our legal procedure. To those of us who have had any experience of foreign legal procedure, as he had in Austria, it is immediately evident how much cheaper and speedier their litigation is. The High Courts in Austria lack the dignity of ours. The reaction of most foreign lawyers is to admire and to praise our legal procedure, but while they admire this tradition at the same time they prefer a simpler, cheaper and more expeditious administration of justice.

As to pre-trial hearing : he confessed he was not familiar with the American pre-trial hearing. In Austria there is a system of examination of the relevant documents, and even of what the witnesses are going to say, before the case comes on. The advantage is that it is possible for the examining judge to determine how long a case will last. Thus it is possible to say of a certain case that it will come on at 10.30 a.m., and it does ! It is tiresome that witnesses, especially professional men such as doctors, should be kept waiting about for a case to come on. The possibility of some kind of pre-trial examination to enable a time to be fixed for the hearing of cases should be considered.

In conclusion he would like to ask with Lord Cooper whether we have not in England too high a respect for the doctrine of precedent. If you take the famous case of *Diplock*, it would be an extremely difficult matter to attempt to explain this to an ordinary man, or even to a foreign lawyer, and one would find it impossible to convince them of the importance of " and/or " in this case. Is not precedent carried too far where cases of that kind are concerned ?

Professor F. H. Newark (Queen's University of Belfast), said he agreed with Lord Cooper that it is a fair question to ask what the judges are going to do about it. He felt that 50 per cent. of these problems which undoubtedly exist are problems where it is for the judges to start the ball rolling.

There is first the loquacity of the judges. One should compare reports with those of the last century to see how modern judges delight to expand their judgments. He invited everyone to compare the short classic judgment of Blackburn, J., in *Rylands* v. *Fletcher* with the meanderings of the House of Lords on the same topic in 1948 in *Read* v. *Lyons*. If the judges will not be more succinct it must be left to the reporters to apply a remedy, but the difficulty of the reporters is that if they condense, some other series will report in full and then their own reports will be criticised as incomplete. The obvious solution is one official series of reports which alone may be cited.

Then there is the terrible state of the law of practice. Anyone with illusions about the state of practice should look at the White Book. Again the remedy is in the hands of the judges. The judges started with virtually a clean sheet in 1875 and the White Book is merely a compilation of judge-made law since that date.

Lord Chorley (University of London), after adding his tribute to Lord Cooper's address, said he agreed that the Courts had been losing work in recent years. Scrutton, L.J., had warned the commercial lawyers years ago that their dilatory methods would have this result. In spite of the efforts which he had made when judge in the commercial Court to speed up litigation the profession had failed to respond, though commercial litigation was less in a white sheet than other branches.

Arbitration, however, had other advantages over litigation. Not only did it avoid publicity, but it enabled small disputes, such as whether a bulk delivery corresponded with a sample, to be cleared up quickly and cheaply. These considerations explained why arbitration clauses were common form in standardised contracts.

With regard to the Workmen's Compensation Acts, while he agreed that the intricate case law which had come to govern the rights of workmen had disgusted them with legal methods, it must not be thought that the bureaucratic method which had replaced them was altogether satisfactory. The centralising system of the Commissioners in London had led to the virtual abnegation of the discretion of the local Appeal Tribunals, and Chairmen who did not toe the line found that they were, in effect, dismissed. There had been a particularly bad instance of this in the case of an old and respected member of the Society which he (Lord Chorley) had raised in the House of Lords, but the Lord Chancellor had not been helpful.

Returning to the problem of speedy decisions, Lord Chorley said that the profession unfortunately opposed almost all the efforts which were made to secure improvement. The New Procedure which had made quite a promising start before the war was abandoned before it had been properly tried out simply because of prejudice, and now the Evershed proposals were being fiercely criticised by the profession. Too many lawyers were more concerned with stepping up their fees ; the refresher system was often disgracefully used, and now he was afraid that advantage was being taken of the arrangements for assisted litigation to keep the legal pot boiling.

The public were only too well aware of these things with the result that the profession was not really respected.

He agreed that if practice and procedure were made a regular part of the work of the law schools it might well lead to an improvement. After all, the work of the school, both in the classroom and in the production of text-books, had led to a marked improvement in the substantive law during the past fifty years. They might produce a similar result on the procedural side.

Mr J. Gordon Stanier (University of Southampton), said he was pleased to hear praise of British Columbia, where he practised for some years. There they had a system of Discovery by Examination, now used throughout Canada, which is something like pre-trial examination. It is far better than Interrogatories, and every Canadian barrister is entirely in favour of it ; it is rather like depositions in criminal cases. After the Statement of Claim and Defence have been delivered either party can examine the opposite party before a Registrar. The witness is examined, cross-examined, and re-examined, and the evidence so adduced, or any part of it, can be used in Court at the hearing if desired. Much time is thereby saved because most of the facts are agreed before trial. Many cases can be settled out of Court, and it works very well. He had sent a note about this to the Evershed Committee, but they considered the system too drastic.

As regards Administrative Tribunals, lawyers are sometimes excluded or discouraged because counsel and solicitors are too eloquent and take too long. If lawyers would learn to state the facts briefly and control their eloquence they could be as efficient as trade union and other officials, especially as they are more familiar with the law of evidence. But the rules of evidence are still much too complicated and ought to be simplified.

Dr A. K. R. Kiralfy (University of London), thought that members would be interested to know that about one-third of one first-year course at London University commencing next month will deal with civil and criminal procedure, under changes suggested by Professor Gower. It remains to be seen whether the teaching of procedure academically would succeed, and he asked for sympathy in such efforts.

He doubted whether precedent in England would ever be eliminated. Consider the precedents of interpretation of deeds and wills, of statutes and even the exercise of judicial discretion. Even where Parliament confers a wide discretion, as under the 1938 Inheritance Act, the judges soon develop consistent principles for the exercise of that discretion.

The enormous expense of appeals to the House of Lords hardly seems justified by any resulting certainty. In the English inductive system every point is narrow. Each decision on a statute is simply the application of some words in some section to some particular circumstances. Hence the decision is often of little assistance in slightly different circumstances, and real certainty is not achieved.

Mr Hamish R. Gray (University of Nottingham), said he would like to put in a plea for the County Courts, in which, after all, five-sixths of the civil proceedings in this country take place. Here the litigant's interests are not forgotten. Here justice is cheap and expeditious, and procedure simple. And who should complain of the law's delays who has seen seven interlocutory applications, seventy-three judgment summonses, eight possession actions and a wrongful dismissal all disposed of in less than two and a half hours?

Mr D. I. C. Ashton-Cross (University of Cambridge), said that as regards Arbitrations, there are several sound reasons for business men preferring arbitration to litigation. The main one is that if they take their business friends to Court they lose them as friends and customers; but another no less important consideration is that in many cases the parties want to know not what they are legally bound to do but what they ought to do in fairness to each other, being agreed that some adjustment is necessary. For this they prefer to sit round a table and put their arguments without any feeling of hostility, and they are happy to accept the arbitrator's decision, which is on equity rather than on law, and is quickly and amicably obtained.

Again, it is sometimes not possible to say precisely what a contractor is legally bound to do. In war time his job included authorising payments to shipbuilders for work done, provided the conditions of the contract had been fulfilled. There was one case where a firm had an Admiralty contract for a submarine, the conditions of contract requiring certain diving tests. The firm's next Admiralty order was for an aircraft carrier, the conditions of contract being stated " as for the last contract." This kind of problem it would be quite useless to take to the law courts for a quick decision.

Dr L. N. Brown (University of Sheffield), dealing with the present unpopularity of the legal profession, said the mention of the Workmen's Compensation Acts reminded him of a trade union pamphlet issued about the time of the change to the new and present system of national insurance, in which this change was summarised in the headline " No more court cases—no more lawyers." The hostility which this reflects is not confined in this country to the working classes but is prevalent even amongst the most educated. In France he did not find that hostility, because there so many university-trained people went through a degree course in law simply as a liberal education, and so had some understanding of the lawyer's work and his problems. And in any French law course there would be at least one series of lectures on Civil Procedure.

Civil Procedure in England cannot be taught from the Annual Practice: give us a text-book and then we might make a go of teaching it.

Lord Cooper, in reply to the discussion, said he was glad to learn that in a gathering such as this there seems to be general agreement as to the desirability of the scientific study of procedure—not the memorising of Rules of Court, but the study of judicial methods, their weaknesses and their improvement.

Emphasis has been well laid upon the methods of the best type of arbitrator, who aims at adjustment of differences and compromise rather than the mere determination of disputes. Whether we could get professional judges to do that may be doubtful, for it would not be easy to discard the formal and leisurely methods of the past. As regards pre-trial procedure, his Scottish experience is a drawback, for in Scotland there are no summonses for directions and no Masters, and it may be that against such a background the introduction of pre-trial procedure in the hands of judges would be difficult. His main complaint against our procedural system is that it obliges the judges to sit back and await the taking of the initiative by the parties.

He was sorry to hear that Professor Newark thought that he favoured judicial loquacity. He did not, and he urged the ruthless use of editorial blue pencils. But, after all, the time consumed in giving judgments added very little to the cost of litigation.

He appealed for the help of the academic lawyers, because if you have fourteen Scottish judges and, he thought, over fifty English judges scattered throughout the country and engrossed in their daily work, it is impossible to get them to apply their minds to procedural reform. The work would have to be done by people like the Evershed Committee and Dr Goodhart, with perhaps the assistance of a few highly conscientious and industrious judges like himself !

1953

Administrative Justice [1]

WHEN I was a law student long ago I was taught the then current view that the stability of the British and American constitutions rested upon the separation of the powers of the three great organs of government—the Legislature, the Judicature and the Executive—or, at least, upon a carefully adjusted balance between them. It was essential to the working of a Parliamentary democracy, so we were assured, that this "separation of powers" should be maintained. The rule was regarded as axiomatic and fundamental, and it had been so regarded on both sides of the Atlantic for a century and a half.

That, as I say, was long ago ; and since then we have learned a lot. Early in the present century the excessive availability of the Common Law courts as a check upon the Executive resulted, especially in the United States, in a threatened paralysis of administration ; and the pendulum began to swing. With the unhappy tendency of all pendulums, it swung too far—stimulated by the First World War, when private rights were almost totally submerged beneath the national necessity, and later by that social and political transformation of which most of us have been eye-witnesses, and of which the prime characteristic has been an enormous expansion in the functions of the State. Since the Second World War the pendulum has oscillated about a position very far removed from that defined by the classical constitutional theory of the eighteenth and nineteenth centuries, and a growing demand has arisen for a new position of stability, a demand which comes from several different sections of the community, and which is even more vocal in America than here.

[1] Translated into Japanese by Professor Noboru, Hayakawa, and published in the Japanese legal journal *Meijo Hogaku* in April 1956.

What is the problem? Stated in its simplest form it has arisen thus. Private law (in the sense of the system of rules which regulate the normal relations of citizen and citizen) has been receding all along the line by comparison with public law (in the sense of the system of rules—if system is not too flattering a word—which determines the rights and duties of public authorities *inter se*, or in a question with individual citizens) ; in that situation the question which is being asked is : " By what agency, and subject to what conditions, should decisions be given in controversies arising under public law between citizens and some organ of the executive, central or local ? " Fifty years ago that question was one which could hardly be asked, for the situation rarely arose. To-day it is being asked repeatedly, and is being eagerly canvassed by the academic jurists of two continents. For myself the question has a special interest, for during the last 40 years or so I have had the privilege (denied, I imagine, to everyone else in this room) of being at different times a member of all three organs of government—the Legislature, the Judicature and the Executive, both on the Ministerial and the official level ; for let me reveal to you that I was once a civil servant, and, as John Bunyan would say, but for the grace of God I might have been a civil servant yet ! Anyhow, I have seen the problem from every possible angle ; I have successively acquired and discarded the peculiar prejudices associated with all three organs of government ; and, though I have ended up as a judge, I have been at that long enough to be free from any tendency to proclaim that " there is nothing like leather."

I intend to be severely practical in my discussion and suggestions, but before I part company with the theorists, to whose detached study of these problems we owe a great deal, let me borrow from their sphere two general propositions.

(1) The first is this. Excessive concentration of arbitrary power in any of the three organs of government will produce for a time the reality of a semblance of increased efficiency, but in the long run, will inevitably prove disastrous. Montesquieu taught that in the eighteenth century. Acton taught it in the nineteenth, in his famous aphorism that " power

always corrupts and absolute power corrupts absolutely."
The American constitution is a running commentary upon that
text ; and the collapse of the Nazi and Fascist regimes is a
recent demonstration of its truth.   It seems that in Western
civilisation of the present time humanity is so constituted that
a system of checks and balances guaranteeing the supremacy
of the rule of law is indispensable to any permanent system
of government, and we have got to recognise that fact as a
condition of the problem of administration.   Despotism,
however benevolent, will not be tolerated long.   During the
last few decades the citizen has been stripped of much of the
protection against arbitrary government on which he had
come to rely—mainly by the central government, partly by
local authorities exercising delegated powers, and partly
by those public corporations which only differ from the central
government in being in some measure accountable to nobody
for what they do or leave undone.   In the last war the threat
was of course redoubled.   The high-water mark was probably
reached in Defence Regulation 18B, as interpreted in the
case of *Liversidge* v. *Anderson* ; and that is a chapter in our
constitutional history on which we shall yet look back with
very mixed feelings.

(2) The second general proposition is this.   While some
issues are clearly appropriate for judicial determination in
the ordinary courts of the country, others are just as clearly
inappropriate, while many are on the border line.   With all
respect to the memory of the late Lord Hewart, I think that
it is now generally accepted that certain areas of territory
once sacrosanct to the lawyers have rightly passed beyond
their ken.   Judicial methods have many admirable qualities,
but in the field of administrative law they have certain
undeniable drawbacks—for they are necessarily cautious,
leisurely, meticulous and costly, and tend to magnify consistency
and uniformity to an undue degree.

If we had tidy minds, like the French, we should not have
drifted blindly into the position we now occupy.   We
should have set up a hierarchy of administrative tribunals,
prescribed the issues over which they should have jurisdiction,

clothed them with the necessary powers, and defined the
conditions under which they should work. There is nothing
unduly difficult about that, for models exist in successful
operation. But that is not the British way. The topic is one
which has small publicity value and therefore makes little
appeal to politicians—I know for I was once one myself :
and so Parliament gave a free hand to half a hundred draftsmen and departmental solicitors to produce whatever appealed
to their taste and fancy, with the result that delegated judicial
powers have been conferred upon all sorts of authorities from
Ministers downwards in such terms as sometimes wholly to
exclude examination or review of any kind ; sometimes so as
to permit examination of their *vires* ; sometimes so as to allow
of a limited appeal on questions of law ; and sometimes so as to
permit of an open appeal. There are all possible permutations
and combinations of these variants, and when a case of this
kind does reach the courts much time has usually to be expended
in discovering how much room, if any, the courts have in which
to move.

The protests against this unsystematic encroachment
upon traditional principles have come from three quarters :
the courts ; the public ; and the constitutional experts, here
and in the United States. I am not concerned with the first
of these protests tonight, for though the sense of indignation still
smoulders, the fire has died down. It is far other with the
second and third classes of protest, for they are of a type which
no government can indefinitely ignore while paying lip service
to the " Western way of life," and eschewing totalitarian
principles. Now I do not wish to be merely descriptive or
merely critical. Equally I do not wish to engage in framing
a long-term programme or in Utopian constitution making.
What I wish to do is to lay before you a short-term policy,
designed to keep the wheels greased and turning over with
the maximum of benefit to the community and the minimum
of just annoyance to the individual. After all that is what we
are all for, and what we all wish to see.

To begin with, let us rid our minds of cant, by ruling out
two answers often given to the critics of the present system.

The first is the common argument that all decisions of the Executive are the decisions of a Minister, answerable to the High Court of Parliament, who, until he is successfully challenged there, must be credited with more than Papal infallibility. Whatever some may think or be induced by a sublime act of faith to believe, you and I know better. In ninety-nine cases out of a hundred the decision is a decision of departmental officials ; and, if the Minister knows anything about it, which he may not, all he knows is derived from a departmental brief provided *ex post facto* to coach him in answering " supplementaries " or in replying to a debate on the adjournment. There is no harm in this so long as it is understood that the Minister is normally the mere mouthpiece of his officials. But as an effective safeguard to an aggrieved individual, a Parliamentary challenge is worth next to nothing, and we may as well admit it.

The second official answer, more often made about delegated legislation than delegated judicial powers, is that the objectionable instrument has been laid on the Table of the House subject to a negative (or occasionally a positive) resolution. I shall not say that that safeguard never works, for I have seen it working ; but in most cases it is nothing but a legal fiction to suggest that instruments which have run the gamut of that procedure embody the considered wisdom of a majority of the House of Commons. We shall never get away with that.

Putting these virtual pretences aside, let us come to positive, constructive ideas. Some of them you will not like, but they will do you good and, if adopted, will save us all infinite trouble in the long run. They are all illustrations of one golden rule with which every professional judge strives to comply, however imperfect his efforts may be, *that it is not enough that justice should be done unless justice is seen to be done.* " Justice visibly done "—that is the ideal. No one should ever be allowed to leave any tribunal with a sense that he has not had a fair run, or with a diminished respect for the law and for those who administer it.

How is this to be achieved in practice by administrative

tribunals ? Chiefly, I maintain, by deliberate action to eliminate the prime vice of all administrative decisions—their *inscrutability*, or, as the American jurists say, their *incognisability*. Let me explain. In the ordinary run of executive work it is second nature to the administrative officer to preserve strict confidentiality and to keep his counsel until a decision is announced by his Minister in a statement in the House or in a White Paper or at a press conference or otherwise. On the other hand, in conducting a judicial process it is second nature to a judge to insist on all the cards being laid face upwards upon the table ; to proceed at every stage in strict conformity with established methods of procedure and accepted principles of evidence ; and to submit the reasons for his every decision to the scrutiny and criticism not only of the parties and of the public but of a trained profession, jealous of the purity of the law, and often of an appellate tribunal, the reasons being embodied in all important cases in the published reports which crowd our shelves. This is a very powerful and exacting discipline, for it compels the judge to treat every problem in a spirit of complete detachment and objectivity. He has no axe to grind. The civil servant acting as judge is normally a specialist, who naturally tends to see everything from the angle of the policy which he is striving to carry into practice, and who genuinely believes that that policy is in the general good. In that sense he has an official axe to grind and is constantly exposed to the temptation, from which the judge is free, to adopt the perilous doctrine that the end justifies the means.

Hence it is that the complaints have arisen—complaints that the tribunals are not truly disinterested ; complaints that established methods of procedure have been replaced by an arbitrary and indefinable discretion ; complaints that a party has not been allowed to know the whole case against him, or to test that case by cross-examination ; complaints that a party has not been afforded a full opportunity of answering that case ; complaints that reports by persons appointed to conduct an investigation have not been made available to him for comment, criticism or answer ; complaints that the grounds of the decision have been withheld ; and complaints of the delays inseparable from departmental methods of handling business, and often excusable and unavoidable.

These are not imaginary complaints. I have encountered them all in practice, some of them again and again ; and the identical complaints are being made in the United States. The distempers of officialdom present the same symptoms wherever officials are found. I shall give you two quite recent examples. In one an enquiry was conducted by an official of a department, and the decision was promulgated without reasons assigned by another official of the same department, in a dispute in which one party was a body partially controlled and financed by that very department ; and the decision was in favour of the body in which the department was interested. Do you wonder that such a proceeding should be attacked and should attract unfavourable comment in court ? In another case the so-called public enquiry was conducted by an independent person, but his report was never published ; and, despite two Parliamentary questions, it was not until eight months after the receipt of the report that the decision was announced. I care not what was the reason for the delay ; the fact of such delay coupled with the silence in which the whole proceedings were enshrouded, needlessly shakes public confidence in the system. These are examples of how not to do it.

To come down to details, there ought always to be available to the subject a right of resort to the ordinary courts in at least two situations :

(1) If the administrative tribunal has exceeded or misinterpreted its powers, or proceeded upon a demonstrably erroneous basis or by reference to inadmissible considerations, the courts must be free to intervene in order to set aside proceedings which, if open to these objections, are fundamentally misconceived. Only the Kremlin could object to that right, for its refusal would be an assertion of arbitrary government.

(2) There ought always to be available to the aggrieved party a right of resort to the courts for an appropriate remedy whenever there has occurred in the course of the proceedings

before an administrative tribunal an infringement of what are universally recognised as " the principles of natural justice "— for instance, if a party were denied a hearing ; or if one party were heard in the absence of the other ; or if the decision rested to any material extent upon facts obtained behind the backs of both parties.

These are only examples, and they are not by any means exhaustive. No claim is made in such cases that the court should review the decision of the administrative tribunal on its merits, or that the court should substitute its own decision, least of all on matters of discretion or administrative policy, for the decision of the tribunal. What is involved is that the proceedings should be liable to judicial scrutiny from the standpoint of the fairness of the methods employed by the administrative tribunal in conducting the enquiry into the dispute and reaching a decision.

I referred a moment ago to the refusal of the right to cross-examine adverse witnesses, whether experts or official witnesses to policy. That practice I condemn as the thin edge of the totalitarian wedge, and the encouragement of half-truths. The evidence of a witness who requires to be protected from the test of cross-examination is worth very little as evidence, and amounts to nothing more than official propaganda for the benefit of the press. The Public Relations people ought to deal with such a pronouncement. It ought never to be permitted to form any part of the material for a judicial or quasi-judicial pronouncement.

I also suggest that when a remit is made to a person to conduct a so-called " public " enquiry, that report should always be made available to the parties for their comments before action is taken upon it. Remember this. For centuries it has been customary, not only in Scotland but in many other countries, for the award of an ordinary arbiter to be embodied in " proposed findings " which are submitted to the parties for their comments, oral or in writing, before the operative award is issued. Why not ? Errors or omissions may be pointed out, and in any event justice visibly done and not inscrutability is the target to be aimed at. If the reporter has

S

embodied something in his report which he or the Department are afraid to reveal to the parties, so much the worse is his report as the basis of a decision.

Again, there are a few provisions in which the zeal of the draftsman has found expression in an instruction to tribunals that they may proceed on evidence less than would be required in a court of law. What does that mean ? It was Mr Justice Stareleigh who laid down in *Pickwick Papers* the self-evident proposition that " what the soldier said is not evidence." Are we to add as a corrollary that " what the soldier said " shall be evidence before an administrative tribunal ? The basic rules of evidence are very few and very simple, and they represent the accumulated wisdom and experience of generations engaged in the search for truth. If a fact is essential to any judicial or quasi-judicial decision, that fact should either be proved in accordance with these simple basic principles, or else it is not proved, and that is an end of the matter.

Lastly, it is well known that every now and then in the course of administrative judicial proceedings there arises a pure question of law, and often a difficult one at that. Whenever that happens I should like to see a general power in the tribunal to state a case for the opinion of the court, and a duty on them to do so on the requisition of either party. After all if our Courts are worth maintaining at all, surely they are the proper tribunal for deciding such points of pure law. Provisions of this type already exist in many statutes, and they work very well. They ought to be standardised. All the court does in such cases is simply to answer the question of law with a reasoned opinion, and with that answer and its reason to remit to the tribunal to proceed with its work. That is the proper business of the courts, in addition to the wider duty already referred to of standing in the background to see fair play and if need be to penalise obstruction and award a free kick or even stop the game.

What I have been trying to do is to suggest certain minimum requirements with which every administrative tribunal could easily comply within the framework of the mass of the existing legislation. If these requirements are complied with, justice will be visibly done in a sense in which that statement cannot be made at present, and I am confident that with these simple precautions the complaints would very largely vanish, and that not one case in a hundred would ever reach the courts. If they are not complied with, and if the authorities yield to the temptation to indulge in inscrutable, oracular pronouncements affecting the private rights of citizens, it will only be a matter of time until we shall have to adopt something like the French system of *droit administratif* or else—what is more probable—Parliament will be forced by the pressure of public opinion and professional protest to retrace its steps, and the pendulum will swing back once again to its position at the beginning of the twentieth century. Such in brief outline is the short-term programme which I commend for your consideration. The person who has to be catered for, and whose reactions must be carefully watched in the interests of the state, is " the man in the street " ; and it is notorious that the " man in the street " distrusts and dislikes both what he calls " the legal mind " and also what he calls " the official mind," these terms being used by him to describe what he regards as different manifestations of incipient ossification of the brain. Both habits of mind have their virtues and their defects, and our aim should be to combine in this field the characteristic virtues of both and to eliminate the characteristic defects of both. Much, I am sure, could be done to achieve that end by the adoption of the expedients I have suggested— above all deliberately discarding the obscurantism which disfigures many of the efforts of the Executive to discharge as amateurs judicial functions.

1954

The Scottish Lawyer's Library in the Seventeenth Century

AFTER THE RESTORATION Scottish lawyers abandoned the attempt to reformulate and modernise the amorphous material which they had inherited from the Dark Age of the previous three centuries, and devoted their attention to fashioning anew an eclectic system in which native material played a relatively small part by comparison with the philosophy of the law of nature and the civilian principles which had been elaborated by generations of Continental jurists. In this task by far the foremost part was taken by Stair ; and the question which is now being asked is how far Stair's work and the new movement of this period of reconstruction were influenced by Continental legal thought.

Difficult of answer as a question of this type always is, it may assist a solution to consider the books which can be shown to have been at the disposal of Stair and his contemporaries and the use they made of them. Of course Scottish law students had been resorting to the law schools of the Continent since the fourteenth century, and must have brought back with them the civilian idiom of legal thinking. But it would only be natural if during the later years of the seventeenth century, when Scotland was engaged in creating a Common Law of its own, concentrated attention were directed to the legal literature of the past and to the views currently held by the jurists of the Western States of Europe. Let us begin with Stair's contemporaries, choosing the three who have left behind a considerable volume of published work—Sir George Mackenzie of Rosehaugh, Sir John Nisbet of Dirleton and Sir John Lauder of Fountainhall.

Neither historians nor lawyers have yet done anything like justice to the wide and profound scholarship of Sir George Mackenzie. It is questionable whether any Scot of his day possessed so extensive a knowledge and so acute a critical appreciation of the entire range of legal literature. That he was not content to absorb blindly the work of previous thinkers and writers is sufficiently proved by his remarkable oration delivered at the formal opening of the Advocates' Library in 1689. The twin propositions on which his thesis was then rested were that the study of comparative law was of supreme importance, and that it was essential to get back to the original *Corpus Juris Civilis*, freed from the superincumbent glosses and commentaries with which it had become overlaid. He had the courage to disparage Accursius, Bartolus and their immediate followers, and to express a preference for the later and more scientific school of Alciatus and Cujacius. The many compilers of repertories, thesauri, lexicons and digests, who flourished in Mackenzie's day, were dismissed by him as " mere slaves," and he had little use for the school of Vigelius who sought to recast the civil law in a new mould. Both in his inaugural address and again in the Introduction to his *Criminals*, he goes out of his way to emphasise the value of the early Byzantine scholiasts—especially the *Basilika* and the works of Theophilus—thus anticipating a viewpoint which is only now finding expression.

In his *Criminals* we can watch Mackenzie at work to better advantage than in any of his other writings. Every proposition which is capable of being vouched or illustrated is supported by at least one quotation or citation and the books thus laid under contribution run into hundreds, including practically everything of note that had been published down to date, beginning with the Greeks of Tribonian's time, and extending through the Glossators, the post-Glossators and the Commentators and most of the civilians and canonists of Italy, France, the Low Countries and Spain. Some of the works relied upon are so little known as to be difficult of identification, but most of them appear in the earliest catalogues of the Advocates' Library, the creation of which was in large measure the work of Mackenzie.

Mackenzie's failing as a jurist (for he is entitled to be so described) is that he relied too much upon book learning and too little upon original reasoning from principle. He tells us not what in his opinion the law is but rather what the law has been declared by others to be. This defect, if it be a defect, coupled with the fact that he was overshadowed by the massive intellect of Stair, accounts for the relatively low esteem in which he has since been held by lawyers. But his writings demonstrate beyond a peradventure the immense range of the legal literature which was available in Scotland and was being skilfully employed by some lawyers about the time when he wrote.

In Sir John Nisbet of Dirleton we find a scholar of a very different type, if indeed he was a scholar at all. The outside of his famous *Doubts* is familiar to every Scots lawyer, though no one seems to have expressed astonishment that any lawyer should have gone to the trouble of publishing a catalogue of the questions to which he did not know the answer. An examination of Dirleton's book reveals that ninety-three of his *Doubts* are vouched by references or quotations, and that of these no fewer than eighty-six are taken from the writings of only four authors, all of whom flourished between 1660 and 1670. Thus there are thirty citations from the *Thesaurus Practicus* of Besoldus (1661) ; twenty-six from the *Exercitationes* and *Jus Fluviaticum* of Fritschius (*circa* 1668) ; twenty from the *De Molendinis* of Heringius (1663) ; and ten from the Commentaries of Perezius (1670). The residue includes one reference to the *De Judiciis* of Scaccia (1669) and two to the *De Causis Matrimonialibus* of Christenius (1663). All these writers belong to the class whom Sir George Mackenzie described as " mere slaves," and their works were little better than text-books or courses of lectures, unfit to be mentioned in the same breath with the classic works of the great jurists. It is true that Dirleton includes a meagre sprinkling of footnote references to Clarus, Cujas and Matthaeus ; but the impression conveyed by the *Doubts* is that its author was content to lift ideas from a superficial perusal of a few second-rate modern handbooks. It is significant that when Sir James Stewart published his *Answers* to the *Doubts*, he did not find it necessary to cite a single reference to earlier works. He disposes of

Dirleton's difficulties more in sorrow than in anger, and rather in the spirit of a patient schoolmaster correcting the exercise of a backward pupil. Be that as it may, Dirleton at least shows us that Scotland was in touch with the latest productions of the Continental presses, and all these books found their way into the Advocates' Library, where for the most part they have since lain undisturbed.

Lauder of Fountainhall offers an example of yet another type of legal scholar. For lawyers he has survived in his series of *Reports*, but he adopted an unusual view of the function of a law reporter. Not content with simply recording decisions, he liberally intersperses his reports with anecdotes, comments and learned lucubrations of his own, so much so that it is often difficult to know whether he is recording the arguments of counsel or the views of the court or is simply expressing his own opinions. This however is plain, that his acquaintance with legal literature was as extensive as Mackenzie's, though visibly less critical and discriminating. Once again the different works cited run into many hundreds, and in a proportion of these instances the citations were evidently made by counsel. When it is plain that they were not, their wholesale invocation by Fountainhall creates a suspicion that he was unduly fond of parading his learning.

Let us now return to Stair, who was of course a professional associate of Mackenzie, Dirleton and Fountainhall, and who as a judge throughout the most of this period must have listened in court to, or perused in written pleadings, the citation of most of the works already referred to. When Stair in writing his *Institutions* sought support for, or illustrations of, the propositions which he formulated, it was almost always to the fountainheads that he went—the Bible, the classics of Greece and Rome and the *Corpus Juris Civilis*. Now and then he prayed in aid the opinions on points of obscurity of such celebrated jurists as Bartolus, Grotius and Cujacius ; and occasionally he made sparing and discriminating use of works which to him must have seemed comparatively modern—the writings of Connanus and Baldinus of the sixteenth century, and of Gudelinus, Corvinus, Rebuffus, Wesenbechius, Faber and

Zoesius of the seventeenth century. It is thus evident that Stair was widely read in the legal literature of the past and of his own day, but it is characteristic of his philosophic and original approach to his task that he did not attempt to perform it by constructing an anthology of quotations from the works of foreigners, however eminent. Stair's *Institutions* is a treatise on the law of Scotland. To this day the authority for what Stair wrote is Stair.

From all this it would seem to be established that modern Scots Law was founded upon a competent knowledge of comparative law—civilian, feudalist and canonist, as seen through the eyes of jurists from all the countries of Western Europe—and that the architects of our system were deeply indoctrinated, according to their several fashions, not only with the best that had been written in the past but with the less admirable works which were still flowing from the Continental law schools.

It is a tribute to the sure instinct of the lawyers of the eighteenth and nineteenth centuries that from the first it was to Stair they looked for a formulation of our Common Law, and not to the academic learning of Mackenzie, the omnivorous reading of Fountainhall, or the superficial curiosity-hunting of Dirleton.

1954

SUPRA CREPIDAM

Foreword

THE FOUR PAPERS which follow contain the substance of Presidential Addresses to the Scottish History Society, delivered at the Annual Meetings of 1946, 1947, 1948 and 1949. They are four variations on a single theme and four sermons from a single text.

A generation ago Science was divided into a dozen water-tight compartments between which there was little or no visible connection. To-day the barriers are down, at least for a time ; and the physicist, the chemist and the astronomer are now working partners in a single adventure, to the immeasurable advantage of all three. The scientist has discovered that if truth is many-sided it is also one ; and that the shoemaker who sticks to his last may make excellent shoes, but he will never make anything else.

It is not only in the field of Science that narrow specialisation has its dangers. There is abundant room for greater co-operation between humanist and scientific scholars, and between those engaged in different branches of humanist studies, by the application of the special technique of one subject to the elucidation of a totally different subject. These papers are experiments conducted to test the validity of this thesis. In the first, a lesser-known chapter of Scottish History has been subjected to the scrutiny of a lawyer. In the second, part of the technique of modern cartography has been applied to the clarification of historical difficulties. In the third, the resources of modern astronomy have been brought to bear upon the question of the reliability of the Scottish Chronicles. In the fourth, fresh light has been admitted into an inspiring episode of Scottish History by the use of certain refinements of literary criticism.

The only claim advanced for these papers is the novelty of the method of approach—a very necessary feature when an amateur addresses specialists on their own subject. Their main justification lies in the support they afford to the plea for the broadening of the basis of higher education and research.

1950

The Scottish Lawyer's Outlook on Scottish History

I wish to speak to you on the Scottish Lawyer's Outlook on Scottish History, and you will find my text in a passage in Sir William Holdsworth's *History of English Law* (v. 412), in which he said : " History can humanise law and law can correct history ; together they can accomplish much that neither can accomplish alone."

Everyone will gratefully acknowledge the fruitful researches which have been conducted by Scottish historians in the field of constitutional law, public administration and the mechanism of government ; and the names of Rait and Hannay, and more recently of Professor Mackie and Professor Dickinson, are as well known to lawyers as to students of history. But to a lawyer such topics lie far away on the outer fringes of his subject. By law he means primarily the rules and principles of the substantive private law, and it is within that special field that I shall plead for a closer measure of co-operation in the interests of historian and lawyer alike.

It is, I think, true to say that the present-day Scottish lawyer is obliged to be more historically minded than the lawyers of any other modern state. The French lawyer when he looks back draws the line at the Code Napoléon. The lawyers of the many states which have built upon the German and Austrian codes seldom penetrate behind codifications of much more recent date. The English and American lawyers, it is true, sometimes submerge themselves in their old common law ; but they soon come up to breathe, and the early statutes of which they have to take account could be counted on the fingers of one hand.

In Scotland, by contrast, many of our most distinctive doctrines are deeply rooted in the distant past ; the bulk of our pre-Stair law is not common law but statute law, dating from the fifteenth century onwards, and many of these old statutes are still the familiar pivots around which masses of modern doctrine continue to revolve. You may be interested to learn that, after the Statute Law Revision Committee had done its best, there was published in 1908 under official auspices a collection of the pre-Union Acts which then were, and (for the most part) still are, in active observance, and that between 1424 and 1707 they number no fewer than 276.

If I were to set in an examination of a Scottish History class the question : " What significant events are associated with the years 1449, 1469, 1573 and 1617 ? " I should not expect very stimulating answers. But if the same question were set to the Scots Law class, I should be surprised if I did not get full and interesting answers. That is a parable of the gap to be bridged. The Scottish lawyer as he looks back over the centuries has a vision of his own. What he chiefly sees is a series of sporadic outbursts of legal reforms in which innovations were made in the private law of Scotland again and again, with results which must have had an immediate and lasting effect upon the social and economic life of the people, and which have permanently and fundamentally affected the legal system under which we still live.

First will you note the irregularity with which these periods of creative legislation are distributed, and the odd fact that the lawyer's interest is generally concentrated at points where the general historian finds little or nothing to record ? The first period was in the closing years of James II and the early years of James III, in the midst of a dispiriting chapter of events from which no-one but the specialist carries away very much except a confused impression of domestic strife and aristocratic turbulence, punctuated by the bursting of that famous cannon at the siege of Roxburgh. Then there is a long silence, broken only by a brief but violent eruption following the Reformation, until we reach the later years of James VI—a period known to historians chiefly because of the reverberations of Church controversy and the first premonitory symptoms of the Scottish inferiority complex. Next, there is a very rich period round about the year 1666, and another during the last ten or twelve years of Scotland's separate existence. To illustrate my thesis I shall choose only three vintage years— 1469, 1617 and 1621—the mere mention of which will bring a gleam of recognition to the countenance of the most Philistine of present-day practitioners, and we shall look at them through a lawyer's spectacles, asking the historian to fit them into the general background of the period, and to tell us why these reforms were undertaken when they were, by what grievances they were inspired, and to whose skill and initiative they were due.

(i) 1469. On 20th November 1469 there passed into law three measures which bear the impress of a political compromise between the conflicting interests of the great feudal landowners and the peasantry. It was a very long conflict, the stages in which can be traced from 1449 onwards to 1500, for it did not end in 1469. Between these extreme dates no fewer than ten separate Acts were passed at brief intervals for the benefit of a class of the community described as " the puir tennentes " or " the puir people that labouris the grund . . . whose heavy complaintes has ofttimes been maid." The first of these Acts, 1449, c. 17, remains to this day the basis of our law of leases—the Scottish answer to the English " term of years."

Twenty years later, in 1469, the landowners yielded their greatest concession, but they only did so in return for a *quid pro quo*. They asked, by no means for the last time, for greater security of title ; and they got two things. In the first place, reversions were made real rights effectual against singular successors,[1] and the first step was taken in setting up the system of registration of deeds which only came to full fruition 200 years later. In the second place, they got the long negative

---

[1] Prior to 1469 a creditor to whom a debtor had conveyed land in security of a debt could defeat the debtor's " reversion " or right of redemption by disposing of the land to a third party. The Act was passed to stop such fraudulent practices by enabling the debtor to force such a purchaser to reconvey the lands on payment of the debt.

prescription in the famous provision that any obligation not insisted on for forty years should be held to be absolutely extinguished, a rule which still holds, though the period has recently been shortened. For the security thus afforded to them the landowners paid dear. By ch. 12 of the same session of 1469, the liability of the tenant for his landlord's debts was restricted to the current year's rent, and the axe was laid at the root of the older feudal system by the imperative requirement that any apprising creditor could insist upon being entered as vassal to a superior by paying one year's rent.[1] The words of that old Act have echoed down the centuries through scores of leading decisions, one of the most illuminating expositions being contained in the judgment of Lord Chancellor Birkenhead in the *Zetland* appeal in 1920, pronounced more than 450 years after the Act was passed.[2]

What I should specially like to know is the nature of the pressure exerted for roughly half a century with the object and effect of extorting such concessions from the rich and powerful few in favour of a politically impotent section of the community. How was effective expression given to the " heavy complaintes " which were " ofttimes maid " ? There may have been in this body of agrarian legislation an element of pure policy aimed at weakening the baronial interests. There may even have been, though I doubt it, an element of enlightened self-interest in the governing classes. But is it an anachronism to suggest that we have here the first emergence in Scotland of that public opinion in which Dicey found the source of nineteenth-century legislation, and which had somehow contrived to make itself not only articulate but menacing ? There is no record of a Tiberius Gracchus in fifteenth-century Scotland, nor even of a William Langland ; but there must then have been a rural population of a quarter

---

[1] Apprising was the original method by which a creditor obtained execution against the lands of his debtor. By assuming the guise of an apprising creditor any purchaser of lands from a vassal could force the superior to give him entry. The statute thus ended the old rule that feus were inalienable, and made lands freely transferable.

[2] *Lord Advocate* v. *Marquess of Zetland*, 1920 S.C.(H.L.) 1, the last stage of a prodigious litigation regarding the method of calculating the compensation due upon redemption of the feudal casualties of a Crown holding.

of a million at least who were quite capable of reacting to oppression as other peoples did in the peasants' revolts ; and I cannot read that series of statutes without concluding that the ruling classes were uncomfortably aware of the fact.

May I commend the year 1469 to your closer attention ? Viewed as legal reforms, these Acts were original, ingenious and of permanent worth. Viewed as political expedients they were statesmanlike and enlightened. Whoever initiated them, it was the Scottish Parliament that gave expression to them ; and an examination of these and many other measures of that period will serve as a useful corrective to the rather disparaging attitude adopted by some historians to the old Scottish Parliament as contrasted with its English counterpart.

(ii) 1617. I pass on to the years after James VI of Scotland had become James I of England, dull years to the ordinary student of history but years of surpassing interest and importance to the lawyer—so much so that I must confine myself to three measures out of many.

The first is 1617, c. 12—" the palladium of our landed proprietors " as Kames called it, " our Magna Carta " in the still more enthusiastic words of Lord Monboddo. In 1469, you remember, Parliament introduced in the negative prescription the rule that a right, however good, could be extinguished by mere lapse of time. In 1617 they introduced in the positive prescription the converse rule that a title to lands, however bad, could be validated by mere lapse of time. Why was this rule, with many refinements and conditions, introduced in 1617 ? The preamble gives us the official answer. Titles to land, it says, were liable to be lost through war, plague, fire or other like occasions. False titles were being counterfeited and forged—the relevance of which preamble is not too clear. The resulting uncertainty was causing great prejudice to the lieges, and had aroused His Majesty's fatherly care to ease and remove the griefs of his subjects. All this, I must say, sounds a trifle unconvincing. The idea of acquisitive prescription must have been familiar to Scottish lawyers for generations, and there had been fewer wars, plagues and fires in Scotland in the reign of James VI than at any period since the days of Wallace and Bruce. One is tempted to conjecture that, with James VI well out of the way, the lawyers had time and opportunity to concentrate upon legal reform, and introduced with variations a well-established rule of Roman Law which was soon acclaimed as a most valuable innovation. However that may be, it is a tribute to the draftsmanship of this intricate statute that it did not require amendment until 1874, and then only in detail, and that it is still the linchpin of Scottish conveyancing.

In the same year there was established, substantially in its present form, that system of public registration of deeds which for nearly two hundred years gave to the Scottish law of heritable rights a unique and envied position in the jurisprudence of the world. The solution was the result of much trial and error, and the successive stages are worthy of examination. Between 1503 and 1609 seven different legislative experiments were tried out and in turn abandoned, and it is clear to demonstration that in this instance there was a real mischief to be remedied—the startling prevalence in sixteenth-century Scotland of calculated fraud, so widespread and habitual as to destroy public confidence in dealings in land. In one year, 1540, three different Acts were passed against three different kinds of fraud. In the same year the new crime of stellionate [1] was invented. Another Act was required in 1555 and two more in 1581. In yet another, in 1583, the preamble plaintively deplores that " falsettes [2] increases daily within this Realm." In a desperate effort to stop the rot a complete system of registration of deeds was set up in 1600 ; but the reform overshot the mark, and the Act had to be repealed nine years later by a further Act which has been judicially described as " a solemn and indignant recantation of a former legislative error." It was public opinion that forced this recantation, for the recital bears that the subjects of all degrees and ranks had received just grief and miscontentment upon the erection of " that unnecessary register." But the register was not " unnecessary." After waiting for the

---

[1] The fraudulent granting of double conveyances of the same lands.
[2] Frauds.

outcry to subside and the frauds to revive, the authorities reintroduced the scheme in 1617 with minor variations, and subject to administrative improvements you can watch that scheme in operation in the Register House to this day.

(iii) 1621, c. 18. My last example is another measure of consummate skill, also directed to frustrating fraud. This was Scotland's first incursion into bankruptcy law, and it strikes at simulate transfers of the debtor's assets to his wife or other " conjunct and confident person " so as to place them beyond the reach of his lawful creditors—a species of chicanery still probably as common as it evidently was in the seventeenth century, and still controlled by that same statute of 1621. The credit in this case goes to the judges, and especially the Earl of Haddington, for the Act simply ratifies and adopts an Act of Sederunt previously passed by the Court. The recital of that Act of Sederunt reveals the same dark background of the overthrowing of honest men's fortunes and the dissolving of trust, commerce and faithful dealings amongst subjects ; and the picture must be a faithful one. It could only have been with many examples of actual frauds present to their minds that the judges could have framed the skilful provisions on which we are still glad to rely.

All these radical and permanent alterations in our private law are more than episodes in legal history. They cannot be accounted for as the product of solitary students working in a vacuum. They usually reflect either an act of high policy or, more usually, the effort to silence protests which could no longer be safely ignored. It is generally when the tide of affairs is slack that the chance is seized by the lawyers for dealing with such matters, and this may explain why the years of special interest to the lawyer are years of which the historian has little to tell. In every instance these Acts reflect a revealing light upon the conditions prevailing before they were passed, and disclose to an unsuspected degree the strength of social forces which might otherwise be overlooked or underestimated. Observe, for example, the chronic impoverishment of old Scotland, and still more the amazing prevalence of fraud ; for there is no legal system of the period which had to devote so much attention for so long a time to the frustration of chicanery as Scots Law had to do in the sixteenth and seventeenth centuries—and I wish John Knox had told us why !

Finally, note with what far-seeing skill these reforms were planned and executed. As Bacon reminded us, the wisdom of the lawyer is one and the wisdom of the lawmaker is another ; for it is not to Balfour or Stair or Erskine that we owe these pivotal statutes, but to unknown legal statesmen whose work is usually their only memorial. If you read the biographies of many who, in the seventeenth and eighteenth centuries, filled the great offices of State and the seats on the Bench, the story brings a blush to the cheek of their humble successors, for it would seem that as a class they were chiefly remarkable for blatant corruption and habitual intemperance. Yet these must be the men to whose profound learning and clear insight we owe so much of lasting worth. Dr Jekyll and Mr Hyde must have been familiar figures in Scotland before Stevenson immortalised the type.

I have only touched the fringe of a line of study which I should like to see pursued. If the historians will enter freely into the inner chambers of Scots Law, we lawyers will be glad to pose to them a good many intriguing questions and to offer in exchange a few provocative ideas for illuminating the dark places in the story of our nation.

1946

A Historical Atlas for Scotland

For maps see pp. 297-308

Anyone who to-day brings forward a project which exhales a scientific or technological aroma, however faint, can count upon being treated as the spoilt darling of officialdom. But we and others like us, whose interests are merely cultural and scholastic and who sometimes split hairs but never atoms, are the Cinderellas of the brave new world, hard put to it to find the paper on which to print our work.[1] Let us refuse to be discouraged. As a defiant gesture against cultural austerity, let us discuss a few ideas of no technical utility whatever, which under present conditions may well be quite incapable of realisation, but which nevertheless may suitably engage our attention this afternoon.

I should like to see a new Historical Atlas of Scotland. There is a great deal to be said for experimentally applying the special technique of one subject to the elucidation of a different subject. The mathematician, the physicist and the engineer would be helpless without their graphical and symbolic methods of recording data and discovering unsuspected relationships—not merely because these methods provide the neatest and most convenient medium for imparting information, but because, when information is so presented, all kinds of valuable inferences which would otherwise elude detection often thrust themselves upon our notice. We are the guests this afternoon of a great scientific society.[2] Let us borrow from them a little more than the accommodation so generously placed at our disposal.

My proposal is not that we should encroach upon the territories of the Royal Scottish Geographical Society. Our concern is not with the history of cartography but with the history of Scotland. Our models will not be the crude representations of Ptolemy or Timothy Pont, nor the finished products of Messrs Bartholomew, but rather the ingenious devices of Mr Horrabin.

Of course this is not virgin soil. Several admirable historical maps are buried in historical treatises—Skene's *Celtic Scotland*, Dunbar's *Scottish Kings* and Cosmo Innes's volumes on legal antiquities, to mention only a few. I single out three other works for special recommendation. There is a remarkable but little-known map of fourteenth-century Scotland in Macpherson's *Geographical Illustrations*, published in 1790 and based upon the charter records, in which you will find much that can be found nowhere else. There are several very fine maps in Lothian's *Historical Atlas* of 1827, showing Scotland under

---

[1] In 1947   [2] The Royal Society of Edinburgh.

the Romans, Scotland in the fifteenth century, the Clan Territories, and the '45 Campaign and its sequels ; but we have learned something since 1827. And there are several magnificent maps appended to the Bannatyne Club volumes, notably the *Origines Parochiales*, covering only a part of the country but excellent for the areas which they cover.

These and other maps blaze the trail which I would follow ; but my quarrel with all of them is that they attempt far too much and that the wood is lost amongst the trees. A score of separate maps would be required to show what Lothian tried to display in one, and it should be left to the student to combine for himself any two or more separate maps so as to derive the information of which he is in search—a process which can be greatly facilitated by printing the series of maps of exactly the same size on transparent paper so that one can be superimposed upon another. Moreover these historical maps should never be encumbered and obscured by irrelevant geo-graphical detail. Little more is usually required than the outline of the coast, the course of the principal rivers and the 500-foot contour line ; for my Highland friends will forgive me for saying that not very much of significance for the history of Scotland occurred more than 500 feet above Mean Tide Level.

The best method of clothing with flesh these skeleton ideas is to display a few specimens constructed for my own use. They are only samples, and random samples at that. Most of them, as it happens, are concerned with medieval Scotland. They would wear a very different aspect if redrawn by experts on the instructions of historians. But they will serve to illustrate my thesis.

The first group of maps is a selection from those used in an investigation into the numbers and distribution of the Scottish population in the thirteenth century. Arguing from the known to the unknown I began with the Census of 1931 and worked backwards at ten-year intervals, placing a dot in every parish for every 1000 of the recorded population, the result being to display with sufficient accuracy and clarity the local density of the population. Even at the comparatively close ten-year census intervals the changes are striking, and if (on the Walt

Disney principle) enough slides were prepared and run through a cinematograph, it would be possible to watch the depopulation of the Highlands and the drift to the south in actual progress.

When the official censuses run out recourse must be had to various unofficial computations, of which the best is that prepared by the Rev. Dr Webster[1] in 1755, a remarkable document which certainly ought to be printed, for it is full of interesting details regarding every parish in the country. As we approach the Middle Ages even unofficial censuses completely fail us, and it is necessary to rely on deduction from indirect information such as can be gleaned from *Bagimond's Roll* and other ecclesiastical returns. As a guide to the distribution of the population in the thirteenth century (but not of course to the numbers) I have plotted on the same scale the sites of every parish church and monastic foundation known to have been in existence in 1300, upon the view that these sites must indicate approximately where aggregations of population were to be found.

Maps 1, 2 and 3 show respectively the position in 1931, when the population was 4,842,980 ; in 1755, when the population was 1,265,380 ; and in 1300, when according to my estimate the population was about 400,000. A comparison of these three maps affords a good deal of food for thought. It is significant how little 1755 differs from 1300, and how widely 1931 differs from 1755—which is exactly what we should expect. It is even more significant to note the relative importance of the Solway coasts, the Moray Firth coasts and Angus and Fife in 1755, and still more strikingly in 1300—a fact which we are very apt to overlook in 1947.

But in Map 3 there is a missing link, for owing to dearth of information the Highlands and Islands are not accurately depicted. The best that could be done for them was to go to the Norse records and re-explore with Haakon the west coast of Scotland. The result is shown on Map 4, and it is surprising to discover how many of these remote places were known by name to a foreign invader as the sites of battles, forays,

---

[1] EDITOR'S NOTE. This document was published in 1952 [see Reference on p. 296].

winter quarters or anchorages. Even Durness and Erribol, now nearly desolate and all but inaccessible, are duly recorded.

The second group of maps is a selection from a number designed to illustrate early feudal government and administration. Map 5 shows all the places named in the first volume of the Record Statutes—a picture of twelfth-century Scotland which may be open to criticism because the place names are often given in their Latinised form. Map 6 rests on surer ground, for it depicts, with the aid of the Sheriff Court Book of Fife, all the sheriff courts which were established by 1300, from which it is plain that the populous parts of the country were by that time fairly well covered by the ubiquitous *vice-comites*. In Map 7 there are shown all the burghs which made returns of their fermes in 1327, and there are also displayed graphically the sums which they returned in that year. The year is not critical, for the figures remain more or less uniform for a decade. It is interesting to note the enormous preponderance of Berwick, Aberdeen and Perth, and the unexpected order in which the remaining names occur. Map 8 shows the sites of seventy-one castles, royal and noble, mentioned as being in existence in 1300, showing curious concentrations in the vicinity of Dundee and Aberdeen.

The last group of maps shows aspects of ecclesiastical Scotland, perhaps the most important key to the life of the thirteenth century. Map 9 depicts the main ecclesiastical divisions, but the boundaries are at many points very difficult to trace. A large-scale map would be required, and a great deal of work would require to be done before it would be possible to show the boundaries of the diocese of Brechin, or the march between St Andrews and Dunblane. Map 10 shows the whole of the 118 monasteries and nunneries ; and the sites chosen by those Orders which worked as well as prayed is a guide to the characteristics of the soil for purposes of arable and pastoral farming. Separate maps should show each of the different orders. Next a map would be required for each of the large monastic establishments to show their appropriated churches and the estates which they owned. It is most revealing to discover by this means the ramification of

the interests of these convents, and the elaborate business
organisation which must have been necessary to control and

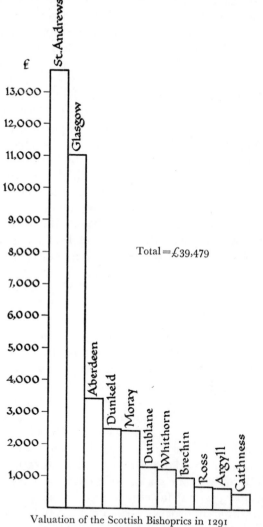

Valuation of the Scottish Bishoprics in 1291
(*Reg. of John de Halton*, Cant. and York Soc., vol. xii)

factor such extensive and widespread possessions. As a sample,
Map 11 shows the position of Arbroath Abbey at the close of

the thirteenth century, but equally striking maps can be made
for Paisley, Holyrood, Kelso and many others.   As a further
sidelight on the educational organisation in medieval Scotland,

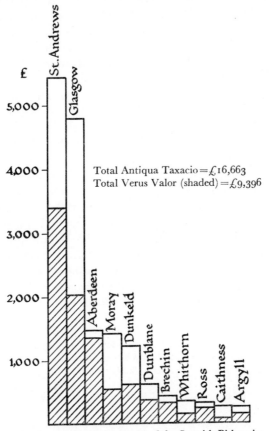

Total Antiqua Taxacio = £16,663
Total Verus Valor (shaded) = £9,396

Valuations of the Endowments of the Scottish Bishoprics
(Antiqua Taxacio and Verus Valor (1366) as given in A.P.S. i, 141)

Map 12 shows the Church schools established by 1300 in
thirteen widely distributed centres.

   The diagrams on page 294 and *supra* would in themselves
provide material for a separate study because of the light they
shed upon the value of land in different parts of thirteenth-
century Scotland, and the inferences they suggest as to the

extent to which the Wars of Independence impoverished different areas of the country.

These maps and diagrams are only a fraction of those which could usefully be constructed for the medieval period alone. One investigation which cries aloud to be undertaken is a map, based on the itineraries and on innumerable charter references to bridges and roads of various types, showing the system of communications which prevailed at the death of Alexander III. It would be a rewarding but laborious task to piece together the evidence which has survived with regard to the *via regia*, the *via superior* and the *via magna* at the one extreme, down to the humble *semita* and *chimagium* at the other.

All that it has been possible to do within the time at my disposal has been to illustrate the possibilities of the project of a Historical Atlas. The scheme could only be carried to fruition by means of co-operative effort over a considerable period of time, the data for different periods and different topics being contributed by specialists in these subjects, and being assembled and presented by draftsmen working under an editorial committee. As the maps would in most cases be simple outline diagrams, requiring no high standard of cartography, the cost would not be great. Whatever the difficulties, the project, I feel sure, would be well worth while. 1947

REFERENCES

SKENE, W. F., *Celtic Scotland*, Edinburgh, 2nd ed. 1886-90.

DUNBAR, Sir ARCHIBALD H., *Scottish Kings*, Edinburgh, 2nd ed. 1906.

INNES, COSMO, *Origines Parochiales Scotiæ*, Bannatyne Club, Edinburgh, 1851-55.

MACPHERSON, DAVID, *Geographical Illustrations of Scottish History*, Edinburgh, 1796.

LOTHIAN, J., *County Atlas of Scotland*, Edinburgh, 1827.

WEBSTER, Rev. Dr ALEXANDER, *Population of Scotland* 1755 (Office of the General Registrar of Scotland). This was published in 1952 under the title *Scottish Population Statistics including Webster's Analysis of Population 1755*, edited by James Gray Kyd (The Scottish History Society, Third Series, Vol. xliii).

DUNLOP, Dr ANNIE, *Bagimond's Roll*, Scottish History Society Miscellany, 3rd series, vol. vi.

ANDERSON, A. O., *Early Sources of Scottish History*, Edinburgh, 1922.

Register of John de Halton, Canterbury and York Society Publications, vol. xii.

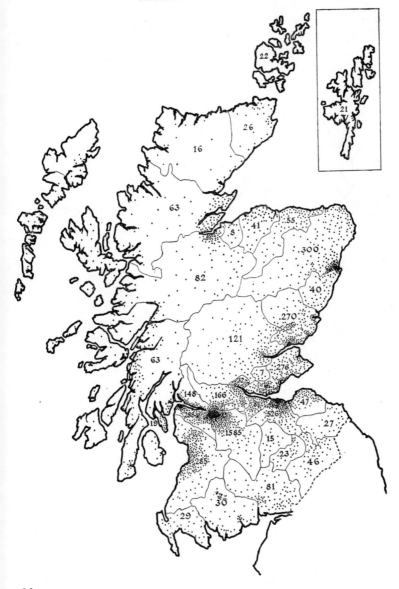

MAP I

1931 Census, 4,842,980

MAP 2

Webster's Census of 1755, 1,265,380

o Monasteries
• Parish Churches

MAP 3

Parish Churches and Monasteries, *c.* 1300

MAP 4

Places mentioned in Norse records, *c.* 1265

MAP 5

Places mentioned in the early Statutes

MAP 6

Sheriff Courts, *c.* 1300

£50   100   150   200   250   300

Berwick
Aberdeen
Perth
Inverness
Stirling
Edinburgh
Ayr
Rutherglen
Haddington
Peebles
Crail
Dundee
Dumbarton
Banff
Roxburgh
Cullen
Forfar
Dumfries
Wigtown
Inverkeithing
Montrose
Lanark
Kintore
Linlithgow
Kirkcudbright
Fyvie

MAP 7

Burghs making returns from 1327 (Exch. Rolls, i)

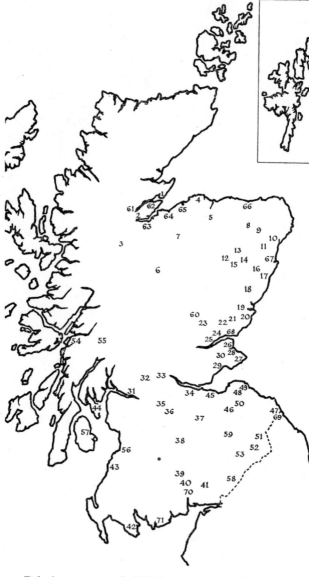

MAP 8

Principal Castles ɪ

1. Dunskaith
2. Edirdouer
3. Urquhart
4. Duffus
5. Boharm
6. Ruthven
7. Lochindorb
8. Shrathbolgie
9. Fyvie
10. Ellon
11. Inverury
12. Migveth
13. Kildrummy
14. Lumphanan
15. Coul
16. Durris
17. Cowie
18. Kincardin
19. Brechin
20. Redcastle
21. Forfar
22. Glammis
23. Kinclevin
24. Balligernoch
25. Mote of Erro
26. Leuchars
27. Crail
28. St Andrews
29. Kennoquhy
30. Cupar
31. Dumbarton
32. Inchmahome
33. Stirling
34. Linlithgow
35. Carpentoloch
36. Bothwell
37. Castel-tarres
38. Douglas
39. Morton

40. Dalswinton	48. Whittinghame	56. New Castel	64. Nairn
41. Lochmaben	49. Dunbar	57. Bradwik	65. Forres
42. Crugelton	50. Yester	58. Hermitage	66. Banff
43. Turnberry	51. Roxburgh	59. Traquair	67. Aberdeen
44. Rothesay	52. Jedburgh	60. Cluny	68. Dundee
45. Edinburgh	53. Hawic	61. Dingwall	69. Berwick
46. Lochorwart	54. Dunstaffinch	62. Cromarty	70. Dumfries
47. Lamberton	55. Kilchurn	63. Inverness	71. Kirkcudbright

Map 9

Dioceses and Episcopal Sees

U

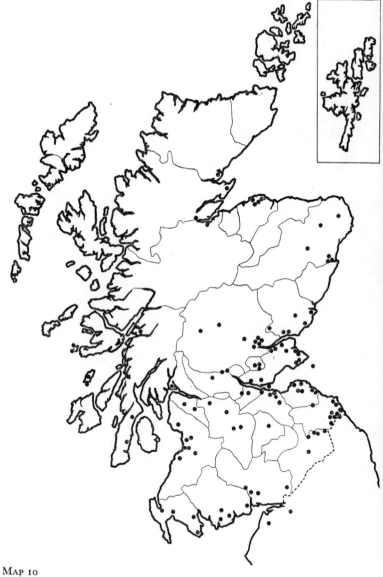

MAP 10

The Monastic Foundations, *c.* 1300
(118 monasteries and nunneries)

MAP 11

Arbroath Abbey: appropriated churches numbered and principal lands marked x

1. Inverness
2. Boyndie
3. Banff
4. Gamrie
5. Aberchirder
6. Turriff
7. Inverugie
8. Fyvie

9. Tarves
10. Coul
11. Banchory
12. Nigg
13. Katerlyn
14. Montrose
15. St Vigeans
16. Monifeith

17. Abernethy
18. Muraus
19. Kirriemuir
20. Glamis
21. Newtyle
22. Haltwhistle
23. Barry
24. Mains

25. Moniky
26. Kingoldrum
27. Dunechtyn
28. Panbryd
29. Arbirlot
30. Ethie
31. Guthrie

Map 12

Church schools in the Thirteenth Century

Solar Eclipses and the Scottish Chronicles

For maps see pp. 317-323

" The historian must not be misled by the tales of the chroniclers
. . . for their accounts cannot be tested." So wrote Thucydides two thousand years ago when laying down the principles
by which the scientific historian should be guided ; and his
warning is still in large measure valid. We have at our disposal,
it is true, many more chronicles and annals than Thucydides
had, and it is sometimes possible by comparing the testimony
which they bear to appraise their reliability by applying the
principle of coherence. But the inference of mutual corroboration and thence of probable trustworthiness depends upon the
several sources of testimony being independent and unconnected. Too often the medieval chronicles are not independent
and unconnected. Too often the same entry, sometimes with
the same mistake, is copied and recopied again and again.
The modern historian can still say with Thucydides when
he turns to the chronicles : " Their accounts cannot be tested";
and he can still learn a lesson from the detective work by which
Ranke undermined the chroniclers of the Renaissance.

Is this counsel of despair completely justified ? Let us
examine the problem a little more narrowly in order to see
whether some objective test of the accuracy of the chronicles
cannot be discovered.

Proceeding by a process of elimination, we may at once
discard the large number of entries dealing with occurrences
of note in the world of political and ecclesiastical history.
Such events cannot often be fixed with exactitude ; and, even
when they can, we have no means of discovering the channel
through which the information reached the chronicler. We
may also discard, for much the same reason, entries of domestic
interest to the chronicler or the religious house to which he
was attached. There remain the entries, common in nearly
all early chronicles, of natural phenomena. Those of a
metereological nature, dealing with storms, great frosts, floods,
droughts and other eccentricities of the weather, do not

carry us any distance ; but we enter a much more promising field when the chronicler lifts his eyes to the heavens and notes the appearance of comets, new stars (*supernovae*) and eclipses. In regard to comets and *supernovae*, reconstruction of the actual event is either impossible, or possible only subject to a wide margin of error.   But total solar eclipses stand in a class apart, and they will repay closer investigation.

Total solar eclipses—and even near-total solar eclipses —are so arresting that chroniclers rarely passed them unnoticed if they were in a position to observe the phenomenon or to learn of it at first hand.   All through written annals, beginning with the Egyptians and the Babylonians, and passing down through Heredotus, Thucydides, Plutarch and other classical historians to the medieval chroniclers, there are numerous references to eclipses, and they are often so phrased as to betray the observer's appreciation of the difference in appearance between a total, an annular and a partial eclipse.   Curiously enough, the total eclipse is most often described in every chronicle in one or other of two phrases :   " day was turned into night," or " the stars appeared."   It is a fairly safe assumption that it would only be during totality that stars (or planets) would be visible to the naked eye in daytime, even in the clear skies of the Mediterranean basin and its hinterlands.

Fortunately for our present purpose an immense amount of labour has been devoted to the task of computing the elements of past solar eclipses.   Every historian is of course acquainted with the approximations given in *L'Art de Vérifier les Dates* and in *Mas Latric* ;   and it is truly amazing that the compilers of these invaluable aids to the study of chronology attained so high a degree of accuracy.   But the matter has been taken up afresh in modern times by highly skilled computers and carried to far closer standards of accuracy by the German Oppolzer, the Scandinavian Schroeter, and several British astronomers whose researches have been published in the proceedings of the Royal Astronomical Society.   The result is that it is now possible with considerable confidence to state, for example, exactly what was visible from Melrose at 2.15 on the afternoon of 1st May 1185.

Using these modern researches for a purpose their authors never intended, I propose to apply their data to seven major eclipses which occurred during the twelfth century, which was a bumper century for eclipses visible in the British Isles, with a view to setting the actual facts against the records in the Melrose and Holyrood Chronicles. It may be safely assumed that the astronomical computations are accurate within a much narrower margin of error than is required for the purpose in hand, namely to meet the requirement of Thucydides that the accounts of the chroniclers should be " tested."

But before embarking upon the details, it is necessary to re-state certain facts and sound certain cautionary notes. Melrose Abbey was founded in 1136 as a Cistercian colony from Rievaulx in Yorkshire and ultimately from Cîteaux in France ; and contacts between the daughter-house and the parent establishments were doubtless frequent. Holyrood Abbey was founded in 1128 as an abbey of the Canons Regular of St Augustine, and the editors of the Holyrood Chronicle give reasons for thinking that the Chronicle may have been written in whole or in part not at Holyrood but at the Cistercian daughter-house of Melrose which was established at Coupar Angus in 1164. We must therefore take account not only of Melrose and Holyrood, but also of Rievaulx, Cîteaux and Coupar Angus. The entries in the Melrose and Holyrood Chronicles for dates prior to about 1150 were in all probability copied from other chronicles, but it seems a fair assumption that the entries for the years from 1150 onwards were based on local observation or first-hand sources of information, at least in part. Next, we must remember that the monkish chroniclers had no clocks. Probably they had sundials, hour-glasses and devices of that kind ; but nothing that would give the time of day within a matter of minutes. Finally, if the sky happened to be heavily obscured by clouds, or if an eclipse occurred near sunrise or sunset, it might very easily pass unnoticed.

In the figures which follow the times have been corrected so as to show apparent or " sundial " time for the longitude of Melrose, Holyrood and Coupar Angus (which happens to be practically the same) ; and while a professional astronomer would probably be at least as cautious as a historian usually is in committing himself to a precise statement of fact, it is my belief that the particulars depicted are correct within a few minutes of time and a dozen miles of space.

Map 1 shows what happened during a period of 4½ minutes at about 11.25 (Melrose apparent time) on the forenoon of 2nd August 1133. It will be noted that the shadow of totality passed diagonally across a large part of Scotland and northern England, obscuring Melrose, Holyrood, Coupar and Rievaulx. The chronicle entries are as follows :

> *Melrose* : 2nd August 1133. " An eclipse of the sun occurred on Wednesday, 2nd August, so that for a time day was turned into night."

> *Holyrood* : " An eclipse occurred on 5th August 1133."

As a comment upon Holyrood's error as to the date, it may be noted that John of Hexham gives the date as 3rd August 1133 ; William of Malmesbury as 5th August 1132 ; and the Chronicle of Man as 2nd August 1133.

Map 2 shows the eclipse of 20th March 1140, which occurred about 2.54 p.m. (Melrose apparent time), and lasted about 3½ minutes. The shadow of totality passed across the Midlands of England, but did not touch any of the centres with which we are at present concerned. Under the date 20th March 1140, Melrose records that " an eclipse of the sun occurred on 20th March " ; but Holyrood makes no entry. It is interesting to note that the Anglo-Saxon Chronicles record that " the candles were lighted at noon," which would be unlikely to be true of any place outside the region of the shadow.

Map 3 shows the eclipse—an annular and not a total eclipse—which occurred near sunrise on 26th October 1147. On a dull autumn morning this eclipse might easily be un-observed in Lowland Scotland, and it is appropriate enough that no entry appears either in the Melrose or in the Holyrood Chronicle. It is pleasing to be able at an interval of over eight hundred years to deduce what the weather was like that morning !

Map 4 is of special interest, for it depicts a total eclipse between 11 a.m. and noon on 13th September 1178, the shadow of which never passed near the British Isles, where the eclipse would be only partial though 80-85 per cent. of the sun's disc would be obscured. Under this date Melrose records that " about midday the sun became invested with pallor and was almost completely obscured "—a description which could accurately have been made by an eye-witness at Melrose. The Holyrood Chronicle contains no entry.

Map 5 shows the annular eclipse of 28th January 1180, which occurred about sunrise, and on a stormy January morning might easily pass unnoticed. There are no entries in either chronicle.

Map 6 shows the position about a quarter past two on the afternoon of 1st May 1185. The eclipse was total in the north of Scotland, but nowhere south of a line between Peterhead and Oban. It is true that 95 per cent. of the sun would be obscured throughout southern Scotland, but there is a vast difference in the result between 95 and 100 per cent. in an eclipse of the sun. The Melrose Chronicle records that " an eclipse of the sun occurred in the afternoon of Wednesday, 1st May, and the stars appeared." Here for the first time the Melrose chronicler is detected in an apparent misstatement if he meant to imply that the stars appeared at Melrose, for it is certain that they did not. Perhaps a returned traveller from the Moray Firth coast supplied this information, which might be perfectly true of these regions. The Holyrood Chronicle records that an eclipse occurred " *circa horam nonam*," which is not a very accurate description of 2.16 p.m. But these old chroniclers were not concerned to give times with much exactitude. Benedict of Peterborough fixes the eclipse " about midday," and Ralph de Diceto says " in the afternoon."

Map 7 depicts the annular eclipse which occurred about 11.3 a.m. on 23rd June 1191, the shadow passing across

Yorkshire, and at Melrose obscuring the sun to the extent of about 90 per cent. The Melrose entry is unusually precise— "An eclipse of the sun occurred in the sixth hour on Sunday, 23rd June, in the vigil of St John the Baptist." Holyrood made no entry.

The results are tabulated on page 315. Melrose scores very highly. With one exception all the entries are consistent with what might have been observed (or excusably not observed) from Melrose, the one exception being the reference to the stars appearing during the 1185 eclipse. It is apparent from earlier entries in the Melrose Chronicle derived from other sources that the editor was quite aware of the difference between a total and partial eclipse, and knew that the appearance of the stars in daytime was characteristic of a total eclipse ; but it may well be that when he passed the entry for 1st May 1185 all he meant to indicate was that the eclipse had been total at some parts of Scotland and not necessarily at Melrose.

On the other hand Holyrood emerges from the test with little credit. Only two out of the seven eclipses are recorded, and one is under the wrong date. The editor ought to have known better, for there is at least one good entry, in his Chronicle, relating to the eclipse of 1133, with regard to which it is stated—on the authority of some other chronicle—that "an eclipse of the sun occurred about 9 a.m. on 14th August, almost the entire disc of the sun being apparently obscured by a kind of black and horrible shield." The eclipse was only partial north of the Wash and only annular south of that, so that the description given would be perfectly accurate for observers in Northumberland, which is probably the original source of this part of the Chronicle.

The experiment, so far as it goes, justifies the guarded conclusion that the accuracy and intelligence of the Holyrood chronicler cannot be rated highly. But, while I make no claim to have examined anything like all the other chronicles of the period, I have found none with a better record than the Melrose Chronicle ; and if the bulk of the later Melrose entries may be assumed to correspond to the sample tested,

Twelfth Century Eclipses Visible in the U.K.

	Date	Type	Melrose	Holyrood
(1)	1133	Total in Central Scotland	Recorded as total	Recorded under wrong date as an eclipse
(2)	1140	Partial (95%) in Lowland Scotland)	Recorded as an eclipse	Not recorded
(3)	1147	Partial (90%) in Scotland but difficult of observation	Not recorded	Not recorded
(4)	1178	Partial in Lowland Scotland (80%)	Recorded as partial	Not recorded
(5)	1180	Partial in Lowland Scotland (90%) but difficult of observation	Not recorded	Not recorded
(6)	1185	Partial (95%) in Lowland Scotland	Recorded as total	Recorded as an eclipse
(7)	1191	Partial (90%) in Lowland Scotland	Recorded as an eclipse	Not recorded

that Chronicle, when its " accounts are tested," sets a very creditable standard of accuracy and reliability.

1948

REFERENCES

L'Art de Vérifier les Dates, Paris, 3rd ed. 1783-87.

MAS-LATRIE, *Trésor de Chronologie*, Paris, 1889.

OPPOLZER, T. R. VON, *Kanon der Finsternisse*, Vienna, 1887.

Royal Astronomical Society, Monthly Notices, xlv, 400 (Maguire) ; xlvi, (Maguire) ; civ. (Fotheringham).

Royal Astronomical Society, Memoirs, xli, (Raynard).

Chronicle of Melrose, facsimile edition, London, 1936.

Chronicle of Holyrood, Scottish History Society, 3rd series, vol. xxx.

SCHROETER, J. Fr., *Kanon der Finsternisse*, Kristiania, 1923.

THUCYDIDES, *Peloponnesian War*, i, 21.

SIMEON OF DURHAM, *Opera Omnia*, Rolls Series, vol. 75.

WILLIAM OF MALMESBURY, *Gesta*, Rolls Series, vol. 90.

Chronicle of Man, Manx Society, vol. 22.

Anglo-Saxon Chronicle, Rolls Series, vol. 23.

BENEDICT OF PETERBOROUGH, *Gesta*, Rolls Series, vol. 49.

RALPH DE DICETO, *Ymagines Historiarum*, Rolls Series, vol. 68.

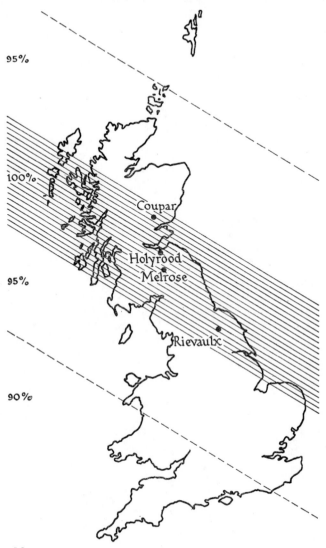

95%

100%

95%

90%

Coupar

Holyrood
Melrose

Rievaulx

Map 1

Total Eclipse, 2nd August 1133
11.25 a.m. Melrose apparent time ; duration 4 mins. 34 secs.

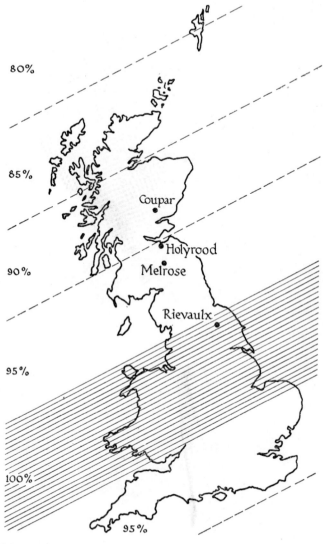

Map 2

Total Eclipse, 20th March 1140
2.54 p.m. Melrose apparent time ; duration 3 mins. 26 secs.

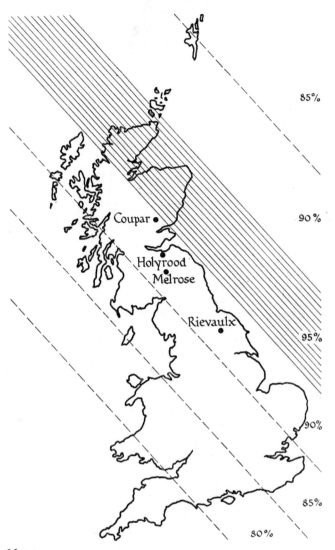

MAP 3

Annular Eclipse, 26th October 1147
near sunrise

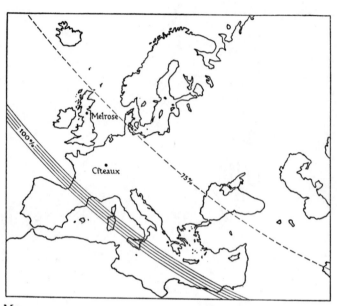

MAP 4

Total Eclipse, 13th September 1178
11 a.m. to 12 noon Melrose apparent time

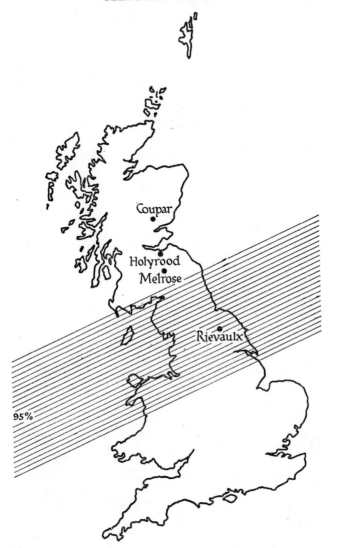

MAP 5

Annular Eclipse, 28th January 1180
at sunset

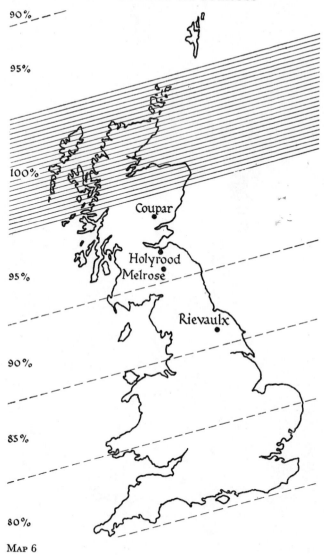

MAP 6

Total Eclipse, 1st May 1185
2.16 p.m. Melrose apparent time ; duration 4 mins. 33 secs.

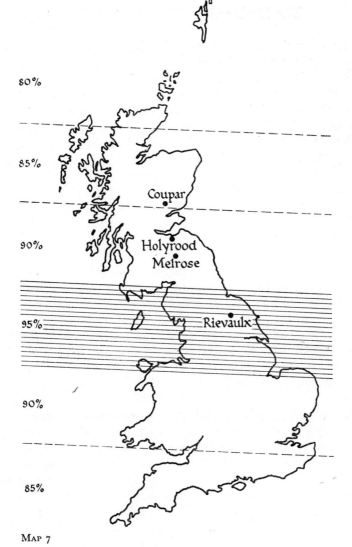

MAP 7

Annular Eclipse, 23rd June 1191
11.3 a.m. Melrose apparent time

The Declaration of Arbroath Revisited

The Barons' letter to Pope John XXII of 6th April 1320 has long been a titbit for the serious student of Scottish History ; but it is now news. All last summer [1] the correspondence columns of our newspapers contained discussions of the Declaration of Arbroath. It figured in the revived Arbroath pageant. It is being sent to our secondary schools. It is being set as an unseen Latin prose in one of our universities. For the last two months Sir Andrew Murray has been distributing facsimiles of it from Halifax to Vancouver, and from Winnipeg to New Orleans. The letter has long possessed a peculiar fascination for myself, and I have been led by this outburst of public interest to engage in a fresh examination of this remarkable document from one or two new angles.

First a word with regard to the text. The so-called original in H.M. Register House was deposited there by the then Earl of Haddington in 1829, and a good deal of curiosity has been aroused as to how that document came to be in East Lothian and not in the Vatican archives. I shall return to that in a moment ; but meantime let me observe that the document in the Register House of which facsimiles were given by Anderson in his *Diplomata* and by Cosmo Innes in the first volume of the Record statutes, will not construe at several points. There is another text in the Edinburgh University MS. of the *Scotichronicon*, and this text will construe, for it contains a number of extra words essential to the sense which have been omitted from the so-called original. There is yet a third text printed in Sir George Mackenzie's *Causae Forenses*, which differs in detail from both the texts already referred to. I commend to this Society the project of a scientifically collated text founded on these sources and any others which may exist [2] ; for I venture the assertion that the document in H.M. Register House is not the original at all but one of several imperfectly copied duplicates.

Let us pass on to matters of greater import than textual

[1] 1949   [2] A collated text is printed as an Appendix

criticism in order to consider the Declaration on its merits as a piece of rhetorical Latin prose, and to analyse some of its intrinsic characteristics. In order to make my first point I must embark upon a brief digression.

In classical and medieval times prose was thought of not as something to be read in silence but as something to be declaimed aloud, to listeners whose ears were attuned to rhythm and assonance to a degree to which we cannot aspire. The discovery was soon made that the quality of prose depended mainly upon the rhythms with which paragraphs, sentences or even phrases end—the *clausulae*, as they were called. You can rediscover that fact for yourselves by examining the great passages of the Authorised Version, and the English Prayer Book. In Greek and classical Latin the rhythms were mainly prosodic, depending on the quantities of the vowels. In medieval Latin the rhythms became mainly accentual and therefore much easier of detection by the modern ear ; and it was not long before the whole process was reduced to rule, and prose composition became (like the writing of heroic couplets after Pope) a mere mechanic art, though a very difficult one. It was in the Papal Curia during the thirteenth century that the *ars dictaminis*, as it was called, attained its highest developments, and it soon came to be accepted that the *clausulae*, or closing cadences, ought to conform in the main to one or other of three patterns, and that rhetorical prose ought to be written in one or other of three keys ; the *Cursus Planus*, for narrative ; the *Cursus Tardus*. for solemn invocation ; and the *Cursus Velox*, for passages of deep urgency or strong feeling. There were several permitted variants, like the accidentals in music, and the key could at any time be transposed to fit the substance of the message. The three primary forms are shown in these examples :

> *Cursus Planus* : cretic-trochee, as in " servants departed "
> *Cursus Tardus* : cretic-cretic, as in " perfect felicity "
> *Cursus Velox* : cretic-ditrochee, as in " glorious under-taking "

Now if any of you find it tolerable in ending a sentence to

transpose any of these pairs of words, I must regretfully inform you that, like Charles Lamb, you have no ear. Anyhow all the great masters of prose from Demosthenes to De Quincey have been unanimous in employing, consciously or unconsciously, these or very similar cadences.

Let us return from that long digression to the Declaration of Arbroath. It is a practically faultless specimen of the *ars dictaminis* of the thirteenth century. It conforms so closely to the accepted standards of its day that it might almost be said to be set to music. The dominant key is appropriately the *Cursus Velox*, with occasional transpositions in the narrative portions into the *Cursus Planus*, changing in the solemn closing invocations into the *Cursus Tardus*. There are in all 89 *clausulae* in the Declaration, and of these no fewer than 78 are in the classic rhythms, the balance being permitted variants. If we confine attention to the 22 main periods or paragraphs, 18 of them are in the three main keys, and 14 in the *Cursus Velox*, 10 in its most perfect form with a final quadrisyllable. In the oft-quoted central passage in which the Declaration soars into the famous eulogy of liberty, the three final cadences are three perfect *clausulae* in the *Cursus Velox* : " *omnibus adhaerere* " ; " *sufficere faciemus* " ; " *volumus subjugari.*"

This method of rhythmic analysis must be taken seriously, for it is being applied with remarkable results to the detection of genuine from spurious works, notably by the American School of Patristic Studies. It appears that no serious writer of prose can alter his characteristic prose rhythms any more than he can disguise his finger-prints.

Let me carry the matter a stage further in order to demonstrate that the finished products which we see in the Declaration of Arbroath were not the casual result of accident, but the fruit of conscious art skilfully applied. The Declaration is replete with apt quotations from or allusions to well-known sources, but never once is the quotation literally exact. In every instance the original has been adapted to fit the composer's rhythmical pattern. Take these examples. There are nine quotations from the Vulgate. The deliverance of Scotland is ascribed to Him who woundeth and His hands make whole (Job v. 18) ;

but while Jerome wrote " *vulnerat et medetur*," which will not scan, the Declaration substitutes " *Qui post vulnera medetur et sanat* "—the *Cursus Planus*. Bruce is described as he by whom salvation was wrought unto our people (1 Sam. xi. 13), but the Vulgate has been turned round from the active to the passive voice in order to produce a *Cursus Tardus*. The reference to Him with whom there is no respect of persons ends in the Vulgate with the cacophonous " *acceptio personarum*," which is discarded in favour of " *pondus nec distinctio*." In the closing invocation " Unto God we commit our cause " and so on, the Vulgate's " *in Eo ponamus eloquium meum* " becomes a sonorous *Cursus Tardus*—" *causam nostram tuendam committimus* " ; and " casting all our care upon Him " is not as in 1 Pet. v. 7 the staccato and unmanageable " *solicitudinem nostram projicientes in Eum*," but another majestic *Cursus Tardus*—" *cogitatum nostrum jactantes in Ipso*." These examples are enough to suggest that, however humbly the draftsman may have respected St Jerome as a theologian, he simply could not abide his discords.

And so with the famous quotation from Sallust's *Catiline* recently rediscovered by Mr Philip in the pages of the Scottish Historical Review. Now Sallust is peculiar amongst Roman prose writers in affecting an archaist style and in despising rhetorical orthodoxy, and the *clausula* of his famous peroration, whether read quantitatively or accentually, is truly rather dreadful. Listen to it : " *Sed libertatem | quam nemo bonus | nisi cum anima | simul amittit* "—the jingle of a very bad hexameter. And look what it became : " *Libertatem solummodo* "—the *Cursus Tardus* ; " *simul cum vita amittit* "—the *Cursus Planus*. Mr Philip and others have discussed the question why the draftsman altered Sallust, and two suggestions have been advanced : first, that he had mislaid his Sallust and was quoting from memory ; and second, that as a good Catholic he could not refer to the loss of a soul—*anima*. I fear that I cannot accept either explanation. In the very next sentence the Declaration again refers to the loss of souls (*animarum exitia*), and a few weeks later in a letter to Edward II the Pope himself (whose orthodoxy was presumably above approach) uses the same expression. Nor can I believe that a document of such importance, drafted with such meticulous care, would be allowed to pass with a slipshod misquotation. The change, I suggest, like the alterations on the Vulgate, was made deliberately and solely for prosodic reasons ; and it was because his sensitive ear would not allow him to jar the Pope's sensitive ear with the painful rhythm of the original that the draftsman did. for Sallust and Jerome what Shakespeare did so often for North's *Plutarch* and Holinshed's *Chronicle*.

All this, I suggest to you, throws a certain amount of light upon the question of who composed the Declaration. Obviously it could only be a Churchman of wide culture and exceptional skill in the *ars dictaminis*. If you compare the Declaration as a piece of rhetorical Latin prose with the surviving records of the period in the charters and state papers of Scotland and England, you will find extraordinarily little worthy of comparison with it. The great bulk of the others, when not written in the vernacular or in Norman French, are written in that pedestrian and undistinguished Latin which marked the last stages of the transition to the Romance languages. This is true of Bruce's own charters, and of the legislation of 1318, and of what little else has survived, with five notable exceptions : the letter to Philip of France in 1308 ; the Church's declaration for Bruce in 1309 ; the manifestos regarding the succession to the throne in 1315 and 1318 ; and the peace terms of 1326. All these formal documents, like the Declaration of Arbroath, closely follow the medieval *cursus* with the *Cursus Velox* predominating. None of them would have disgraced the Papal Curia. And there are a few revealing touches in these other documents. The horrors of war are invariably described in these other documents with the same accumulation of exaggerated epithets as we find in the Declaration. In them, as in the Declaration, the Almighty is usually referred to by an allusive quotation from the Vulgate, but once again the quotation is never literally exact, but is adapted to the rhythmic pattern. Thus in the Church's declaration we find a reference to Him by whom Kings reign and Princes decree justice (Prov. viii. 15), but Jerome's Latin has been rearranged so as to produce a *Cursus Velox*.

The conclusion which at once suggests itself is that all these Scottish state papers dating from 1308 to 1326 were written by the same hand or passed for revision under the same eye. Was there a cultured Churchman who during these years was in a position to discharge such responsibilities? The answer is, of course, the answer of tradition—Bernard de Linton, Abbot of Arbroath, who held the office of Chancellor of Scotland and King's Secretary of State from 1308 to 1328.

Someone ought to write Bernard's biography. He suddenly appears from nowhere in the centre of the stage within eighteen months of Bruce's coronation—a veritable priest after the order of Melchizedek, without father, without mother, without descent, having neither beginning of days nor end of life—so far as our records disclose. When we first see him he is already Bruce's Chancellor, and he was at his royal master's right hand throughout these twenty eventful years, until in 1328 he relinquished his post in order to become Bishop of Sodor, with a pension from the Abbey he had served so well and a gift of £100 from the King to pay his election expenses. Much may be learned from the testing clauses of the charters, and something perhaps from the Latin verses ascribed to him in the *Scotichronicon* by which he celebrated the victory of Bannock-burn, though I do not believe he was there on 24th June 1314. I strongly suspect that Bruce owed everything not attributable to his own martial prowess to the political wisdom and diplo-matic skill of the Abbot of Arbroath, and that we have one outstanding specimen of his scholarship and political wisdom in the Declaration of Arbroath. It is a great pity that in the end of the day he was so shabbily treated.

There is another point. Much ink has been spilt upon speculations as to how the so-called original came to be in Haddingtonshire, and whether the letter ever reached the Pope or indeed was ever intended to do so. Professor Hannay maintained that a notarial transumpt may have gone to Avignon, and that the original was retained at home, pre-sumably for the office file. I cannot think so. In form and substance the Declaration is a letter and not an agreement, and it seems improbable that the punctilious draftsman would have exasperated the precisians of the Papal Curia by sending them a notarial transumpt. It would be just as likely that a Foreign Secretary would send a carbon copy of a dispatch to the ambassador of a foreign power. My impression is that the letter would be executed and sealed in duplicate or in triplicate ; that the principal would go to Avignon ; and that what we have in the Register House is an imperfectly copied duplicate.

Be that as it may, there is no room for doubt that Pope John XXII got the letter ; and I shall tell you why. The Assembly at Arbroath Abbey was on 6th April 1320. Some weeks might easily elapse before the envoys were ready to start on their long and dangerous journey, and they might not reach Avignon and get an audience before the end of May or early June, and possibly later. Let us now pick up the story at the other end in the pages of Theiner and Rymer. The purpose of the Barons' letter was of course to induce the Pope to alter his policy towards Edward II ; and on 29th July 1320 the Pope wrote to Edward II in the precise sense which the Barons desired. In that letter he used with Edward II one of the arguments employed by the Barons in the Declaration of Arbroath and made an exact quotation from it. The Barons had boldly warned the Pope that, if he did not comply, the Almighty would lay at his door the responsibility for the consequences in death and disaster—note the words, *animarum exitia, corporum excidia, et cetera quae sequentur incommoda*. When he wrote to Edward II the Pope warned him that the continuance of the war would entail " *animarum exitia, excidia corporum, vastitates rerum, et alia non facile numeranda incommoda.* Can it be doubted that when the Pope or his Secretary penned that letter, he had the Declaration of Arbroath lying on the table in front of him ?

I was still relishing this item of evidence when I received a letter from Dr Donaldson,[1] who unknown to me was fishing in the same pool, pointing out that on the very next page of Theiner there is a letter from the Pope to the Barons acknowledging the receipt of the Declaration, from which he quotes

[1] Lecturer in Scottish History in the University of Edinburgh

certain passages. The point is thus lifted outside the range of discussion, and we look forward to an early article by Dr Donaldson elaborating his discovery, the credit of which he gains by a very short head.

These papal records deserve more study than they have received. We get the names of the two envoys who carried the letter—Edward de Mambuisson and Adam de Gordon—and we find that they were more than postmen, for they were charged with oral messages to the Pope and had several audiences with him. Moreover the Declaration of Arbroath was not the only letter which they carried, for there was also a private letter from Bruce. That letter has not (so far as I know) been preserved, but by great good fortune we can reconstruct its contents from two letters in reply which the Pope dispatched to Bruce, and from a further letter to Edward II which he wrote to report all that had happened. That is just as well, for this reason. There were " Men of Vichy " at Arbroath on that fateful day when the Declaration was sealed, and the strange passage in the Declaration by which the Barons assert that, if Bruce weakened in his resolution, they would drive him from his throne and choose another king, creates a faint suspicion that Bruce himself was suspected of designs to make peace. The private letter thus becomes very important for the purpose of discovering where exactly Bruce stood. Happily its reconstructed contents refute this suspicion. What did Bruce write ? He raised the question of the vacant Bishopric of Glasgow. He asked the Pope to secure the pardon of certain ecclesiastics who were imprisoned, presumably in England. And he made a spirited protest against the Pope's practice of refusing to give him his title of King of Scots. That was all. There is no hint or trace of weakening ; and by the time we reach September Bruce comes out of that correspondence with much greater credit than John XXII.

And so we may conclude that when Bernard inserted that odd passage in the Declaration, he was not covertly hitting at Bruce, who, by the way, was not the kind of man to tolerate insinuations of that sort. So to read the passage is to miss the point. The draftsman—consummate artist as he was—was working up to his dramatic peroration in which he spoke of the one hundred Scots who might still be left alive ; and his point was that the Pope had to reckon not with one man but with a nation ; that Bruce was no more than the instrument of the people's will ; and that, if Bruce vanished or had to be liquidated, the iron resolution of a nation would remain unbroken and unshaken. Any ruler who betrayed his trust forfeited his position. Bruce, I have little doubt, listened to that passage when it was read at Arbroath Abbey, not with a guilty conscience nor with resentment at any supposed innuendo, but with admiration for its rhetorical skill.

There is still much to be learned from that remarkable manifesto. Read it again, and judge for yourselves whether it does not deserve on its merits to be ranked as one of the masterpieces of political rhetoric of all time.

1949

References

THEINER, *Vetera Monumenta Hibernorum et Scotorum Historiam illustrantia*, Rome, 1864.

RYMER, *Foedera*, 4th ed., London, 1816-30.

CLARK, A. C. *The Cursus in Medieval Latin*, Oxford, 1910.

BROADHEAD, H. D., *Latin Prose Rhythm*, Cambridge, 1922.

Catholic University of America, *Patristic Studies*, Washington, 1937.

HANNAY, R. K., *The Letter of the Barons of Scotland*, Edinburgh Heriot-Watt College, 1936.

PHILIP, J. R., " Sallust and the Declaration of Arbroath," *Sc. Hist. Rev.* xxvi, 75.

DONALDSON, GORDON, " The Pope's Reply to the Scottish Barons in 1320," *Sc. Hist. Rev.* xxix, 119.

APPENDIX

★

*Latin Text and English Translation
of the Declaration of Arbroath*

collated from

A The copy in H.M. Register House (facsimiles in *A.P.S.* vol. i ;
Anderson's *Diplomata*, lii ; and *Nat. MSS. of Scotland*, ii, 17).

B The *Scotichronicon* (Goodall's ed. ii, 275).

C Sir George Mackenzie's *Causæ Forenses* (*Works*, i, 145).

Latin Text

The contractions have been expanded and modern orthography and punctuation employed

Sanctissimo Patri in Christo ac Domino, DOMINO JOHANNI, Divina Providentia Sacrosantae Romanae et Universalis Ecclesiae Summo Pontifici, filii sui humiles et devoti . . .* ceterique Barones et Liberetenentes ac tota Communitas Regni Scotiae, omnimodam reverentiam filialem, cum devotis pedum osculis beatorum.

Scimus, Sanctissime Pater et Domine, et ex antiquorum gestis et libris colligimus, quod inter ceteras nationes egregias nostra (scilicet, Scotorum) natio multis praeconiis fuerit insignita. Quae de Majori Scythia per Mare Tirenum et Columnas Herculis transiens, et in Hispania inter ferocissimos per multa temporum curricula residens, a nullis quantumcunque barbaricis poterat alicubi subjugari. Indeque veniens post mille et ducentos annos a transitu Populi Israelitici, sibi sedes in Occidente quas nunc obtinet, expulsis Britonibus et Pictis omnino deletis, licet per Norvegienses, Danos [1] et Anglos [2] saepius impugnata fuerit, multis sibi victoriis et laboribus quamplurimis adquisivit, ipsasque ab omni servitute liberas, ut priscorum testantur historiae, semper tenuit. In quorum regno centum et tresdecim reges de ipsorum regali prosapia nullo alienigena interveniente, regnaverunt. Quorum nobilitates et merita, licet ex aliis non clarerent, satis tamen patenter effulgent ex eo quod Rex Regum et [3] Dominus, Jesus Christus, post Passionem et Resurrectionem suam,[4] ipsos in ultimis terrae finibus constitutos quasi primos ad suam fidem sanctissimam convocavit. Nec eos per quemlibet in dicta fide confirmari voluit sed per suum primum Apostolum vocatione,[5] quamvis ordine secundum vel tertium, scilicet [6] Andream,

* See p. 342.

[1] Dacos AB.   [2] Anglicos AB.
[3] Omitted C.   [4] Omitted C.
[5] Omitted AC.   [6] Sanctum C.

Translation

Unto the Most Holy Father in Christ and the Lord, JOHN, by the Providence of God Supreme Pontiff of the Holy Roman Church Universal, Duncan, Earl of Fife [here follow 39 names and designations *] and the other Barons and Freeholders and the whole community of the Scottish realm offer all filial reverence with devout kisses to his blessed feet.

WE know, Most Holy Father and Lord, and we find it written in the records and histories of the ancients, that amongst other peoples of renown our Scottish nation has been distinguished by many tributes to their fame. We passed over from Greater Scythia across the Tyrrhenian Sea and beyond the Pillars of Hercules, and sojourned for many a year amid the most savage races of Spain ; but nowhere could any people, however barbarous, reduce us to subjection. From there, twelve hundred years after the Departure of the Children of Israel, we came to our abode in the West where we now dwell. The Britons were driven out ; the Picts were utterly destroyed ; we were assailed again and again by Norse, Angle and Dane : but by many a victory and with endless toil we established ourselves here, and, as the historians of old bear witness, we have ever held our land free from servitude of every kind. Within this our realm there have reigned one hundred and thirteen Kings of our native royal dynasty, and not one of alien birth. If proof be needed of the quality and worth of our people, it shines forth for all to see in this that the King of Kings, our Lord Jesus Christ, after His Passion and Resurrection, chose us as almost the first to be called to His most holy faith, though we dwelt in the uttermost parts of the earth, and He would not that we should be confirmed therein by anyone except the first of His Apostles by calling, though the second or third in rank, Andrew the Meek, the brother of blessed Peter, whom He appointed to be our leader and patron Saint for ever.

* See p. 342.

mitissimum [1] beati Petri germanum, quem semper ipsis praeesse voluit ut Patronum.

Haec autem Sanctissimi Patres et praedecessores vestri sollicita mente pensantes, ipsum regnum et populum, ut beati Petri germani peculium, multis favoribus er privilegiis muniverunt. Itaque gens nostra sub ipsorum protectione liber hactenus deguit et quieta, donec ille princeps magnificus, Rex Anglorum, Edwardus, pater istius qui nunc est, regnum nostrum acephalum populumque nullius mali aut doli conscium nec bellis aut insultibus tunc assuetum, sub amici et confederati specie inimicabiliter [2] infestavit. Cujus injurias, caedes et violentias, praedationes, incendia, prelatorum incarcerationes, monasteriorum combustiones, religiosorum spoliationes et occisiones, alia quoque enormia quae in dicto populo exercuit, nulli parcens aetati aut sexui, religioni aut ordini, nullus scriberet nec ad plenum intelligeret nisi quem experientia informaret.

A quibus malis innumeris, Ipso juvante qui post vulnera medetur et sanat, liberati sumus per strenuissimum [3] principem, regem et dominum nostrum, Dominum Robertum, qui pro populo et hereditate suis de manibus inimicorum liberandis, quasi alter Maccabeus aut Joshua, labores et taedia, inedias et pericula laeto sustinuit animo. Quem etiam Divina dispositio et juxta leges et consuetudines nostras, quas usque ad mortem sustinere volumus, juris successio et debitus nostrorum omnium [4] consensus et assensus nostrum fecerunt principem atque Regem. Cui, tanquam illi per quem salus in populo [5] facta est, pro nostra libertate tuenda tam jure quam meritis tenemur et volumus in omnibus adhaerere. Quem si ab inceptis desisteret, Regi Anglorum aut Anglicis nos aut regnum nostrum volens subjicere, tanquam inimicum nostrum et sui nostrique juris subversorem, statim expellere niteremur, et alium regem nostrum qui ad defensionem nostram sufficeret [6] faciemus.[7]

Quia quamdiu centum viri remanserint, nunquam Anglorum dominio aliquatenus volumus subjugari. Non

---

[1] Meritissimum C.
[2] Innumerabiliter C.
[3] Serenissimum C.
[4] Omitted C.
[5] Populo nostro B.
[6] Sufficiet C.
[7] Faceremus B.

It was after pondering all these things in their minds that the Most Holy Fathers, your predecessors, fortified our realm and people, as the peculiar possession of the brother of blessed Peter, with many favours and countless privileges. So it came about that under their protection our nation lived in freedom and in peace, until that august prince, Edward, King of England, the father of the present King, finding our realm without a king, and our people innocent of evil intent and still unused to the assaults of war, came to us in the guise of a friend and ally and then made a hostile attack upon us. As for the wrongs he inflicted upon us—the slaughter, violence, pillage, conflagration, prelates imprisoned, monasteries burned down and their inmates robbed and slain, and all the other outrages which he perpetrated on our people, sparing neither age nor sex nor religious order—none could describe nor even conceive these things unless he had actually experienced them.

From these innumerable evils, with the aid of Him Who woundeth and His hands make whole, we have been delivered by our most valiant Prince and King, Robert ; who, that he might free his people and heritage from the hands of the enemy, rose like another Joshua or Maccabeus, and cheerfully endured toil and weariness, hunger and peril. He it is that by the providence of God we have made our Prince and King, not only by right of succession according to our laws and customs, which we are resolved to maintain unto the death, but also with the due consent and assent of us all. Unto him, by whom salvation has been wrought unto our people, we are bound for the preservation of our liberties, both by force of law and out of gratitude for all he has done ; and unto him we are determined in all things to adhere. But were he to abandon the task to which he has set his hand or to show any disposition to subject us or our realm to the King of England or the English, we would instantly strive to expel him as our enemy and the betrayer of his own rights and ours, and we would choose another King to rule over us who would be equal to the task of our defence.

For so long as one hundred men remain alive, we shall never under any conditions submit to the domination of the

enim propter gloriam, divitias aut honores pugnamus, sed propter libertatem solummodo, quam nemo bonus nisi simul cum vita amittit.[1]

Hinc, est reverende Pater et Domine, quod sanctitatem vestram omni [2] precum instantia genuflexis cordibus exoramus quatenus, sincero corde menteque pia recensentes quod apud Eum, cujus vices in terris geritis, non sit pondus et pondus, nec distinctio Judaei et Graeci, Scoti aut Anglici, tribulationes et angustias nobis et Ecclesiae Dei illatas ab Anglicis paternis oculis intuentes, Regem Anglorum, cui sufficere debet quod possidet, cum olim Anglia septem aut pluribus solebat sufficere regibus, monere et exhortari dignemini ut nos Scotos in exili degentes Scotia, ultra quam habitatio non est, nihilque nisi nostrum cupientes, in pace dimittat : cui pro nostra procuranda quiete quicquid possumus, ad statum nostrum respectu habito, hoc facere volumus cum effectu.

Vestra enim interest, Sancte Pater, hoc facere, qui paganorum seritatem, Christianorum culpis exigentibus, in Christianos saevientem aspicitis et Christianorum terminos arctari indies. Quantumque [3] vestrae memoriae derogat si [4] (quod absit) Ecclesia in aliqua sui parte vestris temporibus patiatur eclipsim aut scandalum vos videritis. Excitet [5] igitur Christianos principes, qui non causam ut causam ponentes, se fingunt in subsidium Terrae Sanctae propter guerras quas habent cum proximis ire non posse ; cujus impedimenti causa est verior quod in minoribus proximis debellandis utilitas propior et resistentia debilior aestimantur. Sed [6] quam laeto corde dictus Dominus Rex noster et nos, si Rex Anglorum nos in pace dimitteret, illuc iremus, Qui nil ignorat satis novit. Quod Christi Vicario totique Christianitati ostendimus et testamur.

Quibus si Sanctitas Vestra, Anglorum relatibus nimis credula, fidem sinceram non adhibet,[7] aut ipsis in nostram confusionem favere non desinat, corporum excidia, animarum

---

[1] Amittet C. [2] Cum omni C.
[3] Illegible A. Quare ne quid C.
[4] Et si C. The true reading probably is deroget si.
[5] Exhortet C. [6] Set A. Sic C.
[7] Adhibeat C.

English. It is not for glory or riches or honours that we fight, but only for liberty, which no good man will consent to lose but with his life.

For these reasons, revered Father and Lord, we most earnestly pray and from our hearts beseech your Holiness that in all sincerity and piety you will call to mind that with Him, whose earthly vicegerent you are, there is no respect of persons and neither Jew nor Greek, Scot nor English. We entreat you to look with a father's eye upon the tribulations and distress which the English have brought upon us and upon the Church of God : and we ask that you will be pleased to admonish and exhort the King of England (who should rest content with what he has seeing that it was enough to satisfy at least seven kings), urging him to leave us in peace in our poor Scotland, where we live on the uttermost bounds of human habitation and covet nothing but our own. To secure such a peace we are willing in very deed to do anything in our power saving all these our vital interests. So to do, Holy Father, is a matter of real concern for yourself ; for you see how the heathen rage against the Christians through the fault of the Christians, and how the boundaries of Christendom are being narrowed every day. See to it that your good name does not suffer if—which God forbid—the Church in any place suffers eclipse or offence while you are Pope ! Make an appeal therefore to the Christian princes who are alleging as false pretexts for their inability to go on a crusade to the Holy Land that they are at war with their neighbours—the truth being that they consider it more profitable and less dangerous to vanquish their weaker neighbours than to go on a crusade. But if only the King of England would leave us in peace, He from Whom no secrets are hid well knows how joyfully we and our King would go to the Holy Land ; and this pledge we declare and testify to you as the Vicar of Christ and to the whole of Christendom.

But if your Holiness will not place reliance on these our assurances, preferring to lend too credulous an ear to the allegations of the English and continuing to show favour to them to our discomfiture, rest assured that the destruction of

exitia et cetera quae sequentur [1] incommoda, quae ipsi in nobis et nos in ipsis fecerimus, vobis ab Altissimo credimus imputanda.

Ex quo sumus et erimus, in his quae tenemur, parati [2] tanquam obedientiae filii, vobis, tanquam Ipsius Vicario, in omnibus complacere. Ipsique, tanquam Summo Regi et Judici, causam nostram tuendam committimus, cogitatum nostrum jactantes in Ipso, sperantesque firmiter [3] quod in nobis virtutem faciet, et ad nihilum rediget hostes nostros.

Sanctitatem ac sanitatem [4] vestram conservet Altissimus Ecclesiae Suae Sanctae per tempora diuturna.

> Datum apud Monasterium de Abirbrothoc in Scotia Sexto die Aprilis, Anno Gratiæ Millesimo Trecentesimo Vicesimo, Anno vero Regni Regis nostri supradicti Quinto Decimo.

[1] Sequuntur C.
[3] Finem C.

[2] Omitted AC.
[4] Serenitatem et sanctitatem C.

life, the perdition of souls and all the other evils which will ensue and which we shall inflict on the English and they on us, will be laid by the Most High to your account !

Wherefore we are and ever shall be, as in duty bound, prepared as obedient children to do your good pleasure as His Vicar. And unto Him, the King and Judge most high, we commit our cause, casting all our care upon Him, and steadfastly trusting that He will endue us with courage and bring our enemies to nought.

May the Most High preserve your Holiness in health and strength for the service of His Holy Church to length of days.

> Executed at the Monastery of Arbroath in Scotland on the Sixth day of April, in the year of Grace One thousand three hundred and twenty and in the Fifteenth year of the Reign of our said King.

The Declaration of Arbroath

was executed by

Duncan, Earl of Fife

Thomas Randulph, Earl of Moray, Lord of Man and Annandale

Patrick Dunbar, Earl of March

Malise, Earl of Strathearn

Malcolm, Earl of Lennox

William, Earl of Ross

Magnus, Earl of Caithness and Orkney

William, Earl of Sutherland

Walter, Steward of Scotland

William of Soulis, Butler of Scotland

James, Lord of Douglas

Roger Moubray

David, Lord of Brechin

David Graham

Ingeram Umfraville

John Menteith, Guardian of the Earldom of Monteith

Alexander Fraser

Gilbert Hay, Constable of Scotland

Robert Keith, Marshall of Scotland

Henry Sinclair

John Graham

David Lindsay

William Oliphant

Patrick Graham

John Fenton

William Abernethy

David Wemyss

William Muschet

Fergus of Ardrossan

Eustace Maxwell

William Ramsay

William Mowat

Allan Moray

Donald Campbell

John Cameron

Ronald Cheyne

Alexander Seton

Andrew Leslie

Alexander Stratton

Judicial Opinions from
Session Cases

H.M. Advocate v. Rolley [1]

LORD JUSTICE-CLERK (Cooper) : Members of the jury, you are the masters of the facts ; but there is one fact upon which I think you will have very little difficulty in making up your minds, namely, that what I shall call for short a burglary was committed during the week 11th to 18th September at 9 Campbell Road, Edinburgh, and that the unknown burglar appropriated by theft the numerous articles to which Mrs Lindsay and her little boy spoke. The real issue in this case—and probably you will think the single issue in fact—is, who was the person who committed that act of house-breaking ? Now, as Mr Cunningham quite properly reminded you, it is, of course, for the Crown to satisfy you that the accused was the person who was there and who committed that crime. It is not for the accused to satisfy you of his innocence. That means that, if in the end of the day you should still remain in real and genuine doubt—and it must be a real and genuine doubt—as to where the truth of this matter lies, then you would be bound to give the accused the benefit of that doubt. On the other hand, if you were satisfied on what you have heard that the Crown has succeeded in fastening guilt on the accused—if you think that is the just and reasonable inference from the evidence led before you this morning—equally it is your plain duty to convict.

Now, Mr Cunningham for the defence has accepted the position, and I so direct you, that the evidence on which the Crown rely to link the accused with this offence, namely, the palm print, is competent, admissible and sufficient evidence of

---

[1] 1945 S.C.(J) 155.

identification *provided you accept it*. The *value* of the evidence is a matter for you. I would like to explain that very briefly on the lines referred to by the Solicitor-General, by pointing out that in all cases of this kind, unless you have an actual eye-witness, or the housebreaker is caught in the act or in recent possession of the stolen goods, the most common method upon which the prosecution rely for bringing home guilt to the accused is to found upon something that the delinquent has left behind, and then by suitable evidence to show that that something is unquestionably associated and identified with the accused. It may be a footprint, it may be a garment, or a distinctive tool, or something of that kind. In this case it is a palm print ; and it seems to me to make no difference what it is, provided that the evidence in its quality and substance is of a character to carry conviction to the jury, whose duty it is to determine upon its value. Something was said in the course of evidence and in the speeches of learned counsel on the word " infallibility," and on that topic I want to read to you a sentence or two from a case which dealt not with palm prints but with finger prints, and in it the late Lord Clyde as Lord Justice-General said this :

The value of finger-print evidence depends on the reliance which can be placed on the result of expert investigation and experience—in an immense number of cases, examined over a very extended period of years—to the effect that identity is never found to exist between the skin ridges of two different persons' fingers. This is what leads the experts to claim infallibility for the finger-mark method. I deprecate the use of the word " infallibility " in this connection at all. What the experts obviously mean is, not absolute, but practical infallibility—that is to say, a presumption of truth, the reliability of which may be accepted, not because it is irrebuttable in its own nature, but because long and extensive experience is shown to provide no instance in which it has ever been successfully rebutted. All proof depends at bottom on presumption ; even the evidence of two credible and uncontradicted witnesses who speak to the same occurrence in *probatio probata* not because it is impossible that they should both be mistaken, but because of the high presumption that what two credible witnesses say happened in their presence did actually happen.

[*Hamilton* v. *H.M. Advocate*, 1934 J.C. 1, at p. 4.]

Now that is very like what the Solicitor-General said, and to apply it to this case, you might figure the situation which would arise if Mrs Lindsay and her little boy had come and said they saw the thief and recognised him. That would not be infallible in any sense. They might be wrong. You are presented not with that type of evidence but with a different type of evidence, and it is for you to consider, and for me in a very few words to assist you in considering, the evidence which has been led on the topic of the palm print and its sufficiency for justifying the conclusion spoken to by the expert witnesses that the palm print impression left on the sideboard of the morning room of 9 Campbell Road was made by the left hand of the accused, and by no one else. You have had the evidence of four witnesses, and I feel bound to point out to you that they are men of wide and prolonged experience in the matter, and that the witnesses adduced from Scotland Yard are probably as rich in experience in this subject as anybody alive. On the basis of that long experience and study of the subject, including contributions to its study in the shape of the book to which Superintendent Cherrill referred, all four of them, as you will remember, said that as a result of a comparison of the original prints—I mean by that the small prints—and of the enlargements which were subsequently made, they had— and I think they all used the same words or almost the same words—*no doubt whatsoever*. In order to make the ground of their conviction more clear to you, they have prepared two sets of photographs, and, in accordance with Mr Cunningham's suggestion, I am willing that you should take them with you when you retire in a few moments—No. 5 the small pair of photographs made in Edinburgh and No. 7 the big pair of enlarged photographs made in London. The photographs made in Edinburgh indicate sixteen points of alleged identity, and the photographs made in London indicate twenty-five points of alleged identity. Please remember what the witnesses said—that the identity on which they rely is the identity of the ridge characteristics, and in particular the sequence of the ridge characteristics, and that they discount and allow for any differences between the impressions which are due to the degree of pressure with which the palm may have been pressed on the surface when the impressions were taken, or any difference in the character of the surfaces on which the palm may have been placed. So that in asking you to look at the photographs I would ask you not to look at them with an uninstructed eye, but with the eye of a person who has heard the explanations of those expert witnesses.

The criticism that was directed by Mr Cunningham against those powerfully-expressed views was, I think, two-fold. He said the area was too small to enable a proper conclusion to be drawn, and you heard the justification which the four witnesses gave—I think all four were questioned on these lines—for rejecting that suggestion and showing they had enough to warrant the conviction which they felt and expressed. He said, in the second place, that, as the experts had not examined the palms of everybody in the world or in Great Britain, they could not be certain that the identity of ridge characteristics and of sequence of ridge characteristics was as complete as they asserted. I think the point to keep in view when considering that criticism, as you must, is the very point in the passage from the late Lord Clyde which I read a moment ago, that in this imperfect world absolute certainty is unobtainable by any method known to the law or to science, and that what we are looking for is practical infallibility. The real question for you will be whether you are satisfied, from the explanations given by these four gentlemen, that their experience has been gathered over a sufficiently long number of years—I think twenty-six years in one case—and has extended to a sufficiently large number of cases to justify the confidence with which their conclusion was expressed. On the other side you will keep in view that the accused, in addition to tendering a plea of not guilty, to which he has adhered—and that is why we are here to-day—has gone into the witness-box and has in effect repeated that plea of not guilty under oath, and this also is an element that you will take into account. But the main point for your consideration will be whether, on a consideration of the police and expert evidence, you are satisfied beyond reasonable doubt that the just and proper inference is that the accused was the person who broke into that house, or whether you are not so satisfied.

The jury returned a verdict of guilty.

H.M. Advocate v. *Rutherford* [1]

LORD JUSTICE-CLERK (Cooper) : Ladies and gentlemen of the jury, both learned counsel began by saying that this case was unique. So it is. I do not think that such a story as was told in this court yesterday has ever been told in this court before, and on that account there is a special responsibility on you in relation to your duty, and on me in relation to mine.

In the first place, not only has nearly every critical fact in the Crown's story been established by evidence which was hardly challenged by cross-examination, but in substance the case for the Crown has been admitted by the accused in the witness-box to be a true and accurate story. You are the masters of the facts ; but in all I am going to say to you I am going to assume that you accept it as abundantly established, if not admitted, that about one o'clock on the morning of 16th July last, at or near that boat-house at St Margaret's Loch, the accused, Rutherford, strangled this woman and left her dead upon the staging. If that is your view, ladies and gentlemen—and frankly I do not not see what other view is possible—the question is not the question customary in trials of this kind, of whether the accused did this dreadful thing, but what crime, if any, he committed by doing it.

One word by way of digression. In the latter part of the address which he has just delivered, Mr Milligan threw out the suggestion that the woman Paton was of an emotional and excitable nature, and might die very quickly or very easily. That is a factor which will arise at a later stage in our consideration of the matter ; but I wish to guard against any misapprehension on your part by telling you now with emphasis that it is no answer for an assailant who causes death by violence to say that his victim had a weak heart or was excitable

[1] 1947 S.C.(J.) 1, at p. 3.

or emotional, or anything of that kind. He must take his victim as he finds her. It is just as criminal to kill an invalid as it is to kill a hale and hearty man in the prime of life. That by way of digression, because it was referred to in the concluding part of the argument to which you have just listened.

Now, if, as I am assuming, these broad stark facts which I have just summarised are proved, and if there were nothing more to be said in the case, then unquestionably there is no escape from a verdict of murder. But, of course, a great deal more has been said : and what has been said centres primarily if not entirely, upon the accused's own story as told to us in the witness-box. What was that story ? I think I am summarising it accurately and almost in his own words if I put it thus : " She asked me to strangle her to death. She asked me more than once." As Mr Milligan said, rightly enough, " she pestered me. She put my tie round her neck. I pulled it. She asked me to get on with it. I pulled it again. I had no intention of doing her harm. I only did it to humour her. I only meant to frighten her." That, in brief summary, is the very remarkable, and, I think, unprecedented, story which was put forward, and we have got to consider two things. In the first place—a question for you—whether that defence is to be accepted, and, in the second place—partly for myself and partly for you—what would be the effect of its acceptance or its rejection ?

Let me consider very briefly, because learned counsel have devoted much attention to it, the first point. Can you take this story off his hands ? Is it true in whole or in part ? Because I do not shrink from emphasising to you that you are not bound to look at the matter as if it were a question of accepting the whole story or nothing. Parts of it may be true, parts of it may be understated or overstated ; but the broad question is—Is this in substance a true story, or is it an afterthought invented to save the accused from an obviously desperate situation ? (His Lordship reviewed the evidence which told in favour of or against the acceptance of the accused's explanation of the occurrence, referring, *inter alia*, to the nature of the considerable injuries to the woman's throat, the indications both of strangulation by a ligature and also of manual throttling, her peculiar character, and evidence of certain attempts at suicide upon her part, one of them apparently genuine, others in the nature of play-acting for effect.)

Well, there the matter stands. You will consider the story as told by the accused both as a whole and in its separate parts, whether it is to be accepted in whole or in part. It is a possible view, and it is a view which I think you must take into account, that the episode at the boat-house began with requests by the woman to implement this alleged promise in writing, by request to the accused to strangle her—possibly to strangle her to death—and that it may later have changed its character, he may have lost his head or his temper or something of that kind. That is a possible view of the occurrence ; but the broad question with which I am concerned is—are you prepared to accept the story or not ? If you reject the story outright as an invention, and are therefore left with the facts in all their naked ugliness, then I have to tell you that your plain duty is to return a verdict of guilty of murder. But if you accept the story as substantially true in whole or in part, what then ?

That brings me to a consideration of certain of the legal questions on which I have been asked to give you directions, and let me tell you, ladies and gentlemen, it is not very easy in short space to cover accurately the propositions in law which rule a case so remarkable as this. Will you therefore give me your close attention for a few minutes longer ? The first thing I would say to you is this—rejecting one of the propositions that Mr Milligan asked me to pronounce—the first direction is this, that, even if you accepted the defence on its face value, there is no material before you in this case which would entitle you to treat the accused as guiltless and to acquit him, and I will tell you why. Mr Milligan said that this is a case to be accounted for as a mere accident, a pure misadventure, what is called in our law casual homicide. Now, casual homicide is a well-recognised category in the criminal law of Scotland, as in other countries, and I am going to read you a short passage from an authoritative work (Alison's *Criminal Law*, vol. i, pp. 139, 140) which explains what it is, and when I read it you will see why I decline this direction. The passage is this, " It is casual homicide where a person kills unintentionally, when lawfully employed, and neither meaning harm to anyone, nor having failed in the due degree of care and circumspection for preventing mischief to his neighbour." Note well the conditions. The writer proceeds, " Under this class are comprehended all those cases, unfortunately too numerous, in which death ensues, not from any fault in any quarter, but from some misfortune or accident, and where, consequently, the person who is the innocent cause of another's death is more the subject of pity than punishment." And then he proceeds to give examples. " Thus, if a person's gun burst in his hand and kill his neighbour ; or if the trigger be caught in going through a hedge, and the contents of the piece lodge in his breast ; or a horse ran away with its rider, in spite of all his efforts, and, though he had no good reason to have believed he would not manage it, and kill a passenger on the road," and so on—cases, ladies and gentlemen, of pure misadventure. Now, the responsibility is mine, and if I am wrong I shall be set right elsewhere, but I have to direct you in law that on no view of the evidence in this case would you be entitled to accept Mr Milligan's submission that this is a case of misadventure or pure accident or casual homicide as known to the law, and therefore no question of acquitting the accused altogether on that ground can arise.

So much for that. The next point which I have to direct you upon is this—it is a point the Solicitor-General raised, and the direction he asked was that anyone who wilfully kills another person at the latter's request or command is guilty of murder. That, in my opinion, is sound law, and I so direct you ; but I would rather put it more specifically with reference to this case in this form, that, if life is taken under circumstances which would otherwise infer guilt of murder, the crime does not cease to be murder merely because the victim consented to be murdered, or even urged the assailant to strike the fatal blow. To put the matter in popular terms ; if there was nothing in this case except the woman's request, and you held that proved, that would not suffice to take the edge off the guilt which otherwise attaches to the assailant. The attitude of the victim is irrelevant. What matters is the intent of the assailant. I think you will see, ladies and gentlemen, that it must be so. It would be a most perilous doctrine to introduce into the law of Scotland, or of any civilised country, that any person was entitled to kill any other person at that other person's request.

But, ladies and gentlemen, that is not the end of the matter. There still remains the issue which is, I think, the one to which your attention must be directed—whether there is enough in the evidence in this case to warrant you in finding the accused guilty not of murder but of the lesser crime of culpable homicide. Here again I must refuse one of the directions that Mr Milligan asked me to give. This is not on any view a case of simple assault. Where violence is used, as admittedly it was used in this case, and it results in fatal consequences, that is not by the law of Scotland assault. It is culpable homicide. And the question to which I now direct your attention is the question of the choice between a verdict of guilty of murder and a verdict of guilty of culpable homicide. That choice depends entirely upon the quality of the criminal intent which, in your view, inspired the assailant, Rutherford, Notice I say " intent " not " motive." The Crown is not obliged in any case of this kind to establish the motive with which the crime is committed. What the law looks for is, not the motive at the back of a man's mind, but the intention, the intent with which he acts ; and of course it is just there that the difficulty arises, because no one can see inside any person's mind, and intent must always be a matter of inference—inference mainly from what the person does, but partly also from the whole surrounding circumstances of the case. Now, note this—and note this particularly—the essence of murder is that the accused should have acted deliberately with intent to kill, or at least with reckless indifference as to the consequences of his violence upon his victim.

I will say that again, " intent to kill or at least with reckless indifference as to the consequences of his violence upon his victim." These words have been used again and again, and no better formulation is known to me. It is not necessary that the murder should be premeditated, and, as I have said, motive need not be proved. But, unless it is established to your satisfaction beyond reasonable doubt that Rutherford when compressing this woman's throat was acting with the intent which I have defined, his crime is not murder, and your verdict ought to be one of culpable homicide. If, on the other hand, on the best survey you are able to form of the whole of the evidence in this strange and dramatic case, you feel that the just and proper conclusion is that the intent was a murderous intent, then, your duty, under your sworn oath as jurors, is plain. Let me consider the choice for a few moments. (His Lordship referred to certain considerations which might influence their decision upon this matter.)

Now, ladies and gentlemen, the position, as I see it, is this —*prima facie*, and without the explanations afforded by the accused, this is a plain case of murder. But the explanations of the accused may be enough to raise in your minds the reasonable doubt as to whether a murderous intent was present ; and reasonable doubt, if it be *reasonable* doubt, is enough, because it is the duty of every jury to give the accused the benefit of a reasonable doubt, provided it is a genuine doubt arising on the evidence and not some fanciful or vague hypothesis. Taking the matter on the footing which I have endeavoured to lay before you, the effective choice which you have now to make is a choice between a verdict of murder or a verdict of guilty of culpable homicide, because, as I have said, if you accept the account of this tragedy which is now to all intents and purposes common ground, there is no material which would justify any jury in returning a verdict of not guilty or not proven.

Macleod v. *Mackenzie* [1]

LORD JUSTICE-GENERAL (Cooper) : In the heart of the Island of Lewis near the head of Loch Erisort there is a clachan called Balallan, in which the complainer keeps the local store, selling articles of clothing, provisions and general merchandise. He also acts as merchant for the local Harris tweed, and he works a croft, and at certain times of the year, particularly in the spring and summer, he also works at cutting, weathering and ingathering peats. His must be a full life, for his activities touch current regulations at countless points. In May 1946 there penetrated into Balallan from Inverness two inspectors of the Price Regulation Committee, and, on visiting the complainer's shop, they either attempted to purchase or found exposed for sale there a curious assortment of articles :— twenty hand towels, eleven pairs of knickers, one pair of boy's boots, and certain other goods. Seven months later, there were served upon the complainer not one, but five separate complaints. Under the first, he was charged with having priced the towels at 4½d. too much, the total excess being 7s. 6d. Under charge (2), he was charged with having priced the knickers at 9d. per pair too much, the total excess being 8s. 3d. and under the third with having priced the pair of boots at 22s. 6d. instead of 22s., the excess being 6d. Under the fourth and fifth complaints, the gravamen of the charge was that he had failed to preserve for a period of twelve months from the date of delivery the invoices relating to these and certain other miscellaneous goods. The maximum penalties stated (in some cases inaccurately) in the complaints are, as usual, Draconian, and, a plea of guilty having been tendered by a solicitor on behalf of the accused, the learned Sheriff-substitute has imposed under charges (1), (2) and (3) three fines of £10, and under charges (4) and (5) two fines of £15, making £60 in all.

It appears from the bill of suspension and answers to be

[1] 1947 S.C.(J.) 103, at p. 108.

Z

abundantly plain that there was no question of dishonesty or of engaging in black market transactions but, at worst, of an unsuccessful effort to comply with all the regulations. Indeed, the inspectors on the occasion of their visit found various articles undercharged. Moreover the facts indicate that the complainer made a full disclosure and gave every assistance to the inspectors and the authorities, and that the truth of the matter is that he has been guilty under the first three complaints of a technical infringement involving relatively trivial sums, and under the fourth and fifth complaints of inability to do that which in the case of such a store in such a place must be far from easy of performance in the absence of skilled clerical aid.

There is this further consideration that, although the maximum penalties under the first three complaints differed from those applicable under the last two, though the articles and the number of articles differed in the different complaints, and though the amounts involved vary from 6d. in the case of charge (3) to 8s. 3d. in the case of charge (2), the penalty is, as I have stated the same under the first three charges and 50 per cent. greater for the fourth and fifth. Mr Hunter has satisfied me that this is a case which may fairly be described in the language of the Lord Justice-General in *Stewart* v. *Cormack* [1] as one in which the penalty is not properly related to the offence, and taking the whole circumstances into consideration I feel that justice would be done by substituting under each of the five heads for the penalty imposed by the Sheriff-substitute an admonition.

Chalmers v. *H.M. Lord Advocate* [2]

LORD JUSTICE-GENERAL (Cooper) : The appellant was convicted by a majority verdict, after a trial before Lord Strachan and a jury at Stirling, on a charge of robbery and murder, and, in respect that at the date of the crimes he was 16 years of

[1] 1941 J.C. 73.   [2] 1954 S.C.(J.) 66, at p. 73.

age, he was ordered to be detained during Her Majesty's pleasure. The grounds of appeal against the conviction are (1) wrongful admission of evidence, and (2) insufficient admissible evidence to support the conviction.

The crimes were committed in foundry premises at Larbert in the late afternoon of 24th July 1953, and there is no doubt that the deceased was then robbed and seriously assaulted by someone. The live issue at the trial was whether the Crown could identify the appellant as the assailant.

In the course of their investigations the police made many enquiries, and on 26th July, and again on 7th August, questioned the appellant. The statements then given by him were not incriminating. The police later obtained certain information from the witnesses Mrs Oliver and her small son, which tended to cast some doubt upon the truth of the statements made by the appellant, and the police decided to see the appellant again. Their attitude at this point is frankly explained by the detective inspector in charge of the investigation, who says that, from the information received from Mrs Oliver, he was " inclined to suspect " that the appellant might have some connection with the crime, and that the appellant " was under suspicion." In that situation a police car with two officers was sent from Falkirk on 15th August to fetch the appellant from Clackmannan, where he was still in bed ; and he was brought to the police station at Falkirk at 11.10 a.m. and there interviewed by a detective inspector in the presence of another officer of the same rank. The appellant (he was never at liberty again) was told that he was to be further questioned, and was cautioned in the usual terms. The inspector then proceeded to interrogate the appellant, telling him the information which had come into the possession of the police and reopening the statement made by him on 7th August. The inspector admits that he was " cross-examining " the appellant, and making suggestions to him which were contradictory of his previous statement, saying, *inter alia*, that the police had reason to believe that he " might have been " at the locus at the time when the crimes were committed. The interrogation lasted for about five minutes, until the appellant was reduced to tears. He was then cautioned a second time, and asked whether he wanted his father or a solicitor to be present " when he did a certain thing." The appellant declined. The second inspector was then asked to take a note of the appellant's statement, but, before doing so, he gave a third (or fourth) caution to the appellant and repeated the offer that his father or a solicitor should be present. A statement was then taken, which we can only assume was highly incriminating ; but this statement was not tendered in evidence by the Crown.

Matters did not end there. Immediately after the statement had been taken the first inspector questioned the appellant about certain matters contained in his statement, and, in consequence of answers thus obtained, the appellant was taken about 11.45 a.m. in a police van by the inspector and two other police officers to a cornfield near the locus, where the purse of the deceased was found at a spot pointed out by the appellant under the surveillance of the police. The appellant was then taken back to the police station about 12.10 p.m. An interval of about two hours then ensued while the appellant's father was being fetched by the police, and at this stage, though there had been neither charge nor arrest, the appellant is described by the police as being " detained in connection with the murder," whatever that may mean. The father arrived about 2.15 p.m., and the appellant again broke down. At 2.25 p.m. he was cautioned and formally charged in presence of his father, whereupon the appellant is said to have replied : " I did it. He struck me."

A speciality is introduced by the reasons given by the presiding judge in determining to admit the evidence regarding the cornfield. As I have observed, the " statement " was not tendered in evidence, presumably because it was regarded as unfair so to do, and the presiding judge indicated that he would disallow any evidence of statements made by the appellant at the cornfield, but that, in the absence of authority, he would not reject evidence as to the " actings " of the appellant at the cornfield—i.e. the evidence that the appellant when taken to the cornfield, pointed out the place where the purse was found. The whole of the evidence bearing upon the circumstances of the interrogation at the police station and of the subsequent conducted visit to the cornfield was adduced in the presence and hearing of the jury. This evidence the judge left to the jury with certain comments upon its weight and value, and with the direction that, if they thought that there was such unfairness in the police proceedings as to force them to ˜disregard this piece of evidence, they were entitled to do so. According to the argument for the appellant this line of approach indicated a fatal inconsistency. On behalf of the Crown it was maintained (*a*) that the cornfield episode was separable from the proceedings which culminated in the " statement," and (*b*) that " the statement " at the police station, if tendered, would have been admissible. The two contentions are so closely related in argument and in the reasoning of the presiding judge that we allowed the debate to proceed though the second question is not properly before us, and it is right that I should indicate my views upon both questions.

I take first the " statement," with regard to which I am of opinion that in the circumstances a decision to reject this evidence would have been right. The charge, if there was to be a charge, was bound to be one of murder. The accused was a juvenile. On 15th August he was under suspicion of being a murderer ; and, as I read the police evidence, he was then, in their view, not merely a possible but a likely perpetrator of the crime ; and it is very significant of the state of mind of the police that the proceedings began with a caution, and that several further cautions followed within the next five minutes. The process to which the appellant was subjected was one not merely of interrogation but of " cross-examination," and of being confronted with police information contradictory of the statement which he had already made ; and this process was continued until the appellant broke down. It is said that the appellant was not technically in custody, that no warrant for his apprehension had been issued, and that he had not been formally charged. This is true, and I recognise that in several cases distinctions have very properly

been drawn between " routine questioning " during explora-
tory police investigation of a crime, and the interrogation
of prisoners after arrest or in prison awaiting trial.   But
when a person is brought by police officers in a police van to a
police station, and, while there alone, is faced with police
officers of high rank, I cannot think that his need for protection
is any less than it would have been if he had been formally
apprehended. The ordinary person (least of all a youth of
sixteen) is not to know that he could have refused to be taken
to the police station or to answer any questions, and, even if he
knew that, he would be unlikely to adopt such a course and it
would probably avail him little if he did.   Taking all the
circumstances into account I am unable to regard a confession
or other incriminating statement extracted by such methods
as presenting those features of a " voluntary " and " spontaneous " statement on which strong emphasis has been laid
in so many of the cases, and such a confession or statement
cannot be laid before a jury.   I am unable to draw the line
or to describe it in terms universally or generally applicable,
but I am satisfied that in this case the line was crossed and the
statement would have been inadmissible if it had been offered
in evidence.

I take next the episode of the cornfield.   This is related to
the interrogation in two ways.   In point of time the visit to
the cornfield followed immediately after the further interrogation which followed the taking of the " statement."   Moreover it is admitted that during the further interrogation the
appellant was asked what happened to the purse, and that
it was " in consequence of " his answer to that question that
he was taken to the cornfield " to facilitate any search."   I
therefore regard the visit to the cornfield under the surveillance
of the police as part and parcel of the same transaction as the
interrogation, and, if the interrogation and the " statement "
which emerged from it are inadmissible as " unfair," the
same criticism must attach to the conducted visit to the cornfield.   Next I feel unable to accept the distinction drawn by
the presiding judge between statements and " actings," and I
suspect that a fallacy lurks in the word " actings."   The

actings of an accused, if unattended by such circumstances as are here presented, are normally competent evidence against him. For instance, if the police had kept watch on the accused and had seen him go to the cornfield to retrieve the purse, such evidence would have been perfectly competent. Again " actings," in the sense of conduct, may be perfectly neutral as a communication of specific information ; but " actings " in the sense of a gesture or sign, may be indistinguishable from a communication by word of mouth or by writing. The question here was—Where exactly is the purse ? And this question might have been answered by an oral description of the place where it was, or by going to the place and silently pointing to that place. It seems to me to make no difference for present purposes which method of answering the question was adopted ; from which it follows that, if, in the circumstances of this case, the " statement " was inadmissible, the episode of the cornfield was equally inadmissible. The significance of the episode is plain, for it showed that the appellant knew where the purse was. If the police had simply produced, and proved the finding of, the purse, that evidence would have carried them little or no distance in this case towards implicating the appellant. It was essential that the appellant should be linked up with the purse, either by oral confession or by its equivalent—tacit admission of knowledge of its whereabouts obtained as a sequel to the interrogation.

That, I am afraid, is an end of the case ; for I did not understand it to be maintained, and in any event I do not think that it could successfully be maintained, that the verdict could stand in so narrow a case without the evidence of either the " statement " or the cornfield episode. All that is left is some exceedingly imperfect evidence of bare opportunity, and the alleged admission made when the appellant was charged. The presiding judge admitted the evidence of this final admission with express hesitation arising from the fact that, considering the youth and condition of the appellant, and considering also the evidence (*ex hypothesi* inadmissible) of his visit to the cornfield, it is not easy to attach full significance and value to the further statement made when he was charged. The charge was made at 2.25 p.m. after the appellant's father had reached the police station, and the presiding judge found in this interval of time sufficient to separate the charge from the proceedings which had taken place earlier that day. I do not consider that this time interval was sufficient in the circumstances to overcome the difficulty, nor am I satisfied that the appellant's answer to the charge would have been the same if the police questioning had stopped at the line beyond which self-incriminating statements became inadmissible in evidence ; but I prefer to rest my judgment upon the wider ground that, even accepting the final statement, there is not enough left in the case and that the verdict is vitiated by the erroneous admission of the evidence regarding the cornfield episode.

I have sympathy with the police in the difficult position in which they are often placed. We have no power to give instructions to the police, but we have the power and the duty to exclude from the cognisance of a jury evidence which, according to our practice and decisions, is inadmissible ; and the police have an interest to know why such decisions are taken. Were it possible to do so, I should like to be able to lay down comprehensive rules for the guidance of the police in all the situations which may arise in practice, but I am satisfied that this is impossible because in the border-line case so much turns upon the exact circumstances. To such cases it is possible to apply the words of Lord Sumner in *Ibrahim* v. *Rex*,[1] in which, after reviewing a large number of cases, his Lordship said (at p. 614) : " The English Law is still unsettled, strange as it may seem, since the point is one that constantly occurs in criminal trials. Many judges in their discretion exclude such evidence for they fear that nothing less than the exclusion of all such statements can prevent improper questioning of prisoners, by removing the inducement to resort to it. . . . Others, less tender to the prisoner or more mindful of the balance of decided authority, would admit such statements. . . . If, as appears even on the line of authorities which the trial judge did not follow, the

[1] [1914] A.C. 599.

matter is one for the judge's discretion, depending largely on his view of the impropriety of the questioner's conduct and the general circumstances of the case, their Lordships think, as will hereafter be seen, that in the circumstances of this case his discretion is not shown to have been exercised improperly." In quoting this passage I am not to be taken as suggesting that English Law is the same as Scottish, for it is not, the English Courts being in use to admit certain evidence which would fall to be rejected in Scotland and the procedure in the two countries being materially different. But the *dictum* stresses the undoubted fact that it is inherent in the problem that wide generalisation is impossible. This, however, it is possible to say with regard to Scots Law. It is not the function of the police when investigating a crime to direct their endeavours to obtaining a confession from the suspect to be used as evidence against him at the trial. In some legal systems the inquisitorial method of investigation is allowed in different degrees and subject to various safeguards ; but by our law self-incriminating statements, when tendered in evidence at a criminal trial, are always jealously examined from the standpoint of being assured as to their spontaneity ; and if, on a review of all the proved circumstances, that test is not satisfied, evidence of such statements will usually be excluded altogether. The theory of our law is that at the stage of initial investigation the police may question anyone with a view to acquiring information which may lead to the detection of the criminal ; but that, when the stage has been reached at which suspicion, or more than suspicion, has in their view centred upon some person as the likely perpetrator of the crime, further interrogation of that person becomes very dangerous, and, if carried too far, *e.g.* to the point of extracting a confession by what amounts to cross-examination, the evidence of that confession will almost certainly be excluded. Once the accused has been apprehended and charged he has the statutory right to a private interview with a solicitor and to be brought before a magistrate with all convenient speed, so that he may, if so advised, emit a declaration in presence of his solicitor under conditions which safeguard him against prejudice. The practice of emitting declarations has very largely fallen into disuse since the Evidence Act of 1898,[1] but the underlying principle survives, and it may be applicable to situations which arise before apprehension and charge. Much reference was made to a person " detained under suspicion," an expression which has been used ambiguously in many of our decisions, but the emphasis is on the suspicion and not on the detention. Putting aside the case of proper apprehension without a warrant of persons caught more or less red-handed, no person can be lawfully detained except after a charge has been made against him, and it is for this reason that I view with some uneasiness the situation disclosed in this case, and illustrated by the recent cases of *Rigg* [2] and *Short* [3] in which a suspect is neither apprehended nor charged but is simply " asked " to accompany two police officers to a police office to be there questioned. In former times such questioning, if undertaken, would be conducted by police officers visiting the house or place of business of the suspect and there questioning him, probably in the presence of a relation or friend. However convenient the modern practice may be, it must normally create a situation very unfavourable to the suspect. In the eyes of every ordinary citizen the venue is a sinister one. When he stands alone in such a place confronted by several police officers, usually some of high rank, the dice are loaded against him, especially as he knows that there is no one to corroborate him as to what exactly occurred during the interrogation, how it was conducted, and how long it lasted. If under such circumstances cross-examination is pursued with the result, though perhaps not with the deliberate object, of causing him to break down and to condemn himself out of his own mouth, the impropriety of the proceedings cannot be cured by the giving of any number of formal cautions or by the introduction of some officer other than the questioner to record the ultimate statement. In the ordinary case, as many decisions now demonstrate, that statement, if tendered in evidence at the trial, will not be treated as possessing that quality of spontaneity

---

[1] 61 and 62 Vict. c. 36.   [2] 1946 J.C. 1.
[3] 30th May 1950, unreported.

on which our law insists, and its rejection, when tendered in evidence, may, and sometimes does, wreck the prosecution. The practice exemplified by this and other recent cases in substance puts the suspect in much the same position as if he had been arrested, while depriving him of the privileges and safeguards which are extended by the statute and the decisions to an accused person who has been apprehended. The police have, of course, the right and the duty to produce all the incriminating evidence they can lay their hands on, from whatever source they may legitimately derive the clue which leads to its discovery, so long as any admission or confession by the accused is not elicited before the jury as an element in proof of guilt. The matter may be put in another way. The accused cannot be compelled to give evidence at his trial and to submit to cross-examination. If it were competent for the police at their own hand to subject the accused to interrogation and cross-examination and to adduce evidence of what he said, the prosecution would in effect be making the accused a compellable witness, and laying before the jury at second-hand, evidence which could not be adduced at first hand, even subject to all the precautions which are available for the protection of the accused at a criminal trial.

In expressing the above views I am only reiterating principles which have been stated and restated in over a score of decisions in the last eighty or ninety years. All these cases turned upon their own facts (as every case of this kind must inevitably do) ; but there are numerous *dicta* of high authority, which latterly founded upon the principle of " fairness " as the ultimate test of the propriety or otherwise of admitting self-incriminating evidence of the type here in question. In Alison on *Criminal Law*, vol. ii, p. 584, there is a singularly apt passage which was founded upon by the appellant as negativing the admissibility of the evidence about the cornfield. So long ago as 1842 Lord Justice-Clerk Hope observed [1] that " it is not the duty of a criminal officer to act as the examinator of prisoners " ; and in 1858 Lord Justice-Clerk Inglis said [2] : " When a person is under suspicion of a

[1] *Martin,* (1842) 1 Broun, 382.   [2] *Hay,* 3 Irv. 181, at p. 184.

crime, it is not proper to put questions, and receive answers, except before a magistrate." In *Hodgson* v. *Macpherson* [1] Lord Kinnear said (at p. 74) : " A criminal officer is not entitled to examine a person suspected of a crime in order to obtain confessions or admissions from the criminal, and so in fact to obtain from him what is to serve the purpose of a declaration without giving him the protection of the magistrate, before whom alone declarations have to be taken." In *Costello* [2] Lord Justice-Clerk Scott Dickson (at p. 12) drew a distinction between the truly voluntary or spontaneous statement and statements elicited by cross-questioning by the police ; and the same distinction was central to the decision in *Waddell* v. *Kinnaird* [3] where the earlier authorities are reviewed. There are numerous recent illustrations of these principles to which I need not refer.

There is one final matter which merits consideration. In this case, following certain precedents (such as *Cunningham*), [4] the presiding judge excluded the jury during the argument as to the admissibility of the evidence as regards the cornfield, but took the evidence as to the circumstances attending the interrogation in the police station and its sequel in the cornfield in the presence and hearing of the jury. In my view, this course is open to objection and should no longer be followed. In some cases (of which the present is an instance) such a course not only unduly ties the hands of counsel in examining and cross-examining witnesses, but almost inevitably leads to the disclosure to the jury, directly or by inference, of matters which ought to be withheld from their knowledge. When objection is taken to a line of evidence based upon the alleged unfairness of the methods used in eliciting it, the jury ought to be excluded, and the evidence bearing upon the attendant circumstances should be heard by the judge in the absence of the jury, including, if so advised, the evidence of the accused himself. If, in the light of such evidence and argument, the judge sustains the objection, the jury should be told nothing about the matter. If on the other hand the judge repels the

[1] 1913 S.C.(J.) 68.
[3] 1922 J.C. 40.
[2] 1922 J.C. 9.
[4] 1939 J.C. 61.

objection, the case will proceed in the presence and hearing of the jury, and, if either prosecution or defence choose to do so, the evidence bearing upon the attendant circumstances can be made the subject of examination and cross-examination a second time. In the end of the day it will be for the judge to direct the jury that, in considering the weight and value of the evidence to which objection has been taken and repelled, it is for the jury to have regard to the attendant circumstances as proved before them, and, in so far as they may consider that the evidence objected to is not to be relied upon by reason of the circumstances in which it arose, to discount it or exclude it from their deliberations. I recognise that this procedure may give rise to difficulty and may not always achieve the desired ideal of avoiding prejudice to the accused. But it will at least minimise the risk of such prejudice to an extent unattainable by our past practice. In a murder trial the jury, being enclosed, will hear nothing of evidence which the presiding judge has ruled to be inadmissible. In other types of cases the jury may acquire information through the medium of the Press ; and all that can be done in such cases is to request the Press not to report the matter pending the conclusion of the trial, and to warn the jury to refrain from discussing the case with others, and from reading newspaper reports, during any overnight adjournment. I have had an opportunity of considering the supplementary opinion of the Lord Justice-Clerk and I concur with it.

As regards the present appeal, I am of opinion, as already announced, that the conviction must be quashed.

MacCormick v. *H.M. Advocate* [1]

LORD PRESIDENT (Cooper) : This is a petition of suspension and interdict against the Lord Advocate as representing Her Majesty's Ministers and Officers of State praying for interdict against them from publishing a Proclamation entitling Her

[1] 1953 S.C. 396.

Majesty as *inter alia* " Elizabeth the Second of the United Kingdom of Great Britain." Some of the questions which would have arisen as to the feasibility of such a remedy were largely superseded by the Petitioners' invocation of section 21 of the Crown Proceedings Act, 1947, in terms of which they asked only for " an order declaratory of the rights of parties." Where such an order is asked I consider that it should be formulated with precision, and this has not been done. But it was made sufficiently plain in the pleadings and argument that what the Petitioners sought was a finding from this Court that the use in Her Majesty's title of " the numeral " was not only inconsistent with historical fact and political reality, but involved a contravention of the Treaty of Union of 1707 and of the relative Scottish and English legislation passed at that time.

The Lord Ordinary dismissed the Petition upon these grounds—(1) that the adoption of " the numeral " had been expressly authorised by the Royal Titles Act, 1953, and that an Act of the Parliament of Great Britain was not challengeable in any Court as being in breach of the Treaty of Union or on any other ground ; (2) that in any event Article One of the Treaty did not expressly or by implication prohibit the use of " the numeral," and that the action therefore failed on relevancy ; and (3) that the petitioners had no legal title or interest to sue.

In the first place, the argument has not satisfied me that the Royal Titles Act, 1953, has any proper bearing upon the sole issue here in controversy. That Act only received the Royal Assent on 26th March 1953. More than thirteen months previously, on 6th February 1952, Her Majesty was proclaimed at her Accession Council (and immediately thereafter throughout the Realm and the Dominions) under the name of " Elizabeth the Second." It was under the same name and " numeral " that Her Majesty on 8th February 1952 subscribed the statutory Oath in relation to the Rights and Privileges of the Church of Scotland. We have judicial knowledge of these facts because the original Oath, together with the relative Instrument and Order in Council, was presented to this Court on 12th February 1952, and was directed to be recorded in the Books of Sederunt and to be transmitted to the Keeper of the Records of Scotland. Identical procedure *mutatis mutandis* was followed on the occasion of the Accessions of Their Majesties Edward VII, George V, Edward VIII and George VI. In all these instances the name and " the numeral " were adopted without the authority of any Act of Parliament (anticipatory or retrospective), and were never altered during the reigns of the several Sovereigns concerned. There have been several statutes in the last 150 years dealing with the " Royal Style and Titles," but it is plain from an examination of them and of the Royal Proclamations which followed that each and all were concerned not with the name and the " numeral " but with the appendant designations and with the necessity for varying those appendant designations because of some supervening change in the status of some part of the territories still or previously acknowledging allegiance to the British Crown—notably the differing positions at different times of Ireland, India, and what are now the Dominions. The Act of 1953 is in my view in the same general category as the earlier Acts of this type, its occasion (as the preamble discloses), being a meeting with the Dominion representatives in December 1952. There is however this significant difference that the Act of 1953 merely signifies the " assent " of the United Kingdom Parliament to the adoption of unspecified styles and titles, whereas the earlier Acts (notably those passed in 1876, 1901, 1927 and 1947) bore to authorise the alteration by the expression " it shall be lawful for Her (or His) Majesty." The Proclamation issued on 28th May 1953 in pursuance of the Act of 1953 substitutes " Northern Ireland " for " Ireland " ; alters the formula applicable to the Commonwealth and Empire overseas ; but leaves the name and " the numeral " and the rest of the style and title unaffected. I find it impossible to hold that the Act of 1953 authorised, either retrospectively or by anticipation, the adoption by Her Majesty of the name and " numeral " by which she was initially proclaimed and has ever since been officially known.

I interpose this observation that, if it were necessary to construe the Act of 1953, I should find it impossible to do so because the Act is not self-contained. All the other Acts dealing with a change in the Royal Style and Titles simply authorised the Sovereign to adopt such changed styles and titles as the Sovereign might think fit. But in 1953 the Sovereign's discretion in the matter is not unqualified. The changed style and titles to which Parliament assented must be such as Her Majesty may think fit " *having regard to the said Agreement.*" What agreement? Plainly the agreement said to have been concluded with the Dominion representatives in December 1952. But this agreement is not scheduled or otherwise detailed, the only reference to it being in the vague words of the preamble of the Act, which are entirely lacking in specification. The Lord Advocate admitted that the Act was not self-explanatory, and offered in supplement a " White Paper," which he indicated had been made available in the Vote Office prior to the consideration of the Bill. But Parliament can only speak through the medium of a statute. A court of law is not entitled to investigate the Parliamentary history of a bill, whether in the pages of Hansard or in their equivalent a " White Paper," and I am therefore forced to the conclusion that this Act must remain incapable of being fully understood or intelligently interpreted by any court, the Legislature having withheld the material necessary for that purpose. Be that as it may, I consider that the Lord Advocate failed to show that there is, or ever was, Parliamentary authority for the adoption by Her Majesty of the name and the " numeral " which in fact were adopted on Her Majesty's Accession and have been used ever since.

Upon this view a part of the Lord Ordinary's judgment and of the argument before us disappears. But lest this case should go further, I shall briefly express my opinion.

The principle of the unlimited sovereignty of Parliament is a distinctively English principle which has no counterpart in Scottish constitutional law. It derives its origin from Coke and Blackstone, and was widely popularised during the nineteenth century by Bagehot and Dicey, the latter having stated the doctrine in its classic form in his *Law of the Constitution*. Considering that the Union legislation extinguished the Parliaments of Scotland and England and replaced them by a new Parliament, I have difficulty in seeing why it should have been supposed that the new Parliament of Great Britain must inherit all the peculiar characteristics of the English Parliament but none of the Scottish Parliament, as if all that happened in 1707 was that Scottish representatives were admitted to the Parliament of England. That is not what was done. Further, the Treaty and the associated legislation, by which the Parliament of Great Britain was brought into being as the successor of the separate Parliaments of Scotland and England, contain some clauses which expressly reserve to the Parliament of Great Britain powers of subsequent modification, and other clauses which either contain no such power or emphatically exclude subsequent alteration by declarations that the provision shall be fundamental and unalterable in all time coming, or declarations of a like effect. I have never been able to understand how it is possible to reconcile with elementary canons of construction the adoption by the English constitutional theorists of the same attitude to these markedly different types of provisions.

The Lord Advocate conceded this point by admitting that the Parliament of Great Britain " could not " repeal or alter such " fundamental and essential " conditions. He was doubtless influenced in making this concession by the modified views expressed by Dicey in his later work entitled *Thoughts on the Scottish Union*, from which I take this passage (pp. 252-53) : " The statesmen of 1707, though giving full sovereign power to the Parliament of Great Britain, clearly believed in the possibility of creating an absolutely sovereign Legislature which should yet be bound by unalterable laws." After instancing the provisions as to Presbyterian Church government in Scotland with their emphatic prohibition against alteration, the author proceeds : " It represents the conviction of the Parliament which passed the Act of Union that the Act for the security of the Church of Scotland ought to be morally or constitutionally unchangeable even by the British Parliament.

2 A

. . . A sovereign Parliament in short, though it cannot be logically bound to abstain from changing any given law, may, by the fact that an Act when it was passed had been declared to be unchangeable, receive a warning that it cannot be changed without grave danger to the Constitution of the country." I have not found in the Union legislation any provision that the Parliament of Great Britain should be "absolutely sovereign" in the sense that that Parliament should be free to alter the Treaty at will. However that may be, these passages provide a necessary corrective to the extreme formulations adopted by the Lord Ordinary, and not now supported. In the latest editions of the *Law of the Constitution* the editor uneasily described Dicey's theories as "purely lawyer's conceptions," and demonstrates how deeply later events, such as the Statute of Westminster, have encroached upon the earlier dogmas. As is well known the conflict between academic logic and political reality has been emphasised by the recent South African decision as to the effect of the Statute of Westminster (*Harris* v. *Minister of Interior*, 1952, 1 T.L.R. 1245).

But the Petitioners have still a grave difficulty to overcome on this branch of their argument. Accepting it that there are provisions in the Treaty of Union and associated legislation which are "fundamental law," and assuming for the moment that something is alleged to have been done—it matters not whether with legislative authority or not—in breach of that fundamental law, the question remains whether such a question is determinable as a justiciable issue in the Courts of either Scotland or England, in the same fashion as an issue of constitutional *vires* would be cognisable by the Supreme Courts of the United States, or of South Africa or Australia. I reserve my opinion with regard to the provisions relating expressly to this Court and to the laws "which concern private right" which are administered here. This is not such a question, but a matter of "public right" (Articles XVIII and XIX). To put the matter in another way, it is of little avail to ask whether the Parliament of Great Britain, "can" do this thing or that, without going on to enquire who can stop them if they do. Any person "can" repudiate his solemn engagement but he cannot normally do so with impunity. Only two answers have been suggested to this corollary to the main question. The first is the exceedingly cynical answer implied by Dicey (*Law of the Constitution*, 9th ed. p. 82) in the statement that " it would be rash of the Imperial Parliament to abolish the Scotch Law Courts and assimilate the law of Scotland to that of England. But no one can feel sure at what point Scottish resistance to such a change would become serious." The other answer was that nowadays there may be room for the invocation of an " advisory opinion " from the International Court of Justice. On these matters I express no view. This at least is plain, that there is neither precedent nor authority of any kind for the view that the domestic Courts of either Scotland or England have jurisdiction to determine whether a governmental act of the type here in controversy is or is not conform to the provisions of a Treaty, least of all when that Treaty is one under which both Scotland and England ceased to be independent states and merged their identity in an incorporating union. From the standpoint both of constitutional law and of international law the position appears to me to be unique, and I am constrained to hold that the action as laid is incompetent in respect that it has not been shown that the Court of Session has authority to entertain the issue sought to be raised.

Upon the question of the relevancy of the Petitioners' averments of breach of the provisions of the Treaty I agree in the result with the Lord Ordinary. Only Article One of the Treaty was founded upon, and it was conceded that there was nothing explicit in that Article dealing with the point in controversy. I am unable to find in that Article any sufficient implied prohibition against the adoption of the " numeral " complained of, and this view is supported by the practice of 120 years. That practice is doubtless correctly explained in Phillip's *Principles of the English Law and the Constitution* (1939) (at pp. 229-30) as follows : " The number attached to the name of a king refers to the Kings *of England* since the Norman Conquest " ; for, if this is not the rule, all the kings of the name of Edward since Edward I have been wrongly numbered.

Whether the rule is good or bad, and whether it is politically wise to continue to apply it, it is not for this Court to say ; but in so far as I am entitled to look at Article One of the Treaty, I am unable to affirm that any breach has been committed.

Finally I agree with the Lord Ordinary on title to sue. There is no plea by the Respondent to this point and it is of minor significance.   It is true that we in Scotland recognise within certain limits the *actio popularis*, in which any member of the public may be entitled as such to vindicate certain forms of public right.   But the device has never been extended to such a case as this.   I cannot see how we could admit the title and interest of the present Petitioners to raise the point in issue before the Court of Session without conceding a similar right to almost any opponent of almost any political action to which public opposition had arisen.

For these reasons, which differ in certain respects from the views expressed by the Lord Ordinary, I am for adhering to his Lordship's interlocutor.   I desire to place it on record that the Petitioners expressly disclaimed any attempt to criticise Her Majesty or any disloyalty to Her, their action being based upon considerations of which the present issue is merely symbolical.

1953

Bibliography

Excluding Addresses and Speeches reported in the contemporary press and Opinions to be found in the volumes of Session Cases from 1941-1954. An asterisk signifies that the paper has been included in the present volume.

Law of Housing and Town Planning [with Sir W. E. Whyte]. Edinburgh and London (Hodge), 1920.

Select Scottish Cases of the Thirteenth Century. Edinburgh and London (Hodge), 1944.

The Register of Brieves, 1286-1386, as contained in the Ayr MS., *the Bute* MS. *and Quoniam Attachiamenta.* Edinburgh (Stair Socy., vol. x), 1946.

Regiam Majestatem and Quoniam Attachiamenta, based on the Text of Sir John Skene. Edinburgh (Stair Socy., vol. XI), 1947.

* *The Scottish Legal Tradition.* Saltire Pamphlets No. 7. Edinburgh and London (Oliver and Boyd), 1949.

* *Supra Crepidam.* Presidential Addresses delivered to the Scottish History Socy. [1946-1949]. Edinburgh and London (Nelson), 1951.

* *The Dark Age of Scottish Legal History, 1350-1650.* Being the nineteenth Lecture on the David Murray Foundation in the University of Glasgow delivered on 12th November 1951. Glasgow University Publications XCII. Glasgow (Jackson), 1952.

★   ★   ★

*Legal Education in Scotland : A criticism. *Scottish Law Review,* vol. XXXVIII (1922), pp. 71-75.

*Accountancy Evidence from an Advocate's Point of View. Being a Lecture delivered to the Chartered Accountants Students' Society of Edinburgh on 12th January 1928, and to the Glasgow Chartered Accountants Students' Society on 25th January 1928. *Accountants' Magazine,* vol. XXXII (1928), pp. 95-110.

*The Limitations of the Judicial Functions of Public Authorities. An Address delivered to the Institute of Public Administration : Summer Conference, July 1929. *Scots Law Times,* 1930, pp. 1-6. Reprinted from *Public Administration,* vol. VII (1929), pp. 260-268.

*Some Classics of Scottish Legal Literature. An Address delivered to the Institute of Bankers in Scotland at Edinburgh on 29th October 1929. *Scottish Bankers Magazine,* vol. XXI (1929-1930), pp. 259-271.

*The Length of the Chancellor's Foot. *Juridical Review*, vol. XLV (1933), pp. 145-150.

*Trial by Jury in Scotland : Is there a case for Reform ? Being a lecture delivered to the Glasgow Chartered Accountants Students' Society on 15th February 1935, and to the Chartered Accountants Students' Society of Edinburgh on 26th October 1934. *Accountants' Magazine*, vol. XXXIX (1935), pp. 207-219.

Devotion to Professional Ideals. A Speech at the Annual Dinner of the Edinburgh and East of Scotland District of the Institute of Journalists, 29th January 1938. *The Journal*, March 1938, pp. 51-52.

*The Administration of Criminal Justice in Scotland. An Address delivered at the Annual Meeting of the Scottish Justices and Magistrates' Association in Edinburgh on 26th January 1939.

*The Legal Profession. An Address to the Faculty of Law of Edinburgh University delivered in March 1939.

*Melrose Abbey *versus* the Earl of Dunbar. *Juridical Review*, vol. LV (1943), pp. 1-8.

*The First Law Reform (Miscellaneous Provisions) Act. *Juridical Review*, vol. LVI (1944), pp. 1-5.

A Scottish Law Student at Oxford in 1250. *Juridical Review*, vol. LVI (1944), pp. 57-61.

*Curiosities of Medieval Scots Law. *Proceedings of the Royal Philosophical Society of Glasgow*, vol. LXIX ; Pt. 5 (1945), pp. 51-64.

Freehold in Scots Law. *Juridical Review*, vol. LVII (1945), pp. 1-5.

*The Sheep, the Horse, and the Mill. *Scottish Law Review*, vol. LXI (1945), pp. 109-110.

*Cromwell's Judges and Their Influence on Scots Law. *Juridical Review*, vol. LVIII (1946), pp. 20-25.

*The King *versus* The Court of Session. *Juridical Review*, vol. LVIII (1946), pp. 83-92.

*Frustration of Contract in Scots Law. *Journal of Comparative Legislation*, 3rd ser. vol. XXVIII (1946), pp. 1-5.

The Berne Legal Manuscript. *Edinburgh Bibliographical Society Transactions*, vol. II (1946), pp. 379-381.

*The Numbers and the Distribution of the Population of Medieval Scotland. *Scottish Historical Review*, vol. XXVI (1947), pp. 1-9.

*The Importance of Comparative Law in Scotland. An Address delivered in the University of Aberdeen on 15th April 1947.

*The Future of the Legal Profession. The Inaugural Address delivered to the Edinburgh University Law Faculty Society on 10th October 1947.

*The Authorship of the Berne MS. *Scottish Historical Review*, vol. XXVII (1948), pp. 114-123.

George Watson : Founder's Day Oration at George Watson's Boys' College, Edinburgh, 9th July 1948. *The Watsonian*, vol. XLIII (1948), pp. 92-97. Reprinted in *The Watsonian, 1904-1954. A Jubilee Volume*, 1955, pp. 12-16.

*The Common and the Civil Law—A Scot's View. The Substance of an Address delivered to the Summer School, Edinburgh University, July 1946. *Harvard Law Review*, vol. 63 (1950), pp. 468-475.

*The Profession of the Law To-Day. An Address to the Law Society of Glasgow University on 27th October 1950. *Scottish Law Review*, vol. LXVI (1950), pp. 249-256.

*Early Scottish Statutes Revisited. *Juridical Review*, vol. LXIV (1952), pp. 197-203.

*Defects in the British Judicial Machine : an Address delivered before the Society of Public Teachers of Law at the Annual Meeting, Sheffield, on 18th September 1953. *Journal of the Society of Public Teachers of Law*, New Series, vol. II (1952-1954), pp. 91-100. Discussion, pp. 100-105.

*Administrative Justice. A Lecture to the Edinburgh Group of the Royal Institute of Public Administration, 26th March 1954. *Public Administration*, vol. XXXII (1954), pp. 165-171.

*A Scottish Lawyer's Library in the Seventeenth Century. *Juridical Review*, vol. LXVI (1954), pp. 1-5.

★　　　★　　　★

Report of the Committee on Hydro-Electric Development in Scotland. [Lord Cooper, Chairman.] Scottish Office, Edinburgh. H.M.S.O. Cmd. 6406, 1942.

Report of the Clyde Estuary Committee. [Lord Cooper, Chairman.] Ministry of War Transport, London. H.M.S.O., 1945.

Report of the Special Committee appointed in March 1946 to inquire and advise regarding an Application by the University Courts of the Universities of Scotland for an increased Grant from the Education (Scotland) Fund. [Lord Cooper, Chairman.] Scottish Education Department, Edinburgh. H.M.S.O. Cmd. 6853, 1946.

Report of the Inquiry [by Lord Cooper, with two Assessors] *appointed in February 1949 to review and report on the organisation of University education in Dundee and its relationship with St Andrews University*. Scottish Office, Edinburgh. H.M.S.O., 1949.

Subject Index

This Index does not iuclude all names mentioned in the
text ; it is intended simply as a guide to the main topics
discussed.

377